LYLE PRICE GUIDE
SILVER

The publishers wish to express their sincere thanks to the following for their involvement and assistance in the production of this volume:

TONY CURTIS (Editor)
EELIN McIVOR (Sub Editor)
ANNETTE CURTIS (Editorial)
DONNA RUTHERFORD (Editorial)
CATRIONA DAY (Art Production)
ANGIE DE MARCO (Art Production)
JAMES BROWN (Graphics)

A CIP catalogue record for this book is available from the British Library

ISBN 86248-151-1
Copyright © Lyle Publication MCMXCV
Glenmayne, Galashiels, Scotland.

Typeset by Word Power, Berwickshire.
Printed and bound in Great Britain by
Butler & Tanner Ltd., Frome and London.

LYLE PRICE GUIDE

SILVER

TONY CURTIS

CONTENTS

ACKNOWLEDGEMENTS

Anderson & Garland, Marlborough House, Marlborough Crescent, Newcastle upon Tyne NE1 4EE
Auction Team Köln, Postfach 50 11 68, D-5000 Köln 50 Germany
Auktionshaus Arnold, Bleichstr. 42, 6000 Frankfurt a/M, Germany
Bearnes, Rainbow, Avenue Road, Torquay TQ2 5TG
Boardman Fine Art Auctioneers, Station Road Corner, Haverhill, Suffolk CB9 0EY
Bonhams, Montpelier Street, Knightsbridge, London SW7 1HH
Bonhams Chelsea, 65–69 Lots Road, London SW10 0RN
Bonhams West Country, Dowell Street, Honiton, Devon
Butterfield & Butterfield, 220 San Bruno Avenue, San Francisco CA94103, USA
Butterfield & Butterfield, 7601 Sunset Boulevard, Los Angeles CA90046, USA
Canterbury Auction Galleries, 40 Station Road West, Canterbury CT2 8AN
Christie's (International) SA, 8 place de la Taconnerie, 1204 Genève, Switzerland
Christie's Monaco, S.A.M, Park Palace 98000 Monte Carlo, Monaco
Christie's Scotland, 164–166 Bath Street, Glasgow G2 4TG
Christie's South Kensington Ltd., 85 Old Brompton Road, London SW7 3LD
Christie's, 8 King Street, London SW1Y 6QT
Christie's East, 219 East 67th Street, New York, NY 10021, USA
Christie's, 502 Park Avenue, New York, NY 10022, USA
Christie's, Cornelis Schuytstraat 57, 1071 JG Amsterdam, Netherlands
Christie's SA Roma, 114 Piazza Navona, 00186 Rome, Italy
Christie's Swire, 1202 Alexandra House, 16–20 Chater Road, Hong Kong
Christie's Australia Pty Ltd., 1 Darling Street, South Yarra, Melbourne, Victoria 3141, Australia
Diamond Mills & Co., 117 Hamilton Road, Felixstowe, Suffolk
Hy. Duke & Son, 40 South Street, Dorchester, Dorset
Eldred's, Box 796, E. Dennis, MA 02641, USA
Finarte, 20121 Milano, Piazzetta Bossi 4, Italy
Peter Francis, 19 King Street, Carmarthen, Dyfed
Galerie Koller, Rämistr. 8, CH 8024 Zürich, Switzerland
Galerie Moderne, 3 rue du Parnasse, 1040 Bruxelles, Belgium
Graves Son & Pilcher, 71 Church Road, Hove, East Sussex BN3 2GL
Greenslade Hunt, Magdalene House, Church Square, Taunton, Somerset, TA1 1SB
G. A. Key, Aylsham Saleroom, Palmers Lane, Aylsham, Norfolk NR11 6EH
Kunsthaus am Museum, Drususgasse 1–5, 5000 Köln 1, Germany
W. H. Lane & Son, 64 Morrab Road, Penzance, Cornwall TR18 2QT
Langlois Ltd., Westway Rooms, Don Street, St. Helier, Channel Islands
Lawrence Fine Art, South Street, Crewkerne, Somerset TA18 8AB
Lawrence's Fine Art Auctioneers, Norfolk House, 80 High Street, Bletchingley, Surrey
David Lay, The Penzance Auction House, Alverton, Penzance, Cornwall TA18 4KE
Lots Road Chelsea Auction Galleries, 71 Lots Road, Chelsea, London SW10 0RN
Phillips Manchester, Trinity House, 114 Northenden Road, Sale, Manchester M33 3HD
Phillips Son & Neale SA, 10 rue des Chaudronniers, 1204 Genève, Switzerland
Phillips West Two, 10 Salem Road, London W2 4BL
Phillips, 11 Bayle Parade, Folkestone, Kent CT20 1SQ
Phillips, 49 London Road, Sevenoaks, Kent TN13 1UU
Phillips, 65 George Street, Edinburgh EH2 2JL
Phillips, Blenstock House, 7 Blenheim Street, New Bond Street, London W1Y 0AS
Phillips Marylebone, Hayes Place, Lisson Grove, London NW1 6UA
Phillips, New House, 150 Christleton Road, Chester CH3 5TD
Phillips/Spencer, 20 The Square, Retford, Notts. DN22 6BX
Riddetts, Richmond Hill, Bournemouth
Russell, Baldwin & Bright, The Fine Art Saleroom, Ryelands Road, Leominster HR6 8JG
Selkirk's, 4166 Olive Street, St. Louis, Missouri 63108, USA
Skinner Inc., Bolton Gallery, Route 117, Bolton MA, USA
Sotheby's, 34–35 New Bond Street, London W1A 2AF
Sotheby's, 1334 York Avenue, New York NY 10021, USA
Sotheby's, 112 George Street, Edinburgh EH2 4LH
Sotheby's, Summers Place, Billingshurst, West Sussex RH14 9AD
Sotheby's Monaco, BP 45, 98001 Monte Carlo
Tennants, Harmby Road, Leyburn, Yorkshire
Woolley & Wallis, The Castle Auction Mart, Salisbury, Wilts SP1 3SU

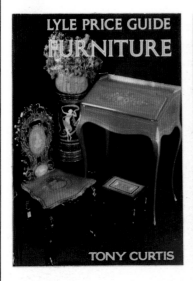
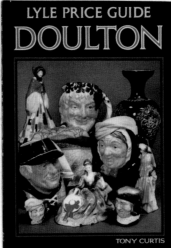

SILVER

There are few media more versatile or more timeless than silver, for while gold may suggest greater magnificence, silver has always offered special opportunities for the genius of artists and craftsmen. All the ancient civilisations delighted in silver – there are frequent references to it throughout the Old Testament, and in the writings of the Classical authors and historians.

The use of silver did, however, present certain problems, in that pure silver was too soft to work, while the addition of other white metals rendered it brittle. Finally, copper was found to be a suitable alloy, and experiments showed that the addition of 11oz 2dwt of silver to 18dwt of copper was a satisfactory mix. This was the standard adopted in Britain, which is now esteemed throughout the world as Sterling. There were always those prepared to cut corners, however, through the addition of higher proportions of alloy, which is very difficult to detect. It was for this reason that in the main European silvermaking centres medieval master silversmiths formed themselves into guilds to protect themselves against such unfair competition. They established a hallmarking system, which, in addition to guaranteeing the purity of the metal, incorporated the date, assay centre and maker of each piece, and it is a system which has lasted successfully to the present day.

During the Middle Ages and, indeed, until the 16–17th centuries, much of the wealth of the country resided in the hands of a few noble families and, of course, the Church. Thus it is that so many early silver pieces found today are ecclesiastical in origin. Nor did the Reformation change things so completely, for even the Puritans still had their Communion cups and plate. It was not until the mid 17th century that the use of domestic silver became more widespread and only in the 18th and 19th centuries that the 'family silver' became a reality for most members of the middle classes. The phrase itself reflects the esteem in which such pieces were held. They would be passed down through the generations and 'having to sell off the family silver' meant that one was destitute indeed.

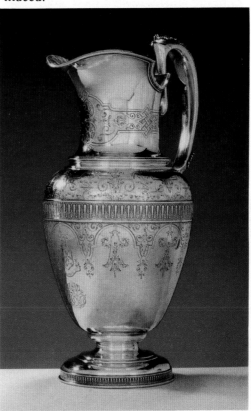

A silver water pitcher by Tiffany & Co., New York, circa 1869, of vase form on stepped pedestal base, engraved on front with a monogram below armorials, 13³/₄in. high, 44oz. (Christie's)   £2,226 $3,450

In the 18th century something of a revolution took place, which greatly assisted the proliferation of 'silver'. This was the discovery of Sheffield Plate – a way of replicating the silver of the rich so cheaply that it became generally affordable.

The process was discovered by Thomas Bolsover in 1743, and consisted of fusing a thin sheet of silver to an ingot of copper. These were then passed through heavy hand rollers so that their thickness was reduced while the relative proportions remained unchanged. By the end of the century the process had become a huge commercial success. Almost all silver forms were being copied in plate – for about one fifth of the cost of the originals!

The popularity of silver as a collectable has never waned, though there are those who, in the last year or so, have claimed that there is not now the interest in it that there used to be, and for two main reasons. Firstly, with the current rise in crime, it is a ready target for burglars, being, of course, highly portable. In the rash of recent robberies from stately homes up and down the country, a high proportion of the 'loot' consisted of silver items, many of which have never been recovered.

A silver hot water kettle on stand by Tiffany, Young & Ellis, New York, circa 1850, of baluster form, with circular base on four scroll supports, 12³/₈in. high, 51oz.
(Christie's)   £4,080 $6,325

A Queen Anne circular partly-fluted punch bowl, on spreading gadrooned foot with grotesque masks and drop ring handles, by Gabriel Sleath, 1713, 10in. diameter, 33 oz.
(Christie's)   £4,950 $7,771

10

Secondly, silver does involve a certain amount of upkeep. Gone are the days when an army of servants would be detailed each Thursday to 'polish the silver', and it has been claimed that people nowadays have neither the time nor the inclination for this frankly messy task.

That said, though, the lie seems to have been given to such arguments by the results at recent silver sales. As in so many fields, there has been a certain polarisation of the Best and the Rest. For the Best, the sky is the limit. Pieces by the great names such as de Lamerie, Storr, and latterly Omar Ramsden, regularly fetch enormous sums at auction. Christie's and Sotheby's New York sales recently netted between them over £2.75 million, with a pair of tureens by George Wickes fetching £920,000 plus premium at Sotheby's.

A mixed-metal and silver bud vase by Tiffany & Co., circa 1878, designed by Edward C. Moore, in the Japanese taste, 6³/₈in. high, gross weight 6oz. (Christie's) £5,935 $9,200

As for the rest, the results may be much more pedestrian, but they are certainly steady, and the strength of silver at this level seems to rest firmly with the private buyer. This is hardly surprising when you consider the wealth of different items produced in silver, items to suit every taste and pocket. You don't have to go in for terribly serious soup tureens or elegant épergnes. Novelty vinaigrettes, cigar cutters or table bells, for example, can be great fun in themselves and can be found at reasonable prices. Indeed, there is a strong case for arguing that silver, especially flatware, is consistently undervalued. This then could be an excellent time to begin or expand a collection, as it seems certain that silver continues dear to our hearts and thus can only appreciate as time goes on.

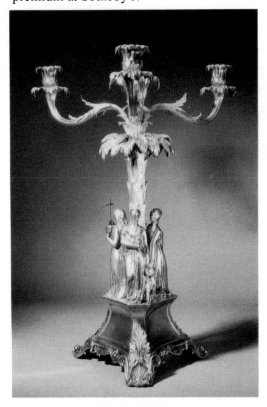

A Victorian silver-gilt four-light candelabrum centrepiece, by Edward Barnard & Sons, 1846, 27¹/₂in. high, 195oz. (Christie's) £5,500 $8,635

A cylindrical tankard by Abraham Drentwett,
embossed with cherubs, Augsburg circa 1650,
22cm. high, circa 1900 gr.
(Auktionsverket Stockholm) £20,898 $32,078

A pair of George II plain vase-shaped casters,
each on spreading circular foot and with
pierced detachable domed cover with baluster
finial, by John White, 1732, 6¹/₂in. high, 19oz.
(Christie's)   £2,070 $3,167

A fine silver teapot, by Samuel Johnson, New York, circa 1765, 10in. long, gross weight 24oz.
10dwt.
(Christie's)   £30,492 $46,200

A mixed-metal and silver berry bowl by Gorham Mfg. Co., Providence, 1879, in the Japanese taste, the interior gilt, length over handles 11in., gross weight 31oz. 10dwt. (Christie's)   £3,709 $5,750

A George III cow creamer, the curved tail forming the handle and with hinged back-flap with applied bee, probably by John Schuppe, 5³/₄in. long, 4oz.
(Christie's)   £4,025 $5,917

A George II inverted pear-shaped tea kettle, stand and lamp, the stand on three shell and dolphin's mask feet, by John Swift, 1742, 14¹/₂in. high, 72oz. gross.
(Christie's)   £3,220 $4,733

A large Edwardian silver-gilt centrepiece, by John Bodman Carrington, 1904, 30in. long, 584oz.
(Christie's)   £19,550 $28,739

A fine silver cake basket, by Fletcher & Gardiner, Philadelphia, circa 1825, 17in. long, 66oz. 10dwt.
(Christie's)   £15,972 $24,200

A William IV silver mounted mantel clock, with gilt engine-turned dial signed *Vulliamy London*, the case by Benjamin Smith, 1836, 15in. high, 162oz. gross.
(Christie's) £9,775 $14,369

A silver mounted patinated copper coffee pot by Gorham Mfg. Co., Providence, 1883, 13in. high.
(Christie's) £1,484 $2,300

An important George III circular 'ragout' dish, cover and liner, the dish with detachable fluted ivory handle, by Paul Storr, 1801, 15in. long, 71oz.
(Christie's) £25,300 $37,191

A pair of Victorian two-handled melon-fluted soup tureens, covers and liners, by Robert Garrard, 1843, 14³/₄in. wide, 288oz.
(Christie's)   £16,500 $25,905

A silver water pitcher, by John C. Moore and Tiffany & Co., New York, circa 1853, 9³/₄in. high, 26oz.
(Christie's)   £4,822 $7,475

A fine five-piece silver tea and coffee service, by Gorham Mfg. Co., Providence, 1881, in the Persian taste, height of coffee pot 7¹/₂in., 93oz.
(Christie's)   £25,967 $40,250

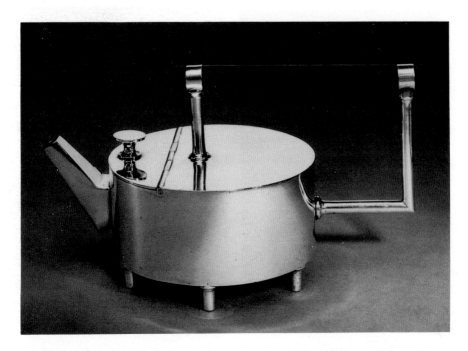

An electroplated teapot, by Christopher Dresser for James Dixon & Sons, 1879, shallow
drum-shaped body with hinged lid and angular ebonised handle, 12cm. high.
(Sotheby's)   £65,300 $99,909

A French large silver-gilt shaped-oblong centrepiece and mirror plateau, stamped *D.R.*
Camus, late 19th century, 31½in. long.
(Christie's)   £18,400 $27,048

A rare Indian-trade silver cross, by Francois Paul Malcher, Detroit, circa 1790, 12¼in. long, 3oz. 10dwt.
(Christie's)   £5,808 $8,800

A George III vase-shaped tea kettle, stand, lamp and tray, by John Emes, 1802, 14in. high, 96oz. gross.
(Christie's)   £2,640 $4,144

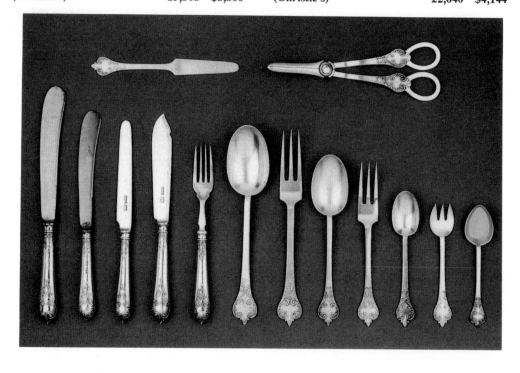

An extensive trefid-end pattern table service, the handles stamped with foliage, by Mappin and Webb, 1911, 503oz.
(Christie's)   £8,050 $12,316

18

A pair of unusual George IV silver-gilt mounted frosted glass wine coolers formed as the Warwick vase, by Samuel Jackson, 1825, 10¹/₂in. high.
(Christie's)   £6,325 $9,487

An important George I two-handled octagonal wine cooler, by David Willaume, 1718, Britannia Standard, fitted with a pierced detachable unmarked strainer, 104oz.
(Christie's)   £133,500 $196,245

An important and documented porringer by Paul Revere II, Boston, 1782, length to handle 8¹/₄in., approx. 9oz.
(Bonhams)   £10,000 $16,000

A fine silver tankard, by Ephraim Brasher, New York, 1770–1780, the front engraved with a coat-of-arms and crest within an elaborate foliate scroll, 8³/₄in. high, 40oz.
(Christie's)   £47,190 $71,500

A Dutch silver-gilt two-handled shaped-oval basket, by Johannes Janse(n), Rotterdam, 1777, 15³/₄in. wide, 1251 gr.
(Christie's)   £8,625 $12,679

A rare Elizabeth I silver-gilt mounted tiger-ware jug, winged demi-cherub thumbpiece, 1561, maker's mark GW, 6¹/₂in. high.
(Christie's)   £12,650 $19,860

A pair of Victorian tea caddies, matching sugar box and silver-mounted tortoiseshell veneered casket by Charles and George Fox, 1844, 39oz.
(Christie's)   £10,450 $16,406

A pair of George III soup tureens by Paul Storr, liners, covers and two handled stands of oval form, 12in. high, approx. 435oz.
(Bonhams)   £41,000 $65,600

GLOSSARY OF TERMS

ACANTHUS
Stylized foliage decoration derived from capitals of Corinthian columns, popular on 17th century silver and revived on neo-classical 18th and early 19th century pieces.

ALMSDISH
Broad-rimmed circular plate of large diameter, made for ecclesiastical use throughout Europe from Middle Ages onwards.

ANTHEMION MOTIF
Stylized flower or leaf shape based on honeysuckle flower, common on late 18th-early 19th century flat and hollow ware in neo-classical style.

APOSTLE SPOONS
Spoons made from 15th-17th century in Britain and Europe in sets of 13, with knops in the form of Christ and the 12 apostles. Revived in 19th century England.

APPLIED
Ornament separately shaped and worked, then fixed to an object with solder.

ARABESQUE
Roman, usually symmetrical pattern of interlaced branches, leaves etc., often found as pierced or embossed ornament on 16th and early 18th century silver and revived in 19th century.

ARGENTINE SILVER
Also known as German silver, an alloy of copper, nickel and zinc, of Chinese origin. Used as a base for late Sheffield plate and for electroplating.

ARGYLE
A silver or Sheffield plate vessel for warming gravy, with lining for hot water. Shape often based on coffee pots with spout set low at right angles to handle. Popular from circa 1770–1820.

ARMADA JUG
Silver or cut-glass and silver-mounted claret jug or wine ewer with slender neck, scrolling handle and spreading foot, made from circa 1860.

ASPARAGUS TONGS
Used in Britain from early 18th century, earlier types were scissor shaped with corrugated ridges on the inside of the arms. Later examples, with pierced, flat grips, resemble sugar tongs.

ASSAY MARK
Mark stamped on silver by assay offices, guaranteeing the metal is of required purity.

ASSOCIATED
Used on silverware sets where a piece is of similar design to the rest but not originally made for the set.

BALLIN, CLAUDE I & II
Silversmiths, uncle and nephew, working in Paris in 17th and 18th century. Claude I was Royal goldsmith to Louis XIV. Both worked in baroque style, making many commissions for royalty.

BALZAC, EDMÉ PIERRE
18th century French silversmith best known for domestic silver in rococo styles.

BANNOCK RACK
Silver rack for oatmeal bannocks, shaped like outsize toast rack. Most examples are 18th century Scottish.

BAPTISMAL BASIN
Silver basin used for holy baptism, mainly in America.

BARBER'S BOWL
Bowl with curved piece cut from rim to fit against neck. Most silver examples date from 17th and 18th century.

BARNARD, EDWARD & SONS
19th century London silversmiths, continuation of Emes and Barnard.

BASKET
Serving container for bread, cake or fruit. Earlier examples mainly circular, with oval shapes introduced from circa 1730.

BATEMAN FAMILY
18th/19th century family of English silversmiths. Hester took over husband's business in 1760, producing at first mainly flatware, then full range of domestic items. Sons Peter and Jonathan, daughter-in-law Ann, and grandson William continued production until after 1815.

BEADING
Moulding in form of a string of beads, common on 18th century silver.

BEAKER
Stemless cylindrical drinking vessel popular in much of Europe between 15th-18th century, though silver examples exist from the Middle Ages onwards.

BEKERSCHROEF
17th century Dutch silver wineglass stand, shaped like stem of large cup.

BELL SALT
Bell-shaped salt container, English, mainly 16th/17th century. Most in three sections, two for salt and the upper pierced, used as spice or pepper caster.

BIGGIN
18th/19th century English cylindrical coffee pot with short lip spout and built-in strainer for coffee grounds, often with stand and spirit lamp.

BLACKJACK
17th/18th century English silver-mounted leather jug of tankard shape.

BOGAERT, JOHANNES (1626–c.1677)
Amsterdam silversmith working in Dutch grotesque style, making domestic and church plate.

BOGAERT, THOMAS (c.1597–1653)
Father of Johannes, working in Utrecht, specialised in ecclesiastical pieces.

BOLSOVER, THOMAS (1704–88)
English silversmith who invented Sheffield plate in 1742. Mainly known for his production of buttons and boxes.

BOMBÉ
Convex curved vertical surface, common in 18th and early 19th century silver, and Sheffield plate teapots, tureens etc.

BOULTON, MATTHEW (1728–1809)
Major 18th century silver manufacturer, working in Birmingham. Largest producer of Sheffield plate in the later 18th century.

BRADBURY, THOMAS (1763–1838)
English Sheffield plate manufacturer, working in Sheffield.

BRANDEWIJKOM
Oval, two-handled brandy bowl, 17th-18th century Dutch, where it was used to hold raisins steeped in brandy on festive occasions.

BRANDY BOWL
Scandinavian flat, two-handled bowl used in 17th century for serving hot brandy.

BRANDY SAUCEPAN
Small silver saucepan of bulbous or baluster shape with long handle at right angles to spout, for warming and serving brandy.

BRATINA
Form of Russian loving-cup, often richly decorated with enamel and gems, the narrower lipband often engraved with sententious inscription. Sometimes with pointed domed cover.

BRIGHT CUT
Faceted engraving in which lines on the edges of the design are bevelled to catch the light and appear more brilliant. Developed in late 18th century in Birmingham.

BRITANNIA STANDARD
Standard of silver purity higher than Sterling silver, of 928 parts pure per 1000. Introduced 1697 to prevent silversmiths melting down coinage for domestic ware, and usually stamped with figure of Britannia.

BULLET TEAPOT
Early 18th century form with spherical body, the lid cut out of the upper part. Revived in mid 19th century.

BUTTER DISH
Found mainly in Ireland from 18th century, shallow pierced bowls with glass liner and cover. English examples rare until 19th century, when some were tub shaped, and others had stand, glass dish and cover.

BUTTER KNIFE
Small silver knife with scimitar-shaped blade and mother-of-pearl or ivory handle. Dates from late 18th century in Britain.

CADDY SPOON
Short stemmed spoon, often with broad ornamental bowl, used from late 18th century to transfer tea leaves from caddy to teapot.

CANDELABRUM
A branched form of candlestick with two or more curved branches radiating from a central stem. In use from the Middle Ages in Europe and becoming steadily more ornate.

CANDLESTICK
Individual candle holders in use from at least 10th century. Silver one of most popular materials and later often made in pairs or sets of four.

CANN
Late 17th/18th century American drinking vessel rather like English mug, with rounded sides and on moulded base. Later, bellied forms became popular.

CANTEEN
Individual set of eating utensils, cased and used for travelling, from late 17th-late 18th century. Later applied to full set of cutlery.

CASTER
A pierced container for sugar, pepper or other spices, of cylindrical form, the cover usually attached by a bayonet joint. Later replaced by cut-glass examples with silver covers.

CAUDLE CUP
A handled cup with straight sided or baluster body and flared mouth, often with domed lid with finial. Used in 17th and 18th century for feeding caudle (a hot spiced drink) to invalids.

CENTREPIECE
Also known as an épergne, a large and elaborate device with various fittings used as a table ornament. It was often equipped with dishes from which guests could serve themselves.

CHAFING DISH
A silver container with a long turned wooden side handle for hot charcoal. The bowl has pierced ornamentation and rests on cast supports. Used in 17th/18th century to keep silver dishes hot.

CHALICE
A stemmed cup in which wine is served at the Eucharist.

CHAMBER CANDLESTICK
A candleholder set in a greasepan, with attached carrying handle and sometimes also with snuffer.

CHARGE MARK
Mark struck on unfinished French silver before testing by the guild wardens.

CHASING
A design produced by using a hammer and punches, as opposed to carving or engraving.

CHAWNER, HENRY
18th century London silversmith. Went into partnership with John Emes, probably 1796.

CHEESE SCOOP
A utensil with crescent-shaped scoop blade and solid silver or ivory handle in use in Britain from late 18th century.

CHOCOLATE POT
A vessel almost identical to a coffee pot except for some which have a hinged or sliding finial in the lid for insertion of a rod to stir the contents. Very popular in England and France in the late 17th-early 18th century.

CIBORIUM
An elaborate stemmed, covered cup used for the reservation of the Eucharist and for carrying it in procession.

COASTER
Circular stand with raised gallery for holding bottle or decanter and 'coasting' it on a polished table top after the cloth has been removed. In use from early 18th century.

COFFEE POT
Container for coffee in use from late 17th century. Early examples of straight tapering form. After 1730 pear shapes appear and baluster shapes about a decade later.

COFFEE URN
A container for coffee with spout replaced by a spigot and tap at the base of the body. In use in Britain and Europe from mid 18th century.

COFFIN END SPOON
A 19th century American spoon with a square ended stem clipped at the corners to resemble a coffin.

COMMONWEALTH OR PURITAN TANKARD
A British tankard with cylindrical body, wide skirt foot and stepped lid with projecting point on surrounding flange opposite the handle. Of one pint capacity. Dates from Commonwealth period.

COMMUNION CUP
Used by the Reformed churches for holding communion wine.

COW CREAMER
Cream jug in the form of a cow, the tail as handle and mouth as spout. Introduced by John Schuppe in the mid-18th century and popular for many years.

CRIPPS, WILLIAM (d. after 1767)
English silversmith producing mainly domestic silver, some in rococo style.

CUPPING DISH
A flat shallow bowl with one pierced and shaped handle. Many have been used for bleeding patients, but more likely used as a porringer, especially in America.

CUT-CARD WORK
Gold or silver applied ornamentation much used from mid-17th to early 18th century. Often pierced and engraved and then soldered to object.

DE LAMERIE, PAUL (1688–1751)
Huguenot silversmith settled in London circa 1691, appointed goldsmith to George I in 1716. Produced all kinds of domestic ware in Huguenot and rococo style.

DELAPIERRE, MICHEL II (d. after 1785)
French silversmith producing domestic and some church plate in rococo style.

DESSERT SERVICE
Gilt set of plates, dishes and baskets, then also special dessert cutlery from early 18th century.

DISC-END SPOON
A flat stemmed spoon, the face of the terminal sometimes engraved with a skull and the back with a motto. Made in 16th and 17th century Scotland and N. England.

DISCHARGE MARK
A mark struck on finished silver indicating that the duty on that piece had been paid. Generally took the form of animals, birds, human heads, etc.

DISH CROSS
A support for hot dishes to prevent them damaging table tops. Generally with decorative handle at top. Most date from mid-18th to 19th century.

DIXON, JAMES & SONS
Manufacturers of Sheffield plate, Britannia ware, silver and electroplate in Sheffield, founded 1806.

DOUBLE CUP
German drinking vessel in the form of two matching cups on pedestal foot. The smaller, when inverted, fits into the larger as lid. Date from 15th-17th century.

DRAM CUP
Small, two-handled silver cup, similar to wine-taster.

DREDGER
Cylindrical vessel with pierced top like a caster, but usually larger and with finer holes for sprinkling powdered sugar etc.

DRESSER, CHRISTOPHER (1834–1904)
British designer who designed in various media, but in silver for Hukin & Heath, James Dixon and Elkington, in characteristic angular styles.

DUBOIS, ABRAHAM (fl. 1777–1807)
American silversmith working in Philadelphia. Produced domestic silver in neo-classical style.

DUMMER, JEREMIAH (1645–1718)
Boston silversmith who produced tankards, beakers, candlesticks, spoons and bleeding bowls.

DURAND, ANTOINE SEBASTIEN (d. after 1785)
Paris silversmith working in rococo style.

DUTCH GROTESQUE STYLE
Early 17th century style developed by Dutch silversmiths, characterised by fluid, curving forms and grotesque figures and masks. Motifs were always embossed.

DWT
Abbreviation for 'pennyweight', the smallest weight in the Troy system.

ECUELLE
Shallow, two-handled lidded bowl, sometimes with salver or stand, originally used for giving nourishment to women in childbirth. Made from late 17th to mid 18th century, mainly in France and Germany.

EDWARDS, JOHN (1671–1746)
English-born Boston silversmith, probably apprenticed to Jeremiah Dummer. Produced domestic wares and succeeded by his sons Samuel and Thomas and grandson Joseph.

EGG BOILER
A cylindrical vessel with flat cover and two handles, on stand with spirit lamp under, and wirework frame within body to hold four to six eggs. Used from late 18th century in Britain, usually en suite with eggcups.

EGG FRAME OR CRUET
Openwork frame holding two or more eggcups with spoons, and sometimes also a salt cellar. In use from late 17th century.

ELECTROPLATE
Silver coating deposited by electrolysis on base metal. The object is immersed in electrolytic solution, a current passed through and the silver particles transfer from anode to object which acts as cathode.

ELKINGTON & CO.
Firm manufacturing mainly electroplated wares founded by George Elkington with his uncle and cousin Henry, in 1829. Produced wide range of domestic articles, copying contemporary silver styles.

EMBOSSING
General term used to describe relief work on metal, produced by hammering reverse side, which is supported on a pliable bed.

EMES, JOHN (d. 1808)
London silversmith, partner of Henry Chawner. On his death, Emes' widow Rebecca went into partnership with Edward Barnard.

ENTREE DISH
A large covered dish for serving food, the lid often with detachable handles which could be used as another plate. Later examples often have heater stands en suite.

ENGRAVING

Decorative technique whereby pattern or inscription is traced with a graver, which removes fine threads of metal. Probably oldest decorative technique for metal.

EPERGNE

Fashionable silver or plate centrepiece for table, intended to save guests the trouble of passing dishes. Often had containers and plates suspended from branches, sometimes also fitted with candle sockets. Popular from mid 18th century.

ETCHING

Tracing of an incised pattern on silver or glass by means of acid. Rarely found on silver before 19th century, when it became common.

EWER

Large pouring vessel, originally with lid, for serving wine or water. Most were vase shaped, on a spreading foot. Earliest silver examples date from 16th century.

FEATHER EDGE

Engraved ornament of fine oblique lines on the edge of silver, much used on flatware.

FIDDLE PATTERN

Common stem pattern of 18th/19th century flatware, the flat stem end resembling a violin shape and narrowing to just above the bowl where it forms shoulders.

FILIGREE

Lacy ornamentation made from very fine gold or silver wire. Often used for openwork panels in baskets and boxes etc. Birmingham was a principal production centre in 18th and early 19th century.

FISH KNIFE

Knife with blunt shaped blade like contemporary fish slice, the handle often of ivory or mother-of-pearl. In use from early 19th century. Many later examples electroplated.

FISH SERVERS

Used in Britain from circa 1790, large knife and fork type implements for serving fish.

FISH SLICE

A utensil with a wide flat, engraved or pierced silver blade, introduced mid 18th century. Later examples conform to table service patterns and are comparatively plain.

FLAGON

Large pear-shaped or cylindrical vessel for serving wine or other liquors, closely related in form to contemporary tankards. Most were used for ecclesiastical purposes. Few secular silver flagons made after 17th century.

FLAT CHASING

A low relief linear surface decoration on silver, achieved without removing any metal, by hammering with small blunt tools. Popular in late 17th century.

FLATWARE

Term now used to mean cutlery, forming part of a service. Generically means flat vessels such as dishes, saucers, salvers etc.

FOX, CHARLES (d. c. 1838)

London silversmith who founded firm which continued till 1890s, producing domestic items characterised by advanced styling and decorative use of plant forms.

FROSTING

A rough or matt surface produced by heating object then dipping in hot dilute sulphuric acid, leaving film of pure silver on surface. Common 19th century form of ornamentation.

FREEDOM BOX

British or American box like a snuff box used in 18th and 19th century for conferring freedom of city, and engraved with appropriate city arms.

FUETER, DANIEL (fl. 1753–76)

Swiss-born silversmith who worked in London and then New York, making domestic items in rococo style.

GADROONING

An ornamental relief pattern used often as a border in the form of repeated parallel lines or lobes, at right angles or slanting from the edge of the object.

GARRARD & CO.

London silver retailers and jewellers founded 1792, and still in existence. Goldsmiths to Queen Victoria, and produce many trophies and cups.

GERMAN SILVER see ARGENTINE

GOLDSMITHS & SILVERSMITHS CO.

English gold, silver and jewellery designers, manufacturers and retailers founded in London by William Gibson in 1890. Taken over by Garrards in 1952.

GORHAM CORP.

American manufacturing silversmiths founded Rhode Island 1815. One of first manufacturers to use mass production techniques.

GRAPE SCISSORS

In use in Britain from late 18th century, earliest examples have ring handles and straight blades, while later have handles decorated with vine leaves, and blades cross over.

GUILLOCHE

An ornament of interlaced ribbon-like bands enclosing foliage rosettes, engraved or chased on 16th and late 18th century silver.

HALLMARK

The symbol struck at assay office on silver and gold items to indicate that they conformed to legal standards of purity. Used to denote whole group of marks employed, i.e. maker's, standard, date letter, hall.

HATCHING

Creation of shade or tone on silver surface with engraved parallel lines.

HENNELL FAMILY

An extensive family of London silversmiths working in the 18th and 19th century. Confusingly, there were two firms of cousins who totalled between them four Roberts, an uncle (1741–1811), nephew (b. 1769) and his son and grandson (1826–1892).

HOLLOW WARE

Generic term for vessels with raised sides, such as bowls and cups.

HOLY WATER BUCKET

A bucket or vase-shaped container with swing handle, and separate sprinkler, used for holy water.

HONEY POT

A honey container shaped like a bee skep, the top of the hive as lid, with ring or bee finial. Used in Britain from 18th century.

HUKIN & HEATH (1879–1953)

British manufacturers of tea and coffee sets and wide range of silver and electroplate articles in Birmingham. Christopher Dresser artistic director from c. 1880.

HUSK ORNAMENT
A stylized corn-husk used as decoration on baroque and neo-classical silver in 18th-early 19th century.

ICE PAIL
A footed, two-handled silver bucket, with central cavity for bottle and outer cavity for ice.

INKSTAND
A tray or box for holding writing materials, with containers for sealing wax, wafers, tapersticks, etc., either fitting into box or resting on tray.

JACK-IN-THE-CELLAR
A trick cup made in 17th century Holland and Germany with short, hollow column in centre of bowl. The figure of a child, concealed in the column, shoots up as the cup is tilted.

JENSEN, GEORG (1866–1935)
Danish silversmith, best known for cutlery, hand-hammered coffee pots and milk jugs and later, jewellery.

JOUBERT, FRANÇOIS (1742-after 1793)
Paris silversmith working in rococo style, making range of domestic items.

JUNGFRAUENBECHER
16th and 17th century German marriage or wager cup in the form of a girl with widespread skirt holding a swivel bowl above her head, the skirt forming a larger cup.

KETTLES
Tea kettles were made in silver from the late 17th century. Many were made in rococo style, with stand and small spirit lamp.

KINGS PATTERN
19th century British flatware pattern, fiddle stem edged with scroll design with shell in relief on face of stem end and on bowl back and anthemion in relief on face and back half way along stem.

KITCHEN PEPPER
Small cylindrical container for spices with scroll handle, spreading foot and domed pierced cover.

KOVSCH
Russian drinking ladle with boat shaped body and flat handle. Often richly decorated and used for ceremonial purposes.

LADLE
Spoon with deep round or ovoid bowl and long stem, for serving soups, punches, sauces etc. Most examples date from early 18th century onwards.

LAP JOINT
The method of joining a spoon finial to the stem, by cutting the two pieces into opposing L shapes.

LAPPED EDGE
In Sheffield plate, the sheet silver turned over the edge of a vessel to disguise the copper core, or an extra band of silver applied to achieve the same effect.

LEMON SQUEEZER
A hinged utensil with cuplike clamp to contain the fruit, used from early 19th century for extracting juice from lemons, limes etc.

LINWOOD, MATTHEW (1754–1826)
British silversmith working in Birmingham, best known for snuff boxes and vinaigrettes with die-stamped views of buildings or portraits.

LOADING
The use of material such as resin to give weight to the hollow section of an object (candlesticks etc.) stamped from thin sheet silver or Sheffield plate.

MARROW SCOOP
A silver implement with long narrow elongated bowl and narrow hollowed-out stem in use from 17th century for scooping marrow out of bones.

MATTING
Use of a punch or hammer to give a textured appearance to metal. In 19th century often used as a background for chased ornamentation.

MAZARINE
18th century pierced dish fitted into larger dish for straining fish or other similar foods.

MAZER
Silver mounted wooden (usually maple) drinking bowl, possibly of German origin, in use from 13th to 16th century.

MELON CUP
A British and European standing cup with melon shaped bowl and cover, a spiral plant stalk or tree trunk usually forming the stem. Popular in 16th and 17th century.

MILLS, NATHANIEL (fl. 1826–50)
Birmingham silversmith noted for his boxes and vinaigrettes, of oblong form with high-relief engine-turned panels of views and buildings.

MONSTRANCE
Glass or crystal cylinder set into a gold or silver structure used to display the Host in Catholic churches, and dating from Middle Ages onwards.

MONTEITH
A large silver bowl with scalloped, often detachable rim, from which wine glasses were suspended to cool over iced water. First appeared late 17th century.

MOTE SKIMMER
A small spoon with pierced bowl and circular tapering stem with spiked end, designed for removing floating tea-leaves from tea, the spike to clear leaves from perforations at base of spout.

MUFFINEER
Small caster used for sprinkling salt or sugar on muffins. Made from late 18th century.

MUSTARD BARREL
A barrel-shaped container for mustard with lid and sometimes scroll handle, in use in Britain and Europe from 18th century.

MUSTARD POT
A pot for mustard paste with cylindrical, ovoid or octagonal body and lid with aperture for mustard spoon. In later 18th century many had pierced bodies with blue glass liners.

NEF
Model ship of silver, gold or other precious materials used to mark the place of honour at table or hold the lord's eating utensils. Most made from 19th century as decoration only.

NICKEL SILVER
Alloy of 25% nickel and 75% copper, its white colour making it an inexpensive alternative to silver for cutlery and coinage.

NIELLO
A black metal alloy of silver, copper, lead and sulphur used for filling engraved designs on silverware.

NUTMEG GRATER

A tiny silver box with lid containing a rasp for grating nutmeg and a container to catch the powder. Made in a variety of novelty shapes. In use from mid 18th to mid 19th century.

OIL AND VINEGAR STAND

Also known as cruet stand, a silver or plate frame to hold cruets and sometimes casters, in use from 18th century.

OLD ENGLISH PATTERN

A cutlery pattern wherein the flat, rounded stem end turns downwards. In use from mid-18th century.

OLIVE SPOON

See strainer spoon.

ONSLOW PATTERN

English flatware pattern with stem end turned back to form rolled scroll and face of stem moulded into ridges converging at a point midway along it. Plain or leaf drop reinforcement along spoon back. Mid 18th century.

ORLOFF SERVICE

Circa 3,000 piece dinner service in neo-classical style commissioned by Catherine the Great from Roettiers of Paris for her favourite, Prince Orloff, in 1770s.

OSTRICH EGG CUP

A ceremonial cup with ostrich egg bowl set in silver, silver-gilt or gold mount. Mainly English or German, 15th and 16th century.

OVERSTAMPING

Where retailer puts his stamp on a piece already stamped with maker's mark.

OVTCHINNIKOV, PAUL AKIMOVICH (1851–c.1917)

Russian Imperial silversmith who revived Old Russian style. Pieces designed for Russian market rather than international clientèle.

PAKTONG

Chinese alloy introduced into Europe in late 18th century. Polishes to brightness of silver and does not tarnish. Used for grates, candlesticks etc.

PAP BOAT

Boat shaped small container used in 18th and 19th century for feeding semi-liquid food to infants.

PARCEL GILT

Medieval term meaning partially gilded. Often used for the inside of vessels where the contents (e.g. salt) might damage the silver.

PATEN

Small circular dish for holding Communion bread.

PEDESTAL SALT

Standing salt shaped like architectural column pedestal. Usually English, 16th century.

PEG TANKARD

Basically Scandinavian tankard form with vertical row of studs or pegs inside to measure the liquid contained. Some also made in Scotland and N. England.

PENNER

Tapering hollow silver tube with compartments for ink and quills, often with seal finial. Used from 17th century in Britain.

PENNYWEIGHT

The smallest Troy weight, 24 grains or $1/20$oz. Troy.

PERFUME OR PASTILLE BURNER

Small silver container with pierced cover for burning perfume or pastilles, in use from 16th century.

PIERCING

A technique of metal decoration whereby the background to the pattern is cut away by hand or machine. Much used in 18th century for baskets, slices, etc.

PILGRIM BOTTLE

A bottle with flattened ovoid body, narrow neck, moulded foot and chain stopper made from 16th century in Europe and Britain. Made in 17th and 18th century as sideboard plate.

PINEAPPLE CUP

A highly decorated German 16th and 17th century standing cup with the bowl formed as a pineapple, the stem as a tree trunk or a figure.

PLANISHING

Levelling a metal surface using a broad, oval-faced hammer.

PLATE

Old term used to describe articles of gold or silver, not to be confused with Sheffield plate or plated wares, where silver is fused to a base metal alloy.

PLATEAU

A silver or plated base with glass or mirror top, placed on table beneath épergne or candelabra for display purposes. Can also mean a shallow dish on a short stem, mainly of Iberian origin.

POMANDER

Small silver box for sweet-smelling spices carried up to 17th century to ward off infections. Superseded by vinaigrette.

PORRINGER

A two handled eating or drinking bowl, sometimes lidded; dates from 17th century onwards.

POT POURRI BOWL

Small silver bowl with footring and pierced cover for holding sweet-smelling herbs. Very popular in 18th century Netherlands.

POTATO RING

Incorrect name for a dish ring, an Irish hollow, spool shaped support for hot dishes and bowls, in use from mid 18th to early 19th century.

POUNCE BOX

A baluster or vase shaped pot with pierced cover used for sprinkling pounce (gum sandarac) on writing paper. Made from 18th century, often as part of an inkstand.

PRICKET CANDLESTICK

Earliest type of candlestick with spike for impaling candle, seldom found for domestic use after 17th century though ecclesiastical use continued.

PUNCH BOWL

Large bowl, sometimes with two, usually ring, handles and footrim, used from late 17th century for serving punch.

PUNCHED WORK

Relief decoration on metal made by grouping two or more blunt tools in a pattern and punching them onto the object.

PUNCH LADLE

Ladle with deep bowl and sometimes with serving lip, and long handle for serving punch. Used in Britain from 18th century.

PYX

Small box, often richly decorated and surmounted by a cross on the lid, in which the sacrament was conveyed to the sick and dying.

QUAICH
A Scottish silver drinking bowl, circular, with two flat handles and sometimes a low circular foot. Made in the 17th and 18th century in various sizes.

QUEEN'S PATTERN
19th century British flatware pattern, resembling King's pattern but with a reinforcing palmette on the bowl back instead of a shell.

RAISING
The technique of forming a hollow vessel from sheet metal by successive rows of hammering on a stake from base upwards. Hammer marks removed from outside by planishing.

RAMSDEN, OMAR (1873–1939)
English silversmith associated with Arts & Crafts Movement. Specialised in ceremonial pieces, and later work shows Art Deco style, while earlier pieces often show Celtic and Tudor influence.

RAT-TAIL SPOON
A spoon with elongated V shaped extension of stem on back of bowl for reinforcement.

REED-AND-TIE MOULDING
A neo-classical border ornament of reeds bound with ribbon.

REPOUSSÉ
Relief ornament hammered from the under or inside of the metal, usually heightened with surface chasing.

REVERE, PAUL II (1735–1818)
Son of Paul Revere the Elder, a Huguenot silversmith who emigrated from Guernsey, Paul the Younger worked in Boston. Made range of domestic silver in English styles; became famous also for his political involvement during the War of Independence.

RIESENPOKAL
Huge 16th century German standing cup with cover, with some examples over 3ft. high. Made for display rather than use!

ROSEWATER BOWL
Silver table bowl, often en suite with a ewer, in which diners rinsed their fingers at table before the introduction of forks. Some still made in 18th century, and smaller versions for toilet services.

SALAD SERVERS
British and European utensils for serving salad, in use from late 18th century, comprising large spoon and fork with spoon-like bowl ending in prongs.

SALT
A container for salt, originally called a saler.

SALT CELLAR
A small salt container, at first in shape of a small bowl with gadrooned border and on feet or a low stem. From 18th century often made with pierced body and glass liner.

SALT SPOON
Small spoon with shovel-shaped, round or oval bowl, used from 18th century.

SALVER
A flat plate or tray used for serving food or drink.

SAMOVAR
A Russian tea urn with one or more taps, and domed lid with finial, in use from 18th century. Also made elsewhere.

SAUCEBOAT
Container for sauce with boat shaped body, some with spouts at each end, others with one spout and handle. In use from 18th century.

SAUCEPAN
Silver vessel with cylindrical, bellied or pear-shaped body, generally with handle set at right angles to spout or lip. Small examples often used to warm brandy. Most are 18th century.

SAUCE TUREEN
Container for sauce in shape of soup tureen but smaller, in use from late 18th century.

SCHUPPE, JOHN (fl. 1753–73)
London silversmith, possibly of Dutch origin, especially associated with cow creamers.

SCONCE
Wall light for candles, consisting of a plate with branches especially fashionable in 17th century. Now used to refer also to other candlesticks.

SEAL SPOON
15th to 17th century spoon with finial shaped like a wax seal.

SECOND COURSE DISH
A circular dish for serving entremets and puddings, which conforms in style and pattern to contemporary meat dishes.

SERVING SPOONS
Large spoons which followed patterns of smaller spoons, called hash spoons in Scotland and Ireland.

SHEFFIELD PLATE
Process developed in Sheffield circa 1742 by T. Bolsover, whereby two rolled sheets of silver are fused with a copper core. Cheaper than silver and used for same types of vessels.

SILVER GILT
Silver with applied surface of gold.

SNUFF MULL
Box made of horn, ivory, shell, deer's hoof etc. and silver mounted and sometimes set with semi-precious stones. Made in Scotland in late 18th-early 19th century.

SNUFFERS
A silver implement for trimming candle wicks, basically of scissor form with a box attached to one arm for catching the snuffed wick.

SNUFFER TRAY
Oblong or oval tray, sometimes footed and with handle, for holding snuffers.

SOAP BOX
Spherical box with moulded foot for holding soap, with hinged, pierced or plain cover, 18th century.

SOY FRAME
Oblong or oval stand with ring frame for holding soy or sauce bottles. Introduced in late 18th century and sometimes en suite with larger cruet frames.

SPICE BOX
Small silver box with hinged cover to hold spices, sweetmeats etc. 16th and 17th century examples often in the form of scallop shells. In 18th century shaped like oval caskets.

SPOOL OR CAPSTAN SALT
Mid-17th century salt container with spool shaped body and scroll brackets around top edge for holding napkin or plate.

SPOON TRAY

Used before introduction of saucers for holding tea-drinkers' spoons. Usually of oval shape with plain or ornamental edge.

STEEPLE CUP

16th-17th century British standing cup with trumpet shaped base and stem, egg shaped bowl and cover with steeple finial.

STERLING MARK

Lion passant mark (Thistle in Scotland) used since 1544 by Goldsmith's Company as guarantee that article was of Sterling standard.

STERLING STANDARD

Established standard of purity of English silver since Anglo-Saxon times – 925 parts per 100 pure.

STORR, PAUL (1771–1844)

London silversmith who worked for a number of aristocratic and royal patrons and was noted for silver on a grand scale. Worked in rococo and classical Roman styles.

STRAINER

A utensil with a circular, shallow, pierced bowl with one or two handles, used in 17th and 18th century for straining particles from punch.

STRAINER SPOON

Small spoon with pierced bowl and circular tapering stem with spiked end, the spike used to clear the clogged holes in teapot spouts. British, in use from end 17th century.

STRAWBERRY DISH

Small saucer-like dishes made in the 17th and 18th century, early examples with punched decoration, later with scalloped rim. Sometimes found in sets with serving dish.

SUCKET SPOON

Implement with rat-tailed spoon at one end and two or three prongs at the other, used from 17th century in Britain for eating candied fruit.

SUGAR CRUSHER

A rod with disc at one end and ring at the other, circa 5in. long. Used in 19th century Britain for breaking lumps off sugar loaf.

SUGAR NIPPERS

Usually of George I and II vintage, an early form of sugar tongs of scissor-like shape.

SUGAR SPOON

A small spoon, shovel-shaped or with pierced circular bowl for sprinkling, used in 18th and 19th century Britain.

SUGAR TONGS

Used from late 17th century for handling lumps of sugar. Early examples modelled as miniature fire tongs, later of spring bow form with spoon-shaped pans.

SWAGE

A shaped border on a salver or tray etc. Also a tool for forming border or shaping up small objects from flat.

TABLE SERVICE

Set of matching silver dishes, tureens, etc. made for wealthy families from early 18th century.

TANKARD

Drinking vessel for beer, ale or cider with single handle and usually with hinged lid.

TAPERSTICK

Small candlestick, 5–7in. high, for holding taper. Made from late 17th century.

TAZZA

Wine cup with shallow circular bowl. Also now applies to wide, shallow dish on stem and/or foot.

TEA CADDY or CANISTER

A small oblong or octagonal canister for holding tea. Silver examples date from late 17th century onwards. From 18th century made in other shapes and materials and known as caddies from end of 18th century.

TEACUP

Small, circular, handleless, drinking vessel for tea dating from late 17th and early 18th century. Superseded by porcelain and rare.

TEA KETTLE

Introduced circa 1690 and resembles tea pot in form. Some had tripod stand and spirit lamp, and later some examples had tap instead of spout. Superseded by tea urns circa 1765.

TEAPOT

Container for brewing tea. Silver examples date from 18th century onwards.

TEA SERVICE

A set comprising teapot, milk jug and sugar bowl made en suite from early 18th century in Europe and America.

TEASPOON

Small silver spoon made as part of tea service. In use from late 17th century on, and styles followed those of larger spoons.

TEA TRAY

Tray or salver for serving tea, made in a variety of shapes and sizes.

TEA URN

Large, vase-shaped hot-water urn introduced around 1760 in Britain and Europe, and largely replaced tea kettle. Usually has a compartment for red-hot iron to keep water hot.

THISTLE CUP

Scottish mug made from late 17th century with slightly bulging body, decorated round base and with everted rim, the whole shape reminiscent of a thistle.

THREAD AND SHELL PATTERN

Decoration most common on fiddle-pattern cutlery, where stem is edged with a moulded thread line, with relief shell form on face of stem end and back of bowl.

TIFFANY & CO.

New York manufacturing jewellers who also produced silver from 1850. Large factory built 1892 in Newark NJ, for production of electroplate.

TIGERWARE JUG

German silver-mounted stoneware jug with mottled surface resembling tiger markings. Of big-bellied form, and imported into England in 16th century.

TOAST RACK

A wire rack fitting into and sometimes detachable from, a tray base. In use in Britain from late 18th century.

TOBACCO BOX

Small metal box with tight-fitting lid for storing tobacco. In use from late 17th century and often finely engraved with armorials or ciphers.

TOILET SERVICE

Set of toilet articles made for rich British and European ladies from the 16th century. Some elaborate 17th century sets comprised over 50 items.

TOUCHSTONE

A piece of dark flint or other hard stone on which a piece of silver of known quality could be rubbed to compare its mark with that of a piece being assayed.

TREFID SPOON
Spoon with rounded stem end divided into three sections by two small cuts then flattened. Known from circa 1650.

TREFOIL
Gothic ornament in form of three leaves, similarly, quatrefoil (four leaves) and cinquefoil (five).

TREMBLEUSE
Saucer with deep recess and raised ring, made mainly in Europe to hold tea or chocolate cup.

TRENCHER SALT
Small individual salt cellar with solid sides, lying flat on the table. Most silver examples date from mid 17th to mid 18th century.

TROY WEIGHT
Standard weight system in English-speaking countries for gold, silver and precious stones.

TULIP ORNAMENT
Popular ornamental motif for silver in 17th century.

TUMBLER
Small cylindrical drinking cup on thick hemispherical base to steady it, made in Britain and Europe in 17th and 18th century.

TUREEN
Circular or oval serving bowl for soup etc., used from early 18th century. Often on spreading base or feet with domed cover with finial. Smaller versions introduced mid-18th century for sauces.

VEGETABLE DISH
Covered serving dish similar to entrée dish but with domed cover with fixed handle. Often comes with stand and burner. In use from circa 1800.

VENISON DISH
Large oval meat dish with ribbed base (forming cross) and well at one end to collect gravy. Often on two stud feet, the well forming the third foot. In use in Britain early 19th century.

VINAIGRETTE
A small box with hinged lid and inner pierced grille, containing a sponge soaked in aromatic vinegar. Dates from circa 1800 onwards, for ladies' use against faintness.

WAFER BOX
An inkstand fitting, comprising a box for thin adhesive discs or wafers. In use from mid 16th to 19th century.

WAGER CUP
A trick cup dating from the 16th and 17th century, most having two tilting bowls, the larger of which had to be drunk first. Mainly Dutch or German.

WAITER
Small tray in use during 18th and 19th century for handing letters, wine etc. Often forms part of a set.

WAKELIN, EDWARD (d. 1784) AND JOHN (d. c. 1802)
Father and son, silversmiths working in London. John Wakelin one of the original partners in Wakelin & Garrard, predecessors of the modern Garrards.

WARWICK FRAME
A British silver cruet frame with quatrefoil or cinquefoil base, each leaf having a guard ring of moulded wire to hold the bottle, and usually with a central vertical ring handle.

WAXJACK
An open frame stand for a coil of sealing wax threaded round a central pin and fed through nozzle above. Dates from late 17th century onwards.

WHISTLE TANKARD
A silver tankard with a hole in the lower part of the hollow handle. Unlikely, as sometimes claimed, that hole was used to whistle for another drink, rather to let hot air escape during soldering to body.

WILLAUME, DAVID THE ELDER (c.1658–1741)
French-trained Huguenot silversmith working in London, specialized in wine cisterns and made a range of domestic silver. Succeeded by his son, David the Younger.

WILLKOMM
German 'welcome' cup, a standing cup used by the guilds, presumably to toast visitors.

WINDMILL CUP
Late 16th and 17th century Dutch, windmill-shaped, wager cup, the body acting as a bowl, the sails set in motion first and the contents to be drunk before they stopped.

WINE CISTERN
A large oval vessel on feet or base for cooling wine bottles. Usually had two handles. Most surviving examples date from 17th and 18th century.

WINE COASTER
A circular decanter or bottle stand for the table, generally with wood base and pierced silver sides. Most come in pairs or sets. In use from mid 18th century.

WINE COOLER
A two handled vessel on low foot or base, for cooling individual wine bottle. Mostly of urn or tub shape and with detachable liner. In use from late 17th century until about 1850.

WINE FOUNTAIN
A large, urn-shaped vessel with lid and two handles and tap at base of body. Used from late 17th to mid 18th century to hold large quantities of wine.

WINE FUNNEL
Cone shaped silver funnel with detachable strainer used for decanting wine. Often came with domed saucer-like stand on which it could rest inverted.

WINE LABEL
Made in England from about 1725 to identify contents of glass decanters, hung by chain around the neck. Most can be dated by style of decoration.

WINE TASTER
Shallow-bowled vessels, with or without handles, used by vintners for sampling wine.

WINE WAGON
A two-bottle coaster raised on wheels like a wagon, for passing wine around the table after the cloth was lifted.

WIREWORK
A rod of metal drawn out to form a thin wire and repeatedly annealed to retain malleability. Much used to make baskets, toast racks and filigree work.

WODEWOSE SPOON
15th century English spoon with knop in form of a wild man of the woods with a club.

WRIGGLEWORK
A form of engraving using a zig-zag line cut by a rocking motion. Particularly in late 17th century, often used in conjunction with line engraving.

WRYTHEN
Twisted or coiled decoration, in which cast ribs spiral round the object.

Birmingham

Chester

Dublin

Edinburgh

Exeter

Glasgow

London

Newcastle

Sheffield

York

Example for 1850

	B	C	D	Ed	Ex	G	L	N	S	Y
1730										
1731										
1732										
1733										
1734										
1735										
1736										
1737										
1738										
1739										
1740										
1741										
1742										
1743										
1744										
1745										
1746										
1747										
1748										
1749										
1750										
1751										
1752										
1753										
1754										
1755										
1756										
1757										
1758										
1759										
1760										
1761										
1762										
1763										
1764										
1765										
1766										
1767										
1768										
1769										
1770										
1771										
1772										
1773										
1774										

	B	C	D	Ed	Ex	G	L	N	S	Y
1700										
1701										
1702										
1703										
1704										
1705										
1706										
1707										
1708										
1709										
1710										
1711										
1712										
1713										
1714										
1715										
1716										
1717										
1718										
1719										
1720										
1721										
1722										
1723										
1724										
1725										
1726										
1727										
1728										
1729										

	B	C	D	Ed	Ex	G	L	N	S	Y
1775	C	Y	C	D	C			U	I	N
1776	D	a	a	I	D	O	a	K		R
1777	E	b	E	F	E		b	L		h
1778	F	C	F	Z	F		C	M	H	C
1779	G	d	G	G	G		d	N	A	D
1780	H	e	H	A	H		e	O	C	E
1781	I	f	I	B		I	f	P	D	
1782	K	g	K	C			g	Q	G	
1783	L	h	L	D	K	S	h	R	B	H
1784	M	i	M	E	U		i	S	I	J
1785	N	k	N	F	M	S	k	T	V	K
1786	O	l	O	G	N		l	U	U	L
1787	P	m	P	O			m	W	T	A
1788	Q	n	Q	H	P		n	X	m	B
1789	R	O	R	IJ	q		O	Y	M	C
1790	S	P	S	K	R	S	p	Z	L	D
1791	T	q	T	L			q	A	P	e
1792	U	r	U	M	t		r	B	U	f
1793	V	S	W	N	u		S	C	G	g
1794	W	t	X	O	W		t	D	m	h
1795	X	u	Y	P	X	S	u	E	q	i
1796	Y	V	Z	Q	y		A	F	Z	k
1797	Z	A	A	R			B	G	X	L
1798	a	B	B	S	B		C	H	V	M
1799	b	C	C	T	C		D	I	E	N
1800	C	D	D	U	D	S	E	K	N	O
1801	d	E	E	V	E		F	L	H	P
1802	e	F	F	W			G	M	O	
1803	f	G	G	X	G		H	N	F	R
1804	g	H	H	Y	H		I	O		S
1805	h	I	I	Z	I		K	P		T
1806	i	K	K				L	Q	A	U
1807	J	L	L	b	L		M	R	S	V
1808	k	M	M	C	M		N	S	P	W
1809	l	N	N	d	N		O	T	K	X
1810	m	O	O	e	O		P	U	L	Y
1811	n	P	P	f	P		Q	W	C	Z
1812	O	Q	Q	g	Q		R	X	D	a
1813	P	R	R	h	R		S	Y	R	b
1814	q	S	S	i	S		T	Z	W	C
1815	r	T	T	j	T		U	A	O	d
1816	S	U	U	k	U		a	B	T	e
1817	t	V	W	l	a		b	C	X	f
1818	u	A	X	m	b		C	D	I	g
1819	V	B	Y	n	C	A	d	E	V	h

	B	C	D	Ed	Ex	G	L	N	S	Y
1820	W	C	Z	O	d	B	e	F	Q	i
1821	X	D	A	P	e	C	f	G	Y	k
1822	y	D	B	q	f	D	g	H	Z	l
1823	Z	E	C	r	g	E	h	I	U	m
1824	A	F	D	s	h	F	i	K	A	n
1825	B	G	E	t	i	G	k	L	b	O
1826	C	H	F	u	k	H	l	M	C	p
1827	D	I	G	v	l	I	m	N	O	q
1828	E	K	H	w	m	J	n	O	e	r
1829	F	L	I	x	n	K	O	P	g	S
1830	G	M	K	y	O	L	P	Q	g	t
1831	H	N	L	Z	P	M	q	R	h	u
1832	J	O	M	A	q	N	r	S	k	V
1833	K	P	N	S	r	O	S	T	l	w
1834	L	Q	O	C	s	P	t	U	m	r
1835	M	R	P	D	t	Q	u	W	P	P
1836	N	S	Q	E	u	R	A	X	q	z
1837	O	T	R	F	A	S	B	Y	r	A
1838	P	U	S	G	B	T	C	Z	S	B
1839	Q	A	T	H	C	U	D	A	t	C
1840	R	B	U	J	d	V	E	B	U	D
1841	S	C	V	K	e	W	f	C	V	E
1842	T	D	W	L	f	X	G	D	X	F
1843	U	E	X	M	G	Y	H	E	Z	G
1844	W	F	Y	A	h	Z	J	F	A	H
1845	x	G	Z	O	J	A	K	G	B	I
1846	Y	b	a	P	K	B	L	H	C	K
1847	p	J	b	O	l	C	M	I	D	L
1848	Z	R	C	R	D	A	N	J	E	M
1849	A	L	d	S	A	E	O	K	F	N
1850	B	M	e	T	f	P	P	L	G	O
1851	C	A	f	u	O	G	Q	M	H	P
1852	D	O	g	W	H	R	R	N	I	Q
1853	E	P	h	W	i	S	S	O	K	R
1854	F	Q	i	X	J	T	T	P	L	S
1855	G	R	k	Y	K	U	U	Q	M	T
1856	H	S	l	Z	L	V	V	R	N	V
1857	I	C	m	A	A	W	b	O		
1858	J	a	n	B	B	A	C	T	P	
1859	K	b	O	C	C	D	d	U	R	
1860	L	c	P	D	D	E	e	W	S	
1861	M	f	q	E	E	f	f	X	T	
1862	N	g	r	F	F	R	g	Y	U	
1863	O	Z	S	G	G	S	h	Z	V	
1864	P	t	t	H	H	T	i	a	w	

	B	C	D	Ed	Ex	G	L	N	S	Y
1865	Q	b	u	i	I	k	b			X
1866	R	c	v	K	K	l	c			Y
1867	S	d	w	L	L	m	d			Z
1868	T	e	x	M	M	x	n	e		A
1869	U	f	y	N	N	o	o			B
1870	V	g	z	O	O	z	p			C
1871	W	h	A	P	P	A	q	h		D
1872	X	i	B	Q	Q	B	r	i		E
1873	Y	k	C	R	R	C	s	k		F
1874	Z	l	D	S	S	D	t	l		G
1875	a	m	E	T	T	E	u	m		H
1876	b	n	F	U	U	F	A	n		J
1877	c	o	G	V	A	G	B	o		K
1878	d	p	H	W	B	H	C	p		L
1879	e	q	U	X	C	I	D	q		M
1880	f	r	K	Y	D	J	E	r		N
1881	g	s	L	Z	E	K	F	s		O
1882	h	t	M	a	F	L	G	t		P
1883	i	u	N	b		M	H	u		Q
1884	k	A	O	c		N	I			R
1885	l	B	P	d		O	K			S
1886	m	C	Q	e		P	L			T
1887	n	D	R	f		Q	M			U
1888	o	E	S	g		R	N			V
1889	p	F	T	h		S	O			W
1890	q	G	U	i		T	P			X
1891	r	H	V	k		U	Q			Y
1892	s	I	W	l		V	R			Z
1893	t	K	X	m		W	S			a
1894	u	L	V	n		X	T			b
1895	v	M	Z	o		Y	U			c
1896	m	N	A	p		Z	a			d
1897	x	O	B	q		A	b			e
1898	y	P	C	r		B	c			f
1899	z	Q	D	s		C	d			g
1900	a	R	E	t		D	e			h
1901	b	A	F	u		E	f			i
1902	c	B	G	w		F	g			k
1903	d	C	H	x		G	h			l
1904	e	D	H	y		H	i			m
1905	f	E	K	z		G	k			n
1906	g	F	L	A		G	l			o
1907	h	G	M	B		K	m			p
1908	i	H	A	C		L	n			q
1909	k	J	O	D		M	o			r

	B	C	D	Ed	Ex	G	L	N	S	Y
1910	l	K	P	E			N	p		S
1911	m	L	Q	F			O	q		t
1912	n	M	R	G			P	r		u
1913	o	N	S	H			Q	s		v
1914	p	O	T	I			R	t		w
1915	q	P	U	K			S	u		x
1916	r	Q	A	L			T	a		y
1917	s	R	B	M			U	b		z
1918	t	S	C	N			V	c		a
1919	u	T	D	O			W	d		b
1920	v	U	E	P			X	e		c
1921	w	V	F	Q			Y	f		d
1922	x	W	S	R			Z	g		e
1923	y	X	h	S			a	h		f
1924	z	Y	i	T			b	i		g
1925	A	Z	B	U			C	k		h
1926	B	a	c	V			D	l		i
1927	C	B	m	W			e	m		k
1928	D	C	n	X			f	n		l
1929	E	D	O	Y			g	o		m
1930	F	e	P	Z			h	p		n
1931	G	ff		A			i	q		o
1932	H	G	Q	B			j	r		p
1933	J	B	R	C			k	s		q
1934	K	J	S	D			l	t		r
1935	L	K	C	E			m	u		s
1936	M	L	U	F			n	A		t
1937	N	m	V	G			O	B		u
1938	O	n	W	H			P	C		v
1939	P	O	X	J			Q	D		w
1940	Q	P	Y	K			r	E		x
1941	R	Q	Z	L			s	F		y
1942	S	R	A	M			t	G		z
1943	T	S	B	N			u	H		A
1944	U	T	C	O			v	I		B
1945	V	U	D	P			W	K		C
1946	W	V	E	Q			X	L		D
1947	X	W	F	R			Y	M		E
1948	Y	X	G	S			Z	N		F
1949	Z	Y	H	T			A	O		G
1950	A	Z	I	U			B	P		H
1951	B	A	J	V			C	Q		I
1952	C	B	K	W			D	R		K
1953	D	C	L	X			E	S		L
1954	C	D	M	Y			F	T		M

In the 1760s a rather strange looking addition was made to the repertoire of dishes on the fashionable dining table. This was the argyle, a vessel about 7in. high, reminiscent of an ill-proportioned teapot, designed for the purpose of keeping gravy hot.

The spout was set low, so that the best of the gravy was poured, and they came with heating units consisting either of a central box iron or a hot water chamber positioned either centrally, below the gravy chamber, or between an outer and inner lining. Those with box irons tend to have a more slender stem, while a central hot water heater is found in straight sided or hexagonal argyles towards the end of the century.

By and large, during the period of their popularity, which lasted until about 1820, argyle design followed that of teapots. Earlier examples tended to lack a footrim, but later a loose stand was introduced, either on four ball or moulded feet to protect the table, and this in turn was followed by a flaring footrim.

A Sheffield plate argyle with engraved ribbon-tied festoons and fronds, with beaded edging, detachable cover and wood scroll handle, 4³/₄in. high. (Bearne's) £550

A Regency plain argyle on circular domed foot, by Wm. Burwash, 1819, 6¹/₈in. high, 17oz.15dwt. £1,425

A George III plain cylindrical argyle, with elongated curved spout, short curved spout with hinged flap, wicker-covered scroll handle, and reeded borders, by Andrew Fogelberg and Stephen Gilbert, 1791, 4³/₄in. high, gross 11oz. (Christie's) £2,750

A George III argyle, of urn shape, on a pedestal foot, wood handle, 20cm. high overall, by Henry Green, 1791, 14oz. (Phillips) £2,600

A George III plain vase-shaped argyle, by Wm. Elliott, 1818, 8½in. high, gross 25oz. £2,420

An Edwardian gadrooned cylindrical argyle, in the late 18th century taste, with a wicker-covered scroll handle, Charles Stuart Harris and Son, London 1907, 4³/₄in., 14.25oz. (Christie's S. Ken) £418

A George IV Sheffield plate argyle, in the manner of Robert Gainsford, the baluster body chased with foliage, 6¹/₄in. high. (Woolley & Wallis) £380

Apart from simple vessels for washing in, basins have been adapted for a number of specific purposes. Barbers' basins, for example, were characterised by a piece cut out of the rim for placing against the neck. Though in use from the late 15th century by the versatile barber-surgeons of the day, most silver examples date from the late 17th or 18th century and are either circular or oval in form.

Then there are rose water basins, used from the 16th century onwards for finger washing at table. These had their religious counterpart in the baptismal basin, similar in shape and design but decorated with Biblical figures and scenes. Used from the 17th century, most are of American origin. European examples are rare, owing to the prevalence there of the baptismal font. Basins were also an integral part of the afternoon tea ritual. Silver sugar containers had been in use since the early 18th century, but it was only in the 1790s that a squat basin form emerged, by now usually part of a matching tea service.

A French silver-gilt oval basin, the everted rim applied with oval vignettes, a nymph riding hippocamps, sea monster, palmettes and scrolls, by Marc-Augustine Lebrun, Paris 1821–1838, 14¹/₂ in. long, 942grs. (Christie's) £4,950

A rare silver barber basin, maker's mark of William Moulton IV, Newburyport, circa 1815, 10¹/₄ in. diameter, 24 oz. 10 dwt. (Christie's) £3,080

A Hukin and Heath silver sugar basin designed by Dr Christopher Dresser, with hinged loop handle, the hemispherical bowl with raised double-rib decoration, with stamped maker's marks and London hallmarks for 1879, 12.5cm. diam. 182 grams. (Christie's) £3,960

A George III beaded, pierced and bright-cut oval swing-handled pedestal sugar basin fitted with a blue glass liner, London 1784, incuse mark, 6³/₄ in. overall, 8oz. free. (Christie's S. Ken) £506

A George III Irish punch-beaded and spiral-fluted cauldron sugar basin on shell and hoof feet, Matthew West, Dublin 1787, 5in., 5.25oz. (Christie's S. Ken) £572

A Louis XV basin, by Gilles Degage, Nantes, 1766, 12in. diam., 30oz. £1,360

A George III Irish cauldron sugar basin on lions' mask and paw feet, later-decorated with punch-beaded spiral fluting, 5³/₄ in., 9oz. (Christie's S. Ken) £385

BASKETS

Baskets were variously used for bread, cakes or fruit, while smaller examples were also popular for sweets and sugar.

The earliest cake baskets tended to be round, and are very rare. After 1730, however, they became very popular and it was at this time that oval forms with swing handles and pierced bodies were introduced. It is always worth while examining the piercing very carefully, as any damage is very difficult to repair.

Wirework bodies with applied foliage, wheat and flowers became fashionable about 1770, while later examples more often have engraved solid bodies, and gadrooned or reeded rims. Most cake baskets tend to have armorials on the bottom.

Early examples often lack a hallmark, but from 1760 one is more likely to find a lion passant mark, sometimes with the maker's mark as well. After the introduction of the duty mark in 1784, handles should definitely be marked. After 1800, circular gilt baskets for dessert use were reintroduced.

A George III silver-gilt oval basket, on spreading foot pierced and chased with palmettes and anthemion ornament, by Thomas Arden, 1805, 13¼ in. long, 54oz.
(Christie's)   £7,150

A good late Victorian basket by William Comyns, of bombé flared quatrefoil form, raised upon an elaborately cast and pierced foliate and knurl foot, London 1888, 1492 grammes, 38cm. wide.
(Spencer's)   £1,650

A pair of highly important George II two-handled circular baskets, each on pierced spreading foot with applied rope-twist band above, by Paul de Lamerie, 1734, 12½in. wide, 81oz.
(Christie's)   £572,000

George II silver basket, by Samuel Herbert & Co., London, circa 1757–58, in the rococo taste, of oval cross section, with a pierced and cast border of C and S scrolls, cast arched swing handle.
(William Doyle Galleries) £6,710

A 19th century German silver basket, the sides of leaves, terminating in external hanging spheres, with spiral border and filigree handle, 845gr.
(Duran)   £556

German silver reticulated basket in the Louis XVI taste, late 19th century, oval, of cast parts, the body with openwork sides of vertical ribs overlaid with ribbon tied floral garlands, 15in. long, 43oz. 12dwt.
(Butterfield & Butterfield) £1,426

An attractive late Victorian basket by Martin Hall & Co., the beaded border enclosing pierced arcading and strapwork engraving, London 1877, 645 grammes, 30cm. wide.
(Spencer's)   £500

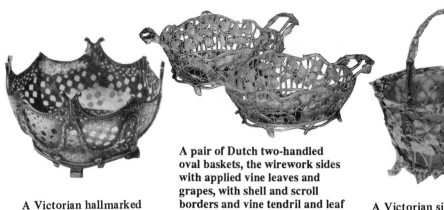

A Victorian hallmarked
silver basket with scroll
base and feet, London
1886, 19oz.   £400

A pair of Dutch two-handled
oval baskets, the wirework sides
with applied vine leaves and
grapes, with shell and scroll
borders and vine tendril and leaf
handles, Rotterdam, 1769,
12½in. overall, 1,253grs.
(Christie's)   £17,600

A Victorian silver gilt basket,
by Barnard & Co., 1846,
6¼in. diam., 13oz.3dwt.
        £850

A good early Victorian silver gilt
basket by Robert Hennell, of
shaped oval form with
openwork overhead swing
handle, London 1858, 1,052
grammes, 36cm. wide.
(Spencer's)   £1,050

A pair of George III silver-gilt
oval baskets and covers, the
spreading sides and domed
covers pierced and chased with
fruit and vines, by William Pitts,
1808, 12½in. wide, 94 oz.
(Christie's)   £6,600

A German oval basket with
swing handle and oak leaf
border, on oval base with four
paw and ball feet, date for 1833,
1,130gr.
(Kunsthaus am Museum) £1,016

Large German silver basket,
early 20th century, the flat oval
base a cast plaque showing a
group of winged putti gathering
flowers, 14in. wide, 25oz.
12dwts.
(Butterfield & Butterfield)
        £1,557

A pair of Edwardian baskets, the
sides pierced in scroll and star
designs, leafy borders and
pierced scroll feet, by Messrs.
Elkington, Sheffield, 1901,
21.5cm., 21.5oz.
(Lawrence Fine Art)   £902

A Dutch small two-handled oval
basket, the pierced sides applied
with portrait busts, husk
festoons and ribbon ornament,
by Johannes Janse(n),
Rotterdam, 1777, 7½in. overall
width, 266grs.
(Christie's)   £2,420

BREAD

A George II shaped oval bread basket, with shell and scroll border and swing handle, by John Swift, 1746, 12¾in. long, 45oz.
(Christie's) £13,200

A parcel gilt and enamel bread basket of circular form with rope-twist handles, Moscow, 1884, 38cm. wide. £3,300

A Victorian shaped-oval bread basket, with applied border incorporating female masks, trailing vines, wheat ears and scrolls, by Robert Hennell, 1843, 16in. long, 61 oz.
(Christie's) £5,500

A fine George II shaped-oval bread basket, the everted border cast and pierced with wheat ears, flowers, scrolls and ribbons, by Paul de Lamerie, 1747, 13¾in. long, 72oz.
(Christie's) £121,000

A George I circular bread basket, by Thomas Farren, 1725, date letter struck twice, 12¾in. diam., 94oz.
£72,600

A George III circular bread basket, with openwork basket-work sides, basket-weave border and twisted and foliage swing handle, by John Wakelin and Robert Garrard, 1795, 11¼in. diameter, 42 oz.
(Christie's) £5,280

A George III bread basket, with everted wire work sides, the swing handle of cable design, 1762 (maker's mark poorly struck), 32cm., 22 oz.
(Lawrence Fine Art) £1,265

A George I two-handled circular bread basket, on pierced and ropework foot, the basketwork sides with similar ropework border, by David Willaume, 1723, Britannia Standard, 11¼in. diameter, 32oz.
(Christie's) £6,600

A George II shaped-oval bread basket, the rim applied with wheat ears, fruits, vines and foliage and with dolphin's mask and scroll swing handle, by Samuel Herbert & Co., 1755, 14¼in. long, 48 oz.
(Christie's) £5,060

BREAD

An Art Deco style roll basket, 13in. long, rounded rectangular, ribbed interior and angled side handles, Birmingham, 1937, 19 ozs.
(Bonhams) £330

A fine George II two-handled bread basket, by Paul de Lamerie, the sloping sides of simple pierced trellis-work with interlaced flat-chased grooved strands, 8.5cm. high, 33cm. long, 1731, 40.5 ozs.
(Phillips) £100,000

An oval roll basket, 13in. diameter, bar-pierced sides with everted gadrooned border on raised oval base, Chester 1932, 28oz.
(Bonhams) £460

A George II shaped oval bread basket, the sides pierced and chased with quatrefoils, scrolls and beading, by Edward Aldridge, 1759, with blue glass liner, 17¼in. wide, 52oz.
(Christie's) £7,480

A George III oblong bread basket, chased with a broad band of flutes and with shell, foliage and gadrooned border and cornucopia, shell, fruit and foliage swing handle, by James Barber and William Whitwell, York, 1818, 12in. long, 39 oz.
(Christie's) £1,430

A George III circular bread basket, chased with a broad band of flutes and engraved with a band of anthemion ornament, by Joseph Felix Podio, 1806, 10½in. diameter, 32oz.
(Christie's) £2,090

A George II Irish shaped oval bread basket, by Geo. Hill, Dublin, 1760, 15in. long, 72oz. £18,150

A large George II circular bread basket, the spreading foot chased with a band of acanthus leaves, by Louis Laroche, 1733, 12¼in. diameter, 79oz.
(Christie's) £41,800

A George III shaped oval bread basket, by Sarah Buttall, 1770, 14in. long, 37oz. £3,150

CAKE

A Victorian shaped oblong cake basket on spreading base with reeded borders and swing handle, by Bradbury and Henderson, Sheffield, 1881, 11½in. wide, 21oz.
(Christie's) £828

A George II large oval cake basket, by David Willaume II, 1730, 15¼in., 86oz.
£20,200

George IV silver cake basket, John Edward Terry, London, 1823–24, approximately 34 troy oz.
(Skinner) £839

A circular cake basket, the lobed body with engraved and repoussé decoration of game birds, London 1842, probably by Joshua Taylor, 34cm. diameter, 45oz.
(Langlois) £1,400

A pair of American shaped-oval cake baskets, each on four scroll feet, inscribed *J.H.I.* and stamped made for Tiffany & Co., 10½in. wide, 46oz.
(Christie's) £1,840

A fine early Victorian cake basket, embossed with rococo foliage sprays, having a swing handle, on a shaped floral embossed foot, 10½in. diameter, George John Richards, London 1848, 21 oz.
(Woolley & Wallis) £820

A silver cake basket, maker's mark of R&W Wilson, Philadelphia, circa 1830, with die-rolled Greek-key borders, 12in. diameter, 38 oz.
(Christie's) £616

A late Victorian quatrefoil pierced cake basket on applied shell and scrolling foliate feet, James Dixon & Son, Sheffield 1900, 12¼in., 20.25 oz.
(Christie's S. Ken) £660

A George IV silver gilt oval cake basket in George III-style, by P. Rundell, London, 1822, 13¾in. wide, 39oz.10dwt. £8,230

CAKE

A George III shaped oval cake basket, the centre engraved with a crest, 1802 by Robert and Samuel Hennell, 39.2cm., 31.5oz. (Lawrence) £1,265

A George III shaped oval cake basket, by John Romer, 1765, 13in. long, 34oz. £1,900

A George III reeded oval swing handled cake basket on a rising foot, maker's initials M.H., London, 1799, 14in., 24oz. (Christie's S. Ken) £715

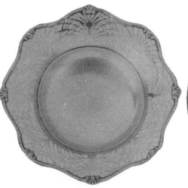

George II cake basket, makers possibly Thos. Blackett and another, Newcastle 1756, 14in. wide, 50oz. £2,475

A shaped circular cake basket pierced with stylised shells and with an applied shell and foliate tim, on a rising circular foot, Adey Brothers, Birmingham, 10in., 14oz. (Christie's S. Ken) £418

A panelled circular cake basket with shaped pierced border and swing handle, Birmingham, 1923, weight 10oz., 7in. diameter. (Christie's) £176

George II style silver cake basket, clover piercing and engraved crest, side bearing marks of Wm. Plummer, 1759–60, 13in. wide. (Skinner Inc.) £950

A George III swing-handled oval cake basket, with foliate festoons and openwork swing handle on spreading base, 12in. long, William Plummer, London 1774, 592 gms, 19.0 oz. (Bearne's) £820

A Victorian gadrooned shaped oval swing-handled cake basket on a beaded rising oval foot, John Newton Mappin, Sheffield 1882, 12in., 21.25 oz. (Christie's S. Ken) £462

CAKE

A George II cake basket, by Eliz. Godfrey, 1743, 35.3cm. across, 64.2oz. **£6,050**

A George III Irish cake basket, by J. Graham, Dublin, circa 1765, 35.2cm. long, 38oz. **£2,660**

A George III boat-shaped cake basket on spreading foot, by Paul Storr, 1801, 14³/₄in. long, 30oz. **£3,565**

William IV shaped circular cake basket by Henry Wilkinson & Co., Sheffield, 1832, 13in. diam., 45oz. **£1,606**

A late Victorian slat and roundel-pierced moulded circular cake basket, J.J., Sheffield 1900, 12¹/₄in., 27.75oz. (Christie's S. Ken.) **£550**

George III style silver cake basket, 19th century, bearing marks of London, 1766–7, 14¹/₂in. long., approximately 29 troy oz. (Skinner Inc.) **£732**

A George III oval cake basket, the body with fruiting vine and wheatear decoration, spiral swing handle, London 1762, maker A.S., 33oz. (Russell Baldwin & Bright) £700

A George III shaped oval cake basket, pierced and engraved with foliage, by Robert Breading, Dublin, 1794, 39.7cm. long, 38oz. (Christie's London) **£2,530**

A George IV floral and foliate chased shaped circular swing-handled cake basket, William Bateman, London, 1823, 11in., 25¹/₄oz. (Christie's) **£605**

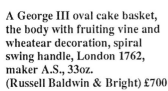

CAKE

A George II shaped oval cake basket, by Edward Wakelin, 1749, 14½in. long, 59oz. £3,330

A George III shaped oval cake basket with pierced swing handle rising from shells, 1763, 37cm., 35.5oz. £700

A George II shaped oval cake basket, by Philip Garden, 1753, 14¼in. long, 58oz. £3,920

An early George III swing handled fruit or cake basket, with an applied cast border of gadrooning, 38cm long, by S.Herbert & Co.,1767, 48½ozs. (Phillips) £3,600

A George IV shaped circular cake basket, 12½in. diam., marked Joseph Angell, London, 1832, 39oz.4dwt. £485

A Victorian swing handled circular cake basket with trailing wheatsheaf rim, by Harrison Bros & Howson, Sheffield, 1857, 44.5oz. (Phillips) £2,000

An oval cake basket, 14¾in. long, with reeded borders, above bright-cut engraved foliate sides, London, 1795, by Robert and David Hennell, 27 oz. (Bonhams) £1,900

A plated cake basket by Rogers & Bro., Waterbury, last quarter 19th century, the everted brim with a die-rolled border in a geometric Aesthetic pattern, 9½in. high, overall. (Christie's) £138

An early Victorian shaped circular cake basket, the plain centre within a band of well chased swirl leafage, 1838, by Joseph and John Angell, 36.5cm., 42.2oz. (Lawrence Fine Arts) £990

FRUIT

A French oval fruit basket, the bowl formed from woven wirework, the rim and crossed scroll handles formed as grape laden vine tendrils, circa 1880, 20¹/₂in. long, 5,593grs. (Christie's) £5,500

An oval fruit basket, 8¹/₄in. diameter, scroll pierced sides, leaf chased border on four pierced foliate feet, Sheffield 1919, by the Dixons, 17oz. (Bonhams) £480

A George V fruit basket of shaped circular form with swing handle, Sheffield, 1934, 25cm. diam., 806gr. £145

German hallmarked silver fruit basket, 19th century, 800 fine, reticulated and chased figural and floral decoration, approximately 46 troy oz. (Skinner Inc.) £1,236

A Georg Jensen moulded oval grape basket, on pedestal feet, the handle with ribbed scroll-work terminals, the bases of the handle applied with grapeclusters, import marks for London 1930, 37oz, 13in. high. (Christie's) £1,800

A George III circular fruit basket, with looped wirework sides, reeded borders and similar swing handle, by John Wakelin and Robert Garrard, 1797, 11³/₄in. diameter, 41oz. (Christie's) £6,050

Sterling silver fruit basket, London, circa 1891-92, maker's mark G.A., 14in. long, 50 troy oz. £770

Adam style fruit basket on stand by C.C. Pilling, London, 1905, 6¹/₂in. high, 32oz., 9¹/₄in. diam. £330

Large silver fruit basket with pierced sides and swing handle, Sheffield, 1907, 44oz., 13¹/₄in. high. £1,250

SUGAR

A George III small sugar basket, by Charles Hougham, 1790, 8cm. high, 4oz. £330

A Victorian pedestal sugar basket, Sheffield, 1853, 4½in. high, 8oz., and a sifting spoon, London, 1862. £290

Late 19th century sterling silver sugar basket, by S. Kirk & Son Co., Maryland, 7in. high. £290

Peter & Ann Bateman, a George III swing-handle sugar basket, the curved oval body finely pierced with an upper and lower frieze of bright-cut leaf motifs and festooning, 8in. high, 1791, 5oz.
(Phillips) £500

A George III sugar basket, with swing handle, the body with floral bright cut engraved decoration, by Solomon Hougham, 1793, 17cm., 7.5 oz.
(Lawrence Fine Art) £550

An attractive George III Irish swing handle sugar basket, the shaped oval body of bat's wing panelled fluting design, by Christopher Haines, Dublin, 1790, 12oz.
(Phillips) £850

Good quality Victorian silver sugar basket in Neo-classical style, boat shaped with rope twist edges and swing handle, Birmingham 1861, 8¹/₂oz.
(G.A. Key) £310

Charles T. and George Fox, early Victorian naturalistic sugar basket, blue glass liner, London 1840, 8.5 oz.
(Woolley & Wallis) £520

George III silver sugar basket, Peter, Anne & William Bateman, London, 1800–1801, approximately 8 troy oz.
(Skinner Inc) £259

44

SUGAR

A George III sugar basket, by Abraham Peterson, 1795, 17cm. across. **£390**

A Dutch 19th century silver sugar basket, oval chased with plinth, swags and scrolls, circa 1880, and a pair of sugar tongs. (Bonhams) **£115**

A George III pierced swing handled sugar basket, by Edward Aldridge, 1771, 11cm. high to top of handle, 1.75oz.
(Phillips London) **£500**

A George III Provincial sugar basket of pedestal form, the body embossed with foliate festoons and tassels, and pierced with slots and lozenge motifs, 8cm. diameter, by Henry Tudor & Thomas Leader, Sheffield, 1777, 2³/₄oz.
(Phillips) **£380**

A fine pair of oval boat shape sugar baskets, makers Samuel Roberts Jr, George Cadman & Co., Sheffield 1798, together with a pair of ladles, maker Richard Crossley, London 1794, 14¹/₂oz.
(Woolley & Wallis) **£1,000**

A sugar basket, pierced and chased with a cartouche, scrolls and paterae amongst pales and flutes, by Burrage Davenport, London 1772, 7³/₄oz., 5¹/₂in. high. (Tennants) **£500**

A George III sugar basket, 1792 maker's mark of George Smith II and Thomas Hayter overstriking another, 14cm. overall height.
(Lawrence) **£528**

A sugar basket of hemispherical shape chased and pierced with flowers, scrolls, and a cartouche, by Richard Meach, London 1770, blue glass liner, 4¹/₂oz., 4¹/₂in. diameter.
(Tennants) **£350**

A George III small boat-shaped sugar basket, on moulded foot and with reeded borders, and swing handle, by Henry Chawner, 1790, 5in. long, 5ozs.
(Christie's) **£805**

BASKETS

SUGAR

A George III swing handled sugar basket of shaped and pleated oblong form, 8cm. high, by William Abdy II, 1792, 5oz.
(Phillips London)　£300

An attractive George III sugar basket, with scrolling foliage within wrigglework scroll borders, London 1778, 202gr., 20cm. high.
(Henry Spencer)　£300

A George III sugar basket, with bright cut engraved floral decoration, swing handle and pedestal foot, 1786, 15.5cm., 8.5oz.
(Lawrence Fine Art)　£440

SWEETMEAT

A Victorian sweet basket in the style of the 1760s, the shaped oval basket pierced with crosses above raised lozenges, 1866 by Robert Harper, 16.6cm., 5oz.
(Lawrence)　£374

A George III sweetmeat basket, by Henry Chawner, the sides with linear and foliate bright-cut decoration, on shaped pedestal base, London, 1792.
(Bonhams)　£380

An attractive William IV sweetmeat basket, chased and embossed with scrolling foliage, 5in., maker's Taylor & Perry, Birmingham 1836, 3oz.
(Woolley & Wallis)　£300

A George III sweetmeat basket, pierced in a design of scrolls between swags and paterae, by Thomas Daniell, 1783, 17cm., 4.5oz.
(Lawrence Fine Art)　£495

A Victorian sweetmeat basket, the wirework sides applied with trailing oak leaf and acorn tendrils and with pierced swing handle, by Hawksworth, Eyre & Co., Sheffield, 1846, 3³/₄in., 7oz.
(Christie's)　£308

A Victorian sweetmeat basket, with beaded borders and beaded swing handle, the sides engraved with ferns and ivy, on oval pedestal base, London, 1856.
(Bonhams)　£320

These stemless drinking cups are functional, simple items which were popular in various parts of Europe from the 15th to the 18th century, and they continued unchanged in shape for some 200 years from 1600. All are raised in one piece, with feet or base moulding.

Nevertheless, clear national characteristics do appear in their decoration. In the 15th century, for instance, they were particularly popular in Germany, where they often had covers decorated with overhanging gothic leaf decoration around the rim. They were made of thick gauge metal, and usually came in pint or half-pint sizes. Early examples may have ball feet, but a moulded or gadrooned foot rim was more usual. Hamburg, Breslau and Strasbourg were the major production centres.

Many fine beakers were made also in Holland, where, after the Reformation, they were used as sacramental cups, sometimes gilded, and engraved with arabesques, sacred subjects, Biblical scenes or churches. By the 17th century, they were usually engraved all over and had a moulded circular foot and slightly spreading sides. 16th century Norwegian beakers, on the other hand, usually rested on feet in the form of lions or female busts.

In their typically English form, beakers tended to be simple, and uncovered, whereas the Hungarians favoured a very tall style with nationalistic decoration. In Italy, they were sometimes covered with filigree work. The earliest American examples were straight sided with a flaring rim, followed by a Queen Anne bell shape.

One of a pair of cylindrical beakers with an applied moulded strap handle, Boston, 1790-1810, 3¹/₈in. high, overall, 8oz.　£760

A silver beaker, maker's mark of Nicholas Geoffroy, Newport, Rhode Island, 1795–1817, 2⁷/₈in. high, 3oz. (Christie's)　£363

A pair of George III plain beakers, each on moulded rim foot, engraved with a crest and monogram, 1773, maker's mark M.S. or S.W., 2⁷/₈in. high, 5oz. (Christie's)　£1,870

A tall beaker by John Burt Lyng, New York, 1760–1780 with a flaring rim, engraved with a ruffle border, 4¹/₂in. high, 5oz. (Christie's New York)　£4,496

An Art Nouveau beaker, the body stamped with flowers, foliage and scrollwork decoration, Mappin and Webb, Sheffield 1901, 6in., 13.5oz. (Christie's S. Ken)　£352

A silver beaker of historical interest, maker's mark of Churchill & Treadwell, Boston, 1805–1813, 3¹/₂in. high, 4oz. 10dwt. (Christie's)　£2,904

A German parcel gilt beaker, by Christoph Muller, Breslau, circa 1710, 5oz.5dwt., 5in. high. £1,700

A small beaker, the sides engraved with opposed leaves and initials and date 1756, 18th century, Scandinavian, 5.5cm. (Lawrence Fine Art) £418

A Commonwealth tapering cylindrical beaker, 1658, maker's mark RF between pellets, 4in. high, 5oz. £2,970

A Charles II beaker, of thistle form, the upper part chased with stylised frieze of seeded flowers and leaves, 9cm. high, punched with the letters TD for Thomas Dare, circa 1660, 3oz. (Phillips London) £2,500

A pair of late 18th century tapering beakers engraved with simulated staves and applied with hoops, possibly Joseph Walley, Chester, circa 1775, 3in., 8.25oz. (Christie's) £660

A German silver gilt tapering cylindrical beaker, the body with a broad band of tear drop ornament on a punched ground, by Christoph Zorer, Augsburg, 1570–1575, 4³/4in. high, 208grs. (Christie's) £7,700

A Hungarian parcel-gilt beaker, engraved with initials and dated *1670*, the base inset with a medallic 1¹/2-Thaler, 1541, struck at Kremnitz, 4in. high, 207grs. (Christie's) £1,760

A rare silver beaker by Samuel Kirk, Baltimore, circa 1840, deeply repousse and chased with buildings surrounded by flowers and trees, 3½in. high, 4½oz. £1,100

An 18th century German white metal beaker, engraved with two bands of strapwork on a matt ground, engraved *Joachim Blecken 1752 8th September*, 8.5cm. high. (Spencer's) £900

A William IV beaker, by Joseph and John Angell, London, 1836, 5oz.2dwt. £330

A German silver gilt beaker, Strasbourg, circa 1700, maker's mark perhaps EB, 3¾in. high, 4oz.18dwt. £1,780

A silver gilt and niello beaker of cylindrical form, maker's mark J.N. in script, Moscow, 1838, 7.7cm. £365

A Victorian parcel-gilt prize beaker in the late 17th/early 18th century Continental style, engraved with portraits of famous people with Liverpool connections, by George Fox, 1890, 13.5cm. high, 11 ozs. (Phillips) £1,300

A pair of George III parcel-gilt beakers, engraved with panels of cupids between festoons and flowers, foliage and husks, by Thomas Balliston, 1818, 3½in. high, 9 oz. (Christie's) £3,630

A Swiss tapering cylindrical beaker, punched with a broad band of matting and with moulded rim, Sion, circa 1700, maker's mark possibly that of Francois-Joseph Ryss, 3¼in. high, 111grs. (Christie's) £3,080

A plain beaker by Jens Bierring (1762–1801), engraved with three cartouches with laurel leaves, initials and date 1798, Danish, 11cm. high, 180gr. (Herholdt Jensen) £513

A William and Mary slightly flaring beaker on rim foot, scratch-engraved with stylised foliage, London 1692, 3¼in., 3.75oz. (Christie's) £1,925

A beaker, by William A. Williams, Alexandria, Virginia or Washington, D.C., early 19th century, with reeded rim and footrim, marked, 8cm. high, 4oz. (Christie's New York) £1,037

A small beaker designed by Jean Puiforcat, 4.8cm. high, silver coloured metal. **£200**

A William III silver gilt beaker, circa 1700, 8cm. high. **£580**

A silver beaker, maker's mark of Jesse Churchill, Boston, circa 1800, 3³/₄in. high, 6oz. (Christie's) **£436**

A Russian gilt-lined and parcel-gilt plain tapering beaker and cover, the body engraved with simple reeded lines, probably Moscow, 18th century, 5¹/₂in., 5oz.
(Christie's) **£792**

An early Provincial silver beaker of waisted circular form having gilt interior, the exterior having scroll engraved frieze, bears initials *C, T.E.* and *E.H.* and bearing date 1579, 3¹/₂in. high.
(Russell Baldwin & Bright) **£700**

One of two George III interlocking beakers, each pair forming a barrel, by C. Aldridge and H. Green, 1778, overall height of a barrel 5¼in., 16oz.18dwt. **£240**

Swedish parcel gilt silver beaker, Olof Fernlof, Goteberg, 1739, inscribed under the lip with period script initials, fluted base, 3³/₄in. high, 2oz. 18dwt.
(Butterfield & Butterfield) **£600**

A German parcel gilt beaker, late 17th/early 18th century, maker's mark only DL struck twice, 3¾in. high, 4oz.17dwt. **£890**

A William and Mary plain beaker, pricked with initials AL.IM, by James Daniel, Norwich, 1689, 3½in. high, 3oz.3dwt. **£2,420**

BELL SHAPED

A French inverted bell shaped beaker, the bowl with a moulded rim and engraved with bright cut swags of fruit and flowers, 4¼ in.
(Christie's)   £440

A Portuguese beaker with bell-shaped body, 16.5cm. high, circa 1740, 360gr.   £790

A French inverted bell-shaped beaker on a part-fluted domed circular foot, Charles-Joseph Fontains, Paris 1774, 5in., 6.25oz.
(Christie's)   £500

A French mid 18th century inverted bell-shaped beaker on a fluted rising circular foot crudely engraved with two names, Orleans circa 1770, 4½ in.
(Christie's S. Ken)   £770

French silver beaker with Russian inscription, Russian Import mark, 1899–1908, neoclassical style footed tumbler with ring base chased with leaf and dart band, plain top with Russian inscription, 4in. high, 4oz. 8dwt.
(Butterfield & Butterfield) £206

A French silver-gilt inverted bell-shaped beaker, on spreading circular foot cast with a band of guilloche ornament, by François Joubert, Paris, 1781, 5¼in. high, 298gr.
(Christie's)   £2,000

A late 18th century Channel Isles beaker, with an everting rim and a moulded circular foot, 9.5cm. tall, by George Mauger, Jersey, circa 1780–1800, 3oz.
(Phillips)   £450

An 18th century christening beaker, plain, of good gauge, 9cm. high, maker's mark IL, possibly for Jacques Limbour Jersey (of French origin), circa 1775.
(Phillips London)   £500

A French late 18th/early 19th century bell-shaped beaker engraved with foliage and shells, Louis-Jacques Berger, Paris 1798/1809, 5in., 5.75 oz.
(Christie's S. Ken)   £308

FOOTED

A Danish beaker on three ball feet chased with a band depicting horses at various pursuits with presentation inscription, Copenhagen, 1886, 5in. high.
(Christie's)   £264

A late 17th century German parcel gilt covered beaker, with repoussé busts of Roman Emperors, on ball feet, 6¹/₂in., Augsburg, circa 1685.
(Woolley & Wallis)   £2,150

A Continental late 19th century tapering circular beaker on spherical feet and with a moulded rim, London 1885, 3¹/₂in., 5.75oz.
(Christie's)   £165

A German silver-gilt cylindrical beaker, on three ball feet, chased with a broad band of flowers and stylised foliage, by Reinhold Riel, Nurnberg, circa 1670, 4in. high, 111gr.
(Christie's)   £1,035

A German parcel-gilt cage-work beaker and cover, by Frederick Klemm, Dresden, circa 1640, 7¹/₂in. high, 731gr.
(Christie's)   £39,600

An Augsburg beaker on three ball feet, densely chased in repoussé with scenes of children playing, late 17th/early 18th century, 15.5cm. high, 450gr.
(Finarte)   £1,928

A Continental late 19th century tapering circular beaker, depicting the Philosopher Diogenes and Alexander the Great, Berthold Muller, 5¹/₂in., 8.75oz.
(Christie's)   £605

A late 17th century Continental covered beaker, maker's mark EA conjoined, perhaps for Everhard Alffen of Cologne, circa 1680, 14.5cm. high, 8oz.
                              £935

A German tapering cylindrical beaker, by Philipp Jacob Drentwett III, Augsburg, circa 1690, 5½in. high, 10oz. 12dwt.   £1,310

TRUMPET

A trumpet-shape parcel gilt beaker by P. Semyonov, maker's mark, Moscow, circa 1775, 18cm. £960

A tapering cylindrical beaker by Antoni Magnus, Deventer, ?1664, 18.4cm. high, 362gr. £39,640

A Swedish parcel gilt trumpet shaped beaker, by P. Eneroth, Stockholm, 1776, $8^3/4$in. high, 14oz.5dwt. £830

A German wine beaker of shaped cylindrical form cast to either side with a satyr mask and vine foliage, by B. Muller, import marks for Chester, 1900, 5in. high, 8oz.
(Christie's) £440

A Swedish early 19th century gilt-lined tapering beaker on a fluted rising circular foot, engraved with wriggle-work, stylised foliage and trellis-work, $8^1/2$in., 14.25oz.
(Christie's S. Ken) £902

A Hungarian silver-gilt slightly-tapering cylindrical beaker, applied with a band of wriggle-work and chased overall with masks, plumes, shells and stylised foliage, by Johannes (Hans) Bausnert, Nagyszeben, circa 1640, $7^1/2$in. high, 273gr.
(Christie's) £3,450

A Continental silver-gilt beaker, on domed spreading foot chased with fruit, flowers and foliage, inset with 16th century thalers, unmarked, $11^1/2$in. high, 1,304 grs.
(Christie's) £8,250

A C.R. Ashbee hammered silver beaker, the base with an openwork frieze of stylised trees set with seven cabochon garnets, London hallmarks for 1900, 11.5cm. high, 205 grams. gross.
(Christie's) £1,980

Russian silver Catherine the Great period beaker, Moscow, 1769, the sides densely chased in repoussé with exuberant rocaille, scrolls and vegetation, $8^3/4$in. high, 10oz. 14 dwts.
(Butterfield & Butterfield) £504

BELLS

Table bells were first introduced in the 16th century, and their style tended to follow the taste of the times. They are rare, particularly any dating from before the 18th century, and are consequently much sought after. They usually have a baluster handle, and until the mid-18th century frequently featured as the centre piece of an inkstand. Any inkstand so adorned will greatly increase in value, provided the bell is original. Later examples more usually have wooden or ivory handles.

Spanish 17th century table bell with baluster handle, 9oz. 14dwt.
£475

Elkington & Co. a cast table bell, the handle a putto playing a tambourine.
(Woolley & Wallis) £220

A French table bell, 10.2cm. high, maker's mark *J.D.*, Paris, 1761, 138gr. £3,965

Mid 19th century Dutch table bell with fluted handle, 5³⁄₄in. high.
(Christie's) £385

A fine cast table bell, having a cherub handle, the interior and clapper gilded, 6in., maker Henry Bourne, London 1901, 13oz.
(Woolley & Wallis) £540

A table bell by Godert Van Ysseldijk, 14.5cm. high, maker's mark, The Hague, 1767, 306gr. £5,445

A silver figural bell, maker's mark of Tiffany & Co., New York, circa 1875, the handle formed as a classical maiden, marked, 5¹⁄₂in. high, 6oz. 10dwt.
(Christie's) £585

A table bell, of domed form decorated with scrolls and with two winged cherub masks, stamped *925F*, 4in. high.
(Spencer's) £190

A French 19th century table bell with ivory baluster handle, the bell itself decorated with scrolling foliage and strapwork, 4³⁄₄in. high.
(Christie's) £418

A William IV table bell, the slender baluster handle engraved with scroll foliage, 1832 maker's mark rubbed, 11.5cm.
(Lawrence Fine Arts) £550

A George IV silver-gilt cast table bell designed as layered acanthus leaves, 5¹⁄₄in. high, Charles Fox, London 1826, 8.8oz.
(Bearne's) £1,700

BOWLS

Bowls were made in silver for a multitude of purposes. There were bleeding bowls, used by the barbers and apothecaries of the day, brandy bowls, bratinas and charkas (peculiarly Russian drinking vessels), broth bowls, écuelles, mazers, monteiths, punch bowls, quaichs and sugar bowls.

Many have their own separate sections in this book.

The form provided plenty of scope for imaginative styling and decoration, and attractive and valuable examples are found in all categories.

A Charles I plain circular bleeding bowl, with pierced trefoil handle, 1632, maker's mark indistinct, but possibly that of Valerius Sutton, 6in. wide. (Christie's) £4,180

A George II Irish plain circular bowl, on spreading foot and with moulded rim, by Peter Racine, Dublin, 1734, 7¹/₂in. diameter, 19oz. (Christie's) £3,080

Tiffany sterling round serving bowl, late 19th century, everted rim with pierced clover design, 10¹/₄in. diameter, approx. 16 troy oz. (Skinner) £502

Silver bowl with red glass liner, on four cartouche feet, with fluted edge and with open pierced mouldings, flower baskets, garlands and Chinese scenes, German, 24.5cm. high. (Kunsthaus am Museum) £373

Danish silver circular bowl by Georg Jensen, Copenhagen, circa 1940, with lobed sides rising to everted horizontal border, 14in. diameter, 35oz. 4dwts. (Butterfield & Butterfield) £1,384

A late Victorian low pedestal bowl, the everted scroll crimped rim over a band of scrolling acanthus leaves, Sheffield 1898, 712 grammes, 25cm. diameter. (Spencer's) £520

A Liberty & Co. Cymric silver and copper bowl, the shallow conical silver bowl with everted rim set with band of cabochon nephrites, with Birmingham hallmarks for 1901, 20.7cm. diameter, 680 grams. gross. (Christie's) £1,100

A late Victorian pedestal bowl by Walker and Hall, with ribbon tied swags of flowers on a fluted pedestal and domed foot, Sheffield 1898, 1139 gram 26cm. diameter. (Spencer's) £980

A circular silver-gilt bowl, the lower part of the body with a detachable calyx of acanthus leaves, with everted reeded rim, unmarked, late 17th century, 7³/₈ in. diameter, 16oz. (Christie's) £3,300

Kalo sterling silver bowl with attached underliner, Chicago, circa 1915, squat bulbous form, approximately 15 troy oz. (Skinner Inc.) £550

A Liberty and Co. Cymric christening bowl, of circular form repoussé with two Celtic symbols and engraved *Diana From Her Godmother Edith 1904*, Birmingham 1900, 221 grammes, 5in. diameter. (Spencer's) £200

Sterling silver infant bowl and undertray by Gorham, with applied design of four children, date mark, 1903, bowl diameter, 5in. (Eldred's) £1,023

A Hukin & Heath electroplated twin sweetmeat bowl designed by Dr. Christopher Dresser, the two bowls with straight collars and a strap handle positioned at the junction, 27cm. high. (Christie's) £550

A foliate rimmed silver bowl chased and modelled in relief with a foliate band of irises on a stippled ground, stamped *jungin*, Meiji period, 20cm. diam. (Christie's London) £1,980

A Victorian fluted shell design bowl on reeded supports, by George Unite, Birmingham, 1870, 6¼in. high, 11oz. £330

A German shaped circular bowl, the ground decorated with a pastoral scene, 9in. diam. £290

A late Victorian spiral fluted bowl, by James Dixon & Sons, Sheffield, 1893, 9¼in., 22.75oz. £425

A nut bowl in the form of a barrel-stave bucket, by Gorham Manuf. Co., 1869, 2¹/₄in. high, 4³/₄in. wide, 3oz. £409

A Scottish silver bowl, designed by D. Carleton Smythe, 48.5cm. across, bearing Glasgow hallmarks for 1905. £420

An American silver bowl, George Ridout, New York, circa 1750, with flared rim and moulded foot, 16oz. 15dwt., diameter at rim 7¹/₈in. (Sotheby's) £10,592

An Edwardian bowl, the centre and shaped border pierced with scrolls and trellis work, by J. Dixon & Sons, Sheffield, 1908, 33cm., 52oz.
(Lawrence Fine Art) £1,815

A Sibyl Dunlop Celtic silver stemmed bowl, applied on the exterior with Celtic entrelacs and beast masks in relief, 9.5cm. high, 1923.
(Phillips) £620

A 19th century Russian and shaded enamel circular bowl decorated with bats, clouds and circular panels, 4¼in. diameter, maker's mark A. Postnikov, Moscow 1874, 254 gms.
(Bearne's) £780

A parcel gilt circular bowl, by Anton Gunter Dieckmann, initialled and dated 1732, 15.4cm. diam.
£2,050

A silver gilt two-handled bowl by Jakob Kessbayr, 17cm. wide, Augsburg, circa 1625, 280gr. £4,955

A George II Irish circular bowl on a rim foot, by Alexander Brown, Dublin, 1735, 6in. wide, 13oz.7dwt.
£6,180

A chrysanthemum shaped silver bowl chased with a profusion of chrysanthemums, some in gilt, plum blossoms and other foliage, signed Toshinaga, 19th century, 28.5cm high.
(Christie's) £3,105

Rare Sterling silver bowl, circa 1930, by William Waldo Dodge, Jr. of Ashville, NC, hand hammered body, 10in. diameter, 20 troy oz.
(Eldred's) £544

A C. R. Ashbee hammered silver bowl, with pierced design of stylised fruit-laden branches, stamped C R A with London hallmarks for 1899, 430 grams.
(Christie's) £1,210

An inlaid silver Indian-style bowl, by Tiffany & Co., for the Columbian Exposition, circa 1893, 6¼in. high, 56oz. 10dwt. £88,425

An Omar Ramsden silver gilt bowl, London hallmarks for 1935, 46.2cm. wide. £10,285

A Charles Boyton silver stemmed bowl, 12.5cm. diam., 5.75oz., maker's mark for London 1937. £210

A bowl, circular with flaring rim, by Josiah Austin, Boston, circa 1750-70, 3in. high, 5¾in. diam., 6oz. (Christie's) **£8,894**

An Art Nouveau Continental white metal bowl in the style of J. Hofman, 14in. across. **£510**

A silver bowl with Thos. Farrer mark, hallmarked London 1731, 9½in. diam **£1,050**

Unusual Art Deco silver and silver gilt bowl by Jean E. Puiforcat, 24oz. **£4,000**

Whiting sterling chowder bowl and spoon, round form with flaring fluted rim, coordinating spoon, 10in. diameter, approx. 30 troy oz. (Skinner) **£1,961**

Victorian circular bowl on three supports, by Elkington & Co., Birmingham, 1880, 20oz. **£280**

Late Victorian silver reticulated bowl, Thomas Bradbury & Sons, London, 1899, engraved with period overlapping strapwork monogram, the sides decorated with bands of pierced paling, 18¹/₂in. long, 54oz. 2dwt. (Butterfield & Butterfield) **£1,689**

Danish sterling three compartment serving bowl, Georg Jensen, Copenhagen, circa 1925–1932, circular, on ring foot, the interior divided into three equal segments, the dividing walls centred with a bud finial, 9in. diameter, 24oz. 18dwt. (Butterfield & Butterfield) **£1,689**

A large silver-mounted Chinese kraak porcelain bowl, decorated in blue and white with panels of trees, flowers and birds between columns, the silver rim engraved with acanthus leaves, early 17th century, 14¹/₄in. diameter. (Christie's) **£7,150**

A 19th century Indian bowl, heavily chased in the usual manner, 24cm. diam., 37oz. **£350**

Georg Jensen sterling bowl, 20th century, diameter 8in., approx. 17 troy oz. (Skinner) **£151**

A sterling silver bowl, by Arthur Stone, 1910-37, 5³/₈in. diam., 7 troy oz. (Skinner Inc.) **£881**

CENTREPIECE

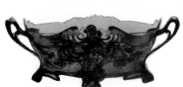

A WMF electroplated metal centrepiece of boat form, circa 1900, 46cm. wide.
£495

A silver centrepiece, maker's mark of S. Kirk & Son, Baltimore, 1880–1890, 15in. long, 22oz. (Christie's)
£1,335

An Art Nouveau centrepiece of open boat shape, 57.5cm. long, silver coloured metal, possibly Austrian or German.
£1,760

Fine Sterling silver centrepiece bowl marked *Tiffany & Co.*, applied spiral shell bosses, twelve-lobed rim, probably circa 1873–91, 10in. diameter. (Eldred's)
£3,006

A large Continental shaped oval centrepiece embossed and chased overall in rococo style, 12¼in. high, import marks for 1906, 149oz.
£5,830

A centrepiece bowl with a scalloped rim, the sides fluted, by Simeon Coley, N.Y., circa 1768, 8⅞in. diam., 21oz. 10dwt. (Christie's)
£17,987

Sterling hand chased centrebowl, Jenkins & Jenkins, Inc., Baltimore, Maryland, circa 1908–1915, circular, on a floral chased domed pedestal base, bowl with curled over sides, 12in. diameter, 26oz. (Butterfield & Butterfield)
£900

A Continental oval centrepiece bowl on four hoof supports, with London import marks, S.B.L., 1896, 14½in. wide, 52oz. (Christie's)
£3,565

Danish silver centrepiece frame with cut glass liner in the rococo taste, dated *1901*, of oval form, the bombé spiral fluted framework applied with pair of cartouches and multi-scroll bracket handles, height 6in. (Butterfield & Butterfield)
£1,203

Austrian Jugendstil silver centrebowl with cut glass liner, F R, circa 1910, the vertical sides pierced with palmettes and scrolls, 12¾in. wide, 39oz. 12dwts. (Butterfield & Butterfield) £761

A centrepiece bowl marked 'Milton A. Fuller, Inc. New York/Palm Beach', circa 1900, on four lion's-paw feet, 14in diam, 68 oz. (Christie's)
£2,629

Sterling silver centrepiece bowl, circa 1896–1903, by Mauser Manufacturing Company, applied and pierced floral decoration, 14in. diameter, 64 troy oz. (Eldred's)
£1,791

A sterling silver Martele oval centrepiece, by Gorham Mfg. Co., dated 1881 to 1906, 38 troy oz., 12¾in. long. **£1,887**

A fine silver bowl, maker's mark of Whiting Mfg. Co., circa 1890, the sides elaborately repoussé and chased with clam, oyster and mussel shells amid seaweed on a matted ground, 10⅝in. diameter, 32 oz. 10 dwt. (Christie's) **£7,392**

Sterling silver centrepiece bowl by A. Stone & Company, maker's mark *G*, for Herman Glendenning (active, 1920–37), 30.4 troy oz. (Eldred's) **£895**

A George III Irish bowl, maker's mark script IL for John Laughlin Jnr., J. Lloyd Snr., or J. Locker, Dublin, 1784, 23.5cm. diam., 19.8oz. **£605**

An Art Nouveau spot hammered centre bowl on a domed circular foot, Albert Edward Bonner, London, 1909, 7½in., 23.25oz. (Christie's S. Ken) **£418**

George V silver bowl with stand, S.B. & S. Ltd., Birmingham, 1920, applied fine ribbed rim band set into a frame with four fluted pilaster-like supports, pierced apron band with cast floral swag and drape below, 8¾in. diameter, 48oz. 4dwt. (Butterfield & Butterfield) **£750**

A silver Martele centrepiece bowl, maker's mark of Gorham Mfg. Co., Providence, circa 1905, the undulating rim repoussé with strawberries, leaves and flowerheads, 15¼in. long, 58 oz. 10 dwt. (Christie's) **£5,790**

A silver-gilt mounted two-handled coconut bowl, the straps pierced with latticework, the bowl carved with stylised foliage, the mounts unmarked, Central European, probably 16th century, 4¼in. high. (Christie's) **£3,300**

An unusual Indian table centrepiece, the large bombé-shaped bowl chased with elephants and scrolling foliage. (Bonhams) **£380**

COVERED

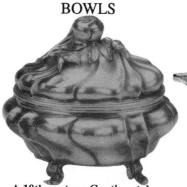

A Ganetti silver Modernist powder bowl and cover, the lift off cover with copper loop handle and mirrored interior, 7in. diameter.
(Henry Spencer) £100

A 19th century Continental shaped oval bowl and cover, with bulbous spiral reeded and fluted body, 5¹/₂in. long, 335gm.
(Bearne's) £400

A 17th century two-handled silver gilt circular bowl and cover, probably Flemish, maker's mark only CD, diam. of bowl 7½in., 39oz. £4,750

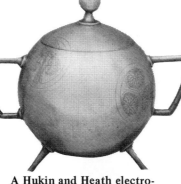

George II silver gilt bowl and cover, Phillips Garden, London, 1751, the upper body chased with flowers and a rococo scrollwork band incorporating two blank cartouches, 4¹/₄in. diameter, 9oz. 2dwts.
(Butterfield & Butterfield) £968

A Hukin and Heath electroplated two handled bowl with hinged cover decorated with four engraved roundels of stylised floral motifs, designed by Dr C. Dresser and date code for 26th March 1879, 19.1cm. high. (Christie's) £9,900

A French late 18th of early 19th century two-handled oval bowl and cover, the sides pierced, stamped and chased with classical figures, Etienne Janety, Paris, 6¹/₂in. overall.
(Christie's S. Ken) £682

A Georg Jensen circular bowl and cover of bulbous form and hammered finish, 6.5in. high, London 1921, 414gms., 13.3oz.
(Bearne's) £600

A Scandinavian circular two-handled bowl and cover, 14.8cm. high, maker's mark C.M., circa 1760, 560gr. £2,975

A Georg Jensen bowl and cover, stamped with C. F. Heise assay mark 100B and with London import marks for 1925, 11.9cm. high, 242gr.
(Christie's) £715

FOOTED

A Tiffany white metal footed bowl, one side cast in relief with a scene of a rabbit being pulled along in a straw basket by a duck, 13.5cm. diameter. (Christie's) **£495**

A footed bowl designed by J. Rohde, stamped Dessin J.R. 925 S Georg Jensen 242, circa 1920, 12.6cm. high, 16oz. **£1,310**

Large oval footed bowl, marked with a crown, post 1950, the navette form body raised on a collet base of overlapping leaves supported by four feet of pierced scrolls and flowers, 23³/₈in. long, 113oz. (Butterfield & Butterfield) **£1,876**

A circular shallow bowl, on tapering shaped hexagonal foot, with openwork knop above, by Omar Ramsden, 1928, 5⁵/₈in. high, 12oz. (Christie's) **£1,980**

A silver footed bowl, maker's mark of Samuel Williamson, Philadelphia, 1795–1810, on a flaring pedestal base over a square foot, 6⁵/₈in. diameter, 15 oz. 10 dwt. (Christie's) **£1,232**

A Georg Jensen footed bowl, with openwork leaf and berry stem, on flared circular foot, with stamped maker's mark for 1925–32, 11cm. high, 305 grams. (Christie's) **£2,420**

Tiffany Sterling footed bowl, circa 1860, approximately 30 troy oz. (Skinner) **£1,158**

A Georg Jensen footed bowl, the lightly hammered gadrooned bowl decorated beneath with trailing vines, on a stepped foot, 25.5cm. diameter, 1050 grams. (Christie's) **£1,760**

A footed bowl, by Whiting Manuf. Co., circa 1875-85, 5in. high, gross weight 22oz. **£3,665**

FRUIT

Gorham Martelé sterling footed fruit bowl, circa 1907, the hand hammered finish with chased flowers, 14in. long, approx. 52 troy oz.
(Skinner) £4,525

A footed fruit bowl by Whiting Manufacturing Company, North Attleboro or Newark, circa 1885, on a spreading cylindrical foot with a serpentine border, 4³/₄in. high, 21 oz. 10 dwt.
(Christie's) £4,497

A Hukin and Heath oval plated fruit bowl with waved rim, the foot applied with flowers, buds and foliage, 38cm. diameter.
(Christie's) £220

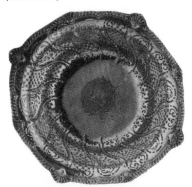

Victorian pedestal fruit bowl by Horace Woodward & Co. Ltd., London, 1898, 26oz. 13dwt., 7½in. high. £550

George III silver fruit bowl by John Parker & Edward Wakelin, London, 1761, the sides chased with swirling flutes, pierced in panels of alternating diaperwork and scrolls, 11in. diameter, 29oz. 4dwts.
(Butterfield & Butterfield) £2,500

A late Victorian foliate-chased boat-shaped pedestal fruit bowl on a shell and foliate-chased domed circular base, Goldsmiths & Silversmiths Co. Ltd., London 1900, 12³/₄in., 34.75oz.
(Christie's S. Ken) £1,210

A Continental moulded oval fruit bowl on openwork rococo floral, foliate and trellis-work feet, bearing import marks for London 1899, 13¹/₄in., 55oz.
(Christie's S. Ken) £3,080

A French 19th century foliate-pierced shaped oval fruit bowl applied with a rococo scrolling foliate rim, 16in., 27 oz.
(Christie's S. Ken) £418

A German late 19th/early 20th century circular fruit bowl, fitted with a clear glass liner, Eugen Marcus, 8in. diameter.
(Christie's S. Ken) £330

MONTEITH

This was a wine glass cooler first introduced in the 1680s and characterised by its indented rim, which was at first part of the body, but became detachable about a decade later. The name is said to be derived from a Scottish adventurer with a notched cloak, but ironically enough, Scottish examples are quite rare. The notches are intended to support drinking vessels by their feet, so that the bowls may cool in the iced water. Often monteiths have lion's mask and ring handles.

An Edwardian part spot-hammered and fluted tapering circular monteith rose bowl, J. B. Carrington, London 1905, 12in., 58.25oz.
(Christie's)　　　　£990

A rare James II monteith, the body plain apart from simple lobing in panels, by George Garthorne, 1685, 31cm., 42oz.
(Lawrence Fine Art)　£41,800

Edwardian silver monteith, London, 1902-03, Charles Stuart Harris, two ring handles hanging from modelled lion's heads, diameter 11in., approx. 68 troy oz.
(Skinner)　　　　£2,074

A George III two-handled circular bowl with monteith rim, the body chased in high relief with oriental figures, flowers, scrolls and foliage, 11in. diameter, maker's mark W.B., London 1817, 100.8oz.
(Bearne's)　　　　£4,800

George V silver monteith style rose bowl, Hawksworth, Eyre & Co. Ltd, London, 1912, panelled sides with fluted borders and notched rim with applied border, 10^{1}/8in. diameter, 34oz.
(Butterfield & Butterfield) £713

A George I two handled circular monteith, with two winged grotesque mask and drop ring handles, by John East, 1718, 10¼in. diam., 52oz.
(Christie's London)　£16,500

A Queen Anne two-handled circular monteith, by R. Syng, 1705, 11in. diam., 69oz.　　　£11,880

Kirk repoussé silver monteith, Baltimore, 1846–61, chased floral decoration, removable goblet holder with 1852 inscription, 10¾in. diameter, approximately 46 troy oz.
(Skinner Inc.)　　£1,458

PUNCH

The punch bowl, with or without drop ring handles, was used contemporaneously with the monteith from the 17th century, the chief difference being that the punch bowl lacks the monteith's characteristic notched rim. Punch bowls seem to have fallen from favour rather between 1760–1800, though some continued to be made in Scotland. Few were made during the greater part of the 19th century, and then copies of earlier styles started to be produced.

Japanese silver repoussé punch bowl, Meiji period, with lush flowering kakitsubaki (iris) plants executed in high relief on a graduated ground, the base impressed *STERLING K & CO.*, 54oz. 6dwts.
(Butterfield & Butterfield)
£3,805

A Queen Anne circular punch bowl, chased with a broad band of flutes and with two applied grotesque male mask and drop-ring handles, by William Fordham, 1706, 11¹/₂in. diameter, 65oz.
(Christie's)
£13,200

Georg Jensen Sterling punch bowl, circular moulded edge resting on leaves and berries, circular base, 9¹/₂in. diam, approximately 42 troy oz.
(Skinner Inc)
£2,402

Hand wrought sterling punch bowl and ladle, Porter Blanchard, Pacoima, California, circa 1980, the bowl shaped as a large hemisphere set on a ring base with horizontal everted lip and peened finish, 542 grams.
(Butterfield & Butterfield)
£2,814

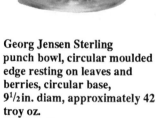

An Edwardian large two-handled punch bowl, chased with scrolls and foliage and engraved with a presentation inscription and coat-of-arms, by Elkington and Company Limited, Birmingham, 1902, 14in. high, 153oz.
(Christie's)
£4,830

A punch bowl, with repoussé band of floral swags suspended from ribbons, engraved with an inscription, Fordham & Faulkner, Sheffield 1897, 10³/₄in. diameter, 17¹/₂oz.
(Lawrence Fine Art)
£748

An American silver punch bowl, William Gale & Son, New York, 1852, the hemispherical bowl chased with rococo ornament, 63oz., diameter 13¹/₄in.
(Sotheby's)
£1,967

Oriental silver punch bowl, of lobed form, the sides worked in deep repoussé with flower heads, 18in. diameter, approximately 214oz.
(William Doyle Galleries)
£10,125

PUNCH

A mid-18th century Irish 7⅝in. circular silver punch bowl engraved a crest in the form of a double headed eagle, maker John Moore, 19¾oz. (Phillips) **£2,700**

A George III hemispherical punch bowl, by Paul Storr, on fluted circular foot, 1867, 30.5cm. diam., 91oz. (Phillips) **£6,200**

Danish raised and chased silver punch bowl, late 19th century, marked Asteffensen, floral swag and leaf decoration, 13in. diameter, approx, 52 troy oz. (Skinner) **£830**

A presentation punch bowl, by Tiffany & Co., N.Y., 1890-91, 9in. high, 15¾in. diam., 101oz. **£18,630**

A Gorham Sterling and mixed metal punchbowl and ladle. (Skinner Inc.) **£11,000**

A George II plain circular punch bowl, by Edward Vincent, 1730, 9½in. diam., 38oz. **£11,290**

A Victorian circular punch bowl with shaped rim in monteith style with masked scroll edging, 13in. diameter, London 1900, 1685 gms, 54.1 oz. (Bearne's) **£1,600**

An Omar Ramsden silver punch bowl with everted rim, London hallmarks for 1931, 23.6cm. wide, 65oz.14dwt. **£4,840**

A silver punch bowl, maker's mark of Redlich & Co., New York, circa 1900, the openwork rims with trailing vine and flowerhead decoration, 10½in. diameter, 56 oz. 10 dwt. (Christie's) **£1,602**

Sterling punch bowl, chased with scroll and floral swag decoration, 13½in. diam, approx. 64 troy oz. (Skinner) **£466**

Silver punch bowl, 19th century, overall chased with the Rajah's hunting party, 9½in. diameter, approx. 45 troy oz. (Skinner) **£646**

A punch bowl, the hemispherical body divided into arched panels, maker's mark probably that of Chas. S. Harris & Sons, 1929, 28.2cm. diam., 37.5oz. **£560**

PUNCH

A fine silver and glass punch bowl by Gorham, Providence, 1893, with a flaring scalloped brim repoussé and chased with grapes and mixed fruit, 16¼in. diam, 352 oz. (Christie's) **£15,220**

A large Thai punch bowl, the sides chased in high relief with deities and mythological creatures, 20cm. diam. (Bonhams) **£450**

A punch bowl by Herbert A. Taylor for Stone Associates, Gardner, Massachusetts, 1908-1937, the sides partly fluted, marked, 39cm. diam., 106oz. (Christie's) **£5,880**

William III style Victorian punch bowl, by Walker & Hall, Sheffield, 1898. **£850**

Fine Sterling silver punch bowl by Old Newbury Crafters, engraved monograms and dates, 16¼in. diameter, 107 troy oz. (Eldred's) **£640**

A large punch bowl, by Walker & Hall, Chester 1906, 21.7cm. high, 69oz. **£1,800**

Large Victorian silver classical style Bacchic punch bowl by Elkington & Co., Birmingham, 1898, 16¾in. high, 178oz. (Butterfield & Butterfield) **£3,782**

An American silver octagonal punch bowl and ladle, Tiffany & Co., New York, 20th century, matching ladle, 162oz., length over handles 16½in. (Sotheby's) **£5,486**

Stieff Sterling repoussé punch bowl, Baltimore, heavily chased with roses and assorted flowers, 12in. diam, approximately 75 troy oz. (Skinner Inc) **£5,519**

A Victorian punch bowl, chased with foliate swags pendent from ribbon ties, 1890, by Walter and John Barnard, 30.4cm. diam., 44oz. (Lawrence Fine Arts) **£1,760**

A fine copper and silver Viking style punch bowl set with stones, maker's mark of Tiffany & Co., New York, finished November 20, 1902, designed by Paulding Farnham, length over handles 21in. (Christie's) **£11,129**

A Limited Edition tapering circular punch bowl, the body applied with four shaped oblong cartouches cast and chased with vignettes of animals, retailed by Tessiers, 10¼in., 47.75oz. (Christie's S. Ken) **£605**

ROSE

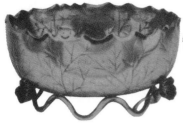

A Hukin & Heath electroplate rose bowl with crimped rim, the sides stamped with stylised branches and engraved with initials, 10in. diameter. (Christie's S. Ken) **£66**

A Scottish Art Nouveau spot hammered rose bowl, applied with three bracket handles, J.F., Glasgow, 1904, 12½in., 49oz. (Christie's S. Ken) **£715**

A silver rose bowl, circular form with part swirl fluted decoration and gadrooned border, London 1899. (Bonhams) **£320**

A silver rose bowl by Bernard Cuzner, the rounded bowl with rolled rim decorated with a repoussé rose briar frieze with five applied stylised rose heads, Birmingham hallmarks for 1911, 18.5cm. high. (Christie's) **£13,200**

An Edwardian silver-gilt and cut-glass rose bowl, the circular lobed cut-glass body with foliate decoration, by William Comyns, 1904, 15cm. (Lawrence) **£1,232**

An A. E. Jones hammered silver rose-bowl, with everted rim decorated with a repoussé frieze of Tudor Roses amid foliage, mounted in wooden plinth, 1909, 22.7cm. diameter, 990 grams. (Christie's) **£1,650**

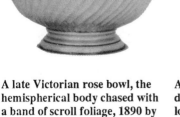

A late Victorian rose bowl, the hemispherical body chased with a band of scroll foliage, 1890 by George Maudsley Jackson, 21cm. diameter, 21.5oz. (Lawrence) **£770**

A presentation rose bowl on domed circular base with fluted lower body and shaped foliage rim, Sheffield, 1910, weight 12oz., 7¼in. diameter. (Christie's) **£308**

A large rose bowl, engraved with a coat of arms and presentation inscription to *A.J. Webbe, 1893*, the interior gilt, by C.S. Harris, 1892, 35cm., approximately 60 oz. (Lawrence Fine Art) **£1,650**

ROSE

A late Victorian pedestal rose bowl, repousse with rococo scrolls and two vacant car-touche panels, London 1897, 1207gr., 29cm. diam. (Henry Spencer) £860

An Edwardian gilt-lined two-handled rose bowl on four stylised bracket feet, the bowl embossed with a Celtic band, London 1908, 10in. diameter, 64oz. (Christie's S. Ken) £1,430

A rosebowl, with leafy scroll and female mask border, Chester 1906, by Walker and Hall, 25cm., 33oz. (Bonhams) £700

An Edward VII circular rose bowl, 26cm. diameter, W. H. Sparrow, Birmingham 1907, together with a metal grille and ebonised wood plinth, 33.2oz. weight of silver. (Bearne's) £720

A Victorian novelty rose bowl modelled as a waterlily, supported by leaves at either side, the junction applied with a frog, by Hukin & Heath, 1885, 25.6cm. diameter, weighable 40.5 ozs. (Phillips) £1,500

An important Keswick School of Industrial Arts silver presen-tation rose bowl and cover, made to commemorate James William Lowther being elected as Speaker to the House of Commons in 1905. (Phillips) £3,400

An Art Nouveau large circular rose bowl on domed base, richly chased and embossed with flowerheads and matted foliage, maker H.W., Sheffield, 1902, 12¼in. diameter, 50oz. (Christie's) £1,092

A late Victorian part oxidised fluted moulded circular rose bowl, Henry Wilkinson & Co Ltd., London, 1900, 10¼in. 37.75oz. (Christie's) £748

A late Victorian part spiral-fluted rose bowl on a rising circular foot and with a moulded rim, William Hutton & Sons Ltd., London 1895, 8¾in., 20oz. free. (Christie's S. Ken) £495

A plain hexagonal sugar bowl, on six curved feet and with foliate pierced rim, by Omar Ramsden, 1935, 4½in. wide, 7oz. (Christie's) **£605**

A George III Scottish swing-handled, boat-shaped sugar bowl, by John Leslie, Aberdeen, circa 1785, 9.5cm. high, 10.5oz. **£550**

A Faberge sugar bowl, set with two 18th century Russian coins, St. Petersburg marks, circa 1890-95, 3in. diam. **£2,200**

An Indian circular sugar bowl and cover on four fluted lion's paw supports, by Davd. Hare, Calcutta, circa 1820, 6½in. high, 21oz. **£2,850**

A James Dixon & Sons sugar bowl and cover, designed by Dr. Christopher Dresser, the spherical body flanked by two curved handles, model number 2273 and registration lozenge for 1880, 9.5cm. high. (Christie's) **£330**

A George II circular sugar bowl and cover, engraved with a band of palm leaves and below the shaped rim with a band of strapwork, latticework and female masks, by John Le Sage, 1730, 4in. high, 17oz. (Christie's) **£8,580**

Coin silver sugar bowl. Christof Christian Küchler for Hyde & Goodrich, (1816-1866), New Orleans, c. 1850, 6¼in. high. (Skinner Inc.) **£2,013**

A Hukin & Heath silver sugar bowl designed by Dr. Christopher Dresser, in the form of a basket with folded rim and loop handle, London hallmarks for 1881, 14.1cm. high, 195 grams. (Christie's) **£352**

A Maltese sugar bowl and cover, probably by Mario Schembri, circa 1775, in Italian style, 10oz.16dwt., 6in. high. **£910**

TWO HANDLED

A shaped circular bowl with two S-scroll twisted wire handles, by B. Schaats, N.Y., circa 1690-1700, 5³/₈ in. diam., 6oz. £48,785

A circular two-handled bowl, the handles each formed as a child sitting astride a reeded scroll branch, by Omar Ramsden, 1937, 7¹/₄in., 10oz. (Christie's) £2,090

A Dutch two-handled octagonal brandy bowl, Bolsward, circa 1685, maker's mark indistinct, 8oz.12dwt. £3,565

A Connell two-handled bowl, designed by Kate Harris, with bottle-green glass liner, London hallmarks for 1904, 39.1cm. diam., 22oz.15dwt. without liner. £1,090

A rare and large American silver two-handled bowl, Cornelius Vander Burgh, New York, circa 1690, 19oz. 3dwt., length over handles 12¹/₄in. (Sotheby's) £153,618

An 18th century two handled marriage bowl, with cast double scroll handles either side, maker's mark PA, for Pierre Amiraux (II), Jersey, circa 1770, 4oz. (Phillips) £850

A heavy Celtic Revival bowl, the almost hemispherical body with a lightly hammered finish, 1937 by the Goldsmiths and Silversmiths Company Ltd., 17.5cm. across handles, 13.3oz. (Lawrence) £132

Late 19th century Viennese circular jewelled and silver gilt mounted striated agate bowl, 5½in. high. £2,380

A Victorian two-handled oval bowl, with leaf-capped handles and on spreading base, 16¹/₂in. over handles, Atkin Brothers, Sheffield 1896, 2216 gms, 71.2 oz. (Bearne's) £1,850

An Edwardian two-handled shaped-oval bowl, on four leaf-capped shell and scroll feet and with openwork mask and scroll handles, by Gibson and Co. Ltd., 1905, 28in. long, 157oz. (Christie's) £8,800

An Edwardian Arts & Crafts circular hammered bowl, by A.E. Jones, Birmingham, 1908, 10in. across handles, 9oz. £210

A G. L. Connell Ltd. silver bowl, applied with exaggerated angular handles and leafage, on flared bracket feet, London hallmarks for 1903, 36.5cm. wide, 2804 grams. (Christie's) £3,300

BOXES

Silver was used to make boxes both for practical and decorative purposes. Principal among practical examples were, perhaps, biscuit and sugar boxes, the latter predating sugar bowls as a receptacle and fetching correspondingly high prices. Biscuit boxes originated in Holland in the late 18th century, and many were produced in the 19th century by English electroplate manufacturers.

Decorative silver boxes included those for tobacco and toilet items. The former were introduced in the late 17th century and were flat, oval or circular boxes with hinged or detachable lids. Again, they originated in Holland, though they were much copied elsewhere. Toilet boxes were usually highly ornamental and mostly formed part of elegant ladies' dressing table sets.

An Austrian hammered silver and silver gilt box with carved ivory finial, Austrian silver marks for 1925, 12oz. 10dwt., 8.2cm. high. **£595**

A Guild of Handicrafts hammered silver box and cover, London hallmarks for 1907, 2oz., 7.25cm. long. **£275**

An attractive late 19th century French enamel and silver gilt box depicting courting couples in 18th century costume, circa 1890, 5.2cm. long. (Phillips) **£320**

A sterling silver box with pierced enamel hinged cover, Worcester, Mass., 1925, 3¾in. wide. (Skinner) **£256**

A Guild of Handicraft silver and enamel box and cover, London hallmarks for 1901, 10cm. diam., 6oz.5dwt. gross weight. **£510**

An Arts & Crafts hammered silver box, by Chas. Horner, Birmingham hallmarks for 1902, 15.3cm. long, 5oz. 12dwt. (Christie's) **£440**

Early 19th century silver mounted coquilla nut with bird finial, 6in. high. **£595**

A 19th century Swiss oblong silver gilt and enamel singing bird box, by Chas. Bruguier, 3.⁷/₈in. long. **£3,565**

A French pepperbox, by Simon-Thadee Puchberger, Aix, 1769, 3¼in. wide, 150gr. **£700**

A William and Mary plain circular box and cover, by Elizabeth Haslewood, Norwich, 1691, 2½in. diam., 1oz.9dwt. **£1,545**

BOXES

An Italian silver gilt trinket box, the lid enamelled with a semi naked woman reclining on rockwork, 3½in.   £308

A silver gilt box with three rounded corners, the lid inset with an enamel plaque signed W. Sawers 1922, 2oz. 17dwt., 9cm. long.   £200

A German oblong dressing table box with hinged cover, 7¼in. long.   £420

A small Liberty & Co. silver and enamel pill box, Birmingham, 6.75cm. diam., 1914.   £130

An Omar Ramsden silver mounted shagreen box, inscribed *Omar Ramsden me fecit* with maker's marks and London hallmarks for 1930, 13cm. wide, 390 grams gross. (Christie's)   £2,420

A Swiss silver gilt and enamel singing bird box, the movement stamped C. Bruguier a Geneve, 9.5cm. wide.   £5,500

An early George II circular box by Charles Kandler, London, 1727, 5in. diam., 15oz.18dwt.   £5,080

An Eastern parcel-gilt shaped oblong box with rising flattened hinged cover, the sides decorated with scrolls and stylised stiff foliage, 5in. wide. (Christie's)   £418

A George IV circular box with a portrait medallion by J. Henning, 1809, 3¼in. diam.   £465

A silver gilt box, the lid inset with an enamel plaque, Birmingham hallmarks for 1922 and maker's monogram SB, 9cm. long, 2oz.17dwt. gross wt. (Christie's)   £165

An attractive Edwardian silver box and cover by Nathan and Hayes, of plain rectangular form, Chester 1901, 37 grams. 6cm. wide. (Spencer's)   £75

A French silver box and cover, the hinged cover chased, engraved and repoussé with an inn interior with figures, London 1897, 399 grammes, 15.5cm. wide. (Spencer's)   £400

73

BOXES

A silver rimmed box, the top with a panel richly decorated in carved shell with chrysanthemums, peonies and other flowers, signed *Shinryosai Masayuki saku,* 19th century, 15.8 x 12cm.
(Christie's) £3,520

An Eastern gilt box and cover modelled as a parrot with crocidolite eyes, a red enamelled beak and green, yellow, white and brown enamelled crest, 6¼in.
(Christie's S. Ken) £462

A Continental fan-shaped box decorated all over with cherubs, flowers and scrolling foliage, 6³/₄in. wide, import mark for London 1913, 7.9oz.
(Bearne's) £400

A Danish white metal and ivory box and cover, stamped marks W/G and CF Heise assay mark, circa 1925, 13.5cm. high. £440

A Guild of Handicraft hammered silver box and cover, the domed cover with painted enamel decoration of a river landscape at sunset, hallmarks for 1902, 11cm. diameter, 320 grams.
(Christie's) £1,320

A Liberty & Co. silver box and cover, the tapering swollen cylindrical body and domed cover set with small turquoise stones, together with two silver match box covers. £315

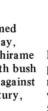

A rectangular silver rimmed Ryoshibako and inner tray, decorated in hiramakie, hirame and other techniques with bush clover and pampas grass against the full moon, 19th century, 22.5cm. wide.
(Christie's) £6,600

H.L., Girl with Poppies circular pill box, 1899, silver-coloured metal, the whole with opalescent white enamel, Birmingham, 5.25cm. diameter.
(Sotheby's) £667 $1,081

A Continental trinket box, French, mid-19th century, shaped rectangular with repoussé scroll and cherub decoration, import marks, 1896 by E.T.B., 9cm.
(Lawrence) £319

Large German silver table box, early 20th century, the lid and long side panels decorated with cast scenes of putti at various pursuits, 12¼in. wide, 46oz. 18dwts.
(Butterfield & Butterfield)
£1,903

An Arts & Crafts rectangular silver box, by W. Hutton & Sons Ltd., London hallmarks for 1901, 11.1cm. long, 11oz. 4dwt. gross weight.
(Christie's) £242

A silver box by Joachim Henrich Dysterdijk decorated in relief with a woman playing a spinet and a listening man, 1760, 145gr.
(Herholdt Jensen) £513

A Ramsden and Carr box, 1910, silver and enamel, maker's mark, London, and inscribed on the underside *Omar Ramsden et Alwyn Carr Me Fecervnt*, 4in. high.
(Sotheby's) £880

Continental silver table box with English import marks for Maurice Freeman, London, 1900, the top and sides with machine embossed die rolled scenes depicting a Renaissance hunt, 4oz. 10dwt.
(Butterfield & Butterfield) £188

A silver and enamel circular box and cover, painted in white, pink and green enamels with the head and shoulders of a long haired maiden, 11.2cm. diam. (Phillips) £700

Continental silver table box in the Louis XV taste, with pseudo French hallmarks, circa 1900, the lid showing a scroll framed scene from antiquity with four figures before a colonnaded building, 3½in. long, 3oz. 18dwt.
(Butterfield & Butterfield) £131

An early George V dressing table box, with escallop shell terminals, the hinged cover repoussé with figures in a public house interior, Chester 1911, 11cm. square overall.
(Spencer's) £340

An Edwardian silver mounted ring box with velvet padded hinged cover and apricot silk and velvet fitted interior, Birmingham 1908, 10cm. wide.
(Spencer's) £100

BISCUIT

A Hukin & Heath electroplated biscuit barrel, designed by Christopher Dresser, of spherical form on three feet, 20cm. high, March 1879.
(Phillips) £3,000

A late Victorian Aesthetic style biscuit barrel, hinged cover on integral two handled stand, all over engraved with storks, bamboo, and bulrushes, the oval stand raised upon four claw feet, 30cm. wide overall.
(Spencer's) £180

A Victorian lozenge shaped plated biscuit box, with formal engraving and panel feet. £95

A Guild of Handicraft silver biscuit barrel, designed by C.R. Ashbee, with green Powell glass liner, the lid with red enamel and wirework finial, with London hallmarks for 1900, 20.5cm. high, 475 grams. gross.
(Christie's) £3,960

An Art Nouveau silver and enamel oval biscuit box richly chased and embossed with sinuous stylised foliage, by Ramsden & Carr, 1902, gross weight 24oz., 7in. wide.
(Christie's) £2,640

A C.R. Ashbee hammered silver box and cover, set with seven cabochon garnets, stamped *C R A* with London hallmarks for 1899, 9.5cm. high, 145 grams. gross.
(Christie's) £1,485

A late Victorian wafer box, of fluted rectangular form, centrally hinged and opening to reveal two pierced liners with wreath cast handles, 24cm. high.
(Spencer's) £240

A Liberty & Co. silver biscuit box with Birmingham hallmarks for 1902, 20oz.14dwt., 14cm. high. (Christie's) £432

A Victorian biscuit box on stand with hinged action opening to reveal pierced liners with cast handles and ornate cast legs, 19cm. wide.
(Phillips) £310

SPICE

A Charles II circular silver gilt spice box, circa 1680, maker's mark FS/S, 3¾in. wide, 4oz.13dwt. **£8,315**

A German silver-gilt double spice box, the interior with central divider, the hinged cover engraved with latticework and scrolls on a matted ground, by Johann Pepfenhauser, Augsburg, 1735–6, 2in. long, 80grs.
(Christie's) **£1,870**

A Spanish oval spice box, on four cast lion's paw feet and with central hinge, Valladolid, circa 1780 and with the mark of Juan A. Sanz de Velasco, 4¹/₂in. long, 438grs.
(Christie's) **£3,520**

SUGAR

A Continental oval box, possibly Dutch 19th century, the hinged cover and sides decorated with repoussé classical figures and foliate scrolls, 1889, Chester, 9cm.
(Lawrence) **£495**

A silver sugar box and scoop of scuttle form, maker's mark S.D.L.D., London, 1911, 17½oz. **£430**

A Scandinavian 19th century oval sugar box or tea caddy on floral and foliate feet, Zethelius, 6¹/₂in., 19oz.
(Christie's S. Ken) **£638**

An oval sugar box by Soren Jensen Klitgaard, Copenhagen, 1754, 10.9cm. wide, 200gr. **£1,240**

An Austro-Hungarian 19th century gilt-lined part-fluted bombé-shaped oblong sugar box, 5¹/₂in., 11.25oz.
(Christie's) **£440**

An Italian sugar box and cover, maker's mark G.T., Venice or Padua, circa 1780, 4in. wide, 130gr. **£1,210**

TOBACCO

A Norwegian mid 18th century oval tobacco box, the lid engraved with birds, trees and a garden urn, 4⁴/₅in.
(Christie's S. Ken)   £462

A Dutch silver-gilt shaped-oblong tobacco-box, the hinged cover engraved with a scene of hounds attacking deer in a wooded landscape, circa 1730, 5¹/₂in. long, 183grs.
(Christie's)   £1,380

A Russian rectangular gilt lined tobacco box, with a nielloed band picking out the word *Souvenir*, Moscow 1878, 4in.
(Christie's S. Ken)   £330

A Charles II plain oval silver tobacco-box, the detachable cover engraved with a coat-of-arms, the base engraved with a monogram, 1671, maker's mark indistinct, 3³/₄in. high.
(Christie's)   £1,430

A William and Mary plain oval tobacco box, with corded borders, the detachable cover engraved with a coat-of-arms within foliage mantling, 1694, maker's mark *NL* probably for Nathaniel Lock, 3³/₄in. long, 5oz.
(Christie's)   £3,220

A Charles II oval silver gilt tobacco box with detachable cover, maker's mark W H only, circa 1675, 4in. long, 5oz.10dwt.   £1,210

A late 17th/early 18th century oval tobacco box engraved with armorials, unmarked, circa 1700, 9.8cm. long, 5 ozs.
(Phillips)   £400

Victorian silver tobacco box, Birmingham, 1900, 3¹/₂in. high, 10oz.   £340

An 18th century Dutch tobacco box of square form with curved corners, Amsterdam marks, 6½in. high, 22½oz. (Prudential)   £5,400

TOILET

A Charles II toilet box, maker's mark only IL a flower below, London, circa 1680, 4¼in. wide. £1,450

A shaped circular toilet box by Francois Thomas Germain, 9cm. diam., Paris, 1750, 275gr. £7,600

A George II silver gilt shaped oblong toilet box, by Ayme Videau, 1755, the cover, unmarked, 6¾in. long, 36oz. £2,970

A late Victorian toilet box in the Carolean taste, engraved with chinoiseries, Ho-ho birds, stylised flowers, foliage and fruit, George Lambert, London 1886, Britannia Standard, 5in., 17oz. (Christie's S. Ken) £935

One of a pair of George III spherical soap boxes, the circular spreading foot and cover border cast with a band of foliage, 1808, maker's mark W P, perhaps for William Pitts, 2¹/₂in. diameter, 7 oz. (Christie's) £2,200

A German oval toilet box and cover, the sides chased with flowers and acanthus foliage, by Daniel Michael II, Augsburg, circa 1675, 5¼in. long, 170grs. (Christie's) £1,210

Late 17th century Estonian parcel gilt toilet box, by F. Lemke, Reval, 4oz.6dwt., 3½in. diam. £785

A George I spherical soap box, by William Fawdery, 1720, Britannia Standard, 3½in. high, 8oz.19dwt. £4,160

A silver gilt double lid toilet box, probably German, circa 1750, unmarked, 3in. wide. £970

BRANDY SAUCE PANS

These were vessels with bellied, pear-shaped or cylindrical bodies, usually with a straight handle which was often of turned wood set at right angles to the pouring lip or spout. Occasionally they come en suite with a spirit burner or stand.

The bodies were made from one piece, usually with a cast lip. Some exceptionally large ones can hold up to two pints, but most were much smaller, and the smaller types are called pipkins. They were in use from the 17th century for warming brandy, though most extant examples date from the 18th century. A few were also made in Sheffield plate.

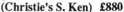

A George III brandy warming saucepan with gadroon edging and turned wood handle, 9in. long, London 1807, 8.5oz. (Bearne's) £280

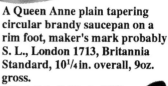

A Queen Anne plain tapering circular brandy saucepan on a rim foot, maker's mark probably S. L., London 1713, Britannia Standard, 10¼in. overall, 9oz. gross. (Christie's S. Ken) £880

A George III compressed brandy saucepan, by Wakelin & Taylor, London, 1782, 13.5oz. £365

An early George III Chester brandy saucepan, by Richard Richardson, 4.3cm. high. £485

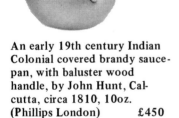

An early 19th century Indian Colonial covered brandy saucepan, with baluster wood handle, by John Hunt, Calcutta, circa 1810, 10oz. (Phillips London) £450

A George II plain baluster brandy saucepan, with moulded rim and lip and turned wood side handle, engraved with initials, by Robert Bailey, 1729, gross 6oz. (Christie's) £605

A George IV brandy warmer and cover, with a turned wood handle at right angles to the lip, Sheffield, 1821, by Samuel Roberts Jn and George Cadman and Co., 16.3cm. overall height, 13.3oz. all in. (Lawrence Fine Arts) £594

A late Victorian plain bellied brandy saucepan in the 18th century taste, James Dixon and Son, Sheffield 1896, 9¾in. overall, 7.25oz. gross. (Christie's) £165

A Queen Anne plain circular brandy saucepan, with turned wood handle, tapering stem and moulded lip, by Nathaniel Lock, 1708, 13in. long overall, gross 20oz. (Christie's) £2,070

William III plain brandy saucepan by John Martin, Stockar, 1698, 7oz.11dwt. £825

BUCKLES

Buckles were an early essential form of ornamentation, known at least since Roman times, and were worn on knee breeches, shoes, girdles, stocks, and cloaks.

Gothic tracery designs became very popular in the 14th and 15th centuries, and this theme was picked up again later, notably in the Art Nouveau period, which drew strongly on Gothic styles.

Buckles for shoes reached the height of their popularity in the 17th and 18th centuries.

A Guild of Handicrafts Ltd., cloak clasp, the design attributed to Charles Robert Ashbee, its body picked out with opal cabochons, 13cm. wide. (Phillips London) £900

A Guild of Handicrafts Ltd. silver enamel and amethyst buckle/cloak clasp, designed by C. R. Ashbee, circa 1902, 13.75cm. wide. £7,150

A Liberty hammered silver and enamelled belt buckle, the pierced floral decoration enamelled in blue and green, Birmingham hall marks for 1910. 7.5cm. long. (Christie's) £550

A Faberge silver-gilt and enamel buckle, 1899-1903. £790

A Liberty & Co. Glasgow style silver and enamel waist buckle with openwork decoration of stylised foliage with enamel details, with Birmingham hallmarks for 1902. (Christie's) £880

A Liberty & Co. silver and enamel waist clasp designed by Jessie M. King, circular openwork decoration of stylised flowers and birds with blue-green enamel details, Birmingham hallmarks for 1906. (Christie's) £1,650

A leaf-form belt buckle by Frank M. Whiting, North Attleboro, circa 1885, applied with a spider, a fly, a bee, and a butterfly, 3^1/$_8$in. long, 1 oz. (Christie's) £291

Sterling silver Arts & Crafts belt buckle, England, circa 1900-1904, two turquoise stones in symmetrical openwork organic design, 3¼in. wide. (Skinner Inc.) £108

A W. H. Haseler, Liberty silver and enamel waist clasp designed by Jessie M. King, each circular openwork section of stylised birds in flight and floral motifs, Birmingham hallmarks for 1906. (Christie's) £2,090

A William Comyns silver buckle in two pieces, of sinuous outline, formed by interwoven foliage, 11.5cm. wide, 1902. (Phillips London) £160

CADDY SPOONS

These originated in late 18th century Britain and were characterised by their short stem and large bowl, which could be in various ornamental forms, such as a leaf or a shell. Some were also made in the form of a jockey cap or an eagle's wing, but these are very rare indeed.

They were used for the transference of tea leaves from caddy to tea pot.

Generally speaking, the more ornamental they are, the more desirable.

A large George IV "Lily Pad" pattern caddy spoon, the looped handle formed as twigs, Robert Hennell, London 1829. (Christie's S. Ken) £660

A Victorian naturalistic leaf bowl caddy spoon with a hollow vine decorated handle, George Unite, Birmingham 1869. (Woolley & Wallis) £120

A Victorian caddy spoon with scalloped bowl, the openwork handle of vine leaf, tendril and grape bunch design, by George Unite, Birmingham, 1869. (Phillips) £110

A George III caddy spoon, with heart-shaped bowl and bifurcated 'mushroom' handle by Josiah Snatt, 1808. (Phillips) £120

A rare William IV die-stamped eagle's wing caddy spoon, the bowl chased with overlapping feathers, by Joseph Willmore, Birmingham, 1832. (Phillips) £800

A good and realistic George III caddy spoon with acorn bowl, the bifurcated handle ending in an octagonal 'fiddle' terminal, by Hart & Co., Birmingham, 1806. (Phillips) £440

An unmarked George III filigree jockey cap caddy spoon, the corrugated cap with wide filigree peak, circa 1800. (Phillips) £260

A good George III caddy spoon with acorn bowl engraved with diaperwork, the shaped handle with central oval panel, by Elizabeth Morley, 1809. (Phillips) £260

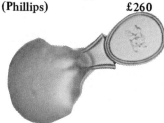

A George III silver-mounted natural shell caddy spoon, the bifurcated octagonal handle with double-thread edge, by Matthew Linwood, of Birmingham, circa 1800. (Phillips) £350

A George III die-stamped caddy spoon, chased with overlapping stylised feathers enclosing an oval centre, by Wardell & Kempson, Birmingham, 1818. (Phillips) £130

A George IV caddy spoon, with plain scallop-shaped bowl and ovoid handle, by Joseph Willmore, Birmingham, 1822. (Phillips) £110

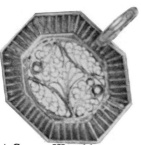

A George III caddy spoon with octagonal bowl, the sides with ribs separated by bands of chevrons, by Samuel Pemberton, Birmingham, 1806. (Phillips) £250

An unusual George III scuttle-shaped caddy spoon, engraved with diaperwork, by Cocks & Bettridge, Birmingham, 1804. (Phillips) £220

A George III caddy spoon with gilt oval fluted bowl and oval filigree central panel, by Samuel Pemberton, Birmingham, 1807. (Phillips) £240

A George III filigree caddy spoon, the bowl of near anthemion shape, each flute terminating in a disc motif, unmarked, circa 1800. (Phillips) £120

A George III right-hand caddy spoon, the flat handle with curved top and incurved sides, by Josiah Snatt, 1805. (Phillips) £350

A George III silver-mounted natural shell caddy spoon, the bifurcated octagonal handle with double-thread edge, by Matthew Linwood, of Birmingham, circa 1800. (Phillips) £340

A George III shovel caddy spoon, engraved with wriggle-work on a hatched background, by William Pugh, Birmingham, 1808. (Phillips) £160

A George III jockey cap caddy spoon, of ribbed design with reeded surfaces, by Joseph Taylor, Birmingham, 1798. (Phillips) £220

A rare George III cast caddy spoon, decorated in relief with a Chinese Mandarin holding a tea plant, by Edward Farrell, 1816. (Phillips) £1,250

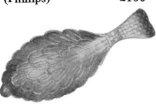

A George III caddy spoon, the feather-shaped bowl chased with stylised overlapping feathers, by William Pugh, Birmingham, 1808. (Phillips) £420

A Victorian caddy spoon, the thistle or bellshaped bowl parcel gilt and embossed with grapes and vine leaves, by Hilliard & Thomason, Birmingham, 1852. (Phillips) £100

A George III 'frying pan' caddy spoon. the circular, engine-turned bowl with central rosette, by Matthew Linwood, Birmingham, 1807. (Phillips) £200

18TH CENTURY

These are branched candlesticks where the stem and base conform to candlestick design with detachable or fixed scroll branches for two or more lights, with finials of various forms. Virtually none exist dating from before the 18th century. Later examples became highly elaborate and many branched, sometimes with interchangeable épergne dishes. Candelabra tend to fetch much higher sums than candlesticks, therefore made up branches are rather more common than the genuine article. To be quite genuine, the marks on the branches should, of course, correspond to the sticks, and should be marked on the sleeve which fits into the candlestick. Then the wax pans below the capitals should bear a lion passant and maker's mark, the capitals should have a lion passant, and the nozzles should bear a lion passant or maker's mark, or, if after 1784, these plus the duty mark. Most fake branches are marked only on the sleeves.

Pair of Louis XVI four-light candelabra, by Antoine Boullier, Paris, 1787, with the charge of Henri Clavel and export discharge mark, 26in. high, 269oz. **£76,710**

One of four Louis XV four-light candelabra, Paris, 1732, fermier-general Hubert Louvet, 217oz. **£53,460**

Pair of Spanish four-light candelabra, by Juan de San Fauri, Madrid, 1762, with the warden's mark of Melun, 19¾in. high, 180oz. **£68,185**

A Danish three-light candelabrum, with baluster stem and vase-shaped socket, by Christian Werum, Copenhagen, probably 1762, 18½in. high, 1439grs.
(Christie's) **£2,090**

19TH CENTURY

One of a pair of Victorian five-light Corinthian column candelabra, dated 1886, 26½in. high, weight of branches 116oz. **£5,700**

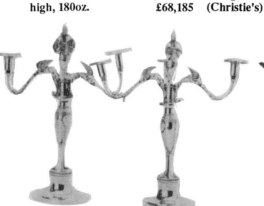

An impressive pair of Austro-Hungarian three branch candelabra, 17⅛in. long, the branches supported by winged beasts, circa 1830.
(Bonhams) **£2,700**

A Victorian three-light candelabrum/centrepiece, by W. & G. Sissons, Sheffield, 1865, 24¾in. high, 165oz. **£5,630**

84

19TH CENTURY

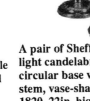

Fine late Victorian silver five light candelabrum in Adam style having a beaded sloped stepped square base, Sheffield 1896, 20in. tall.
(G. A. Key) £1,700

A pair of Sheffield plate three-light candelabra, each on circular base with tapering stem, vase-shaped sconces, circa 1820, 22in. high.
(Christie's) £1,705

A Victorian three-light candelabra, on three foliate and scroll feet and with floral border, by John S. Hunt, 1844, 18in. high, gross 99 oz.
(Christie's) £2,200

One of a pair of Victorian massive seven-light candelabra, the scroll stem entwined with vine tendrils and with frolicking putti, shamrocks and a harp, by John S. Hunt, 1844, 31¹/₂in. high, 741 oz.
(Christie's) £38,500

A pair of Continental seven-light candelabra, each supporting a naturalistic stem and one with a stag, the other with a hind, by L. Janesich, 19th century, 23in. high, 3,779grs.
(Christie's) £3,300

One of a pair Sheffield plate four light candelabra, English, early 19th century, with gadroon bands, fluted decoration and distinguished by square form knops, 23³/₄in. high.
(Butterfield & Butterfield)£1,557

One of a pair of plated five-light candelabra, maker's mark of Tiffany & Co., New York, circa 1885, with foliate decoration, 15¹/₄in. high.
(Christie's) £2,341

A pair of William IV style candelabra each with four scrolling reeded branches emanating from a central nozzle, 16in. (Hy. Duke & Son) £280

One of a pair of Old Sheffield plate three-light candelabra applied with rococo scrolling foliate decoration, 20in. high.
(Christie's) £935

A Victorian candelabrum
centrepiece, by Paul Storr,
1837, 24½in. high, 297oz.
£8,910

A fine pair of sterling silver
five candle candelabra, Adams
style, 16½in. high, 75 troy oz.
£1,620

One of a pair of late 19th
century silver candelabra,
St. Petersburg, 20.5cm:
£1,254

A Victorian six light
candelabrum centrepiece, the
fluted stem with foliage
terminals, with three bi-furcated
scroll branches and vase-shaped
fluted sockets and detachable
nozzles, by Barnard and Co.,
1842, 30½in. high, 343oz.
(Christie's)   **£8,800**

A pair of French seven-light
candelabra, each on a shaped-
oblong base, by Jean-Baptiste
Harleux, Paris, late 19th
century, 22¾in. high, 7,070grs.
(Christie's)   **£5,720**

A 19th/20th century five-light
candelabrum, with beaded
edging, reeded branches and
sconces decorated with ribbon
tied festoons, William Hutton
and Sons Ltd., London 1899,
19¾in. overall height of
candelabrum, 41.3 oz weight of
branches.
(Bearne's)   **£1,200**

One of a pair of George III
three-light candelabra, by
Paul Storr, 1816, 16¾in.
high, 262oz.   **£100,980**

A pair of Victorian four-light
candelabra, each on waisted
circular base hung with foliage
swags, by Smith and Nicholson,
1862, 23½in. high, 178 ozs.
(Christie's)   **£4,950**

A George III silver gilt four-
light candelabrum, by Paul
Storr, 1815, 20½in. high,
143oz.   **£20,196**

19TH CENTURY

One of a pair of Regency three-light candelabra, by Wm. Eaton, 1815, 21½in. high, 421oz. **£36,300**

Pair of 19th century Regency-style silver candelabra, labelled Peruzzi, Florence, 16½in. high. **£580**

A George III three-light candelabrum, by Digby Scott and Benjamin Smith, 1804, 17in. high, 83oz. **£4,750**

An early Victorian five-light candelabrum centrepiece and mirror plateau, the base engraved with a coat-of-arms, crest and presentation inscription dated 1843, by Richard Sawyer, Dublin, 1843, height overall 25in., 254oz. (Christie's) **£6,050**

A pair of German two light candelabra, with two reeded branches and central openwork tripod with applied rams' masks and flame finial, by Johann Gottlieb Kohlheim, Berlin, circa 1800, 20¾in. high, weight of branches 1437grs. (Christie's) **£2,090**

A Russian Hanukah lamp, 1879, assaymaster OC, possibly Minsk, struck with the name L. Zammer and town mark a crescent between mullets, 21¼in. high, weight of branches 30oz. **£2,420**

One of a pair of William IV Sheffield plate candelabra, by J. Dixon & Sons, 21¼in. high. **£570**

A pair of three light candelabra by Giovanni Casolla, Naples, the stems as female figures holding aloft the branches, circa 1830, 66.5cm. high, 7830gr. (Finarte) **£15,888**

One of a pair of candelabra, in Louis XVI style, by Odiot, 55.8cm. high, circa 1870, 11450gr. **£5,610**

CANDELABRA

A Victorian silver-gilt four-light candelabrum centrepiece, by Edward Barnard & Sons, 1846, 27½in. high, 195oz.
(Christie's) £5,500

Pair of George III candelabra, by W. Tucker & Co., Sheffield, 1809, 23in. high. £4,070

William IV five-light candelabrum by Robinson, Edkins & Aston, Birmingham, 1833, 163oz., 20¼in. high. £3,870

One of a pair of Victorian silver-gilt candelabra, four-light, the circular base with foliate repoussé decoration, by John Bodman Carrington, 1898, 44cm., 168oz.
(Lawrence) £4,950

Sheffield plated pair of three light candelabra, circa 1810, circular bases with gadrooned borders supporting a trumpet shaft, height 15¾in.
(Butterfield & Butterfield) £564

One of a pair French silver seven light cast candelabra, maker's mark: *PB* in a diamond, engraved on base: *Bucheron, Paris*, late 19th century, in the rococo taste, 20½in. high, 413oz. 18dwts.
(Butterfield & Butterfield) £10,377

One of a pair of modern small three branch three light candelabra, from a single stick in the George I style, on stepped hexagonal base, London 1965, maker's mark *RC*., 2309 grammes total.
(Spencer's) £900

A pair of Sheffield plate three-light candelabra, each on a shaped square base, decorated with lion masks and acanthus foliage, early 19th century, 21½in. high.
(Christie's) £1,495

A Victorian large six-light candelabrum centrepiece, the base with the detachable figures of Bacchus and two Bacchante, by Benjamin Smith III, 1844, 30½in. high, 290oz.
(Christie's) £7,475

One of a pair of French six-light candelabra, by J. Chaumet, Paris, 1918, 24½in. high, 471oz.　£17,045

One of a pair of Georg Jensen candelabra with five cup-shaped candle nozzles and circular drip pans supported on U-shaped branches, 27cm. high.　£23,760

Sterling silver and copper candelabra, possibly Metcalf & Co., Upstate New York, circa 1905, 13in. high. (Skinner Inc.)　£185

Pair German silver five light candelabra, Friedlander, early 20th century, 800 standard modified reproduction of George III style, 19in. high, 111oz. 14dwts. (Butterfield & Butterfield)　£1,245

A Harold Stabler silver twin-branch candelabrum, tall ovoid fluted and faceted stem with similarly faceted curved branches, stamped facsimile signature *Harold Stabler*, 1935, 29cm. high, 569 grams. (Christie's)　£880

A pair of Sheffield plate three-light candelabra, the circular bases, tapering stems, drip pans and detachable nozzles with gadroon edging, 20in. high, Matthew Boulton, Sheffield. (Bearne's)　£770

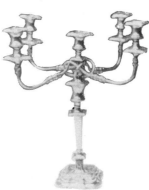

A silver three-branch candel-abrum, no. 159 of a limited edition of 250, London, 1977, 11in. high, 25oz. £145

Pair of Art Nouveau candelabra, silvered metal with stylised arms supporting candle nozzles, impressed marks, 12¼in. high. (Skinner)　£387

A four branch five light candelabrum with shaped square sconces, the whole with foliate stamped angles, 53cm. high. (Spencer's)　£120

20TH CENTURY

A two-branch candelabrum, designed by Soren Georg Jensen, 17.7cm. high, 26oz.10dwt. **£1,575**

One of a pair of Georg Jensen Danish silver candelabra, 9in. high, 76 troy oz. **£3,410**

One of a pair of Georg Jensen five-branch candelabra, designed by Harald Nielsen, 40cm. high. (Christie's) **£15,400**

One of a pair of WMF electroplated candlesticks, each cast as a young woman supporting a flower sprouting to form the four candleholders, 48cm. high, circa 1900. **£2,420**

A pair of Art Nouveau plated metal figural candlesticks, designed by C. Bonnefond, each modelled as a girl with long hair, 36.5cm. high. **£1,300**

A German six-light candelabrum on a rising shaped circular base moulded with flowerheads, laurel leaves and berries, 24in. high. (Christie's S. Ken.) **£1,595**

One of a pair of three-light candelabra, by Thomas Bradbury & Sons, London, 1898/1902, 18¼in. high, 132oz.16dwt. **£1,320**

Silver pair of four light candelabra, Naylor Bros., London, 1961, designed by A. P. Hawksley, plain circular base rising to support a tall faceted bud form, 14in. high, 101oz. (Butterfield & Butterfield) **£1,276**

An Edwardian four branch five light table candelabrum, with detachable square sconces, Sheffield 1906, by Martin Hall and Co., 56cm. high overall. (Spencer's) **£1,250**

18TH CENTURY

The earliest candlesticks were made from sheet, hammered up and hand chased, and these were made until around 1705, though casting was introduced by Huguenot silversmiths in Britain around 1690. From then until the late 18th century all candlesticks were cast, but this method was then abandoned for die stamping from thin silver sheet. The dies were poor at first but rapidly improved and by about 1770 required very little hand finishing, the stampings being soldered together and filled with resin, sometimes with an iron bar up the centre to give weight.

In the 17th century domestic candlesticks were square and solid, providing great scope for the inventions of rococo silversmiths. Baluster forms became more popular in the 18th century.

Few telescopic stems were made in silver, but became common in Sheffield plate from circa 1790.

In the 19th century candlesticks were once again cast, and became massive and ornate in design, while the Classical Revival of the 1870s saw the return of Corinthian column candlesticks about 12in. high. Small cast reproductions of George II styles were also made in the next twenty years, while 1890–1910 saw Commonwealth, Charles II and Louis XVI types recalled.

In the early 20th century candlestick design was influenced by the Arts & Crafts, Art Nouveau and Art Deco movements. Archibald Knox for Liberty, WMF, Georg Jensen and Omar Ramsden all produced candlesticks typical of the styles of the times.

A good pair of late George III telescopic candlesticks by Alexander Goodman and Co., Sheffield 1797, 16cm. high. (Spencer's) £720

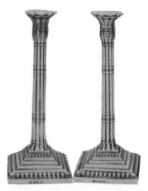

A fine and attractive pair of early George III cluster column candlesticks by Ebenezer Coker, London 1768, 31.5cm. high. (Spencer's) £1,400

A pair of Queen Anne candlesticks, each on spreading gadrooned octagonal base and slightly sunken centre and with partly-fluted baluster stem and vase-shaped socket, by John East, 1702, 6³/₄in. high, 34oz. (Christie's) £11,000

A good pair of George II table candlesticks, the baluster stems and shaped rectangular bases embossed with shells within gadroon borders, by Ebenezer Coker, 1759, 27.5cm., original scratch weight 47.5 oz. (Lawrence Fine Art) £2,640

A pair of late 18th century candlesticks, the lightly channelled stems with slight spiral swirl, stamped with two crowns, Milan, 19cm. high, 700gr. (Finarte) £2,845

A pair of Queen Anne candlesticks, each on spreading decagonal base and with baluster stem and circular vase-shaped socket, by Ambrose Stevenson, 1711, 7in. high, 35oz. (Christie's) £7,290

18TH CENTURY

A pair George I candlesticks, engraved with a coat-of-arms with Bishop's mitre above, by David Green, 1719, 7¹/₈in. high, 30 oz.
(Christie's) £6,600

Pair of George II silver table candlesticks with cherub columns, by Simon Jouet, London, 1747, 9¾in. high, 42oz. £2,090

A pair of George I plain candlesticks, each on hexagonal base and with baluster stem, by William Darker, 1724, 6¹/₄in. high 16oz.
(Christie's) £4,600

John Cafe, a George II cast taperstick, the spool shape holder with a detachable nozzle, 5¹/₅in. high, London 1752, 4¹/₂oz.
(Woolley & Wallis) £620

A set of four table candlesticks, in the Louis XV manner, each on a shaped circular base with shell and scroll borders, 10¹/₂in. high. (Christie's) £1,210

One of a pair of Spanish table candlesticks, Antonio Ruiz, Cordoba, circa 1780, 29oz.3dwt., 9¾in. high.
£1,935

A good pair of late George III candlesticks by John Parsons & Co., on swept circular bases stamped with fluting, Sheffield 1792, 29cm. high.
(Spencer's) £1,000

A good set of four George III Irish candlesticks with 'cotton reel' nozzles and holders, John Walker, Dublin circa 1775, 11.5 oz. (Woolley & Wallis) £5,800

A pair of columnar George III candlesticks, 12in. high, the cylindrical stems chased with spirally fluted masks, London, 1778, by Joseph Heriot.
(Bonhams) £1,300

18TH CENTURY

A George II rare pair of cast candlesticks, 28.5cm. high, by Nicholas Sprimont, 1742, 80oz. (Phillips London) £195,000

An early pair of George III cast candlesticks, in the rocaille style, 28cm. high, by Arthur Annesley, 1760, 52 ozs. (Phillips) £3,800

Pair of George III table candlesticks, London marks of 1776 overstriking the original Sheffield marks, 27.9cm. high. £580

One of four Louis XV/XVI candlesticks, by Joseph-Theodore Vancombert, Paris, two 1771, and two 1775, 10 5/8in. high, 81oz. £10,230

A set of four George III candlesticks, each on a stepped square base with gadrooned border, engraved with a crest, by William Cafe, 1760, 10 1/2in. high. (Christie's) £5,500

One of a pair of William III candlesticks, maker's mark IL, a coronet above and pellet below, circa 1695, 7in. high, 30oz. £4,990

An attractive pair of George III small candlesticks, the baluster urn shaped sockets with flange rims, Sheffield 1780, probably by Fenton Creswick and Co., 19cm. high. (Spencer's) £700

A set of four George II cast candlesticks with fluted baluster columns and shell decorated knops, 23cm. high, by William Gould, 1746, 101.25 ozs. (Phillips) £6,500

A pair of George II cast candlesticks, 8 3/4in. high, the shaped circular bases cast with shells, London 1757, by John Hyatt and Charles Seymour. (Bonhams) £1,700

18TH CENTURY

One of a pair of George II cast table candlesticks, by John Priest, 1754, 20.4cm. high, 27.3oz. **£1,390**

A pair of George I table candlesticks, by David Green, London, 1723, 16.1cm. high, 23oz. **£2,530**

A pair of George III Corinthian column table candlesticks, with detachable square nozzle, by John Carter, 1773, 13in. high. (Christie's) **£2,300**

A pair of George III table candlesticks, with partly-fluted tapering stem and campana-shaped socket, by Joseph Parsons and Co., Sheffield, date letter probably 1788, 11¼in. high. (Christie's) **£1,760**

An almost matching pair of early George II small candlesticks, the cylindrical sockets issuing from inverted octagonal baluster stems, London 1732, by James Gould, 794 grams total, 16.5cm. high. (Spencer's) **£1,800**

Pair of George III silver candlesticks by William Cafe, London, 1765, with spreading shaped stepped circular base chased with acanthus, 10¼in. high, 38oz. 18dwts. (Butterfield & Butterfield) **£1,557**

A pair of George II cast table candlesticks, with shaped circular bases and knopped stems, 7in. high, John Gould, London 1736, 26.6 oz. (Bearne's) **£3,400**

A pair of William III silver-gilt candlesticks, each on spreading circular base and with partly-fluted baluster-stem and vase-shaped socket, one 1701, 7³⁄₄in. high. (Christie's) **£6,325**

A pair of George III Corinthian candlesticks, on plain sloping square bases and with gadroon borders, engraved with a crest, 31cm. high, by John Carter, 1770. (Phillips) **£2,500**

Pair of George III coffee house candlesticks, by E. Coker, 1765, 28.6cm. high, 29oz.
£1,210

A pair of early George III cast table candlesticks, 1762, maker's mark DM over a star and 1763, by E. Coker, 26.1cm. high, 42oz. £1,450

Pair of early George III cast table candlesticks, by Wm. Cafe, 1760, 22.6cm. high, 30oz. £1,090

A pair of George III table candlesticks, the circular bases with fluted borders and engraved with a coat of arms, by John Parsons & Co., Sheffield, 1790, 28cm., wood based.
(Lawrence Fine Art) £2,310

A pair of George I plain hexagonal cast candlesticks, engraved with a coat-of-arms within a scroll cartouche, by Matthew Cooper, 1719, Britannia Standard, 7in. high, 25oz.
(Christie's) £7,700

A pair of George II candlesticks, each on spreading octagonal base with slightly sunken centre and with baluster stem and spool-shaped socket, by Paul de Lamerie, 6½in. high, 31oz.
(Christie's) £29,700

A George III pair of Corinthian candlesticks, with cast acanthus capitals and incurved square nozzles, 29cm. high, by John Parsons & Co., Sheffield, 1789.
(Phillips) £2,200

A George II candlestick and matching snuffers and tray, the candlestick on spreading square base with incurved angles and baluster stem and spool-shaped socket, by James Gould, 1729, gross 22oz.
(Christie's) £10,450

A pair of George III table candlesticks, the cast sticks with fluted knopped stems and shaped square bases, London 1777, by Jonathon Alleine, 21.5cm. high, 34½oz.
(Bonhams) £2,000

A pair of George III telescopic candlesticks, by John Roberts & Co., Sheffield, 1805, 26cm. extended, loaded. **£1,070**

A pair of silver candlesticks, maker's mark of Tiffany & Co., New York, 1883–1891, of shaped square form, 9³/₄in. high, 31oz. (Christie's) **£3,710**

A pair of Old Sheffield Plate telescopic candlesticks, on fluted circular spreading bases. (Bonhams) **£140**

A pair of late Victorian Corinthian capital candlesticks on foliate-stamped rising square bases, Elkington and Co. Ltd., Birmingham 1898, height of candlesticks 12¹/₄in. (Christie's) **£1,155**

A set of four Sheffield plate candlesticks by Waterhouse, Hatfield & Co., Sheffield, circa 1840, 9¹/₄in. high. (Butterfield & Butterfield) **£693**

Pair of Continental silver candlesticks, apparently unmarked, 19th century, fitted with detachable nozzles, 12in. high, 18oz. 16 dwts. (Butterfield & Butterfield) **£630**

A pair of Sheffield plate table candlesticks, the stems designed as bound palms on tapering square bases with beaded edging, 12³/₄in. high. (Bearne's) **£380**

A pair of Victorian Corinthian column dressing table candlesticks, 6in. high, Mappin Brothers, Sheffield 1898, loaded. (Bearne's) **£550**

A pair of Victorian candlesticks, on square shaped bases with foliate swag motif, and corinthian capitals, by H.E., Sheffield 1898, 23cm., loaded. (Lawrence) **£440**

Pair of Victorian table candlesticks embossed, on square bases, Sheffield, 1844, 9½in. high. **£790**

Pair of French silver candlesticks, early 19th century, 8¾in. high, approx. 32 troy oz. (Skinner) **£1,282**

Silver pair of candlesticks, William Gale & Sons, New York, 1852, 23oz. 16dwt. (Butterfield & Butterfield) **£1,876**

A pair of late Victorian table candlesticks in the George III manner, decorated with neo-classical urns and trailing oak leaves, by L. A. West, 1898, 12in. high.
(Christie's) **£1,100**

A pair of Victorian dressing table candlesticks, each square base with a gadrooned edge and stiff leaves to the corners, by Turner Bradbury, 1895, 6in. high.
(Lawrence Fine Art) **£1,540**

A pair of late Victorian tapersticks in the George III style, with detachable square sconces, London 1890, by Henry Wilkinson and Co., loaded, 12cm. high.
(Spencer's) **£450**

Pair of Victorian pillar candlesticks in the Adam style having garland, ribbon and ram's head moulded decoration London 1892, 12in. high.
(Russell Baldwin & Bright) **£880**

Pair of Russian silver gilt and enamel candlesticks, Moscow, late 19th century, approximately 25 troy oz.
(Skinner) **£1,158**

A pair of late Victorian table candlesticks, spirally fluted Corinthian columns on stepped square bases, London, 1892, 11½in. high.
(Bonhams) **£1,200**

19TH CENTURY

A very fine pair of late George III candlesticks by John Roberts and Co., with detachable circular sconces, Sheffield 1810, loaded, 32cm. high. (Spencer's) **£1,600**

A pair of George III Sheffield plated candlesticks, circa 1800, each with reeded rims above fluted candle cups, 12¼in. high. (Christie's) **£925**

A pair of German early 19th century baluster candlesticks on foliate and berry-decorated rising square bases, 9½in., 17 oz. (Christie's S. Ken) **£880**

A pair of George III candlesticks, each on shaped square bases and baluster stem cast and chased with cherubs' masks, by Joseph Craddock and William Reid, 1810, 12in. high, 107oz. (Christie's) **£4,400**

A pair of Victorian novelty bedroom candlesticks, each modelled as three grotesque faces; one sleeping, one yawning and one smiling; 21cm. high, by Henry William Dee, 1878, 19½ozs. (Phillips) **£4,400**

A pair of George III candlesticks, decorated with vertical fluting, with vase-shaped sockets, detachable nozzles and gadrooned borders, by Matthew Boulton, Birmingham, 1801, 12in. high. (Christie's) **£2,200**

A pair of table candlesticks, the tapering stems headed by double sided Bacchanalian masks, possibly central European, circa 1800, 30cm., loaded. (Lawrence Fine Art) **£2,420**

Pair of table candlesticks, by J. M. Wendt, the stems in the form of a male and female Aboriginal, Adelaide, circa 1875, 20.5cm. high, 1330gr. **£9,075**

Pair of Austrian silver candlesticks with Egyptian influence, circa 1810–1824, campagna form sconce with detachable nozzle, 11½in. (Butterfield & Butterfield) **£1,426**

20TH CENTURY

One of a pair of Art Deco silver candlesticks by Walker & Hall, Sheffield, 1934. £2,000

A pair of Georg Jensen white metal candlesticks, designed by Harald Nielsen, the cylindrical candle holder with everted rim, 14cm. high, 1.425 grams. (Christie's London) £2,420

One of a pair of Edwardian candlesticks with trumpet-shaped foot, by Gilbert Marks, 1902, 13in. high, 41oz. (Christie's) £3,672

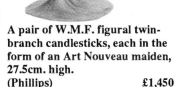

A pair of Georg Jensen candlesticks, with slightly flared sockets, decorated with four pendent buds with berries, on broad circular feet, with stamped maker's marks for 1925–32, 10.2cm. high, 315 grams. (Christie's) £2,640

A pair of W.M.F. figural twin-branch candlesticks, each in the form of an Art Nouveau maiden, 27.5cm. high. (Phillips) £1,450

A pair of Liberty & Co. silver candlesticks, tapered fluted stems beneath flared sconces, on flange feet, each with blue and green enamelled entrelac medallions, 16.7cm. high, 345gr. gross. (Christie's) £1,610

An unusual pair of George V candlesticks, raised upon three openwork supports, London 1920, 464 grams total. (Spencer's) £280

An Art Nouveau silver 'counter-balanced' candlestick, 16.5cm. high, marked KK, London, 1905. £220

Pair of WMF Art Nouveau silver coloured metal candlesticks, 11in. high. £330

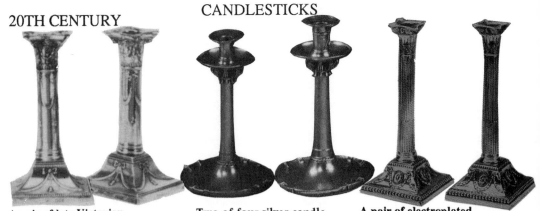

A pair of late Victorian Corinthian capital candlesticks on beaded rising square bases, Thomas Bradbury, London 1901, 7¼in. high. (Christie's) £825

Two of four silver candlesticks, by Omar Ramsden, two 1919, two 1922, loaded, 22.5cm. high. £3,300

A pair of electroplated Corinthian column table candlesticks, the square bases decorated with rams masks, 11¾in. high. (Bearne's) £180

Pair of candlesticks designed by S. Bernadotte, stamped Georg Jensen 355B Sigvard and London import marks, 25.9cm. high, 25oz.11dwt. £1,010

A pair of Edwardian dwarf candlesticks on scroll-decorated rounded square bases applied with scroll feet, Thomas Law, Sheffield 1902, 4¾in. high. (Christie's) £352

A pair of candlesticks, the faceted knopped stem on stepped and cut square bases gadrooned borders, Sheffield 1909. (Bonhams) £650

A pair of silver candlesticks with a round base chased and worked in repoussé with flowering irises among water, impressed on the base *Arthur & Bond, Yokohama* and *yogin* Meiji period (1868-1912), 28 cm high. (Christie's) £1,840

A pair of George V silver mounted oak barley twist candlesticks by Albert Edward Jones, with planished silver cylindrical sockets, Birmingham 1920, 21.5cm. high. (Spencer's) £210

A pair of table candlesticks of Regency design, the baluster stems and shaped circular bases embossed with cartouches between flower swags, by Leopold Ltd., 1908, 25cm.. loaded. (Lawrence Fine Art) £880

A pair of Edwardian cast shell-decorated baluster candlesticks in the mid 18th century taste, E. J. G., Birmingham 1906, 9in., 31.50oz.
(Christie's)　　　　£660

A pair of reproduction cast candlesticks in the William III manner, by Carrington & Co., weight 24oz., 6¹/₄in. high.
(Christie's)　　　　£715

A pair of plain table candlesticks each on a sunken circular base with knopped baluster stem, London, 1911, 9in. high.
(Christie's)　　　　£385

A pair of George VI candlesticks, the plain oval sockets raised upon swept oval columns, Birmingham 1945, by A & J Zimmerman Ltd., 6in. high.
(Spencer's)　　　　£360

A pair of Edwardian table candlesticks in the Neo Classical revival style, 1903, by William Hutton and Sons Ltd., 30.7cm., loaded.　　£1,100

A pair of modern, cast, desktop candlesticks with shaped square bases and knopped stems, 4¹/₄in. high, Asprey, London 1962, 27.81oz.
(Bearne's)　　　　£280

A pair of Edward VII table candlesticks, the octagonal bases, knopped stems and detachable nozzles with reeded edging, 7¹/₂in. high, Thomas Bradbury, London 1902, loaded.
(Bearne's)　　　　£450

Pair of Danish silver single candlesticks by Georg Jensen, Copenhagen, circa 1940, designer Harald Nielsen, both with circular stepped base, 2³/₄in. high, 10oz. 14dwts.
(Butterfield & Butterfield)　　　　£1,384

A pair of James Dixon & Sons silver candlesticks, the concave drip pans with everted rim and cylindrical detachable candleholder, 1907, 22cm. high, 780 grams gross.
(Christie's)　　　　£1,320

CANNS

The cann was a late 17th and 18th century American drinking vessel based on the English mug. The capacity was usually one pint, and the earliest type had a tapering cylindrical body, moulded rim, rat tail handle, with or without a moulded foot. From around 1730 rounded sides became common. Makers include Paul Revere and Samuel Edwards of Boston.

A silver covered cann, maker's mark of Simeon Soumaine, New York, circa 1710, 4³/₄in. high, 10oz. 10dwt.
(Christie's) £4,081

A silver cann, maker's mark of William Taylor, Philadelphia, circa 1775, 5¹/₄in. high, 11oz.
(Christie's) £1,452

A silver cann, maker's mark of William Homes, Sr., Boston, circa 1750, the S-scroll handle with moulded drop and bud terminal, 5¹/₄in. high, 10 oz. 10 dwt.
(Christie's) £739

A rare silver cann, maker's mark of John Bayley, Philadelphia, 1760–1770, the double scroll handle with acanthus-leaf grip, on moulded circular foot, 5in. high, 13 oz. 10 dwt. (Christie's) £1,725

An American silver small cann, Edmund Milne, Philadelphia, circa 1770, with leaf-capped double-scroll handle, 9oz., height 4¹/₂in.
(Sotheby's) £1,967

Silver cann, Ebenezer Moulton, Boston, circa 1790, engraved with foliate monogram, 51/4in. high, 13 troy oz.
(Skinner) £1,723

A rare silver cann, maker's mark of Charles Oliver Bruff, New York, circa 1770, 4³/₈in. high, 9oz.
(Christie's) £5,445

A silver child's cann, maker's mark of Ebenezer Moulton, Boston, circa 1790, 3in. high, 2oz. 10dwt.
(Christie's) £1,888

CARD CASES

The silver card case was much in demand as a social accessory throughout the 19th century, and was a small box for holding visiting cards. (Most were designed to hold six.) It measured around 4 x 3 inches by about ¹/₂in. thick, and had either a sliding lid or a hinge on one of the narrow edges operated by a spring catch. Gentlemens' versions could be rather thicker and opened lengthways like a book with several gilt-rimmed compartments. They were highly decorative, often covered in filigree work, while others were engine-turned or press-embossed. A frequent decorative theme was a famous building, such as Windsor Castle or Abbotsford, embossed in high relief, and most were made in Birmingham, where they were a speciality of Nathaniel Mills. Before the 1840s, hallmarks may be found on the case exterior, and thereafter on the projecting rim. Filigree examples were exempt from hallmarking.

A Victorian shaped rectangular silver card case, by R. Thornton, Birmingham 1866, 11cm.　£65

A Victorian shaped rectangular card case, bright-cut with floral and foliate decoration, George Unite, Birmingham 1891. (Christie's S. Ken)　£187

An Edwardian oblong card case die-stamped with an Art Nouveau profile bust portrait of a maiden with flowing hair and elaborate headdress, Chrisford & Norris, Birmingham 1905, 3³/₄in.. (Christie's)　£330

A Victorian card case decorated in high relief with a panoramic view of a cathedral or minster, by Nathaniel Mills, Birmingham, 1846. (Phillips)　£750

A Victorian shaped rectangular card case, the front chased in high relief with a view of Westminster Abbey, Yapp & Woodward, Birmingham 1854, 3.9in. (Christie's S. Ken.)　£660

A Victorian silver visiting card case by George Unite, of shaped vertical rectangular form, bright cut engraved with strap work panels, Birmingham 1876, 67gm., 10cm. high. (Spencer's)　£120

A Victorian shaped rectangular card case with engine-turned linear decoration and cast with a view of the Scott Monument, Edinburgh, Nathaniel Mills, Birmingham 1851, 4in. (Christie's)　£858

CASKETS

The word 'casket', as opposed simply to 'box', seems to indicate something much more precious, whether it be the contents, or the receptacle itself. Large caskets of silver were made in 16th century Germany, though elsewhere they tended more often to be of other materials and silver mounted. In Holland, too, in the 17th century, there was a vogue for wedding caskets for jewellery, no more than 3in. high, and shaped like miniature chests.

The Victorians continued this use, albeit in a larger form, and silver jewel caskets graced many a lady's dressing table in the 19th century.

A 17th century Dutch silver oblong marriage casket, maker's mark only PH conjoined, 2⁷⁄₈in. long.　£2,140

A late Victorian jewellery casket by William Comyns, of swept rectangular form, the cover and sides stamped with the cherub choir, London 1898, 20.5cm. wide.
(Spencer's)　£440

A shaped square silver casket, by Omar Ramsden, 1929, 4½in. high, 18oz.4dwt. £1,190

A William Hutton & Sons silver casket, the hinged cover inset with high relief panel in mother-of-pearl, pewter, enamel and copper of a lakeside scene, 1902, 31.5cm. long.
(Christie's London)　£4,620

A 17th century Dutch silver oblong marriage casket on four ball feet, 3¹⁄₈in. long.　£2,850

A casket in 17th century style, the octagonal body and domed cover with repoussé decoration of panels of fruit, Continental, 18cm., 20oz.
(Lawrence Fine Art)　£968

An Austro Hungarian silver gilt oval casket, chased overall with eagles, foliage and rococo ornament, the hinged cover containing two oval portrait miniatures, the box apparently 1855, 6in. wide.
(Christie's)　£1,870

W.G. Connell, an Arts & Crafts Movement rectangular casket, the hinged cover with a female portrait medallion, the clasp with copper bolts, 5¹⁄₂in. overall, London 1899, 8¹⁄₄oz.
(Woolley & Wallis)　£480

17TH CENTURY

These started to be made in the late 17th century and usually came in sets of three, for sugar, jamaica and cayenne peppers. The larger one would be about 5½–8in. high and the smaller ones 1in. less. Up to about 1705 they were plain and cylindrical in shape, with high-domed, fret-cut covers, the body and cover secured by bayonet fastenings. After 1705 a pear-shaped body became more fashionable and covers had a sleeve which push-fitted into the body. By 1715 another change occured, and the upper half of the body became visibly concave, a shape which was retained for the next thirty years. The octagonal outlines so often associated with George I styles were also common. After 1745, the lower part of the body acquired a double curve, the cover was often pierced less elaborately in diagonal patterns, and there was frequent use of embossed scrolling on the body. Not many sugar casters were made after 1775, as sugar bowls and baskets with sifter spoons then became fashionable.

After 1760, the spice dredger acquired the name of muffineer, as it was used for sprinkling muffins. These then became vase-shaped or high-shouldered baluster vessels with a tall dome cover drilled with circular holes. The stemmed muffineer evolved from this, followed by a short necked version with a low domed cover, before the cylindrical shape was readopted in the 1790s. In the late 18th century blue glass lined muffineers were also introduced.

Many forms were reproduced in Victorian times, so the collector should be on guard for these.

A set of three late 17th century West Country casters, by Gabriel Felling of Bruton Co., Somerset, circa 1690, 28oz. £35,200

A Charles II caster, the cap pierced with a variety of scattered motifs below gadrooning and baluster finial, London 1679, 7¹/₂oz., 7¹/₈in. (Tennants) £1,300

A rare and important silver sugar caster, maker's mark of Jacobus van der Spiegel, New York, 1690–1708, the domed cover pierced with fleurs-de-lys and florettes and varied shapes including hearts and scrolls, 8¹/₄in. high, 16oz. (Christie's) £65,340

A fine pair of Charles II cylindrical casters, with rope turned borders, by F. Garthorne, 1683, 5in. high, 11oz.7dwt. £12,500

A set of three William III cylindrical casters, the bodies with central moulded rib, the covers with bayonet fittings, by Joseph Ward, 1698, 6¹/₄in. and 7³/₄in. high, 23oz. (Christie's) £9,350

A rare Commonwealth plain cylindrical caster, with rope twist borders and pierced domed cover, engraved with a coat-of-arms, Latin inscription dated 1658, unmarked, circa 1658, 4¹/₈in. high, 4oz. (Christie's) £18,400

A silver caster, maker's mark of Eleazer Baker, Ashford, Connecticut, circa 1785, 5¼in. high, 3oz. 10dwt.
(Christie's)   £2,541

A pair of George II plain octagonal sugar casters, with pierced domed cover and baluster finial, by Samuel Wood, 1737, 6in. high, 10 oz.
(Christie's)   £1,100

A George I octagonal caster chased with scalework, shells and scrolls, by Charles Adam, 1719, 7½in. high, 10oz.
(Christie's)   £690

A Queen Anne plain baluster caster on circular foot with moulded girdle, engraved with later crest and monogram, early 18th century, 5¾in. high, 6oz.
(Christie's)   £528

A set of three Queen Anne octagonal casters, the pierced domed covers with bayonet fittings and baluster finials, unmarked, circa 1710, 5¼in. and 4½in. high, 14 oz.
(Christie's)   £770

A Dutch late 18th or early 19th century beaded and bright cut vase shaped sugar caster, with a spiral twist finial, 7½in., 8.25oz. (Christie's S. Ken)
                    £682

A George I cast sugar dredger, the domed cover pierced and engraved and surmounted by a finial, 17cm. high, by Thomas Bamford I, 1721, 7.5 ozs.
(Phillips)   £1,200

A pair of 18th century Belgian casters of panelled baluster form with knop finials, probably by Ferdinandus Cornelius Carolus Millé, Brussels, 1747/9, 18.7cm. high, 19oz.
(Phillips)   £9,500

A caster with moulded girdle and foot, the cap pierced with scrolls, maker probably S. Wood, London, 1728, 6½oz., 6³⁄₈in. high.
(Tennants)   £400

An early George III inverted pear-shaped caster on a rising circular foot, Samuel Wood, London 1761, 6³/₄in., 6oz. (Christie's)　£440

A pair of George II plain octagonal vase-shaped casters, each on moulded foot, by Samuel Wood, 1731, 5¹/₄in. high, 11ozs. (Christie's)　£1,265

Early George III embossed silver caster of baluster form, wrythen finial to lid, London 1767. (G. A. Key)　£150

A large 18th century Norwegian sugar dredger of vase shape with waisted neck, by Andreas Lude, also bearing mark of Assay Master Dithmar Kahrs, Bergen, 1787, 23.5cm. high, 11.5oz. (Phillips London)　£1,800

A set of three George III baluster casters, the wrythen pierced high covers with urn shaped finials, London 1778, 337 grammes total. (Spencer's)　£780

A George I plain baluster caster with moulded borders and pierced high-domed cover with baluster finial, by Jacob Margas, 1715, weight 10.5oz., 7in. high. (Christie's)　£1,430

A George I baluster sugar caster on a rising circular foot, with a moulded body band and rim, Charles Adam, London 1714, 6in., 6.25oz. (Christie's)　£682

A pair of George II plain vase-shaped casters, each on spreading circular foot and with pierced detachable domed cover with baluster finial, by John Whyte, 1732, 6¹/₂in. high, 19oz. (Christie's)　£2,070

George III lighthouse caster, London, 1768–9, domed bright-cut and pierced cover with button finial, 9¹/₂ in. high, approximately 25 troy oz. (Skinner Inc)　£519

18TH CENTURY

A George II caster of baluster form by Paul De Lamerie, 1732, 8¼in. high, 17oz.13dwt. £12,475

Three George I plain pear-shaped casters, by Samuel Welder 1716 and 1717, 6¼in. and 7¼in. high, 18oz.5dwt. £3,025

A Belgian octagonal pear-shaped caster, Brussels, 1730-33, maker's mark AL, 7½in. high, 9oz.18dwt. £2,905

A George I cast sugar dredger, of baluster octagonal form, engraved with a crest, 15cm. high, by Charles Adam, 1718, 4.75 ozs.
(Phillips) £800

A set of three George III inverted pear-shaped casters, each on spreading circular foot, by James Mince and Jabez Daniell, 1771, 6¾in. and 8in. high, 20 oz.
(Christie's) £2,200

A George II large inverted pear-shaped sugar caster, the pierced domed cover with baluster finial, by Samuel Wood, 1756, 10in. high, 22oz.
(Christie's) £2,090

A George I West Country muffineer, with the mark of Joseph Collier, circa 1725, 11cm. high. £460

A set of three Queen Anne silver gilt casters, by Charles Adam, 1703, 8in. and 6½in. high, 22oz. £12,100

One of a pair of Dutch spirally fluted pear-shaped casters, by J. Siotteling, Amsterdam, 1765, 8¾in. high, 27oz. gross. £5,940

CASTERS

A George III caster in the form of a turret, by Solomon Hougham, Solomon Royes and John East Dix, 1817, 11.3cm. high.   £2,200

A pair of George III reeded vase-shaped casters, the waisted and engraved tops with vase-shaped finials, London 1804, 5³/₄in. (Christie's S. Ken)   £385

A Victorian part-fluted vase-shaped sugar caster on a fluted rising circular foot, maker's initials C.B., London 1883, 8¹/₂in., 9oz. (Christie's)   £330

A late Victorian spiral fluted lighthouse sugar caster in the early 18th century taste, Nathan and Hayes, Chester, 1898, 7¾in., 9oz.   £242

A pair of Victorian octagonal vase-shaped casters in the George I manner, pierced and engraved high-domed covers with baluster finials, by C. S. Harris, 1899, 8¹/₂in., 27oz. (Christie's)   £880

Sterling muffineer by Tiffany & Co., New York, New York, circa 1891–1902, raised on four ball supports, 6³/₈in. high, 6oz. 18 dwts. (Butterfield & Butterfield) £347

A Victorian spiral-fluted and foliate-chased inverted pear-shaped pedestal caster with baluster finial, London 1894, 7¹/₂in. (Christie's)   £253

A pair of Dutch 19th century spiral fluted pear shaped sugar casters on rising shaped circular bases, 7¾in., 19.75oz. (Christie's S. Ken)   £660

A late Victorian octagonal baluster sugar caster in the early 18th century taste, Thomas Bradbury, London 1898, 8¹/₄in., 7.75oz. (Christie's)   £187

20TH CENTURY

An Edwardian hammered baluster sugar caster by Ramsden & Carr with bun-top, 1907, 17.5cm. high, 8ozs. (Phillips) £575

Liberty & Co. silver sugar caster, Birmingham, 1930, 11cm. high, with detachable domed top. £400

An Art Deco tapering circular sugar caster applied with a stylised shell frieze, H W, Sheffield 1934, 6½in. (Christie's) £154

A William Hutton & Sons silver sugar caster, the cover with openwork decoration set with a cabochon amethyst, London hallmarks for 1902, 19.3cm. high, 320gr. (Christie's) £1,760

A set of four George III style baluster casters, having pierced corners, on cast collet feet, Goldsmiths & Silversmiths Co., London 1935, 16 oz. (Woolley & Wallis) £600

A baluster caster, the pierced domed cover applied with a band of flower buds and with stylised flower finial, by Omar Ramsden, 1936, 6½in. high, 11oz. (Christie's) £1,540

An Elkington silver sugar caster, maker's marks and Birmingham hallmarks for 1938, 5oz.2dwt., 8.5cm. high. £265

A sugar caster designed by Harald Nielsen, stamped Dessin H.N. 925S Georg Jensen S Wendel A/S 645, circa 1949, 11.4cm. high, 7oz.14dwt. £475

An amber, coral and malachite sugar caster, designed by Anton Rosen, stamped marks GJ 826 GJ, 19.9cm. high. (Christie's) £2,200

CENTRE PIECES

Centrepieces, or épergnes, are very grand affairs, suitable for only the largest tables, and in some ways took the place of the ceremonial salt. While they were known from the 16th century, it was the opportunities they afforded for the more fantastic inspirations of rococo artists which heralded their popularity in the 18th century, when they could be equipped with candle branches, and produced in such unusual forms as Chinese pagodas, or five-headed dragons. Their basic form, however, is that of a central bowl with various fittings, such as cake baskets, fruit and sweetmeat dishes or condiment containers hung from the branches. Their function, apart from the decorative, was to enable the various sweetmeats etc. to be passed round the table. In the neo-classical period épergnes were made with elaborate piercing or wirework. 19th century examples were more massive, with cut glass dishes and baskets. Throughout, those with fewer, say four, baskets tend to be less valuable than those with more.

A George IV centrepiece, on shaped triangular base and paw feet, by Matthew Boulton and Plate Co, Birmingham, 1822, 11¼ in. high, 53ozs.
(Christie's) £3,450

A Victorian centrepiece of a putto riding a cornucopia drawn by swans, having a glass nautilus shell bough pot, the rectangular pond base engraved with a crest.
(Woolley & Wallis) £620

A George IV table centrepiece on a fluted rising waisted circular base, Rebecca Emes and Edward Barnard, London 1824, 16in., 134oz.
(Christie's) £4,180

A fine Victorian centrepiece by Edward and John Barnard, the triform base cast on three massive leaf mounted feet, London, 1864, 16¼ in. high, 108 oz.(Bonhams) £5,000

A Victorian table centrepiece on domed fluted base with three foliage and scroll feet and flowerheads, by Hayne and Carter, 1842, 25½in. high, 175oz.
(Christie's) £3,450

A large Victorian sculptural centrepiece, with Richard Coeur de Lion on horseback and with two foot soldiers and crossbowman, by Robert Garrard, 1861, 21in. high, 311oz.
(Christie's) £14,950

A good late Victorian table centrepiece by Messrs. Hancock, supported on the outstretched arms and head of a nude, London 1886, 1950 grammes, 33cm. high.
(Spencer's) £2,000

111

19TH CENTURY

An electroplate centrepiece and mirror plateau, circa 1870, 49cm. high. **£725**

A late Victorian centrepiece formed as a horse beneath an oak tree, on rockwork base with presentation shield plaque dated *1899*, 12in. high.
(Christie's) **£825**

Mid 19th century Australian silver mounted emu's egg table ornament on a wood plinth, by Wm. Edwards, 11½in. high. **£4,600**

A Victorian vase-shaped centrepiece and cover, the stem formed as three female figures, the bowl cast and chased with a horserace and numerous figures on horseback, by John S. Hunt, 1861, 20in. high, 266oz.
(Christie's) **£7,000**

An early Victorian six-light candelabrum centrepiece, by Joseph and John Angell, 1836 and 1837, the basket apparently unmarked, 17¾in. high, 178oz.
(Christie's) **£5,280**

A large French parcel-gilt centrepiece, the central hardstone plinth supporting a detachable loosely draped female figure, the ground signed H. Wadere, circa 1897, 34½in. high, gross 25,860grs.
(Christie's) **£16,500**

An antique German Renaissance Revival solid silver centrepiece in the form of a family tree, hallmarked *Posen* for Lazarus Posen, Frankfurt, circa 1880, 33½in. high, 339 troy oz. (Selkirk's) **£4,802**

'English Sterling' centrepiece, New York, circa 1870, the boat form bowl on a narrow waisted stem over a multi stepped expanding base, 8¾in. high, 42oz.
(Butterfield & Butterfield) **£441**

A William IV vine centrepiece, the fluted base on four foliate scroll feet, the stem formed as a vine tendril with pendant grape and vine leaf dishes, by John Tapley, 1835, 17½in. high, 106oz. (Christie's) **£2,530**

20TH CENTURY

A Chinese centrepiece, the panelled sides chased with ceremonial dragons and prunus blossom, maker's mark *W.S.*, 30cm. high.
(Bonhams) £650

A large and impressive table centrepiece as a gondola, raised upon waves and a shaped rectangular base, 22in. wide overall. (Spencer's) £280

An early George V centrepiece, the central flute trumpet shaped posy vase with undulating rim, Chester 1919, maker's mark *C & S*, 39cm. high.
(Spencer's) £340

A table centrepiece on open work scrolling foliate feet and with presentation inscription, Cooper Brothers and Sons Ltd., Sheffield 1918, 16½in., 93oz.
(Christie's) £2,310

An early George V centrepiece, the central trumpet vase flanked by three smaller trumpet vases, the whole with cast reel and bobbin borders, Sheffield 1913, 906 grammes.
(Spencer's) £520

A George V dessert stand centrepiece, supported on a panelled tapering stem, 13in. high, Walker and Hall, Sheffield 1920, 43.7oz.
(Bearne's) £880

A trumpet-shaped table centrepiece on a rising circular foot, M. Beaver Ltd., London 1913, 12¾in., 38.25oz.
(Christie's) £880

Early 20th century French silver gilt centrepiece, Paris, maker's mark AD, bird between, 10¾in. high, 134oz. £5,115

A large and impressive table centrepiece, the stepped circular clear glass shallow bowl with leaf moulded decoration, 50cm. high.
(Spencer's) £300

CHALICES

A chalice is, strictly speaking, the cup in which wine is consecrated at the Eucharist. As such, from earliest times, it has been a precious object, made in silver, gold and frequently incrusted with precious stones.

After the Reformation many were converted into Communion cups, but the medieval chalice form was revived in the 19th century by Pugin and other adherents of the Gothic Revival.

Sterling silver covered chalice, by Georg Jensen, Denmark, circa 1923, 5¾in. high. **£525**

A 20th century enamelled and jewelled sterling silver chalice, approx. 4 troy oz. **£415**

A Spanish silver-gilt chalice, on large circular foot chased with four coats-of-arms between winged cherubs masks and scrolls, Zamora, 17th century, 9½in. high, 722grs. (Christie's) **£2,860**

A Guild of Handicraft silver chalice, supported on wire work brackets and pentagonal stem, the flanged foot with repoussé decoration, with London hallmarks for 1902, 21.5cm. high, 275 grams. (Christie's) **£418**

Austrian silver chalice, circa 1910, raised repeating geometric and medallion pattern on cup, trumpet base with raised repeating pyramid pattern, 7⅞in. high. (Skinner) **£99**

A Charles I silver gilt recusant chalice, the bulbous knop applied with four angels' heads. **£660**

An Arts & Crafts Movement chalice in medieval style, by Omar Ramsden & Alwyn Carr, London, 1912, 5.2in. high, 10oz. all in. **£835**

An early 19th century Mexican silver gilt chalice, maker's mark possibly that of Jose M. Martinez, 9¼in. high, 22oz. **£1,705**

18TH CENTURY

Chambersticks were utilitarian items, used to light one to bed between the late 17th century and the coming of gas lighting. They have a short moulded socket attached to a usually circular greasepan serving as the base, and the curving lateral handle usually supports a conical extinguisher. On those made before 1715, the handle is usually hollow, or made from sheet, whereas after this time, handles are usually cast. Nozzles were introduced around the 1730s and by the 1760s the socket was vase-shaped, with reeded moulding towards the end of the century. Most made after 1735 have a slot to take the scissor-like snuffers which usually accompanied them. If these are still in place, the value increases greatly.

It is always worthwhile checking the handle of the chamberstick for repairs, as our convivial ancestors who could afford them often did not go to bed entirely sober, and many handles were torn off the bases in the rough usage they received.

One of a pair of early 18th century chamber candlesticks, possibly Jersey, circa 1715, 4¼in. diam., 12oz. 9dwt. **£7,500**

A George III chamber candlestick, the dished circular base with flying scroll handle and extinguisher, by Jonathan Alleine, 1777, 8cm., 14oz. (Lawrence Fine Art) **£275**

A George III chamber candlestick, with flying scroll handle and extinguisher, marked on base and extinguisher by Ebenezer Coker, 1766, 10cm., 10.5oz. (Lawrence Fine Art) **£506**

A George II chamber candlestick and snuffer of circular form engraved with crest and monogram, London 1751, 8oz. (Russell Baldwin & Bright) **£330**

A George III silver chamber candlestick, maker's mark *H.H.*, London, 1780, initialled, beaded circular, openwork stem, detachable nozzle and extinguisher, 245gr., 13.4cm. diameter. (Sotheby's) **£352**

George III silver assembled and matching chamberstick with snuffer, Ebenezer Coker, London, 1768 and 1766, baluster form stem and sconce without nozzle, all with gadrooned borders, 7in. high, 16oz. 12dwt. (Butterfield & Butterfield) **£555**

A George III chamberstick of circular form, the urn-shaped capital applied with a beaded girdle above acanthus leaves, initialled, London 1767, maker John Romer, approximate weight 11oz. (Bonhams) **£750**

18TH CENTURY

George III chamber candlestick, by John Crouch and Thos. Hannam, London, 9oz. **£440**

A George II plain circular chamber candlestick with rising scroll handle and waisted socket, John Cafe, London 1756, 6½in., 9.25oz. (Christie's S. Ken) **£770**

George III chamber candlestick with removable drip tray, maker Thos. Robins, London, 1798, 4in. high, 8oz. **£310**

One of a pair of Queen Anne chamber candlesticks, by C. McKenzie, Edinburgh, 1706, 3⅝in. sq., 13oz.3dwt. **£3,630**

A George II silver chamber candlestick with flying scroll handle and resting on pad feet, London, possibly 1754, 10oz., maker: D.E. (Riddetts) **£500**

A George III chamber candlestick with detachable nozzle and conical snuffer, by E. Coker, London, 1771, 5¾in high, 7.75oz. **£580**

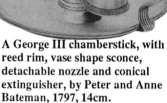

George III Sheffield silver-plated chamber candlestick, Matthew Boulton, late 18th century, with slotted cylindrical sconce, 5¾in. (Skinner Inc.) **£138**

A George III chamberstick, 6½in. diameter, with beaded borders, vase-form socket supporting detachable nozzle, London, 1778, by Richard Carter, Daniel Smith and Robert Sharp, 9 oz. (Bonhams) **£400**

A George III chamberstick, with reed rim, vase shape sconce, detachable nozzle and conical extinguisher, by Peter and Anne Bateman, 1797, 14cm. (Lawrence) **£396**

Georgian silver chamberstick and snuffer, Newcastle stick, 1753-54, Isaac Cookson, London snuffer, possibly 1772-73, approx. 12 troy oz. (Skinner) **£538**

A George II plain chamber candlestick with vase-shaped socket and scroll handle, engraved crest and motto, by James Ker, Edinburgh, circa 1740, weight 8oz. (Christie's) **£1,210**

A George III chamber candlestick, with gadroon border and flying scroll handle, 1772 (no maker's mark but nozzle by Ebenezer Coker), 9.5cm., 7.5oz. (Lawrence Fine Art) **£198**

19TH CENTURY

George III shaped circular chamberstick, by William Stroud, 1805, 13½oz. **£1,100**

An Art Nouveau oil chamberstick with leaf-capped loop handle, 14.25cm. diam. **£330**

A George III circular chamber candlestick, maker John Mewburn, London 1817, 12oz. **£550**

A Swedish shaped circular chamber candlestick with foliate and flute-decorated campana-shaped socket, 5³/₄in. (Christie's) **£748**

A Perry Son & Co. painted metal candlestick, designed by Christopher Dresser, circa 1880, 14cm. **£100**

One of a pair of Victorian fluted shaped circular chamber candlesticks, by Robinson, Edkins & Aston, Birmingham, 1840, 6¼in. high, 24.25oz. **£880**

A Victorian silver gilt small chamber candlestick in the manner of Paul de Lamerie, by S.W., London, 1841, 11cm. diam. **£275**

A Victorian part-fluted and gadrooned boat-shaped chamber candlestick with rising curved spout and detachable conical snuffer, H.S., London 1895, 6³/₄in. (Christie's) **£330**

A George IV chamberstick with conical snuffer, T.B., London, 1822, and a matching chamberstick, London, 1832, each 5½in. diam., total weight 22oz. **£1,030**

One of a pair of shaped chambersticks by Thos., James and Nathaniel Creswick, 1835, 23oz. 8dwt. **£1,150**

An early Victorian chamber candlestick, by Joseph and John Angell, London, 1837, 6½in. high, 8.75oz. **£390**

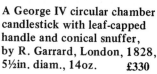

A George IV circular chamber candlestick with leaf-capped handle and conical snuffer, by R. Garrard, London, 1828, 5½in. diam., 14oz. **£330**

A George III circular chamber-stick, with detachable nozzle and snuffer, by Thos. Law, Sheffield, perhaps 1806, 15cm. high, 11oz., and a pair of plated snuffers. £330

A George III chamberstick, 3in. high, with gadrooned border, flying scroll handle and engraved crest, London, 1816, by Samuel Whitford II, 9 oz. (Bonhams) £420

A George III chamberstick, 4in. high, with reeded borders, and vase-shaped socket with detachable nozzle, London, 1807, by William Barrett II, 11 oz. (Bonhams) £320

A matched pair of George III chambersticks complete with scissor-type snuffers and conical extinguishers, one by Robert & Samuel Hennell, 1810, the other by Hennell & Terry, 1813. (Phillips) £2,800

A pair of Russian 19th century chamber candlesticks on domed circular bases applied with stud feet, Khlebnikov, 1886, 4in., 16.75oz. (Christie's) £1,000

A pair of early Victorian Sheffield plate bedroom candlesticks, with leaf scrolls to the borders. (Woolley & Wallis) £380

An unusual George IV silver-gilt chamber candlestick, the base formed as oak leaves and with twig handle and detachable acorn and oak leaf socket, by Paul Storr, 1828, 4³/₄in. wide, 7oz. (Christie's) £1,955

A Hukin & Heath electro-plated chamberstick with snuffer designed by Dr. C. Dresser, stamped H & H 9658 Rd No. 228142, 12.5cm. high. £1,010

A George III miniature chamber candlestick, the circular base, nozzle and conical extinguisher engraved with crest, 3in. diameter, Peter, Anne and William Bateman, London, 1802, 96 gms, 3.0 oz. (Bearne's) £270

19TH CENTURY

One of a pair of German 19th century circular travelling candlesticks with detachable waisted sockets, 4¼in. high.
(Christie's) £1,210

A rare George IV silver-gilt chamber candlestick, with flower petal socket, cylindrical nozzle and tendril handle, by Philip Rundell, 1821, 4¼in. diameter, 6oz.
(Christie's) £1,870

A late George III chamberstick by John Emes, on a dished circular base with reeded border, 292 grammes total.
(Spencer's) £200

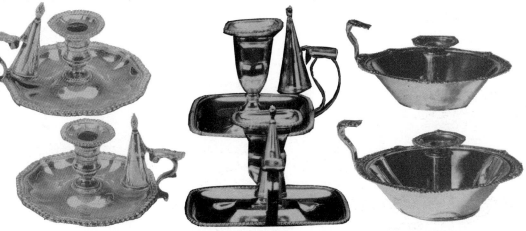

A pair of William IV chamber candlesticks, the shaped circular bases and detachable nozzles with gadroon edging, 6½in. diameter, Paul Storr, London 1832, 28.9oz.
(Bearne's) £3,300

A pair of George III gadrooned rounded oblong chamber candlesticks, Thomas and Daniel Leader, Sheffield 1810, 6in., 22oz.
(Christie's) £902

A pair of George III large chamber candlesticks, each with telescopic cylindrical stem and shell-capped reeded scroll handle, by Crispin Fuller, 1817, 8¼in. diameter, 37oz.
(Christie's) £1,760

A William IV shaped circular chamber candlestick with reeded edging, 5³/₄in. diameter, Henry Wilkinson and Co., Sheffield 1835, 11.2oz.
(Bearne's) £380

Matthew Boulton & Co, an early 19th century circular 'storm' chamber lamp with a matted, globular glass shade, a conical snuffer and gadrooned borders, 15cm. diameter, circa 1815.
(Phillips) £240

A George III chamberstick, 4¼in. high, with gadrooned border, vase-form socket with detachable nozzle and scroll handle, Sheffield, 1803, by John Watson, 8 oz.
(Bonhams) £380

A Victorian chamber candlestick in the Renaissance style,
the cylindrical socket heavily
cast with masks, London 1877,
probably by George Fox,
392gr. (Henry Spencer) £400

A pair of rare George III circular chamber candlesticks, each
with scroll handle, by William
Burwash, 1812, 5½in. diam.,
24oz. (Christie's London) £2,420

Sterling figural chamberstick in
the Empire taste, J. E. Caldwell
& Company, Philadelphia, 19th
century, 5¾in. high, 14oz.
(Butterfield & Butterfield) £667

A Tiffany & Co unusual late
19th century American
Aesthetic Movement parcel
gilt chamberstick, with incurved sides, circa 1880,
11ozs. £6,000

Part of a set of four square
chamber candlesticks with wirework superstructures to hold
storm shades, 5¾in. overall.
(Christie's) (Four) £528

An unusual George IV novelty
small chamberstick by Ledsam,
Vale and Wheeler, with plain
floriform detachable sconce, 29
grammes, 6cm. wide overall.
(Spencer's) £150

A pair of Italian 19th century
dished circular chamber
candlesticks, each with a
campana-shaped socket and
reeded circular detachable
nozzle, Gabriele Sisino, Naples,
circa 1830, 5½in. overall.
(Christie's) £660

C.R. Ashbee, a Guild of
Handicrafts bedroom
candlestick, raised hammered
border chased with branches of
stylised leaves and berries,
London 1900, 7oz.
(Woolley & Wallis) £780

A pair of Victorian chamber
candlesticks, the circular pans
engraved with two crests, 1858
by Daniel and Charles Houle,
13.9cm., 16.2oz.
(Lawrence) £1,430

CHOCOLATE POTS

The chocolate pot is virtually indistinguishable from the coffee pot, except for those which have a detachable or sliding cover finial where a swizzle-stick could be inserted to stir the chocolate.

Chocolate drinking, usually at breakfast, was at the height of its popularity between 1675–1725. Many pots, however, were probably used indiscriminately for both coffee and chocolate.

A cylindrical chocolate pot, by S. C. S. Groth, Copenhagen, 1884, 17.5cm. high, 17oz. £315

Mid 18th century Flemish silver chocolate pot of baluster form, Ghent, 1200gr. £3,025

A Belgian pear-shaped chocolate pot, the body chased with swirling fluting, foliage and festoons of husks, Mons, 1773, maker's mark *G* a coronet above, 13¼in. high, gross 1,206grs.
(Christie's) £22,000

A pair of Edward VII chocolate pots of flared cylindrical form with ebony side handles, 7¼in. high, maker's mark *D.F.*, London 1904, 586 gms, 18.8 oz.
(Bearne's) £450

A Louis XV plain pear-shaped chocolate pot, on three spreading feet, with hinged flap to the curved lip, by Jean Gouel, Paris, 1734, 9½in. high, 840grs.
(Christie's) £3,740

A French 19th century baluster chocolate pot, with a polished rosewood octagonal side handle, applied with shell decoration, 9in., 21.50oz. gross.
(Christie's S. Ken) £638

A silver chocolate pot by Tiffany & Company, New York, tapering cylindrical and partly reeded, on a moulded circular foot, marked, 9¼in. high, gross weight 31oz.
(Christie's) £1,949

A Queen Anne plain tapering cylindrical chocolate pot, with curved spout and detachable domed cover, by Joseph Ward, 1706, 9¾in. high, gross 27oz.
(Christie's London) £6,050

A George II plain tapering cylindrical chocolate pot, Exeter, 1736, 9¾in. high, gross 28oz. £3,564

Late 18th century French silver chocolate pot, 8in. high, 23 troy oz. including wooden handle. £1,650

Late 19th century copper and silver chocolate pot, 9¼in. high. £2,130

A George II chocolate pot, engraved with a crest and with swan neck spout, 9³/₄in. high, Isaac Cookson, Newcastle 1732, 29.2oz.
(Bearne's) £4,100

An early 19th century French silver chocolate pot of bulbous form, marked on body, cover and supports, height 9.25in., makers initials P.L., gross 20.5oz.
(Graves Son & Pilcher) £950

An early George III pear-shaped chocolate pot with hinged cover, maker's mark W.C., London, 1763, 9¾in. high, 18oz. all in. £530

A Queen Anne plain tapering cylindrical chocolate pot, by William Pearson, 1711, 24cm. high, 25oz. £6,600

A sterling silver Martele chocolate pot, by Gorham Mfg. Co., circa 1900, 11½in. high, 23 troy oz.
(Skinner Inc.) £2,083

A Queen Anne plain tapering cylindrical chocolate pot, by Jonah Clifton, 1710, 9¾in. high, gross 20oz. £5,445

CHRISTENING MUGS

Silver mugs given as gifts at a child's christening have been popular for hundreds of years, but it was in the 19th century that the custom became most fashionable, particularly in Britain and America. The ornament is normally engraved or embossed, and the child's name, date of birth, or initials are frequently engraved on the body.

A George III christening mug, dated 1911, with plain curved handle and gilded interior, by Robert and David Hennell, 146 grammes, 7.5cm. high. (Henry Spencer) £130

A Victorian tapering cylindrical christening mug engraved with a pagoda, Oriental figures and birds amidst foliage by Messrs. Barnards, 1840, Britannia standard, 7oz. (Christie's) £276

An Indian Colonial 19th century gilt-lined campana-shaped christening mug, the fluted body chased and applied with flowers and foliage and with a moulded rim, Hamilton & Co., Calcutta circa 1860, 4½ in., 9oz. (Christie's S. Ken) £253

An attractive Victorian silver-gilt christening mug, the baluster body with an overlapping rim embossed on either side with an oval 'disc' cartouche, 12cm. high, E. & J. Barnard, 1862, 7oz. (Phillips) £500

An early Victorian christening mug of panelled waisted cylindrical form, engraved with a presentation inscription, and panels of diapering and foliage, London 1853, maker's mark RD, 127 grams. (Spencer's) £150

A Victorian mug, 5⅜ in. high, the fluted campana-shaped body chased with floral clusters, London, 1840, by Rawlins and Sumner, 10 ozs. (Bonhams) £320

A William IV campana shaped christening mug monogrammed and with acanthus decorated lower body, 11cm. high, Charles Fox, London 1836, 7oz. (Bearne's) £260

A Victorian silver-gilt campana-shaped christening mug on a domed circular base applied with classical musicians, George Adams, London 1858, 5in. (Christie's S. Ken) £396

A Victorian engine-turned christening mug with leaf capped reverse scroll handle, by Rawlings & Sumner, London, 1850, 8oz. **£130**

A Chinese christening mug of tapering cylindrical form, embossed with chrysanthemums, stamped on the base with Chinese characters only, circa 1900, 7.9cm. high, 6oz. (Phillips London) **£220**

A George V christening mug of waisted octagonal form, with foliate cast handle and foot rim, London 1910, 148 grammes. (Henry Spencer) **£85**

A Victorian christening mug of waisted cylindrical form on shell and scroll base, chased and embossed with children playing, by Rawlins and Sumner, 1848, 4$\frac{1}{4}$in. high, 6oz. (Christie's) **£414**

A attractive Victorian christening mug, the cylindrical body panelled and engraved with floral sprays against a shaped background, 13cm. high, by Atherly & Sillwell, 1858, 6oz. (Phillips) **£280**

A Victorian christening mug in the gothic manner engraved with panels of entwined strapwork and foliage and with presentation inscription, Glasgow, 1861. (Christie's) **£462**

Silver christening mug of inverted bell shape with scroll handle and cast foot, London 1869, 2½oz. **£110**

A mid Victorian christening mug by George Unite, of quatrefoil form, Birmingham 1863, 187 grammes, 10.5cm. high. (Spencer's) **£210**

A Victorian christening mug with loop handle, W. E., London, 1878, 4½in. high. **£180**

CHRISTENING SETS

An attractive Arts & Crafts christening set, with blue and turquoise enamelled decoration of seed pods and sinuous tendrils, Sheffield 1906, by Richard Richardson.
(Spencer's) £140

A Victorian silver gilt christening set, comprising a mug, a spoon, fork and knife, the mug 1869 by Robert Garrard, 7.8cm. (Lawrence) £396

A French Christening set, post 1838 guarantee, with maker's mark of Veyrant, 8.8oz. of weighable silver.
£385

CIGAR BOXES

A cigar and cigarette box, engine turned, the twin lidded compartments cedar lined, 9in., makers The Goldsmiths & Silversmiths Co., London 1927.
(Woolley & Wallis) £500

A Cartier cigar box and cover, the exterior veneered in burr maple, the top set with a rectangular clock, 22.5cm. wide.
(Christie's) £935

A Russian silver rectangular cigar box, the cover, sides and base engraved to simulate a wood grain finish, dated 1911, 15.7cm. long.
(Bearne's) £850

CIGAR CASES

An early Victorian cigar case, one side stamped with a view of Windsor Castle, the reverse stamped with a view of Kenilworth Castle, Nathaniel Mills, Birmingham 1839, 4.8in.
(Christie's S. Ken) £209

A hammered silver and silver gilt cheroot case and vesta combined, unmarked, possibly American, circa 1890, 4oz., 9.4cm. long. £420

A William IV slightly curved oblong cheroot case, the front finely engraved with a standing sportsman and two greyhounds, by Henry Wilkinson & Co., Sheffield, 1832, 5¼in. long, 10oz.
(Christie's) £3,300

Silver boxes with a close fitting lid had been used for storing cigars since the early 19th century, and these were later adapted also for cigarettes. Intended to sit on the desk or dining table after dinner, they were often highly ornate and very finely made.

Many were produced during the Art Nouveau and Art Deco periods, when smoking was becoming a more socially acceptable pastime.

A good Irish Arts & Crafts cigarette box, with cut card type hinges, raised upon four peg feet, Dublin 1906, by West & Sons, 19cm. wide. (Spencer's) **£250**

A Chinese wood lined oblong cigarette box ornately moulded with carp, 8¼in. long. **£220**

A Georg Jensen white metal cigarette box, stamped GJ 925S and inscription 6 Oktober 1933, 10¾in. wide. **£1,330**

A Continental oblong wood lined cigarette box decorated in the Art Deco style, 6¼in. long, engraved dated 1938. **£495**

A Victorian part spiral-fluted and foliate-stamped oblong cedar-lined double cigarette box, John Bodman Carrington, London 1894, 7³/₄in. (Christie's) **£605**

A late Victorian oblong cedar-lined cigarette box, the hinged cover cast and chased with an inn scene in the style of Tenniers, Birmingham 1895, 5¹/₂in. (Christie's S. Ken) **£715**

An Art Deco engine-turned square novelty cigarette box, Asprey & Co. Ltd., London 1926, 6¹/₂in. wide. (Christie's) **£330**

A cigarette box, by Ramsden and Carr, the bowed hand-hammered sides with applied entrelac band, London, 1908, 3¾ x 3¼in. (Bonhams) **£650**

A cigarette box, maker's mark HIT, Russian, circa 1890, 21oz. 8dwt. all in, 6⁵/₈in., wide. **£385**

A Ramsden & Carr silver cigarette box and cover, London, 1903, 19cm. wide. **£825**

A rectangular cigarette box, designed by Jorgen Jensen, Dessin JJ, Georg Jensen 857 A, 16cm. wide, 13oz.15dwt. **£725**

These were slim, pocket-sized versions of the cigarette box, popular from the late 19th century. Many were produced on the Continent, particularly in Germany and Russia. The German ones in particular were often finely decorated with painted enamel scenes, which, perhaps because the item was less exposed to the public gaze, very often had an overtly erotic content.

As smoking became more popular among women, following the First World War, elegant jewelled or lacquered versions were also produced for their use by leading jewellers such as Cartier.

Silver and enamel cigarette case by Raymond Templer, 1930. **£1,670**

An enamelled and gilt cigarette case, St. Petersburg, 1908-17, 8.4cm. long. **£415**

A white metal and enamel cigarette case, the enamel by F. Zwichl, circa 1920. **£2,140**

A Victorian cigarette case, the cover enamelled with a nude girl lying beside a stream, Birmingham, 1887. **£440**

A Russian rectangular gilt-lined cigarette case, the lid stamped with a bird of prey in a mountainous wooded landscape, modern, 4¹/₁₀in. (Christie's S. Ken) **£286**

A silver cigarette case, maker's mark A.N.P., Moscow, 1899-1908, 11.5cm. **£425**

A Russian gilt-lined cigarette case, the hinged cover cast and chased with a bear and three bear cubs playing in a pine forest, 4in. wide. (Christie's S. Ken) **£605**

A Russian rectangular gilt lined cigarette case, one side nielloed with a domed building, Moscow, circa 1890, 3¾in. (Christie's) **£385**

A Victorian novelty cigarette case, the name and address and franked postage stamp in enamel to the front, 4in., London 1883. (Woolley & Wallis) **£260**

An enamelled oblong cigarette case, probably German, importer's mark S & Co., Birmingham 1910, 4in. wide. **£510**

An enamelled cigarette case decorated with a naked girl sitting on a wall catching water from a well in a bowl, 9cm. long, stamped *935*.
(Phillips) £420

An amusing German enamelled cigarette case, a gentleman with his female companion, both with cigarettes in their mouths, each smouldering where one touches the other, 9.5 x 7.5cm.
(Phillips) £400

A German enamelled cigarette case depicting a young girl wearing a lacy nightdress, falling from one shoulder, 9cm. long, stamped *935*.
(Phillips) £780

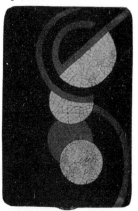

Ferdinand von Reznicek, Lovers cigarette case, circa 1890, with a pair of lovers in evening dress snatching a kiss in the boudoir, 8.75 x 7.75cm.
(Sotheby's) £1,610 $2,608

An enamelled cigarette case, probably German, circa 1910, oblong, painted in pastel shades, 3½in. high. £1,150

A stylish French Art Deco lacquered cigarette case, decorated with egg shell roundels, red roundel and curved bands, 12cm. wide.
(Phillips London) £620

A white metal rectangular hinged cigarette case, decorated in niello to a design by Gerard Sandoz, 5in. long.
(Christie's S. Ken) £1,155

Russian silver and gold cigarette case with gilt medallion, maker L P (Cyrillic), Moscow, 1908–1917, overstamped with Soviet mark 84, 7oz. 6dwts.
(Butterfield & Butterfield) £830

A 1930's cigarette case, silver and two-colour gold coloured metal, with stripes of black lacquer, 11.75cm. wide.
£385

CIGARETTE CASES

A Continental cigarette case, cover enamelled with a nude lying on the edge of the shore, with English import marks for 1906. **£385**

An Omar Ramsden silver cigarette case, with gilt interior, 1923, 9.5cm. **£145**

A Wiener Werkstatte cigarette case, the design attributed to Carl Otto Czeschka, 8.5cm. wide, silver coloured metal. **£715**

A German Art Nouveau silver and enamelled cigarette case, depicting in naturalistic colours a Mucha-style girl, 8.50cm. long, maker's marks for Heinrich Levinger. (Phillips) **£750**

A cigarette case, the cover cast with Napoleon mounted on a rearing horse, white metal, by Konstantin Skvortsov, Moscow, 1908-1917, 4½in. long, 204.6gr. (Christie's) **£440**

A late 19th century Burmese cigarette case, the cover inset with an oval panel of polychrome enamel depicting a girl in Burmese national costume, 9 x 7.5cm., by S.C. Coombes, Rangoon, circa 1900, 4oz. (Phillips) **£200**

An Art Deco sterling silver cigarette case with black and silver ground in a crackle pattern with red enamel zigeraut decoration on one side. **£175**

A Continental white metal cigarette case, of rounded square form, engraved with a dachshund, stamped *800 F.S.*, 9 x 7.5cm. (Spencer's) **£110**

Late 19th century Austrian enamel cigarette case, the cover enamelled with an ancient Egyptian scene, circa 1895. **£660**

CIGARETTE CASES

M.Z., Girl with Fruiting Vine cigarette case, circa 1900, the hinged cover enamelled with a young girl in profile amongst fruiting vines, 8.5 x 8cm. (Sotheby's)   £1,495 $2,422

A Soviet propaganda cigarette case, the foreground with crossed banners and Red Star, white metal, Moscow, 1927, 4½in. long, 162.8gr. gross. (Christie's)   £825

An enamelled oblong silver cigarette case, probably German, importer's mark M & C, Birmingham 1910, 3½in. high.   £680

A German enamelled cigarette case depicting a young woman wearing an off-the-shoulder dress and enjoying the amorous advances of her suitor in a boudoir setting, 8.7cm. long. (Phillips London)   £850

A German cigarette case, one side engraved with an armorial, the lid enamelled with three naked women relaxing by a lake, London 1902, 3²/₅in. (Christie's S. Ken)   £1,045

A silver Imperial presentation cigarette case by Faberge, Moscow, 1908-17, 9.8cm. high.   £1,023

A silver cigarette case with sapphire-set thumbpiece by Faberge, Moscow, 1908-17, 11cm.   £990

A Portuguese enamel cigarette case, the cover depicting a bare-breasted Classical girl, circa 1900.   £420

A silver and enamel cigarette case by I. Khlebnikov, Moscow, circa 1880, 9.5cm.   £760

CLARET JUGS

The claret jug is an English phenomenon, popular in the late 18th and 19th century. They have glass bodies, with ornate silver mounts, as opposed to wine jugs, which are all silver. Some early 19th century versions are stoppered, but most dating from after 1830 have a hinged cover. They come in various body shapes, such as ovoid, pear-shaped etc., and are often of frosted or coloured glass. The mounts are usually ornamented with cast or embossed grape or wine motifs.

A late Victorian glass claret jug in the form of a duck, Sheffield 1894, by Henry Wilkinson, 20cm. high.
(Henry Spencer) £1,500

A Victorian style silver-mounted flaring glass claret jug with star-cut base, the body decorated with vines.
(Christie's S. Ken) £682

A fine silver-mounted cameo claret ewer, probably Thomas Webb and Sons, circa 1884, the deep amber-tinted glass overlaid in opaque-white and carved with dahlias, a raspberry and insects, 10³/₈in. high.
(Sotheby's) £3,300

A pair of Victorian silver-gilt mounted clear glass claret jugs, each on circular slightly spreading foot, by John Figg, 1865, 16¹/₂in. high.
(Christie's) £6,325

A George III vase-shaped claret jug, chased with alternate plain and matted vertical stripes, the shoulder with a band of rosettes and drapery festoons, by James Young and Orlando Jackson, 1774, 13¹/₄in. high, gross 29 oz.
(Christie's) £1,870

A George III reeded vase-shaped pedestal claret or hot water jug with wicker-covered scroll handle, John Denziloe, London 1788, 12in., 20.75 oz. gross.
(Christie's S. Ken) £880

A Hukin & Heath electroplated metal and glass 'crow's foot' decanter, designed by Dr. Christopher Dresser, stamped *H&H*, and with registration lozenge for 1878, 24cm. high.
(Christie's) £13,750

Victorian silver-gilt claret jug, Stephen Smith, London, 1856, with frieze of animals and masks, 13¹/₂ in. high, approximately 39 troy oz.
(Skinner Inc.) £1,563

19TH CENTURY

English silver claret jug, with engraved figural and vintage decoration, bright cut, monogrammed, maker's mark, *E.O.B.*, London 1867, 25.4 troy oz.
(Eldred's) £936

A pair of Victorian pear-shaped claret jugs, by Stephen Smith and William Nicholson, 1858 and 1859, 13$\frac{1}{2}$in. high, 71oz.
(Christie's) £2,420

A French 19th century parcel-gilt silver-mounted spiral-fluted ovoid clear glass claret jug with elaborate scrolling foliate handle, 10$\frac{3}{4}$in. high.
(Christie's) £770

A late Victorian clear glass claret jug, of baluster form with diamond facet cut decoration, Birmingham 1893, by Heath & Middleton, 20cm. high.
(Spencer's) £320

A pair of Victorian silver mounted clear glass claret jugs, each with bracket handle, moulded spout and hinged domed cover, by C.F. Hancock, 1882, 10$\frac{1}{2}$in. high.
(Christie's) £5,720

German silver and cut-glass claret jug late 19th century, silver lid and handle cast with Renaissance-style foliate scrolls, handle marked 800, 11$\frac{1}{2}$in. high.
(Skinner Inc) £422

A Victorian glass claret jug, the mounts richly chased and embossed with fruiting vines and entwined foliage, by W. & J. Sissons, Sheffield, 1867, 10$\frac{1}{2}$in. high.
(Christie's) £1,045

A pair of Victorian vase-shaped claret jugs, one engraved with the 'Triumph of Venus', the other with a 'Sacrifice to Pan', by Roberts and Belk, Sheffield, 1866, 13$\frac{3}{4}$in. high, 43 oz.
(Christie's) £2,750

A Victorian silver-mounted vase-shaped claret jug, the glass engraved with palmettes and beading, with bracket handle, by William Gough, Birmingham, 1869, 11$\frac{1}{4}$in. high.
(Christie's) £1,155

A late Victorian silver-mounted flaring plain glass claret jug with star-cut base, Henry Wilkinson and Co., London 1896, 10³/₄in. high. (Christie's)   £495

A pair of French silver gilt mounted clear glass claret jugs, by Risler & Carre, Paris, circa 1870, 11¾in. high.   £3,565

A late Victorian shaft and globe claret jug, with elaborate fruiting vine mounts, beaded loop handle and hinged cover, 13in. high over handle. (Spencer's)   £380

A late Victorian cut glass claret jug, engraved with flowers and scrolls in a rock-crystal effect, the silver top embossed with foliage and a humming bird, 11in. makers William Hutton & Sons, London 1894. (Woolley & Wallis)   £850

A pair of Victorian silver-gilt mounted glass claret jugs, the neck mounts chased with flowers and foliage on a matted ground, by W. and G. Sissons, Sheffield, 1869, 9¹/₂in. high. (Christie's)   £4,155

German silver mounted cut glass claret jug, Friedlander, late 19th century, 750 standard silver, compressed spherical base with oval and diamond cut panels, 12¹/₂in. high. (Butterfield & Butterfield) £567

A late Victorian silver mounted clear glass claret jug by Martin Hall and Co., the clear glass globular body with star and diamond cut decoration, Sheffield 1890, 21.5cm. high. (Spencer's)   £440

A pair of Victorian silver-gilt-mounted moulded oval clear glass claret jugs, maker's initials C. E., London 1887 and 1888, 13in. and slightly smaller. (Christie's)   £4,950

A crested silver-mounted claret-jug, the flattened oviform body engraved with a crest within an oval cartouche flanked by scantily draped nymphs, London, 1891, 22.5cm. high. (Christie's)   £1,210

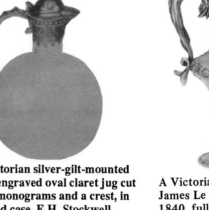

A French claret jug, the ovoid glass body with leaf-chased scroll handle, circa 1880, 10in. high. (Bonhams) **£300**

A Victorian silver-gilt-mounted fern-engraved oval claret jug cut with monograms and a crest, in a fitted case, E.H. Stockwell, London 1871, 7in. (Christie's S. Ken) **£990**

A Victorian claret jug, by James Le Bass, Dublin, 1840, fully marked, 30cm. high, 38oz.4dwt. **£1,270**

A Victorian large vase-shaped claret jug, the cork stopper with melon finial surmounted by two doves, by Hunt and Roskell, 1881, 15½in. high, gross 57oz. (Christie's) **£2,530**

A Frederick Elkington silver barrel-shaped claret jug designed by Dr. Christopher Dresser, London 1866, 17.5cm. high, 20.25oz. (Christie's) **£1,100**

A Victorian silver-mounted bottle-shaped clear glass claret jug with star-cut base, Findley & Taylor, London 1889, 13½in. (Christie's S. Ken) **£770**

A Hukin & Heath claret jug designed by Dr Christopher Dresser, the tapering cylindrical clear glass body surmounted with white metal section, 9½in. high. (Christie's) **£880**

A late Victorian mounted glass claret jug in the form of a cockatoo, by Alex. Crichton, 1882, 27cm. high. **£2,530**

A French silver gilt mounted tapering cylindrical clear glass claret jug, by Charles-Nicholas Odiot, Paris, circa 1860, 11in. high. **£2,500**

A German tapering cut glass claret jug with plain mount, and slightly-domed hinged cover, 14¼in.
(Christie's) £638

A Victorian parcel gilt claret jug formed as a bird, by George Fox, 1877, (patched), 8¼in. high, 22oz. £2,500

A Victorian silver-mounted engraved glass claret jug, 9¾in. high, John Figg, London 1875 (glass foot chipped).
(Bearne's) £700

A Victorian plain vase-shaped claret jug, with entwined double serpent handle, hinged domed cover and bunch of grapes finial, by John S. Hunt, 1860, 12in. high, 30oz.
(Christie's) £1,870

An Elkington electroplate mounted engraved glass claret jug, the cylindrical glass body engraved with fruiting vines on a spreading base, 11in. high, Elkington marks for Newhall Street, 1891.
(Bearne's) £420

A Hukin & Heath silver mounted claret jug designed by Dr. Christopher Dresser, with hinged cover and ebonised bar handle, date registration lozenge for *9th May 1881*, 21.6cm. high.
(Christie's) £1,210

Continental silver claret jug, 19th century, probably French, mermaid handle and conch finial, apparently unmarked, 12in. high, approximately 33 troy oz.
(Skinner Inc.) £1,174

A James Dixon & Sons electroplated claret jug designed by Dr. Christopher Dresser, with angled handle, the conical body with tapering cylindrical neck and triangular spout, 21.7cm. high.
(Christie's) £11,000

A very fine and attractive late Victorian silver mounted claret jug by Elkington & Co. Limited, the clear glass body cut to imitate rock crystal, Birmingham 1893, 17cm. high.
(Spencer's) £850

20TH CENTURY

Gorham Sterling and two-colour cut glass claret jug, ovoid body with green and ruby cutting, 10½in. high.
(Skinner Inc.)   £1,483

A silver and cut-glass claret jug, hinged domed cover with fruit finial, mask spout, vine chased scroll handle. (Bonhams)   £240

A rare, mounted glass, ovoid shaped claret jug on circular foot with coronet pierced gallery collar, 34.5cm. high, 1922. (Phillips)   £6,000

A cut glass and silver-gilt claret jug, marked by Theodore B. Starr, New York, circa 1900, the glass ovoid with melon-reeding, 11⅝in. high.
(Christie's)   £1,107

A pair of silver mounted cut-glass decanters, each cut-glass body with stellar motifs, by Lorie, maker's mark Cyrillic E. Ch, Moscow, 1899-1908, 12¾in. high, 4490gr. gross.
(Christie's)   £5,500

An Edwardian silver mounted claret jug, the silver mount chased and repoussé with an Art Nouveau maiden's head and Bacchus mask surrounded by fruiting vines, London 1907, 27.5cm. high. (Spencer's)   £660

An Edwardian claret jug, with floral repoussé decoration and scroll handle, by J&T, Sheffield, 1901, 28cm.
(Lawrence Fine Art)   £792

A Continental Art Nouveau silver-mounted plain tapering clear glass claret jug with star-cut base, bearing import marks for London 1903, 9in.
(Christie's S. Ken)   £605

A cut glass and silver-gilt claret jug by William B. Durgin Company, Concord, New Hampshire, circa 1900, 12½in. high.
(Christie's)   £4,497

These are circular silver, plate, and/or wooden stands with a raised rim or gallery which were used from around 1760 for coasting, or sliding, a wine bottle or decanter around the polished table top after the cloth had been removed at the end of dinner. The earliest forms were entirely of silver with a concave base, but boxwood bases became common from around 1775, the early everted rim becoming straight, and presswork replacing hand-piercing. They sometimes also had rollers, or a green baize underside to protect the table surface.

Scalloped and undulating rims became common in the 1780s, and in the following decade embossing, piercing and bright-cut engraving were all used as decoration. After 1815, decoration became more florid, with footed stands being introduced in the 1830s.

Double coasters date from the 1790s. Usually coasters were made in pairs or multiples of two.

Most coasters were made to take decanters rather than bottles.

A pair of George III circular wine-coasters, with pierced and engraved sides and reeded rims, by William Abdy, 1790.
(Christie's)   £1,955

A George III silver gilt wine coaster, the sides cast and pierced with bacchantes, lions and trailing vines, 5¾in. diam.
(Christie's)   £7,700

A set of four George III silver-gilt wine coasters, the sides pierced with arcading and applied with husk swags, rosettes and oval cartouches, by Robert Hennell, 1774.
(Christie's)   £4,400

A pair of George III reeded, pierced and bright-cut circular wine coasters with turned wood bases, Richard Morton and Co., Sheffield 1793, 5in. diameter.
(Christie's)   £1,815

A pair of George III circular wine coasters, pierced with slats and with gadrooned borders and wood bases, by Thomas Jackson, 1772.
(Christie's)   £2,420

A pair of George III pierced and gadrooned circular wine coasters applied with paterae and floral and foliate swags, 4¹⁄₂in. diameter.
(Christie's)   £990

A pair of George III decanter stands, the pierced fretwork sides with applied paterae linked swags, London 1775.
(Woolley & Wallis)   £1,000

One of a pair of early Victorian decanter stands, by C., C.T. and G. Fox, London, 1839/41. £1,375

One of a pair of George III circular decanter stands, by John Roberts & Co., Sheffield, 1806/10. £790

One of a pair of George III silver gilt wine coasters by B & B. Smith, London, 1817, 5½in. diam. £3,740

One of a set of four early Victorian shaped circular wine coasters, by Hyman Wilkinson & Co., Sheffield 1842, 14cm. diam. £1,250

Pair of George IV wine coasters by Benjamin Smith, London 1823, 5¾in. diam. £3,630

One of a pair of William IV circular decanter stands, makers Howard, Battie & Hawkesworth, Sheffield, 1832, 10oz. £1,210

Pair of Regency moulded circular wine coasters, by S. C. Younge & Co., Sheffield, 1820, 6¼in. diam. £1,065

A pair of George IV wine coasters, each with similar border, engraved with a crest, by John Bridge, 1825. (Christie's) £7,150

A pair of George III circular decanter stands, by Thomas Robinson I, London, 1809. £1,035

A pair of Regency part-fluted moulded circular gadrooned wine coasters, William Elliot, London 1813, 6¼in. (Christie's S. Ken.) £1,870

A pair of Old Sheffield plate wine coasters, with escallop shell, acanthus leaf and reeded stamped and filled borders, 16cm. diam. (Henry Spencer) £220

Two of a set of four George III circular wine coasters, by R. Emes and E. Barnard, 1809 and 1810, 15.6cm. diam. £2,145

19TH CENTURY

One of a pair of silver mounted Regency papier mâché coasters, each with twin ring handles. **£935**

One of a pair of George III silver coasters decorated with embossed vines, 1816. **£935**

One of a pair of George III plain coasters, by Robert and Samuel Hennell, 1803, 5¼in. **£1,540**

One of a pair of William IV shaped circular wine coaster, by Thomas Blagden & Co., Sheffield, 1830, 18.5cm. diam. **£1,265**

A pair of George III wine coasters, by Paul Storr, London, 1813, 6¾in. diam. **£4,840**

One of a pair of Regency silver-gilt wine coasters, by J.W. Storey and W. Elliott, 1811. **£1,540**

A pair of George III plain, circular wine coasters, by Solomon Hougham, London, 1802, 14.5cm. diam. **£385**

Pair of George IV silver wine coasters by Rebecca Emes and Edward Barnard I, London, 1822, the sides chased with a band of tongue and lotus blossom, diameter 6½in. (Butterfield & Butterfield) **£827**

A pair of early Victorian silver wine coasters with scroll pierced waisted sides, Joseph and John Angell, London 1843. (Christie's) **£825**

One of a pair of George III wine coasters, makers John and Thos. Settle, Sheffield 1816, 7in. diam. **£935**

A set of four Regency part-fluted and gadrooned moulded circular wine coasters, William Elliot, London 1814, 6¼in. (Christie's) **£1,980**

A pair of Old Sheffield plate wine coasters, 5½in. diam., circular fluted sides with everted gadrooned borders, circa 1850. (Bonhams) **£100**

A pair of George IV circular coasters, the everted rims with acanthus, shell and rose bud edging, 6¼in. diameter, maker's mark *W.S.*, London 1823. (Bearne's) **£1,250**

A set of four Victorian plated tall circular wine coasters, the sides pierced with trellis-work and putti harvesting vines, 5¾in. (Christie's S. Ken) **£1,485**

A pair of William IV Sheffield plate decanter stands, the panelled sides with grapevine pierced borders, turned wood bases. (Woolley & Wallis) **£440**

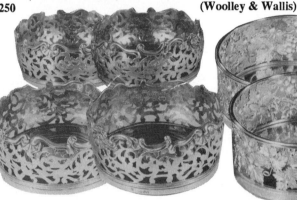

Two of a set of four Regency silver moulded circular wine coasters applied with gadroon, shell and foliate rims, John Edward Terrey, London 1820, 6½in. (Christie's) **£1,760**

A set of four William IV pierced circular wine coasters, each with shell and scroll rim and mahogany base, by Joseph & John Angell, 1832, 5½in. diameter. (Christie's) **£3,410**

A pair of George III silver-gilt wine coasters, the sides cast and pierced with trailing vines and with reeded rim, by Benjamin Smith, 1807. (Christie's) **£13,800**

A pair of Victorian Scottish silver-gilt circular wine coasters, on dragon and ball feet, maker's initials *M.R.*, Edinburgh, 1848, 8½in. overall, 28oz. free. (Christie's) **£1,815**

Four Sheffield plate shaped circular wine coasters with shell and foliate scroll edging on turned wood bases with crested inset plaques, 7in. diameter. (Bearne's) **£410**

A pair of William IV circular wine coasters, with ovolo borders and open wirework sides applied with vines, by John Edward Terrey, 1830. (Christie's) **£3,080**

19TH CENTURY

A pair of George III lobed circular wine coasters with gadrooned borders, central initial disc engraved with a crest, by William Eaton, 1815, 6in. diameter.
(Christie's) £858

A set of four George IV Irish circular wine coasters in the mid-18th century manner, pierced and chased with various animals, fruiting vines and scrolls, by W. Nowlan, Dublin, 1824, diameter 13cm.
(Christie's) £4,200

A set of four William IV silver-gilt wine coasters, each on wood base, the sides pierced and engraved with scrolls, foliage and lattice-work, by Paul Storr, 1833 and 1834.
(Christie's) £12,100

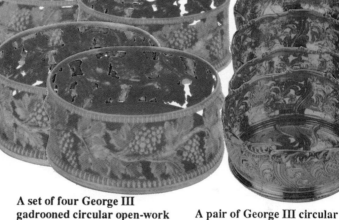

A set of four George IV silver gilt moulded circular wine coasters chased with eagles, flowers and scrolling foliage, William Elliot, London 1822, 6½in. (Christie's) £2,970

A set of four George III gadrooned circular open-work wine coasters applied with die-stamped and chased trailing vine sides, John Roberts & Co., Sheffield 1809, 5½in.
(Christie's S. Ken) £4,620

A pair of George III circular wine coasters, engraved with a crest within a garter cartouche with motto, 1817 by John Houle, 15cm.
(Lawrence) £1,760

A pair of Victorian wine coasters, scroll pierced sides and with floral mounts, by Robinson, Edkins and Aston, Birmingham, 1839, 16cm.
(Phillips) £1,100

A set of four Regency Sheffield plate decanter stands, the turned wood bases with crested bosses.
(Woolley & Wallis) £400

A pair of silver wine coasters, maker's mark of Gale & Willis, New York, 1859, with turned wood bases, 5⅛in. diameter.
(Christie's) £1,815

A pair of early Victorian silver-gilt wine coasters with scroll pierced sides and turned wood bases, Henry Wilkinson and Co., Sheffield 1847.
(Christie's) £800

A pair of George IV circular wine coasters pierced, die-stamped and chased with trailing vines, S. C. Younge & Co., Sheffield 1828 and 1829, 6³/₄in.
(Christie's) £1,430

A pair of William IV silver fluted shaped circular wine coasters applied with trailing vine borders, I. & I. Waterhouse, Sheffield 1831, 7³/₄in. (Christie's) £1,320

A pair of George III 6in. circular silver wine coasters, makers Rebecca Emes and Edward Barnard.
(Phillips) £810

A pair of Old Sheffield plate wine coasters, circular with encrusted scroll and foliate borders, central crest engraved bosses to later wooden bases.
(Bonhams) £160

A pair of William IV wine coasters, each with plain base and cast trailing vine border, by Benjamin Smith, 1831.
(Christie's) £6,210

A pair of William IV silver-gilt wine coasters, the sides pierced with vine leaves and grapes, with reed-and-tie and vine tendril borders, by John Settle and Henry Williamson, Sheffield 1830. (Christie's) £3,960

An almost matched pair of part-fluted moulded circular wine coasters, John Bridge, London 1823 and Messrs. Barnard, London 1834, 6¹/₂in.
(Christie's S. Ken) £1,045

A pair of George IV coasters, plain circular with gadroon rim, wooden bases, engraved with crest, by John Russell, 1822, 15cm.
(Lawrence) £1,012

A Liberty & Co. silver and enamel wine coaster, Birmingham hallmarks for 1905, 9.5cm. diam., 2oz.14dwt. gross wt. (Christie's) £462

One of a pair of Omar Ramsden silver wine coasters, London, 1934, 14cm. diam. £3,872

A good coaster with slightly bevelled sides, the surface hammered and applied with a frieze of stylised leaf motifs, 1926, 5.2cm. high, 11.5cm. diam. (Phillips) £750

A Hutton & Sons silver wine bottle coaster, 16.80cm. high, total weight 19oz., maker's marks for Sheffield, 1905. £285

A set of six Wiener Werkstätte circular wine glass coasters, designed by J. Hoffman and K. Moser, 5.5cm. diam., silver coloured metal. £990

A wine coaster, stamped marks 925.S Georg Jensen & Wendel A/S 289A, 9.5cm. high, 14oz.10dwt. £1,090

A silver tea glass holder, with applied troika horse heads, by V. Akimov, Moscow, circa 1900, overall 4¾in. high, with glass liner, 206.9gr. (Christie's) £495

A George V two handled bottle holder of cylindrical form pierced and cast with stylised flower heads, London 1910, 535 grammes, 16.5cm. high. (Henry Spencer) £340

A cup holder, the openwork frame of a trellis of roses having a leaf decorated handle, inscribed *Omar Ramsden me fecit*, London 1927, 6.5oz. (Woolley & Wallis) £300

COCKTAIL SHAKERS

The cocktail was a phenomenon of the Twenties and spawned a whole host of related items, such as the cocktail cabinet, the cocktail watch and the cocktail shaker. Most examples of the latter are plated or of chrome and often come in novelty shapes. They were used to mix the combined ingredients of the cocktail, and many had recipes on the outer casing.

Chrome metal cocktail shaker, circa 1935, 31cm. high. £1,150

A plated cocktail shaker in the form of a dumbbell. £155

Electro-plated cocktail shaker in the form of a champagne bottle, 13¹/₂in. high. £400

A Sabattini electroplate picnic cocktail set comprising a cylindrical stacking system of six cups and decanter, 15³/₄in. high. (Christie's) £143

Sterling silver cocktail shaker by Shreve, Crump & Low, hammered Art Deco style, San Francisco, circa 1910, 10¹/₄in. high, 12.6 troy oz. (Eldred's) £703

A Georg Jensen cocktail shaker, with two handles each shaped as fruiting vines, stamped maker's mark, 24.5cm. high, 500 grams. (Christie's) £2,200

A Danish white metal cocktail shaker, the cylindrical form on a flared circular foot, Copenhagen marks for 1941, 23cm. high, 440 grams. (Christie's) £330

A Michelsen silver cocktail shaker designed by Kay Fischer, Danish silver marks, circa 1935, 18oz. 5dwt., 24.5cm. high. £615

An Art Deco glass cocktail shaker with silver mounts, Birmingham, 1936, 8in. high. (Dreweatt Neate) £400

A novelty cocktail shaker modelled as a bell, Asprey & Co. Ltd., Birmingham 1946, 10¹/₄in., 25oz. gross. (Christie's) £495

A recipe cocktail shaker, the outer sleeve of which revolves to reveal the correct ingredients. £165

COFFEE BIGGINS

The coffee biggin was an English design of the 18th and 19th century, and was in many ways the forerunner of the modern filter machine. Made in silver and Sheffield Plate, it had a cylindrical body, short lip spout and had a built-in strainer at the top to filter the coffee grounds. It was named after its inventor, George Biggin.

A silver coffee biggin, stand and lamp, maker's mark of Gale & Willis, New York, 1859, the body with elaborate foliate decoration, 11¼in. high, 43 oz.
(Christie's) £924

An early 19th century Continental plain bellied coffee jug with scroll handle and leaf and bud finial, N.B., 6in.
(Christie's S. Ken) £385

A George IV coffee pot, 8in. high, with angled handle and everted cape with beaded border, London, 1824, by William Elliott, 16 oz.
(Bonhams) £620

A Portuguese early 19th century moulded oblong coffee pot on ball feet, maker's initials *T.I.C.*, Lisbon 1814–1816, 9½in., 38 oz. gross.
(Christie's S. Ken) £660

An Edwardian Irish plain cylindrical coffee biggin in the early 19th century taste, with a foliate-decorated spout, J.S., Dublin 1902, 7¾in., 22.75oz. gross.
(Christie's S. Ken) £418

A Regency part-fluted tapering coffee biggin on a spreading circular foot with a part-fluted squat curved spout, Rebecca Emes and Edward Barnard, London 1813, 8in., 22.75oz. gross.
(Christie's S. Ken) £440

A rare silver coffee biggin, maker's mark of Garrett Eoff, New York, circa 1820, with a scroll spout chased with acanthus and a carved wood handle, 9½in. high, 32 oz. 10 dwt.
(Christie's) £1,725

A silver coffee pot by Joyce R. Himsworth, the tapering cylindrical body applied with bands of plaited rope decoration and wirework motifs, Sheffield hallmarks for 1926, 23cm. high, 840 grams gross.
(Christie's) £825

A North Italian coffee jug, maker's mark A.T., circa 1770, 31oz.2dwt. all in, 11½in. high. **£2,785**

A Russian coffee jug, with domed cover, Moscow, 1750, 18.2cm. high, 405gr. **£1,350**

A good Victorian coffee jug, the spirally fluted baluster form body supported on similarly decorated circular base, London, 1885, 10¼in. high. (Bonhams) **£1,100**

A Belgian pear-shaped coffee jug, with fluted curved spout, detachable hinged domed cover with scroll thumbpiece and flower finial, by Jacques-Hermann Le Vieu, Mons, 1753, 11¾in. high, gross 1,180 grs. (Christie's) **£13,200**

A George III coffee jug, 8½in. high, with everted gadroon border and leaf-chased spout and angled wooden handle, London, 1819, 25oz. (Bonhams) **£650**

A George III coffee jug, of slender baluster form, repoussé with ribbon tied drapes centred by rosette medallions, London 1776, 751 grammes gross. (Spencer's) **£1,200**

A George IV coffee jug on circular foot, 8in. high, London, 1824, 26oz. **£440**

A good early Victorian Scottish coffee jug, with a foliate knop finial and corkscrew thumbpiece, Edinburgh 1840 by J. McKay, 22cm., 31.9oz. (Lawrence Fine Arts) **£1.155**

A George IV coffee jug, the ovoid body chased with scroll foliage, 1821 by Joseph Angell, 21.5cm., 23.9oz. (Lawrence) **£748**

A Belgian coffee jug, Tournai, 1771, maker's mark NH below a sunburst, 15½in. high, gross weight 36oz. **£6,390**

A George IV silver coffee jug, Robert Hennell, London, 1823, with fluted domed cover and base, 26oz. 10dwt, 9½in. high. (Sotheby's) **£862**

A silver gilt coffee jug, by J. C. Krause, 24.1cm. high, Konigsberg, 1757, 645gr. (all in). **£2,975**

A German plain pear-shaped coffee-jug, with a moulded drop to the short curved spout, by Martin Friedrich Muller, Berlin, 1735–45, 11½in. high, gross 1056grs. (Christie's) **£7,150**

Paul Storr, coffee jug on stand, of Neo Classical design, with gadroon moulding and engraved with a coat of arms, 13¼in., London 1803, 53.5 oz. (Woolley & Wallis) **£5,200**

A Maltese fluted pear shaped coffee jug, with moulded spout, scroll thumbpiece and flower finial, circa 1770, 8¼in. high, gross 611gr. (Christie's) **£2,640**

A mid 18th century Viennese pear shaped coffee jug, the handle and finial of ebonised wood, 23cm. high, 500gr. (Finarte) **£1,377**

A Belgian coffee jug, maker's mark MH conjoined below a crown, Mons, circa 1730, 9oz.15dwt., 6in. high. **£3,875**

A French small baluster coffee jug, on four scroll supports chased with classical portrait medallions with pendant husk swags between, 8¼in. high. (Christie's) **£352**

18TH CENTURY

Coffee pots were first introduced about 1680, and the earliest were straight-sided, tapering forms, which a little later became polygonal. Pear-shaped bodies were first introduced about 1730 and the Adam period heralded classical vase forms. Continental pots were normally vase-shaped, and many had highly exotic decoration. In America, the shape followed the English style at first, with a severely tapering form, being modified about 20 years later to become rounded at the base, on a narrow, moulded foot. American rococo examples were pear-shaped and tall, with a domed cover, while in the Federal period an inverted pear-shape was preferred, with a simple scroll wooden handle. Side handles went out of fashion about 1715.

In England, no coffee pots made before 1730 are embossed or engraved, apart from armorials. (A good armorial can make a big difference to the value.) From 1730–40 there may be some flat-chasing, but it was not until 1740–60 that any embossing occurs. If the embossed decoration covers the entire pot, there will usually be a distinct decorative theme, such as chinoiserie. If the decoration is floral, it seldom covers more than two-thirds of the surface area. Overall floral decoration, especially on a matted background, is more characteristic of the Victorian era. Between 1780 and 1815 engraving usually consists of bright-cut decorative borders, with beading coming in during the early part of that period followed by thread borders in the 1790s.

A George II coffee pot of tapering cylindrical form, by Edward Feline, 1732, 6.75in. high, 14oz. gross. **£970**

A George II baluster coffee pot, by Thos. Whipham, London, 1755, 23oz.18dwt. **£1,450**

A George III vase-shaped coffee pot, on shaped-oblong foot with incurved angles, bright-cut with two ribbon-tied oval cartouches, by John Scofield, 1795, 12in. high, gross 26oz.
(Christie's) **£2,070**

A late George II plain baluster coffee pot on a gadrooned spreading circular foot, probably Thomas Whipham, London 1757, 10in., 29.25oz. gross.
(Christie's) **£2,310**

An attractive George II coffee pot, 9in. high, on spreading circular foot with leaf-capped curved spout, London, 1748, by Thomas Whipham, 21 oz.
(Bonhams) **£1,600**

A George II coffee pot, 6in. high, on moulded foot with faceted spout and wooden scroll handle, London, 1731, by Samuel Lea, 12oz.
(Bonhams) **£1,200**

COFFEE POTS

An Italian coffee pot with carved wood handle, 31.3cm. high, Genoa, 1768, 1110gr.
£6,275

A George I plain tapering octagonal coffee pot and stand, by John East, 1714, 9¾in. high, gross 33oz.
£28,510

A George II Irish coffee pot, by Thomas Walker, Dublin 1736, 9in. high, 27oz. all in.
£2,200

A George I plain tapering octagonal coffee pot, with curved octagonal spout, moulded borders and domed cover, by Edward Vincent, 1723, 9½in. high, gross 25oz. (Christie's)
£16,500

A George II tapering cylindrical coffee pot, with curved octagonal spout, the upper part of the body engraved with masks, foliage and trellis-work, 1732, 8⅝in. high, gross 26 oz. (Christie's)
£2,200

A coffee pot with straight tapering spout, wood scroll handle and domed cover with bun finial, maker's mark *N.G.*, circa 1730, 23cm., 24 oz. (Lawrence Fine Art)
£2,640

A fine George I plain tapering octagonal coffee pot, with curved spout with duck's head terminal, by John Bache, 1724, 10¾in. high, gross 34oz. (Christie's London)
£33,000

A George III silver partly-fluted coffee-pot, on oval foot and with a band of bright-cut diaper decoration, by Daniel Pontifex, 10in. high, gross 26oz. (Christie's)
£977

A George II tapering coffee pot, the upper and lower parts of the body chased with flowers, foliage and scrolls, by John Swift, 1752, 10½in. high, gross 33oz. (Christie's)
£1,980

18TH CENTURY

A pear shaped coffee pot by Eliza Godfrey, London with richly chased rocaille decoration, 27.5cm. high, 1040gr., 1758/9.
(Finarte) £1,542

A George II plain tapering cylindrical coffee pot, 1727, maker's mark probably IE for John Eckfourd Jnr., 8⅝in. high, gross 20oz. £2,140

George III baluster coffee pot, London, 1770–71, maker script "JS", pineapple finial above a leaf-wrapped spout, 10½in. high, approximately 32 troy oz. (Skinner Inc.) £2,255

An important George II tapering cylindrical coffee pot, with curved spout terminating in an eagle's head and with hinged slightly domed cover and bud finial, by Paul de Lamerie, 1742, 87½in. high, gross 23oz. (Christie's) £44,000

A Queen Anne Irish plain tapering cylindrical coffee pot, on moulded rim foot, the partly octagonal curved spout at right angles to the wood scroll handle, by Thomas Bolton, Dublin, 1706, 9½in. high, gross 29oz. (Christie's) £3,960

A George II plain tapering coffee pot on a spreading circular foot, with a foliate-chased and capped rising curved spout, Thomas Farren, London 1738, 8½in., 22.50oz. gross.
(Christie's S. Ken) £1,540

A George II pear-shaped coffee pot, chased with foliage festoons and rocaille ornament, the cover with an unusual mask, by John Swift, 1744, 10¼in. high, gross 35 oz.
(Christie's) £2,200

George II silver coffee pot by Thomas Farren, London, 1736, with cast faceted swan neck spout, 8¾in. high, gross weight 24oz.
(Butterfield & Butterfield) £2,049

A George III coffee pot, on circular foot, scroll handle and domed cover with pineapple finial, by James Stamp (probably), 1775, 26cm., 25.5 oz.
(Lawrence Fine Art) £2,640

18TH CENTURY

A George III baluster coffee pot on a spreading foot, Alexander Johnston, London 1761, the handle bearing Victorian hallmarks, 12½in., 41oz.
(Christie's) £990

A George II fluted pear shaped coffee pot, on three lion's mask and claw feet, by David Willaume, 1736, 8in. high, gross 28oz.
(Christie's London) £7,700

An electroplated coffee pot in the style of the 1760s, the plain baluster body on a gadrooned pedestal base, by F.B. Thomas and Co., 25.5cm.
(Lawrence) £176

A George III beaded pear-shaped coffee pot on a rising foot, with a bead and foliate-chased rising curved spout, possibly Thomas Heming, London 1779, 12in., 30 oz. gross.
(Christie's S. Ken) £1,870

A fine George II tapering cylindrical coffee pot, the curved spout terminating in bird's mask and with hinged stepped cover and baluster finial, by Paul de Lamerie, 1734, 8¼in. high, gross 25oz.
(Christie's) £17,600

A George III vase-shaped coffee pot, chased with flowers, foliage and scrolls, with beaded and foliage curved spout and domed cover, by Charles Whipham and Thomas Wright, 1764, 11¼in. high, gross 37 oz.
(Christie's) £2,200

A George III coffee pot, the hinged cover, spout and spreading base with banded edging, 10¾in. high, Daniel Smith and Robert Sharp, London 1780, 813 gms, 26.1 oz.
(Bearne's) £3,100

A George II plain tapering cylindrical coffee pot, with wood side handle, curved spout, hinged domed cover and bell-shaped finial, by Paul Crespin, 1732, 7¼in. high, gross 19oz.
(Christie's) £4,400

A George III coffee pot, with gadroon edging, leaf-capped spout, wrythen finial and wood scroll handle, 11¾in. high, maker's mark I.K., London 1772, 29.5oz.
(Bearne's) £1,850

George II silver coffee pot, by Edward Vincent, London, 1738, 8in. high, 19oz. **£1,595**

A George III vase-shaped coffee pot, by Henry Chawner, London, 1789, 11.5in. high, 26oz. all in. **£880**

A George III gadrooned, pear-shaped coffee pot, probably by John Scofield, London, 1776, 10¾in. high, 26.25oz. **£1,210**

George III Irish silver coffee pot by Charles Townsend, Dublin, 1772, on spreading circular base with scroll spout and wooden handle, 12in. high, gross weight 29oz. 6 dwts.
(Butterfield & Butterfield) **£2,049**

A George III Provincial coffee pot with domed cover, acorn finial and gadroon borders, ivory handle and scalloped spout, by Langlands & Robertson, Newcastle, 1784, 33.5cm. high, 29 ozs.
(Phillips) **£2,500**

A George III coffee pot, decorated with scrolls, flowers and foliage and with wood handle on spreading base, 10¼in. high, maker's mark W.C., London 1762, 715gm., 22.9oz.
(Bearne's) **£880**

A George III plain baluster coffee pot on a spreading foot, with a leaf-capped and flute-chased rising curved spout, Samuel Wood, London 1763, 10¼in., 25oz. gross.
(Christie's) **£1,760**

A George I coffee pot, on moulded foot with wooden scroll handle and faceted spout, London, circa 1715, by William Penstone, 24.3cm. high, 25oz.
(Bonhams) **£2,400**

A George III plain baluster coffee pot, with a foliate chased rising curved spout, William and James Priest, London, 1766, 10½in., 19oz. gross.
(Christie's S. Ken) **£1,210**

A George I tapering cylindrical coffee pot on moulded rim foot, by John East, London 1722, 23.2cm. high, 24oz. £3,325

A George II Irish plain tapering cylindrical coffee pot, Dublin, 1734, 9in. high, gross 32oz. £570

A George II pear-shaped coffee pot, by Samuel Courtauld, 1753, 10½in. high, 40oz. £25,410

A George III pear-shaped coffee pot, with leaf-capped curved spout, hinged domed cover and fluted baluster finial, chased with scrolls, flutes and foliage, by Louis Hearn and Francis Butty, 1762, 11in. high, gross 31oz. (Christie's) £1,840

A George II tapering cylindrical coffee pot, engraved with a coat-of-arms and flat-chased with bands of scrolls, shells, strapwork and latticework, by John White, 1737, 8½in. high, gross 24oz. (Christie's) £2,750

A George II baluster coffee pot, later-chased with arabesques and engraved with a contemporary armorial surrounded by rococo flowers and foliage, Benjamin Gignac, London 1750, 10¼in., 30oz. gross. (Christie's) £880

A George II coffee pot, with moulded scroll spout and wood handle, the bun shaped cover with turned finial, by John Pero, 1738, 23cm., 24 oz. (Lawrence Fine Art) £3,080

A George III coffee pot of plain baluster form on beaded circular base, the hinged cover with acorn finial, Newcastle 1784, 25oz., 11½in., makers Langlands and Robertson. (Russell Baldwin & Bright) £950

A George II silver coffee pot, Newcastle, 1744, maker's mark of Isaac Cookson, the hinged stepped domed cover with urn finial, 9in. high, gross weight 18oz. 10dwt. (Christie's) £3,643

A Victorian plain baluster coffee pot in the 18th century taste, with a foliate-chased rising curved spout, Messrs. Barnard, London 1840, 9in., 14³/₄oz. (Christie's) £770

Antique American Empire silver coffee pot, circa 1800–1830, raised petal decoration, wooden handle, ball feet, 11¹/₂in. high, 32 troy oz. (Eldred's) £256

An Italian vase-shaped coffee pot on three scroll supports chased with stylised animal heads and foliage, early 19th century, 9¹/₄in. high. (Christie's) £1,870

A coffee pot by Emanuele Caber, Milan 1812–50, of ovoid shape, the elongated spout ending in a bird's beak, the lid with swan finial, 37cm. high, 1130gr. (Finarte) £4,814

A George IV fluted pear-shaped coffee pot on a rising shaped circular foot, Richard Sibley, London, 1824, overall height 10³/₄in., 46³/₄oz. (Christie's) £1,320

A Victorian coffee pot of George I design, with domed cover and side handle, by Goldsmiths and Silversmiths Co., 1899 (Britannia standard), 23cm., 19oz. (Lawrence Fine Art) £825

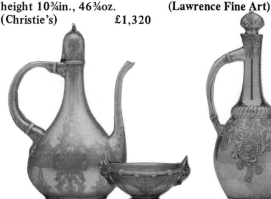

A French 19th century pear-shaped coffee pot on scrolling foliate feet and with a foliate-chased rising curved spout, 9in. high, 18.75 oz. (Christie's S. Ken) £352

A parcel-gilt coffee pot and sugar bowl by Tiffany & Company, New York, 1892–1902, coffee pot 8³/₄in. high; bowl 4in. diam. (Christie's) £2,214

A black coffee pot by Gorham, Providence, 1888, with a narrow curving spout and handle with insulators, 9¹/₂in. high, 14 oz. 10 dwt. (Christie's) £425

19TH CENTURY

A pear shaped coffee pot with broadly reeded body, second half 19th century, Novara, signed with monogram *WB*, 27.5cm. high, 1000gr.
(Finarte)   £1,928

A small cylindrical coffee pot, decorated in relief with chinoiserie motifs and with a Fo dog finial, London 1850, 16.5cm. high.
(Finarte)   £643

A coffee pot by Giuseppe Giovara, Turin, incised with monogram within a cartouche, the lid with fruit finial, 19th century, 24cm. high, 680gr.
(Finarte)   £1,400

An oviform coffee pot on a circular foot, the spout ending in an eagle's head, the cover with pineapple finial, Novara, 1824, 31cm. high, 700gr.
(Finarte)   £2,525

A Swedish 19th century fluted baluster coffee pot with a rising curved spout, and engraved with rococo scrolling foliage, 8¹/₂in., 17oz.
(Christie's)   £495

A coffee pot by Dominick & Haff, New York, 1881, with a domed cover, a pointed finial scrolling handle and a narrow spout, 10³/₄in. high, 23 oz. 10 dwt.
(Christie's)   £1,440

An American silver coffee pot, J. E. Caldwell, Philadelphia, circa 1850–60, derived from German 18th century rococo, 51oz. 10dwt., height 13¹/₂in.
(Sotheby's)   £832

E. E. J. & W. Barnard, a naturalistic coffee pot, melon panelled, with foliage entwined root spout and handle, 8¹/₂in., London 1841, 25oz.
(Woolley & Wallis)   £780

A Victorian Irish melon-fluted baluster coffee pot on a spreading circular foot, J. Smyth, Dublin 1854, 9³/₄in., 37.24oz.
(Christie's)   £880

19TH CENTURY

A Sheffield plated coffee pot, the plain baluster body divided into wide lobes and with a leaf capped scroll handle, 26cm. (Lawrence) **£264**

George III oval vase-shaped coffee pot by R. & D. Hennell, London, 1800, 28oz.13dwt. **£1,120**

A William IV melon panelled baluster coffee pot by E., E. J. & W. Barnard, London 1834, 29oz. **£660**

A Chinese coffee pot, the scroll handle, finial and spout in the form of bamboo, 22.5cm., 26oz. **£485**

A Victorian tapering octagonal coffee pot in the mid 18th century taste, with a leaf capped panelled rising curved spout, W. H., London, 1888, Britannia Standard, 8¾in., 18.25oz. gross. (Christie's S. Ken) **£682**

A German coffee pot, by Gustav Friedrich Gerich, Augsburg, 1805, 22oz. all in, 10½in. high. **£825**

A Continental fluted baluster coffee pot on scroll feet, with a grotesque mask spout, 9½in. high. **£240**

A George III silver coffee pot, London 1817, makers S. Royes and J. E. Dix, 9in. high, 28oz. **£360**

A sterling silver repousse coffee pot, New York, circa 1850, 11½in. high, 35½ troy oz. **£460**

19TH CENTURY

A silver gilt coffee pot by M. Ovchinnikov, in Empire style, maker's mark, Moscow, 1896, 22cm. high.
£2,970

An early Victorian coffee pot, by Charles Reily & George Storer, 1841, 30.7cm. overall height.
£750

A William IV fluted pear-shaped coffee pot, by Paul Storr, 1836, the finial by J. S. Hunt, 8¼in. high, 26oz.
£1,635

Coffee pot attributed to Gaetano Pane, of ovoid shape on three claw feet, the spout ending in a canine head, first half 19th century, Neapolitan area, 31.5cm. high, 1190gr.
(Finarte)   **£2,626**

A German 19th century plain tapering oval gilt-lined coffee pot with rising curved spout, polished wood scroll handle and flattened rising cover, 6in., 17.50oz. gross.
(Christie's)   **£605**

A Genoese oviform coffee pot of three claw feet, the spout ending in a dog's head, the cover with pineapple finial, 25cm. high, 550gr., marks for 1824.
(Finarte)   **£1,377**

A Danish coffee pot, of baluster shape, the wrythen fluted body on four feet, Copenhagen, 10in., 22oz.
(Lawrence Fine Art)   **£198**

A silver demitasse coffee pot, maker's mark of Tiffany & Co., New York, circa 1891, 7³/₄in. high, gross weight 14oz.
(Christie's)   **£1,632**

Baluster form silver coffee pot on round spreading foot, A. Michelson, Copenhagen 1877, 860gr.
(Herholdt Jensen)   **£178**

20TH CENTURY

An Edwardian plain tapering coffee pot in the 18th century taste, Goldsmiths & Silversmiths Co. Ltd., London 1909, 10¼in., 18.25oz. gross.
(Christie's S. Ken)   £352

Tiffany sterling coffee pot, 1902-07, plain Colonial Revival style, the finial cast as a basket of flowers, 10¾in. high, approx. 23 troy oz.
(Skinner)   £641

A Liberty silver coffee pot, designed by Archibald Knox, with Birmingham hallmarks for 1906, 21.5cm. high.
          £2,200

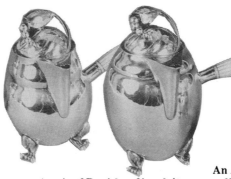

Early 20th century repousse decorated sterling silver coffee pot, Gorham Mfg. Co., 12⅞in. high, approx. 26 troy oz.   £790

A pair of Danish café au lait pots, each of ovoid form, by Georg Jensen, London import hallmarks for 1936 and 1930, 6in. and 5in. high, 20oz.
(Christie's)   £2,070

An American plain vase-shaped coffee pot in the neo-classical manner with reeded borders, domed cover with urn finial, by Tiffany & Co., circa 1900, 11in. high, 17oz.
(Christie's)   £632

A plain baluster coffee jug with panelled lower body, by Brook & Son of Edinburgh, H.M. Sheffield, 1919, weight 16oz.
(Christie's)   £187

A 1960's silver coffee pot and hot water jug, by H. Brown, Birmingham hall-marks for 1963, 29cm. high, 40oz.12dwt. gross weight. (Christie's)   £550

A coffee pot by Samuel Kirk & Son Co., Baltimore, 1903–1907, with a domed cover, curving spout and handle with insulators, 9¼in. high, 23 oz.
(Christie's)   £982

COFFEE URNS

The coffee urn is a rarer version of the tea urn and was in use in Britain and Europe from the mid 18th century. Instead of a spout there is a spigot and tap at the base of the body and there are generally also two handles, either loop, or mask and ring. Usually, too, it is mounted on a footed stand. It was a form particularly popular in the Netherlands, where some very large examples were produced. From the mid 1780s most were made in Sheffield Plate.

A plated coffee urn with applied lion mask ring handles, 13in. high. £395

Sheffield plate coffee urn, circa 1820, on a stepped circular base raised on a square platform with four bun feet, 16¹/₂in. high. (Butterfield & Butterfield) £300

A George III two-handled vase-shaped coffee urn, with fluted body, ivory handle to the spigot and bright-cut engraved borders, by John Denziloe, 1792, the heater-holder and cover, 1903, 13³/₄in. high, gross 42 oz. (Christie's) £1,540

A German two-handled fluted pear-shaped coffee urn, with scroll handles and domed cover, by Johann Georg Kloss, Augsburg, 1747/1749, 11³/₄in. high, 799grs. (Christie's) £1,925

A George III two-handled vase-shaped coffee urn, chased with a band of waterleaves and bright-cut below the reeded rim with rosettes and wheatears, by Peter and Ann Bateman, 1799, 13³/₄in. high, gross 43oz. (Christie's) £1,650

Tiffany sterling coffee urn on stand, 1938–47, tapering fluted body cast with basketweave and Renaissance motifs, 15in. high, approximately 90¹/₂ oz. (Skinner Inc.) £4,509

Bigelow Bros. and Kennard coin silver coffee urn, circa 1845, Greek key and bead detail, bright cut decoration, 16³/₄in. high, approximately 83 troy oz. (Skinner) £1,364

George III silver coffee urn by John Robins, London, 1784, on square platform base supported by four ball feet, 13¹/₂in. high, 38oz. 6 dwts. (Butterfield & Butterfield) £1,009

159

COMPÔTES

Also known as comports or even compostiera, these were large stands or salvers with a round, flat top on a heavy stem, raised on a flared foot, and were used to hold en suite sets of jelly or syllabub dishes. They were popular from the early 18th century in England, but were made almost exclusively of glass, until, in the early Victorian period, silver examples enjoyed a brief vogue. These would be adorned with cutting, enamelling and gilding.

Pair of Black, Starr & Frost sterling compotes, circa 1880, rim and foot pierced with bold flowers, 11in. diameter, approximately 56 troy oz. (Skinner Inc.) £1,383

A footed compote on ring-turned stem, by R. & W. Wilson, circa 1845, 7½in. high, 24oz. 10dwt. £385

A parcel-gilt silver compôte, maker's mark of Gorham Mfg. Co., Providence, 1870, one end forming a handle, elaborately clad with an entwined foliate frosted grape vine and applied gilt fox, 12½in. long, 39 oz. (Christie's) £1,971

A matched pair of Edward VII Art Nouveau comports, supported on openwork pedestal supports of whiplash scroll design, 6¾in. high, Birmingham 1907, 20.6oz. (Bearne's) £320

Austrian silver figural compote, late 19th century, chased shell form bowl supported by Bacchus and child, 14⅛in. high, approximately 44 troy oz. (Skinner Inc.) £1,296

Coin silver compote by Goodnow & Jenks, Boston, cameo reliefs at rim, classical style handle, conical foot with Greek key motif, 8½in. high, 14 troy oz. (Eldred's) £272

Pair of Victorian shaped circular compotes on rising circular bases, by R. Garrard, London, 1880, 9in. diam., 42.25oz. £1,390

A repoussé compote by Tiffany & Company, New York, 1883–1891, the sides formed of a finely repoussé and chased band of mythological figures, 33 oz. 10 dwt. (Christie's) £3,459

CONDIMENTS

While salts, peppers, and mustard pots had long been familiar at the dinner table, it was not until Victorian times that the idea emerged of having them as a set. Many novelty designs were produced, and the condiment set became a standard item of tableware which has continued to this day though few silver examples now regularly grace the average breakfast bar or TV supper table!

A Victorian novelty cruet on an oval ebonised wood base applied: 'Just Out', Robert Hennell, London 1872. (Christie's)   £352

A Victorian novelty cruet in the form of three acorns, C. F., Sheffield, 1876, 4in. high.   £95

A novelty silver plated condiment set, in the form of a small boy seated on a gate, above a pail, the gate flanked by two glass condiments. (Bonhams)   £110

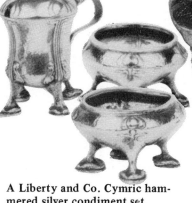

A Liberty and Co. Cymric hammered silver condiment set, comprising two bombe sided salts, similarly decorated mustard pot stamped with maker's marks and London hallmarks for 1897, height of mustard pot 7.8cm. (Christie's)   £770

A pair of thistle shaped cruet stands, each on a foliage base with central ring handle, by Fenton Bros, Sheffield, 1916/18, weight 18oz., with four spoons. (Christie's)   £462

A Liberty & Co. three-piece silver condiment set, Birmingham hallmarks for 1899, pepper-pot 5.5cm. high. (Christie's)   £425

A Charles Boyton hammered silver four-piece condiments set, the mustard pots with spoons and glass liners, 1947, 10oz.   £715

A three-piece condiment set in the Art Nouveau style, by Wm. Hutton & Sons Ltd., Birmingham, 1905.   £170

COW CREAMERS

The cow creamer is simply a silver cream jug in the form of a standing cow. The tail, looped over the back, serves as the handle, while the mouth is the spout. There is an oval lidded opening on the back where the milk is poured in, and this often has a fly or bee in full relief. The cow creamer was introduced from Holland around 1755 by John Schuppe, a Dutchman, and it is his name which is most often associated with the form, though later examples were also produced by other makers.

A Victorian Continental cow creamer, the hinged cover with insect finial, Import mark London 1892.
(Russell, Baldwin & Bright) £620

A George III cow creamer, the hinged back flap with applied bee and curved tail forming the handle, by John Schuppe, 1763, 5³/₄in. long, 4oz.
(Christie's) £5,175

A fine George II silver gilt cow creamer with textured body, by John Schuppe, 1756, 5oz.
(Phillips) £13,000

A George III cow creamer, the curled tail forming the handle and with hinged back-flap chased with foliage and with applied fly, by John Schuppe, 1768, 5³/₄in. long, 4oz.
(Christie's) £9,350

A Dutch silver miniature cow creamer, the loop tail forming the handle, London import mark 1906, maker's mark B.H.M., 107gm., 10.5cm. long.
(Spencer's) £500

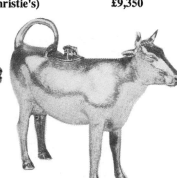

A George III cow creamer, engraved with hair along the ridge of back, the cover chased with flowers and applied with a fly, 9.5cm. high overall, by John Schuppe, 1767, 4 ozs.
(Phillips) £6,200

A good Victorian cow creamer by George Fox in the style of John Schuppe in the mid 18th century, 6¹/₄in., London 1865, 6¹/₄oz.
(Phillips) £4,500

A Dutch cow creamer by Berthold Muller, with a cast and applied buckled collar and flat hinged cover, London import marks for 1895, 195 grammes, 14.5cm. long.
(Spencer's) £420

CREAM JUGS

The earliest milk jugs were in fact hot milk pots which harmonised with the kettles and teapots of the early 18th century. They were usually pear-shaped, sometimes octagonal in cut, with a domed lid and a short, covered spout.

The 1720s saw the introduction of a very small cold milk or cream jug, again of pear or baluster shape, on a spreading foot rim with attached beak spout. The vessel tended to become broader thereafter, on a moulded foot, and the spout became an integral part of the rim, rising upwards and forwards and balanced by a scrolling handle.

Three-footed jugs appeared from the 1720s, firstly with one foot under the lip and subsequently with one under the handle. Shallow boats for cream were usually sold in pairs and could be cast in relief or sometimes shaped as nautilus shells. Others were decorated with engraving or were lightly chased.

Most helmet shaped jugs date from neo-classical times.

A Belgian cream pot with scroll handle, maker's mark T.B. crowned, Namur, circa 1750, 12.3cm. high, 155gr.
£1,320

Fine George III silver cream jug, helmet shaped with bright cut decoration, London 1797, by Peter and Anne Bateman. (G. A. Key) £240

An Irish helmet cream jug on lion mask and paw feet, sides chased with flowers and fish scale decoration, an unrecorded mark of George Moore of Limerick, circa 1765, 6ozs. (Phillips) £620

A fine George II cast cream jug, decorated with cows and a milk maid in naturalistic surroundings, by Elias Cachart, London 1740, 7¹/₂oz., 5in. (Tennants) £3,800

A silver cream jug of inverted pyriform with a scroll handle, by Wm. Hollingshead, Phila., circa 1760/80, 5in. high, 4oz. £2,505

A George III cream jug, with reeded borders and reeded angled handle, London, 1796, by Samuel Hennell. (Bonhams) £190

A George III bright cut fluted helmet cream jug on a reeded rising shaped oblong foot, London 1796, 6in. (Christie's S. Ken) £308

A George II cream jug, 3³/₄in. high, inverted pear-shape, punch bead border and double scroll handle, London, 1770, 2 oz. (Bonhams)   £140

An Irish George III cream jug, with cut away borders and wide lips banded to belly, Dublin, circa 1770, 6 oz. (Bonhams)   £340

A silver cream jug, maker's mark of Samuel Tingley, New York, circa 1775, 5³/₈in. high, 5oz. (Christie's)   £1,597

A George III inverted pear-shaped pedestal cream jug on a gadrooned and reeded domed circular foot, Hester Bateman, London 1781, 4¹/₄in. (Christie's)   £308

A silver cream jug, maker's mark of John Myers, Philadelphia, 1790–1804, helmet-shaped, with a moulded strap handle, on a flaring pedestal base with a square foot, 7¹/₈in. high, 5 oz. 10 dwt. (Christie's)   £1,478

A George III cream jug of helmet shape with gadroon border, scroll handle and pedestal foot, by Charles Clark, 1765, 9cm. (Lawrence Fine Art)   £264

A George II cream jug, with a sparrowbeak lip, 1735, maker's mark possibly for George Hindmarsh, 8.8cm. (Lawrence Fine Arts)   £726

A George III pedestal cream jug, the ogee body chased with an agricultural landscape, 1772 by Thomas Shepherd, 11.8cm. (Lawrence)   £418

A George III silver gilt vase-shaped cream jug, maker's mark only IS, pellet between, 4½in. high, 11oz.2dwt.   £2,615

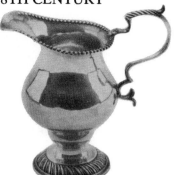

Late 18th century silver creamer, maker's mark INR, Phila., 4½in. high, 4 troy oz. **£300**

A George II silver gilt cast cream jug, unmarked but in the manner of Paul de Lamerie, 4¾in. high, 11oz. **£10,690**

A George III plain, inverted, pear shaped cream jug, London, 1774, 11cm. high. **£85**

A silver cream jug, maker's mark of Daniel Van Voorhis, New York, circa 1795, with cast double-scroll handle, on a pedestal foot, 5¹/₂in. high, 4 oz. 10 dwt.
(Christie's) **£1,232**

A rare George II cast boat-shaped cream jug, the body cast and chased with goats, a cow, bull's masks, shells, scrolls and foliage, by Louis Hamon, 1738, 5¹/₄in. high, 17oz.
(Christie's) **£9,350**

A fine George II pear-shaped cream jug, on three female mask and claw-and-ball feet, chased with two shaped-oval panels, one enclosing goats, the other cows and a milkmaid, by William Cripps, 1749, 5¹/₄in. high, 9oz.
(Christie's) **£12,650**

A silver cream jug, maker's mark of Elias Pelletreau, Southampton, New York, circa 1775, 5³/₈in. high, 5oz. 10dwt.
(Christie's) **£2,904**

A George III inverted pear-shaped cream jug, probably by R. and D. Hennell, London, 1766, 4¼in. high. **£121**

A silver cream jug, maker's mark *WP*, probably Boston, circa 1745, 4³/₈in. high, 3oz.
(Christie's) **£445**

165

A George III gadrooned and gilt-lined moulded shaped oblong cream jug, London 1810, 5¹/₂in. (Christie's) **£100**

A Continental cream jug formed as a pug dog, wearing a link collar and with curled tail, 5in. long. **£330**

A James Dixon & Sons electroplated cream jug, designed by C. Dresser, 1880's, 9.5cm. **£300**

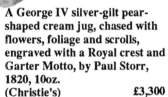

American Empire silver creamer by Garret Eoff, New York, 1845–1858, domed circular pedestal base supporting a squat stem with globular body above, height 6¹/₈in., 15oz. (Butterfield & Butterfield) £358

Late Federal silver cream and sugar set by Fletcher & Gardiner, Philadelphia, 1813–1825, with rectangular body with slightly bowed sides, monogrammed, 29oz. 10dwts. (Butterfield & Butterfield) £376

A George IV silver-gilt pear-shaped cream jug, chased with flowers, foliage and scrolls, engraved with a Royal crest and Garter Motto, by Paul Storr, 1820, 10oz. (Christie's) **£3,300**

A silver cream jug, maker's mark of William Seal, Philadelphia, circa 1815, 6¹/₈in. high, 8oz. 10dwt. (Christie's) **£508**

A George IV cream jug, 3in. high, banded to belly with everted gadrooned border and florally-chased reeded strap handle, London, 1829, by Robert Hennell, 3.5 oz. (Bonhams) **£85**

A novelty cream jug formed as a milk churn with cast handle formed as a cat, by George Angell, 1867, weight 5oz., 4¹/₂in. high. (Christie's) **£3,080**

19TH CENTURY

A late Victorian cream jug, with reeded borders and reeded angled handle, London 1892. (Bonhams) £90

A George IV cream jug, 3½in. high, with gadrooned border and leaf-chased reeded strap handle on four ball feet, London, 1823, by William Burwash, 6 oz. (Bonhams) £120

An early Victorian melon-shaped silver cream jug, 6oz. £190

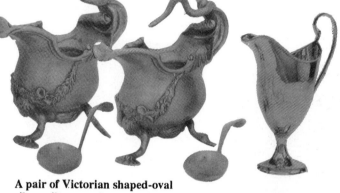

A Victorian gilt-lined vase-shaped cream jug on a foliate and bead decorated rising circular foot, George Adams, London 1861, 5¼in., 9oz. (Christie's) £385

A pair of Victorian shaped-oval silver-gilt cream boats, each supported by a merman, by Andrew Crespel and Thomas Parker, 1869 and 1870 and two Old English pattern silver-gilt cream ladles, 1793 and 1795, 4½in. high, 28 ozs. (Christie's) £5,060

A silver cream jug, maker's mark of John Baptiste Dumoutet, Philadelphia, circa 1800, helmet-shaped, the spreading circular foot on square pedestal base, 7³/₈in. high, 5 oz. 10 dwt. (Christie's) £986

Peter and William Bateman cream jug, with reeded borders, above prick engraved and bright-cut sides, London, 1805, 6 oz. (Bonhams) £160

An early Victorian gilt-lined compressed pear-shaped cream jug on crouching figure feet and with a mask spout, London 1843, overall length 6¼in., 16.75oz. (Christie's S. Ken) £550

A George IV Provincial plain fluted pear-shaped cream-jug, by J Barber & Co, York, 1821, 4½in. high, 9ozs. (Christie's) £1,495

19TH CENTURY

Late 19th century Dutch silver cream jug, 3½oz. £90

Victorian silver cream jug of panelled baluster form chased and embossed with flowers, Birmingham 1864.
(G. A. Key) £85

A Victorian slender baluster cream jug, H. & H. Lias, London 1863, 5¼in., 4.75oz. (Christie's) £154

A George III cream jug, with prick engraved borders, and bright-cut bands, London, 1806, by John Merry.
(Bonhams) £200

A late Victorian Japanesque style barrel shaped cream jug, the planished body engraved with carp swimming amongst weeds, London 1887, by Martin Hall & Co. Ltd., 77 grammes, 7cm. high.
(Henry Spencer) £340

A George III cream jug, the sides later chased with scrolls and foliage, London 1801, by Samuel Hennell.
(Bonhams) £120

20TH CENTURY

A silver oval covered cream jug, by Omar Ramsden, 1925, 11cm. high, 8.5oz. £880

A Continental novelty cream jug modelled as the head of Napoleon, his hat forming two spouts, London 1903, 3¾in.
(Christie's S. Ken.) £495

A Georg Jensen silver cream jug, supported on three foliate feet and having a leaf and magnolia bloom handle, 7.5cm. high. (Phillips) £220

A cream pitcher, by Albert Coles, N.Y., circa 1869, 6¼in. high, 6oz. **£225**

Russian silver cream pitcher, maker T Sokha, St. Petersburg, 1845, 84 standard, melon shaped body on conforming shaped oval foot, 6oz. 8dwts. (Butterfield & Butterfield) **£138**

A silver pyriform cream pitcher, by Samuel Minott, Boston, circa 1750-60, 4¼in. high, 3oz. **£1,525**

A covered cream pitcher, by Chas. Moore and J. Ferguson, Phila., circa 1801-05, 8¼in. high, 8oz. **£1,447**

Sterling Arts and Crafts style cream pitcher and open sugar bowl by Whiting Mfg. Co., Providence, Rhode Island, 1913, 8oz. 14 dwts. (Butterfield & Butterfield) **£173**

A cream pitcher, marked 'ID', probably Phila., 1790-1810, 6¾in. high, 5oz. **£760**

A double pyriform cream pitcher, by Cary Dunn, Newark, circa 1780-90, 5¾in. high, 7oz. 10dwt. **£2,385**

A cream pitcher, helmet-shaped, by Henry J. Pepper, Delaware, 1813-26, 5¾in. high, 7oz. **£465**

A cream pitcher with a scalloped rim and scroll handle, by Z. Brigden, Boston, 1770-85, 4⅞in. high, 3oz. **£1,595**

2 BOTTLE

Originally, cruets were the
vessels used for the wine and
water at the Eucharist. As
table accessories for holding
vinegar and oil, however,
they were introduced into
England from Venice in the
17th century.

The simplest comprised an
openwork frame on a flat
base and a lateral handle,
while by the late 18th century
boat shaped stands with end
handles and stands with
pierced work sides were also
common.

A two bottle cruet frame,
by Adam Jansens, maker's
mark, Maastricht, 1784-86,
27.1cm. wide, 680gr. excluding cut glass bottles and stoppers.   £6,125

A George II oil and vinegar
cruet on scroll and shell
supports, Samuel Wood,
London 1747, 12.75oz.
(Christie's)   £495

A good George III oil and vinegar
bottle stand, with a cast beaded
scroll handle, 1770, by Jabez
Daniell and James Mince, the
bottle mounts with standard and
maker's marks only, circa 1770,
by Robert Peaston, 25cm. high,
25.3oz. of weighable silver.
(Lawrence Fine Arts)   £2,530

Russian silver and glass mustard
set by Nichols and Plinke, St.
Petersburg, 1843, the frame with
threaded octagonal holder for
two glass mustard jars
supported by four vertical
supports, 6in. high, 16oz.
14dwts.
(Butterfield & Butterfield) £692

A George I oil and vinegar
frame, the open work sides
formed as alternating pillars
and brackets, by Paul de
Lamerie, 1723, the bottle
mounts unmarked, $7^{3}/_{4}$in. high,
18oz.
(Christie's)   £11,000

A fine early Victorian oil and
vinegar cruet, by Robert
Hennell, London 1840, 18.5 oz.
weighable silver.
(Woolley & Wallis)   £1,750

A George III boat-shaped oil
and vinegar stand, on four shell-
and-scroll feet with gadrooned
border, by John Parker and
Edward Wakelin, 1774, 11in.
long, 22 oz.
(Christie's)   £3,300

An Italian two-bottle cruet
frame, by Gaspare Ravizza,
Turin, circa 1755, 11oz.
excluding two blue glass
liners, 8in. high.   £1,390

3 BOTTLE

A Hukin & Heath electroplated cruet, designed by C. Dresser, mark April 1878. **£1,000**

A George III two-handled boat-shaped cruet stand, by Robert Hennell, 1781, the bottle mounts by Wm. Abdy II, 1798, 13in. long, 14oz.11dwt. **£1,330**

An Elkington & Co. electroplate cruet stand, 1880's, 12.5cm., together with a dish. **£200**

A James Dixon & Sons electroplated condiment holder, designed by Dr. Christopher Dresser, the wide circular base on three ball feet, 20.8cm. high. (Christie's) **£880**

A Hukin & Heath electroplated metal and cut-glass condiment holder, designed by Dr. Christopher Dresser, complete with two original spoons, registration lozenge for 1878, 9cm. high. (Christie's) **£2,420**

An Elkington three piece cruet and holder, the design attributed to Dr Christopher Dresser, with slender column and T-shaped handle, 12.7cm. high. (Christie's) **£198**

A Hukin & Heath electro-plated cruet set, attributed to Dr. C. Dresser, 4¾in. high. (Christie's) **£200**

Late 19th century Victorian silver plated three-bottle decanter stand, by Martin Hall & Co., 13½in. high. **£350**

A Hukin & Heath electro-plated six-sided cruet frame, designed by Dr. C. Dresser, with lozenge for 11th April 1878, 9cm. high. **£655**

171

4 BOTTLE

A Victorian soy-frame, the four glass bottles with silver neck mounts, covers and handles, by Robert Garrard, 1851, 24oz. £1,430

A boat-shaped cruet stand by Omar Ramsden, 1925, 10in. long, gross 42oz. £4,275

A Hukin & Heath silver condiment set designed by Dr. C. Dresser, London hallmarks for 1881, 14.2cm. high. £1,150

A very rare Scottish provincial four-bottle cruet frame of plain oblong form with rounded corners, maker's mark WF, circa 1825, 17.75oz. (Phillips) £9,000

A James Dixon & Sons electroplated condiment set designed by Dr. Christopher Dresser, the lozenge shaped holder with central handles and four square section compartments, with four faceted clear glass bottles and stoppers, 15.5cm. high. (Christie's) £418

A Hukin and Heath four-piece electroplated cruet, designed by Dr. Christopher Dresser, with patent registration marks for 1879, 13cm. high. (Christie's) £660

A Victorian cruet frame, by Robert Garrard, 1839, 5¾in. wide, the frame 22oz.10dwt. £3,250

A Regency part-fluted rounded square cruet frame on foliate feet and with egg and dart border, Paul Storr, London, 1818, 10¾in., 35.50oz. free. (Christie's) £3,960

George III four bottle silver cruet, by R. & S. Hennell, with blue glass bottles, 9½in. high, 1809. £605

5 BOTTLE

A five-part division Warwick cruet (2 oil bottles missing), by Samuel Wood, London, 1757, 46oz., 27.5cm. high. **£2,000**

A shaped oblong bright cut cruet on shell feet, fitted with cut glass condiment bottles, 9½in. **£165**

Mid 18th century silver and cut-glass cruet set, maker's mark JD, London, 1758, the stand 8½in. high. **£405**

A George III silver circular five division cruet stand, with egg and tongue border, London 1808, maker's mark R.E.E.B. **£900**

A George III gadrooned oval cruet on part-fluted curved feet, the mustard pot with a reeded scroll handle, London 1805, 8¾in.
(Christie's S. Ken.) **£528**

A George III gadrooned and foliate-pierced cinquefoil cruet, Jabez Daniell and James Mince, London 1767, 21oz.
(Christie's) **£550**

A George III cruet stand, by Hester Bateman, 1783, the bottle mounts Birmingham, 1871 by Henry Matthews, 21.5cm. high. **£300**

Silver five-bottle caster frame with scrolled legs, leaf-form feet, turned handle with bright-cut engraving, possible American, 10¼in. high, 36.6 troy oz.
(Eldred's) **£128**

Victorian cruet, oblong with central scrolled handle, London, 1852, 18½oz. **£365**

6 BOTTLE

A Victorian cruet, the six pierced fret holders with a crested cartouche, fitted with a set of glass bottles with stoppers. **£425**

A George III oval boat shaped condiment cruet, by Wm. Simmons, London, 1788, and a later mustard spoon, London, 1809, 29oz. **£1,265**

A Victorian condiment cruet, by James Dixon of Sheffield. **£325**

A Georgian style six bottle cruet stand, of bombé oval form with central spade handle, raised upon four acanthus leaf shell and rosette cast feet. (Spencer's) **£160**

A Hukin & Heath electroplated six piece cruet and stand designed by Dr Christopher Dresser, fitted with three faceted cut glass bottles and stoppers, two similar shakers and mustard pot with hinged cover, 1878, 23.1cm. high. **£4,400**

A George III beaded, pierced and bright cut oval cruet on claw and ball feet, William Abdy, London 1786, 10in. (Christie's S. Ken) **£682**

A silver six-bottle cruet stand, maker's mark of Gorham Mfg. Co., Providence, circa 1855–1860, 14in. high, weighable silver 35oz. (Christie's) **£1,929**

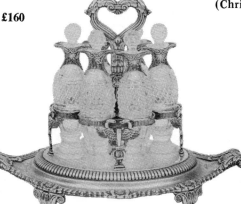

A George III soy frame by Paul Storr, fitted with six contemporary, cut glass condiments on a boat-shaped stand, 30cm. long, 1814, 30oz. **£3,000**

Silver six bottle revolving caster stand fitted with six glass castors by W.K. Vanderslice & Co., San Francisco, California, circa 1875, 14¹/₂in. high, 52oz. (Butterfield & Butterfield) **£1,160**

7 BOTTLE

A silver plated cruet set, the seven cruet bottles in a pierced oval stand with beaded border, on four scroll feet.
(Bonhams)   £260

An EPNS seven bottle cruet stand of rounded rectangular form, with central acanthus leaf sheathed spade handle, 27cm. wide.
(Spencer's)   £240

An early Victorian seven bottle cruet, Sheffield, 1838, by Henry Wilkinson & Co., stand 910gr. (Henry Spencer) £680

A late George III seven bottle cruet, the bombé boat shaped gallery repoussé and chased with scrolling foliage, raised upon four tapering flared feet, London 1866, by Hyam Hyams.
(Spencer's)   £280

George III Sterling seven bottle cruet set by Robert Hennell, London, 1793, with seven original silver mounted glass cruets, the piece properly hallmarked with full and part marks, 10¼in. high.
(Butterfield & Butterfield) £1,729

A George III cruet with four contemporary bottles, two casters and a mustard pot of cut glass with silver mounts, maker's mark *C.C.*, 1804, 20cm.
(Lawrence Fine Art)   £1,210

A George IV cruet and stand, fitted with four cut glass vinaigrette bottles, a mustard jar and two pepperette bottles, one mustard spoon, by Jonathan Hayne, 1822.
(Lawrence)   £715

A George II reeded broad boat-shaped cruet stand on fluted semi-ovoid feet, fitted with seven silver-mounted cut glass condiment bottles and jars, London 1792, 19.25oz. free.
(Christie's)   £1,430

A George III, silver cruet, the stand with gadroon and reeded decoration raised on scrolled lions paw feet, maker Charles Fox, London 1815, 16oz.
(Diamond, Mills & Co)   £600

8 BOTTLE

A late Victorian neo Gothic style eight bottle cruet, of shaped rectangular form, London 1877, 1015 grammes.
(Spencer's)   **£1,300**

A George III silver eight-bottle cruet set, maker's mark of Paul Storr, London 1795, of navette form, 15³/₄in. long.
(Christie's)   **£3,082**

A silver cruet stand, maker's mark of Matthew Pettit, New York, circa 1811, 9¹/₈in. long, weighable silver 25oz. 10dwt.
(Christie's)   **£1,742**

A George III oval boat-shaped cruet stand on four fluted scroll supports, by Robert and David Hennell, 1800, the mustard pot cover, by W.B., 1820, 7¹/₂in. wide.
(Christie's)   **£660**

An attractive George III eight piece cruet and stand, with cast beaded borders enclosing rosette pierced bands and a solid band bright cut engraved with swags of flowers, fruit and pendant husks, London 1787, 18.5cm. wide.
(Spencer's)   **£1,100**

A Regency part-fluted rounded square eight-bottle cruet on scrolling foliate feet, Thomas Robins, London 1814, 8³/₄in., 35oz.
(Christie's)   **£715**

An early Victorian cruet, the mustard pot and caster with contemporary silver mounts, Birmingham 1845, Messrs. Lias, London.
(Woolley & Wallis)   **£340**

A William IV condiment set, the shaped square stand on four foliate shell feet, with eight cut glass bottles, by William Bell Chambers, London 1830, 26cm. high, 27oz.
(Lawrence)   **£418**

An old Sheffield plate eight bottle cruet stand, of slightly shaped rounded rectangular form, Sheffield 1822, by Smith, Tate, Hoult and Tate.
(Spencer's)   **£350**

A Victorian six-cup egg
cruet, by Henry Wilkinson &
Co., Sheffield, 1846, 6in.
high, 20.75oz.   £255

A Victorian basket design
egg cruet, by Robert
Hennell III, London, 1856,
9½in. long, 28oz.   £530

A Victorian circular egg cruet,
with a pair of casters, by John
S. Hunt, 1853, 10½in. high,
76oz.   £2,495

A Victorian large shaped-
circular egg frame, chased with
flowers and scrolling foliage,
with central foliage ring handle
and six cups with shellwork
borders, by John S. Hunt, 1846,
11in. high, 58 oz.
(Christie's)   £1,430

A George III oblong egg cruet,
on four shell and vine feet, fitted
with six egg cups, each with shell
and gadrooned everted rim, by
Philip Rundell, 1818, 8in. long,
28oz.
(Christie's)   £1,650

An unusual six cup egg cruet on
bun feet with a part-spiral-
fluted domed hinged cover with
foliate handle, the latter turning
to open arabesque-decorated
panels concealing the egg cups,
10¹/²in. high.
(Christie's)   £300

A George IV circular egg frame,
on three foliage and paw feet, by
James Fray, Dublin, 1825, with
six fiddle pattern egg-spoons,
1816, 1822, 44oz.
(Christie's)   £1,650

A Victorian breakfast cruet
stand of trefoil form, 1870 by
Joseph and Edward Bradbury,
the red pepper ladle and
mustard spoon Sheffield 1871.
(Lawrence)   £264

Chinese Export silver egg set
and stand, Khecheong, Canton,
mid 19th century, six cups and
spoons, 8in. high, approximately
28 troy oz.
(Skinner Inc.)   £1,404

A Victorian four-cup egg cruet on circular base with scroll supports and central ring handle, by Samuel Whitford, 1848, 7¹/₂in. high, 24oz. (Christie's) £322

A George III Irish Provincial wire-work shaped oval six-cup egg cruet, Carden Terry and Jane Williams, Cork, probably circa 1810, 7¹/₂in., 9.25oz. (Christie's) £209

A silver boat-shaped four-cup egg cruet on reeded curved legs and with central openwork scroll handle, London 1912, 8¹/₂in. high, 21oz. (Christie's) £220

A Regency four-cup shaped square egg cruet on leaf and floral-capped lion's paw feet, Rebecca Emes & Edward Barnard, London 1812, 7³/₄in., 26.50oz. (Christie's S. Ken) £605

A Victorian novelty quatrefoil four-cup egg cruet, the detachable egg cups modelled as riding boots, the centre with crossed riding crops, 6¹/₄in. overall. (Christie's S. Ken) £528

Joseph & Albert Savory, a William IV egg cruet, the circular wire work frame with a central foliage scroll ring handle, London 1836, 22 oz. (Woolley & Wallis) £620

A George IV egg cruet stand with revolving frame, by Robt. Hennell II, fully marked 1823, 19.5cm. high, 29oz. £545

A Regency egg cruet with six matching egg cups, London, 1820, together with six George IV eggspoons, by Eley & Fearn, London, 1824, 32oz. £900

Georgian Irish silver egg cups in circular hallmarked silver stand plus six spoons, 24oz. total. (G. A. Key) £480

WARWICK

A George II Warwick cruet, by Milne & Campbell, Glasgow, circa 1750, 9¼in. high, 49oz.13dwt. £2,750

A George III Irish Warwick cruet, the base engraved 'In all 49oz.9 dwts', 9½in. high, 48oz. £2,660

An early George III cinquefoil Warwick cruet on shell and scroll feet, by J. Delmester, London, 1763, 9¾in. high, 23.5oz. £485

An early George III cruet, the cinquefoil frame with central handle and engraved with a coat of arms on a rococo tablet, maker's mark *ID*, 1763, 23cm., frame 15.5oz. (Lawrence Fine Art) £1,210

George II silver Warwick cruet stand fitted with set of five associated glass casters with silver mounts, Samuel Wood, London, 1751, the stand engraved with original coat of arms and crest, height 9¼in. (Butterfield & Butterfield) £414

A Scottish Warwick cruet stand on four scroll supports with shell feet and central ring handle, by Milne and Campbell, Glasgow, circa 1760, weight 48oz., 9½in. high. (Christie's) £2,200

Sam Wood, a George II Warwick cruet, with central shell and leaf decorated scroll ring handle on a baluster turned stem, London 1746, 54oz. (Woolley & Wallis) £4,100

A George III Warwick cruet, the stand by John Delmester, 1760, the larger caster by Samuel Welder, 1733, the smaller casters by James Mince and Jabez Daniell, 1769, 9½in. high overall, 40oz. £1,750

A George III silver-gilt Warwick cruet, on four shell and scroll feet and with central detachable handle, by John Delmester, 1761, 9in. high, 37oz. (Christie's) £5,060

CUPS

16TH/17TH CENTURY

Silver and gold cups have been used, by those who could afford them, from earliest times, but after the 18th century they passed out of fashion as drinking vessels, and since then they have been used mainly for ceremonial or presentation purposes.

Very many different types of cups exist, including some quite specific examples. These include:

Animal cups. Covered cups in the form of animals made in Germany between the 16th and 18th centuries.

Caudle cups. Two-handled cups, often covered, and generally of gourd shape, used for caudle, a thin gruel mixed with ale or wine. Also known as porringers.

Coconut cups. Although known earlier, the oldest now extant date from the 16th century, when they were popular in both Germany and Holland. Coconuts, polished and sometimes carved, were mounted in fine silver and set on stems. Scottish examples dating from the 16th–18th century are also found, though these are never carved and the mounts are very simple, decorated, if at all, with simple engraving.

Communion cups. The Protestant equivalent of the chalice, introduced under Edward VI. The basic form is of a deep bowl, on a spool-shaped stem, with compressed central knop and circular foot.

Nautilus cups. Nautilus shells elaborately mounted in silver were very popular in Germany in the late 16th/early 17th century and were also introduced in Holland. They are often beautifully mounted and sometimes made to resemble birds and beasts. They were obviously

A parcel gilt standing cup by Marx Merzenbach, 14cm. high, Augsburg, circa 1670, 75gr. £3,965

A German parcel gilt cup and associated cover, Nuremberg, circa 1620, maker's mark IF, 9¼in. high, 6oz.3dwt. £1,090

A highly important Henry VIII silver-gilt standing cup, the circular bowl chased with conforming bands of flutes and foliage and with plain everted lip, engraved with the initials *ER*, 1529, 8½in. high, 28oz. (Christie's) £254,500

A German silver-gilt cup, formed as the standing figure of a lady, her skirt chased and engraved with stylised foliage and scrolls, by Abraham Tittecke (Dittecke), Nuremburg, circa 1600, 5½in. high, 153grs. (Christie's) £29,700

A German parcel gilt standing cup, 20cm. high, probably by Gerhardt Sanders, Wesel, 1692-93, 348gr. £1,450

A silver gilt standing cup by A. Kessbair I, 22.6cm. high, Augsburg, circa 1680, 290gr. £1,320

18TH CENTURY

intended for display rather than use.

Feeding or Spout cups. A small plain cup with one or two handles, shaped rather like a saucepan, with a straight or curved spout. Intended for feeding a child or invalid, these date from the mid 17th century onwards.

Ostrich egg cups. Ostrich eggs, objects of considerable wonder, were often mounted as cups in the later Middle Ages. Most of those now extant are German examples dating from the late 16th and early 17th centuries.

Standing cups. Large ceremonial or decorative cups, usually with cover, with high stems and feet, dating up to the end of the 17th century, when superseded by two-handled cups on a low foot without a stem.

Stirrup cups. Handleless and footless drinking cups, based on the classical rhyton, in the form of a fox's or greyhound's mask and introduced around 1770 as sporting prizes and trophies.

Wager cup – Jungfrauenbecher. A cup in the form of a young girl with wide, spreading skirt, holding a bowl above her head. The bowl is pivoted so that when the figure is turned over the skirt forms the upper cup and the bowl the lower one. They were popular at weddings, especially in 17th century Germany, where the groom was supposed to empty the contents of the larger cup without spilling the lower, which he would hand to the bride.

Wager cup – Windmill. Cup shaped like a model windmill. When inverted, the mill body forms the bowl and the drinker had to empty the contents before the sails stopped turning.

A George III gilt-lined campana-shaped cup on a foliate-chased rising circular foot, maker's initials W.S., London 1797, 9½in., 45.25oz. (Christie's) £1,155

A George III silver-gilt partly-fluted vase-shaped two-handled cup and cover on spreading foot, by Henry Chawner and John Emes, 1797, 14½ in. high, 35ozs. (Christie's) £2,990

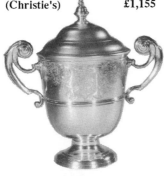

A George II Irish inverted bell-shaped cup and cover, engraved with a broad band of masks, shells, foliage and strapwork on a matted ground incorporating a coat-of-arms and with an Earl's coronet, the cup by John Hamilton, Dublin 1736, 11½in. high, 57oz. (Christie's) £7,130

George III Sterling mounted ostrich egg cup and cover by Allen Dominy, London, 1798, the cup set on trumpet form pedestal base with reeded edge and bright-cut decoration, 12½in. high. (Butterfield & Butterfield) £693

A late 18th century two-handled cup with a domed pedestal foot and reeded handles, the campana shaped body decorated with bands of horizontal convex fluting, 14cm. tall, circa 1780. (Phillips) £160

A George III rare Irish Provincial two-handled cup, the campana-shaped body chased with a foliate festooned classical frieze, by Daniel McCarthy, Cork, circa 1760, 14oz. (Phillips) £550

A Queen Anne two-handled cup and cover on circular fluted foot, by Lewis Mettayer, 1712, 9½in. high, 45oz. **£5,345**

A handled cup, with an S-scroll handle, by Thos. Coverly, Rhode Island, 1730-60, 2½in. high, 2oz. **£2,075**

A George II silver gilt two-handled cup and cover, by B. Godfrey, 1738, 12¼in. high, 81oz. **£7,720**

A George III Scottish gilt lined cup, W. & P. Cunningham, Edinburgh, 1791, 9¼in. high, 21.75oz. **£210**

A George II silver-gilt two-handled cup and associated cover, on domed circular foot, the body with applied rib and with leaf-capped scroll handles, by John Laver, 1771, the cover by Peter Archambo and Peter Meure, 1751, 15in. high, 98oz. (Christie's) **£2,860**

A George III maritime vase-shaped presentation cup and cover, by Robert Salmon, London, 1793, 14in. high, 43 troy oz. **£2,750**

A George II Provincial plain two-handled cup, by John Langlands and John Goodrick, Newcastle, 1755, 7in. high, 31ozs.
(Christie's) **£1,495**

A rare George I stirrup or tot cup of plain circular shape on cast spreading circular foot, by John Chartier, 1717, 3oz. (Phillips) **£1,800**

A rare Queen Anne Irish Provincial two-handled cup, with a moulded rim, the campana-shaped body with a reeded girdle, 13cm. high overall, by William Clarke, Cork, circa 1714, 12oz. (Phillips) **£1,700**

CUPS

A mid 19th century Australian cup, cast in the form of a naked part kneeling Aborigine supporting on his head and with his left arm the cup, circa 1880. (Phillips) £500

A Regency silver gilt two-handled campana shaped cup, by W. & P. Cunningham, Edin., 1818, 10¼in. high. £385

A late Victorian cup and cover, 15½in. high, with two leaf-capped scroll handles, the domed pull-off cover with egg-shaped finial, Birmingham, 1894, 33 ozs. (Bonhams) £400

A George III Irish small two-handled vase-shaped cup, chased and embossed at a later date with foliage and inscription dated *1880*, Dublin, circa 1760, 5¾in. high, 13oz. (Christie's) £319

George III silver cup and cover, William Fountain, London, 1802, engraved with armorial shield and crest, plain ovoid cup on stepped circular pedestal base, 13¾in. high, 38oz. 12dwt. (Butterfield & Butterfield) £600

A small two-handled cup by Charles Fox, 4½in. high, with two foliate mounted scrolling side handles, the sides chased with scrolls and foliage, London, 1834, 7 ozs. (Bonhams) £190

An American silver octagonal standing cup, Hyde & Goodrich, New Orleans, circa 1849, chased with a lake view with swans and sail boat, 5oz. 10dwt., height 7½in. (Sotheby's) £3,216

A late Victorian two handled cup by J. Wakley & F. C. Wheeler, the semi-wrythen fluted lobed cup chased and repoussé with winged cherub masks and foliage, London 1896, 294 grammes, 17cm. wide. (Spencer's) £260

Silver presentation cup, dated *1842*, Oscar T. H. Dibble, Savannah, Georgia, the cylindrical body engraved *Presented by Savannah Rifle Club*, 3½in. high. (Skinner) £407

A George III silver gilt cup and cover by John Houle, London 1812, 38cm. high, 101oz. **£1,815**

A George III cup and cover by Robert Sharp, London 1800, 15in. high, 71oz. **£1,650**

A George IV silver-gilt campana-shaped two-handled cup by Paul Storr, 1821, 5in. high, 15oz.6dwt. **£4,280**

George III silver campana form cup, Story & Elliott, London, 1810, half fluted urn with applied cast band of fruiting vines below the lip, 8³/₄in. high, 33oz. 16dwt. (Butterfield & Butterfield) **£825**

Silver presentation cup, Nicholas J. Bogert (fl. 1801–1830), New York City, the octagonal body engraved *This Goblet was Presented to the Guards by 1st Lieut. W. Bruen as a Prize to be shot for Jan 8th 1845*, 4in. high, 6 troy oz. (Skinner) **£645**

A Victorian two-handled parcel-gilt cup and cover, the handles formed as standing figures of fame, the cover with standing knight in armour finial, by Stephen Smith, 1871, 27¹/₂in. high, 170oz. (Christie's) **£3,190**

A George III two handle cup and cover, the vase shape body engraved with a view of Magdalen Hospital, 1800 by Solomon Hougham, 33.5cm., 37.4oz. (Lawrence Fine Arts) **£2,200**

A William IV two-handled cup, by Paul Storr, 1835, the foot stamped Storr & Mortimer, 10½in. high, 109oz. **£11,495**

A William IV silver gilt two handled cup, on a pedestal foot, the campana shaped body partly plain and with a flared rim, 29cm high, by E.,E. & J. Barnard, 1834, 60oz. (Phillips) **£2,400**

CUPS

A Georg Jensen hammered silver and amethyst cup and cover, Copenhagen mark and London import marks for 1926, 19.9cm. high. (Christie's) £4,400

An Alwyn Carr silver two-handled vase, cylindrical, raised on circular foot, 1920, 16.25cm. high. £440

A Wakeley & Wheeler silver cup and cover designed by R. Y. Gleadowe, Birmingham silver marks for 1938, 30oz.10dwt., 37cm. high. (Christie's)   £8,100

Continental silver wager cup, Foehr, of typical form, female figure in Renaissance dress holding a cup over her head, $10^{1}/_{8}$in. high, 23oz. 2dwt. (Butterfield & Butterfield) £1,201

A pair of German wager cups, in the form of a Jungfrauenbecher and her male companion, Birmingham Import marks for 1902, maker's mark *IS* over *G*, 1187gm. total. (Spencer's)   £2,900

A James Powell & Son silver and green glass two-handled cup, London hallmarks for 1909, 19oz.12dwt., 22.8cm. high.   £660

CAUDLE

A silver caudle cup, London, 1683, 8½oz.   £1,100

Silver caudle cup, Jeremiah Dummer, Boston, (1645–1718), engraved N^SM at base and marked *I.D.* in heart cartouche, approx. wt. 6 troy oz. (Skinner)   £1,290

Silver caudle cup by Henry Greene, London 1720-21, 7oz.   £595

CHRISTENING

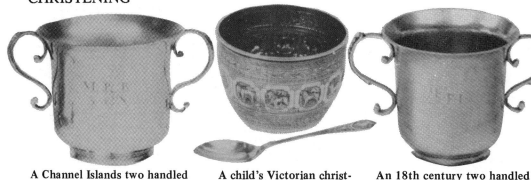

A Channel Islands two handled christening cup, on slightly spreading foot, with everted rim and beaded scroll handles, circa 1784, 7.3cm. high, 108gr. (Christie's)   £1,980

A child's Victorian christening bowl and matching spoon by John Russell, Glasgow 1888, in fitted case.   £110

An 18th century two handled christening cup, 6.5cm. high, maker's mark IH, crown above, (Jean Hardie, probably) Guernsey, circa 1770, 3oz. (Phillips London)   £700

COCONUT

A George III coconut cup, 6½in. high, the bulbous circular bowl carved with figures, palm trees and hearts, silver rim hallmarked for 1809. (Bonhams)   £75

A German silver-mounted coconut cup and cover, the nut with three applied straps and with tapering cylindrical neck and detachable domed cover, by Samuel Kesborer, Ulm, circa 1595, 10¼in. high. (Christie's)   £30,800

A late 19th century Australian silver, rare mounted coconut cup, the body finely carved with Aborigine fish motifs and supported by a calyx of silver-fern-like leaves, 14cm. high, by H. Steiner, circa 1882. (Phillips)   £700

Late 16th century, probably Dutch or German, coconut cup in the form of an owl with parcel gilt mounts, 7in. high. £32,670

A silver mounted coconut cup, by Peter and Anne Bateman, 1792, 4¾in. high.   £605

European 18th century coconut and silver covered chalice, 11in. high.   £255

LOVING

Tiffany sterling silver loving cup, New York, 1891, 9in. high, 13 troy oz. **£380**

Gorham Martelé sterling presentation loving cup, Rhode Island, circa 1902, 11in. high, approximately 92 troy oz. (Skinner Inc.) **£3,510**

Theodore B. Starr Sterling repoussé loving cup, 10¼in. high, approximately 82 troy oz. (Skinner Inc.) **£2,524**

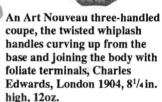

A loving cup, by Gorham, Providence, circa 1905, with an applied grapevine border and three sinuous handles, 19¼in. high, 107oz. (Christie's New York) **£4,842**

Pair of Sterling silver loving cups by Gorham, applied grapevine and Indian chief's head design, 8in. high, 39 troy oz. (Eldred's) **£1,343**

An Art Nouveau three-handled coupe, the twisted whiplash handles curving up from the base and joining the body with foliate terminals, Charles Edwards, London 1904, 8¼in. high, 12oz. (Christie's S. Ken) **£220**

A presentation loving cup by Dominick & Haff, Newark, for J.E. Caldwell & Co., 1895, in original mahogany box, 11½in. high, 82oz. **£6,289**

A trophy loving cup by Tiffany & Co., New York, circa 1889, with a serpentine brim and three curving handles formed as anchors, 9in. high, 57 oz. 10 dwt. (Christie's) **£1,505**

Sterling silver loving cup by Gorham, applied leaf and vine design, gold washed interior, 9⅜in. high, 21.4 troy oz. (Eldred's) **£288**

STIRRUP CUPS

A George III silver gilt fox mask stirrup cup, by Thomas Pitts, 1771, 5½in. long, 5oz. 13dwt. **£3,250**

A Victorian stirrup cup and stand, 1857, the stand by John S. Hunt, 1858, 40cm. high. **£430**

A late Victorian stirrup cup modelled as a fox's head, with circular cartouche, by Elkington & Co., Birmingham, 1897, 7.25oz. **£1,250**

A William IV fox head stirrup cup by Benjamin Smith, with chased and repoussé features, London 1835, 202 grammes, 11cm. long. (Spencer's) **£2,400**

A Dutch stirrup cup, the base naturalistically formed as a fox mask, apparently unmarked, silver coloured metal, 12.6cm. (Lawrence Fine Arts) **£462**

An Austro-Hungarian stirrup cup modelled as a kitten's head, circa 1870, 7.4cm. high, 4.25oz. **£660**

John S. Hunt, a fine Victorian stag's head stirrup cup, with gilt interior, 6in., London 1846, 19oz. (Woolley & Wallis) **£3,650**

A William IV silver stirrup cup, cast and chased as a fox mask, by C.G. Gordon, London, 1833, 6½in. long, 12oz. **£5,500**

A silver stirrup cup in the form of a stag's head, by Samuel Arnd, St. Petersburg, 1863, 8cm. high, 134.5gr. gross. **£2,500**

CUPS

A Regency period silver gilt campana-shape cup and cover by Paul Storr, London 1818, 15in. high, 108oz.
£3,740

Blackpool Aviation Meeting, 1910, a silver cup with three reeded handles on acanthus legs, 8½in. diam.
(Christie's) **£1,100**

A George IV silver gilt two-handled campana-shaped cup and cover, by Wm. Burwash, 1821, 15¼in. high, 136oz. **£5,700**

Important Sterling silver trophy, 19th century, by Tiffany, cast handles in the form of angels holding children, either side with applied full, two-dimensional figures of women in diaphanous clothing, 24.8 troy oz.
(Eldred's) **£1,919**

A Victorian large silver-gilt inverted bell-shaped cup and cover, by James Garrard, 1890, with wood plinth applied with two silver-gilt plaques, one engraved *"THE GOODWOOD CUP, 1892"*, 18½in. high, 163oz.
(Christie's) **£9,900**

A William IV two-handled silver-gilt cup and cover, the campana-shaped body decorated with acanthus leaves, flower-heads and with an applied horse, engraved *RICHMOND RACES 1834*, by Bernard & Co, 17¼in. high, 115oz. (Christie's) **£6,380**

A late Victorian neo-classical style two-handled trophy cup, by Charles S. Harris, London, 1899, 15in. high, 81oz. **£585**

George IV silver gilt trophy cup with ogee-shaped body, by J. Bridge, London, 1824, 54oz. 11dwt., 10½in. high. **£1,390**

A Continental gilt lined rowing trophy cup modelled as a Classical dolphin supporting a nautilus shell, 13½in. high. (Christie's S. Ken) **£275**

TROPHY

A George III silver-gilt campana shaped cup and cover, domed cover with detachable mare and foal finial, by Rebecca Emes and Edward Barnard, 1819, height of cup and cover 17in., 131oz.
(Christie's) £7,820

An Edwardian two handled trophy cup, on a domed foot repoussé with flower heads and scrolls, London 1901, by Stephen Smith, 620 grammes.
(Spencer's) £260

A late Victorian trophy cup, engraved with a fern wreath enclosing a vacant panel, raised upon a single blade knop stem and swept circular foot, London 1879, 229 grammes, 20cm. high
(Spencer's) £80

An Irish two handled Challenge Cup and cover, the cylindrical body on a circular pedestal foot, engraved with a coat of arms, by Charles Lamb, Dublin 1920, 55oz.
(Lawrence) £682

A large Victorian two-handled trophy cup, 10½in. high, the sides engraved with diaper-worked panels and chased with 'C' scrolls, ferns and other foliage, London, 1849, by Samuel Hayne and Dudley Carter, 31ozs.
(Bonhams) £560

A Victorian electro-plated two-handled football trophy of highly ornamental form, the lid surmounted by a female figure depicting Victory, the underside inscribed, *Kerr and Philips, Silversmiths, Glasgow*, 26½in. high.
(Christie's) £550

A George III silver gilt two-handled cup and cover, by Philip Rundell, 1818, the cover 1819, 13in. high, 94oz.
£2,660

A George IV silver gilt racing trophy cup, by Benjamin Smith, 1824, 34cm. high, 116.5oz. £2,750

A 19th century French racing trophy cup, the lower part of the foot electroplate, circa 1870, 38cm. high, weighable silver 115oz. £1,980

TUMBLER

A Charles II plain tumbler cup, maker's mark EG, 1681, 2¼in. high, 6oz. 3dwt. **£3,330**

A Kalo sterling silver tumbler, Chicago, Illinois, 1914-18, 3⅝in. high, approx. 3½ troy oz. **£70**

A Charles II plain tumbler cup, by Robert Williamson, York, 1669, 3½in. diam., 3oz.13dwt. **£3,750**

A William and Mary parcel-gilt tumbler cup, the sides stamped with a broad band of matting and with moulded rim, probably 1694, maker's mark indistinct, 2¼in. high. (Christie's) **£1,100**

A pair of Charles II tumbler cups. (Greenslade Hunt) **£7,800**

A silver tumbler cup, maker's mark of Andrew Billing, Preston, Connecticut, Poughkeepsie area, 1775–1808, engraved with script monogram *JWK* within circular bright-cut reserve, 2⅛in. high, 1 oz. 10 dwt. (Christie's) **£801**

One of a pair of French beakers, by Joseph Moillet, Paris, 1725, 6oz.1dwt., 2¼in. high. **£1,030**

A Charles II large tumbler cup, engraved with crest and beneath the lip, *The Gift from the owners of The Reliant*, 1683, maker's mark *IC*, 3in. high, 6 oz. (Christie's) **£4,400**

A George III tumbler cup, plain, of circular form with a rounded base, 5.5cm. high, inscribed *S.K*, by James Waters, 1770, 2¹/₂oz. (Phillips) **£340**

WINE

A Charles I plain wine cup on circular foot, 1640, maker's mark RW over a cinquefoil, within a dotted heart, 7in. high, 10oz.
£5,940

A Commonwealth wine cup, the hexafoil slightly tapering bowl punched with beading and chased with matted arches, 1652, 3³/₄in. high.
(Christie's) £7,150

An Elizabeth I plain wine cup, engraved 'The Towne of Wollterton, 1568', by Peter Peterson, Norwich, 5¼in. high, 6oz. £3,800

A Commonwealth wine cup, the tapering bowl chased with flutes, the foot and bowl with matted shaped-oval panels, 1650, maker's mark *E.T.* crescent below, 3¹/₂in. high, 2oz.
(Christie's) £8,250

A Charles I shallow wine cup, the hexafoil bowl chased with stylised shells each within shaped-oval surround, 1640, maker's mark *GM*, a bird below, 2¹/₄in. high.
(Christie's) £8,250

A Commonwealth small wine cup, the tapering cylindrical bowl punched with beading and chased with stylised flower-heads, 1656, maker's mark *H.N* 2¾in. high, 1oz.
(Christie's) £4,620

A James I wine cup, on spreading circular foot, the foot and bowl chased with stylised flower heads and pricked with scrolls, 1623, 7¹/₂in. high, 5oz.
(Christie's) £9,200

A Commonwealth wine cup on trumpet-shaped foot, 1655, maker's mark ET a crescent below, 3½in. high, 2oz.18dwt. £2,615

An Elizabeth I wine cup, the waisted stem with plain knop, the tapering bowl engraved with a band of strapwork and stylised foliate scrolls, 1571, maker's mark *HW*, 7in. high, 8 oz.
(Christie's) £8,800

An Imperial silver and enamel Art Nouveau desk folder, Moscow, 1908-17, 43.5cm. high. £2,000

A fine silver and enamel desk set, maker's mark of Tiffany & Co., New York, circa 1886, decorated with polychrome enamel in the Islamic taste, in original fitted leather box dated *1886*.
(Christie's) £3,696

A late George V silver perpeual desk calendar, of vertical rectangular form on a square plinth with engine turned wave decoration, engraved *N.B.27.7.38*, Birmingham 1934, 7.5cm. high.
(Spencer's) £90

DISH RINGS

A George III Irish dish ring, pierced with laurel swags, slats, scrolls and scalework, by William Hughes, Dublin, 1773, 8in. diameter, 10oz.
(Christie's) £1,650

A George III Irish potato ring, pierced and chased with pheasants, S and C scrolls and fruiting vines, by William Homer, Dublin, circa 1765, 20.2cm. diam., 16oz.
(Phillips) £2,600

A waisted dish ring in the Irish 18th century taste, pierced and chased with various animals, birds, fruit, flowers and scrolling foliage, 7½in., 10oz. (Christie's S. Ken) £418

A late Victorian pierced and waisted dish ring in the Irish 18th century taste, Wakelin and Wheeler, London 1896, 8¼in., 12.25oz.
(Christie's) £418

A late Victorian replica of an Irish dish ring by G. Nathan & R. Hayes, Chester 1900, 19.6cm. diam., 12.8oz. £210

A dish ring in the Irish style, the spool shape body chased and pierced, 1911, by Robert Frederick Fox, of C.T. & G. Fox, 20.7cm., 17.2oz.
(Lawrence Fine Arts) £418

There are many types of silver dishes, some of which are accorded individual sections in this book. Among the others, however, principal types include:

Butter dishes. Oval, pierced glass bowl and cover with a glass liner, usually Irish and dating from the later 18th century. Few English examples occured until the 19th century, when they were usually circular, tub-shaped containers.

Chafing dishes. Circular or shaped metal containers usually with a long turned wooden handle at the side, for hot charcoal, the bowl usually with pierced ornament resting on cast supports. In use from the 17th century to keep silver dishes hot. A form especially popular in America.

Ecuelles. A peculiarly French shallow, two-handled, covered dish popular in the rococo and Régence periods. Early 17th century examples usually had flat covers topped by a handle, whereas their 18th century counterparts had domed covers surmounted by a finial.

Late 16th/early 17th century Hungarian parcel gilt circular dish, unmarked, 24.2cm. diam., 415gr. £3,630

A George III silver gilt fluted circular dish of shallow form, by E. C. Farrell, London, 1818, 10in. diam., 17oz.3dwt. £3,410

A Spanish octagonal dish, repoussé and chased with birds, flowers and foliage, Cordoba, early 18th century, maker's mark not identified, Fiel Contraste Francisco Alonso del Castillo, 15½in. wide, 450grs. (Christie's) £1,870

A Louis XVI shaped-oval shaving dish, with detachable neck-notch and reeded borders, engraved with a coat-of-arms, by Jean-Antoine Gallemant, Paris, 1780–81, 13in. wide, 820 grs. (Christie's) £2,860

A Guild of Handicraft silver dish, designed by C.R. Ashbee, the border decorated with a pierced frieze of stylised galleons, London hallmarks for 1906, 20.5cm. diameter, 250 grams. (Christie's) £528

One of a set of four George III silver gilt dessert dishes, by John Wakelin and R. Garrard I, London, 1799, 9in. long, 73oz. £42,615

A late Victorian shaped-circular dish, the broad waved border chased with acorns and oak leaves, by Gilbert Marks, 1898, Britannia standard, 16¾in. diameter, 56oz. (Christie's) £4,840

A German parcel gilt circular dish, by Jeremias Ritter, Nuremberg, circa 1630, 7¾in. wide, 5oz.12dwt. **£2,850**

A George II dish, possibly John Carnaby, Newcastle, circa 1735, 7oz.17dwt., 6¼in. **£850**

A George II silver gilt circular alms dish, by R. Beale or R. Bayley, 21.8cm. diam., 18.9oz. **£2,300**

A German silver, ivory and lapis lazuli-mounted oval dish, the shaped central oval plaque depicting the triumph of Love over War, carved in high relief, inscribed to the reverse *Christoffero Jamnizer Fecit*, circa 1870, 18 x 21in. (Christie's) **£10,350**

A silver and enamel presentation boat-shaped dish, the loop handles surmounted by Art Nouveau winged angels, decorated in polychrome enamel with the arms of the City of Carlisle, by William Hutton and Sons Ltd., Sheffield, 1907, 22in. wide, overall, 98oz. (Christie's) **£2,640**

Sterling 'Japanese Movement' rectangular dish, Whiting Mfg. Co., Newark, New Jersey, 1880–1890, the face engraved with a pair of rabbits under a flowering stalk looking at a crescent moon, length 8⁵/₈in., 14oz. 4dwts. (Butterfield & Butterfield) **£676**

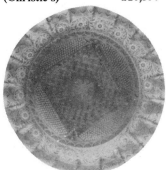

A plated dish by James W. Tufts, Boston, last quarter 19th century, with a flaring lobed brim, the entire surface chased with stylised foliate and geometric borders, 11³/₈in. diam. (Christie's) **£173**

A mother-of-pearl and silver-mounted circular shallow dish, the centre of flowerhead pattern engraved with the date 1568, possibly German, 10in. diameter. (Christie's S. Ken) **£2,420**

A Spanish silver-gilt shaped-circular dish, chased with birds, flowers and foliage, with raised moulded border, late 17th century, possibly Palencia, 17³/₄in. diameter, 1,098 grs. (Christie's) **£1,650**

An Edwardian two handled dish of rounded rectangular form with scroll handles, the border pierced with scrolling foliage, London 1902, 465 grammes, 30cm. wide.
(Spencer's) £260

A George II small shaped circular dish, by Paul de Lamerie, 1738, 6^1/$_8$ in. diam., 9oz.8dwt. £7,020

A Guild of Handicraft electroplated serving dish and cover, with complex intertwining wirework handle, 14cm. high.
(Christie's) £308

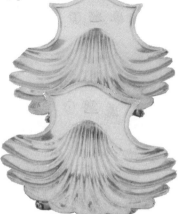

Pair of George III silver shell form dishes by Peter, Ann and William Bateman, London, 1802, both dishes shaped as shells with fluted bodies and scalloped borders, balanced on two nautilus shell feet, length 6^1/$_4$in., 8oz. 12dwts.
(Butterfield & Butterfield) £714

A parcel-gilt silver olive dish and tongs, maker's mark of Gorham Mfg. Co., Providence, 1887, formed as a cured olive with stem, 5^3/$_4$in. long, 5 oz. 10 dwt.
(Christie's) £739

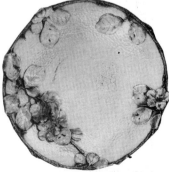

Pair of Sheffield plate covered dishes with liners, by Mappin Bros., circa 1850, the handles reeded and ribbon tied, the covers lifting to reveal removable liners, 10^1/$_2$in. diameter.
(Butterfield & Butterfield) £761

One of a pair of shaped circular silver gilt dishes, circa 1700, maker's mark only WH between rosettes and pellets, 15in. diam., 65oz. £4,280

A Spanish oval dish, the well and border repoussé and chased with flowers and foliage, by Jose Asteiza, Bilbao, circa 1760, 20in. wide, 1,097 grs.
(Christie's) £1,760

A mixed-metal and silver centrepiece dish, maker's mark of Gorham Mfg. Co., Providence, 1881, 12^3/$_4$in. diameter, gross weight 41oz.
(Christie's) £5,194

A late Victorian dish, of shaped lozenge form, stamped and pierced with fruit, scrolls, acanthus leaves and pendant husks, Sheffield 1899, 287 grammes, 27cm. wide. (Spencer's) £240

A French two-handled silver-gilt circular écuelle and cover, chased with bands of flowers, scrolls and shell ornament, Paris, circa 1785, the bowl maker's mark *JDB*, perhaps for Jacques du Boys, 12in. wide, 839 grs. (Christie's) £2,200

Sterling reticulated dish, en suite, Tiffany & Co., New York, 1891–1902, with lobed sides pierced with trellis work, and joined by scrolls and flowers, height 2³/₄in., 31oz. 12dwts. (Butterfield & Butterfield) £1,353

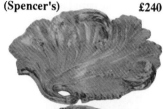

Two leaf-shaped dishes, chased to simulate acanthus-leaves, with matted decoration and tendril handle, Sheffield, 1829 and 1834, one by Robert Gainsford, the other by John Watson, 9¹/₄in. wide, 25 oz. (Christie's) £1,980

A Victorian copy of the Temperantia dish of Francois Briot, chased with panels of Classical figures, by Robert Garrard, 1862, 17in. diam., 66oz. (Christie's London) £2,200

A fine pair of Victorian oval dessert dishes, the sides with repoussé fruit and foliage, 12¹/₄in. across handles, maker William Evans, London 1878, 39oz. (Woolley & Wallis) £1,650

A silver gilt basketweave dish, by Tiffany & Co., New York, circa 1890, in the form of an Indian basket, 5¾in. diam., 5oz. (Christie's) £830

A Japanese pierced silver dish mounted with a central Shibayama panel, signed, decorated with a vase of flowers on a table, 12¹/₄in. diameter. (Bearne's) £1,350

A small ten-sided dish with a moulded border, decorated in the centre with an applied boss, modelled as a Tudor rose, 15cm. diameter, 1932, 6.5 ozs. (Phillips) £280

DISHES

BON BON

A Dutch 19th century pierced moulded oval bonbon dish in the 18th century taste, 5in., 8oz. (Christie's S. Ken) £352

A Hukin & Heath electroplated double bon-bon dish designed by Dr. Christopher Dresser, each oval basket with inverted rim, with loop handle, circa 1881, 14cm. high.
(Christie's)   £462

A silver-gilt swan bon-bon dish, 5in. long, the cut-glass oval body with silver-gilt neck and head.
(Bonhams)   £160

A pair of silver bonbonnières, maker's mark of Tiffany & Co., New York, circa 1910, each with openwork scroll and flower stem terminating with cherub amid rocaille, 13¹/₂in. long, 34 oz.
(Christie's)   £1,971

An almost matching pair of silver-gilt pierced and gadrooned shell-shaped bonbon dishes on cast and applied dolphin feet, Goldsmiths & Silversmiths Co. Ltd., London 1914 and 1917, 6in. and 5³/₄in., 21.25oz.
(Christie's S. Ken)   £1,320

An attractive pair of early George V boat shaped bon bon dishes by Hamilton and Inches, Edinburgh 1910, 330 grammes. total, 13.5cm. wide.
(Spencer's)   £260

BUTTER

A silver butter dish and cover, maker's mark of Bigelow, Kennard & Co., Boston, circa 1880, in the Persian taste, eleborately repoussé with foliate scrolls and fluting, 8in. wide, 16¹/₂ oz.
(Christie's)   £493

A parcel-gilt silver covered butter dish, maker's mark of Tiffany & Co., New York, 1881–1891, the spot-hammered surface applied with silver-gilt leaves and thistles, 5⁷/₈in. diameter, 15 oz. 10 dwt.
(Christie's)   £1,602

A Regency butter cooler, the partly ribbed pail with shell scroll, the cover with a cow finial, by Rebecca Emes and Edward Barnard, London 1813, 23oz.
(Woolley & Wallis)   £1,400

BUTTER

A Victorian octagonal butter dish, cover and stand, with vertical handles to the sides and flower finial to the slightly raised cover, by E.J. and W. Barnard, 1837, 20oz.
(Christie's) **£1,760**

A George III Irish oval butter dish with green glass liner, by Joseph Jadison, Dublin, 1779, 17.1cm. long, 14oz. **£990**

A good William IV butter dish, stand and cover, with a flower-head finial, 1836, by Joseph and John Angell, 19cm. diam of base, 26.9oz. **£825**

A pair of George II butter shells, engraved with an armed griffin crest, on webbed feet, S. Herbert & Co., London 1757, 7.5 oz.
(Woolley & Wallis) **£860**

A William IV circular butter dish, formed as a pail with swing handle, engraved with cypher, crest and Garter Motto, by Robert Garrard, 1834, 4³/₄in. diameter, 11oz.
(Christie's) **£2,200**

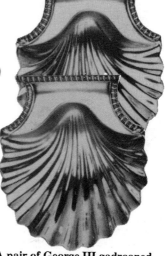

A pair of George III gadrooned shell butter dishes on triple periwinkle feet, Rebecca Emes and Edward Barnard, London 1810, 5¹/₂in., 9¹/₄oz.
(Christie's) **£880**

A medallion butter dish by Gorham, Providence, circa 1865, repoussé and chased with a band of cartouches, scrolls, and foliage, 5in. high, 16 oz.
(Christie's) **£623**

An attractive Arts and Crafts Movement butter dish and cover of compressed circular shape, the hammered surfaces chased with stylised chrysanthemum motifs, 6cm. high, 12.5cm. diameter, by H. Haseler, Birmingham, 1911, 14 ozs.
(Phillips) **£900**

One of a pair of George II butter shells on three shell and rocaille feet, by Paul de Lamerie, 1746, 4¾in. wide, 10oz.6dwt. **£40,395**

ENTRÉE

This covered serving dish was probably based on the chafing dish and was made in Britain from circa 1760. The cover is shaped like the dish but was slightly smaller to fit over the rim within the outer border of the dish. The handles on the cover were usually detachable to allow use as a serving dish. Early shapes were usually circular or polygonal, but later they became oblong or oval. Decoration was mainly simple, consisting often only of gadrooning round the border. Handles were sometimes also made in the form of a family crest.

Victorian silver footed entrée dish, Walker & Hall, Sheffield 1884–85, on reeded legs with paw feet, approximately 54 troy oz.
(Skinner Inc.) £378

A pair of electroplated rounded rectangular entrée dishes with detachable acanthus handles and gadroon edging, 14in. over handles.
(Bearne's) £450

A pair of gadrooned edge rectangular entree dishes and covers, with foliate capped stylised loop handles, on leaf capped paw feet, circa 1820.
(Phillips) £920

One of a pair of Louis XVI entree dishes, by F. Corbie, Paris, 1783, 9½in. square, 40oz. £3,835

A pair of Sheffield plate rectangular entrée dishes, with heavily chased foliate scroll and gadroon edging, the covers with detachable handles, 12³/₄in. long.
(Bearne's) £480

An entrée or breakfast dish of George III design, the domed cover with handle in the form of a crest and with interior liner, by Messrs. Elkington, Birmingham, 1903, 29cm., approximately 75 oz.
(Lawrence Fine Art) £715

Chinese export silver covered entree dish and serving bowl, 19th century, with beaded rim and domed cover, 8in. diam., 54 troy oz.
(Skinner Inc.) £1,688

A mid Victorian entree dish, cover and detachable handle by Martin Hall & Co., of plain oval form with bead cast borders, the cover engraved with two oval panels, within foliate strapwork, Sheffield 1863, 1630 grammes total, 30cm. wide.
(Spencer's) £420

A William IV entree dish by Paul Storr, on four foliate scroll feet, London, 1833, 34oz. £660

A covered entree dish with a figural finial, by Samuel Kirk & Son, Baltimore, 1880-1890, the domed cover surmounted by a figure of a grazing deer, marked, 6¾in. high, 52oz. (Christie's New York) £3,320

One of a pair of Louis XV entree dishes, Paris, 1773, maker's mark apparently that of Jean-Francois Genu, 11in. long, 41oz. £4,260

A pair of Victorian shaped-circular entrée dishes and covers, with gadrooned borders, by William Moulson, 1857, 10½in. diameter, 86oz. (Christie's) £2,420

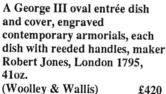

A George III oval entrée dish and cover, engraved contemporary armorials, each dish with reeded handles, maker Robert Jones, London 1795, 41oz. (Woolley & Wallis) £420

A pair of electroplated shaped oval entrée dishes and covers with detachable handles, 14in. over handles, Martin Hall and Company. (Bearne's) £550

A covered entree dish, by Samuel Kirk & Son Co., Baltimore, 1896-1925, the cover and bowl repousse and chased with flowers and scrolls, 23cm. diam., 35oz. (Christie's) £2,214

A George III entrée dish and cover, by Paul Storr, 1801, 28cm., approximately 51 oz., together with a metal handle in the form of a crest of a dog. (Lawrence Fine Art) £1,430

Paul Storr, a George III entrée dish and cover, of plain circular form, the base-dish with a finely applied border of scallop and oak leaf motifs with gadrooning, 20.5cm. high overall, 1810, 61oz. (Phillips) £7,000

201

ENTREE DISHES

One of a pair of oblong entree dishes and covers, by Paul Storr, London 1812, 31cm. wide, 3750gr. **£5,280**

One of a set of four Sheffield plated entree dishes , covers and detachable handles by M. Boulton. 25.3cm. **£375**

One of a pair of silver George III entree dishes and covers, by Paul Storr, 1810, 12¾in. long, 153oz. **£10,690**

One of a pair of oval entree dishes, covers and detachable handles, by Walker & Hall, Sheffield, 1911, 27.7cm., 108oz. **£665**

A George III shaped oblong entree dish, cover and handle, by Paul Storr, 1809, 16½in. wide overall, 68oz. **£3,565**

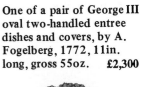

One of a pair of George III oval two-handled entree dishes and covers, by A. Fogelberg, 1772, 11in. long, gross 55oz. **£2,300**

FRUIT

A fruit dish modelled as a shell with a seated merman, by the Goldsmiths & Silversmiths Co., 1910, 37cm. high. **£1,815**

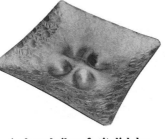

A chased silver fruit dish by Michael Lloyd, on four short cylindrical feet, the grooved central quatrefoil with four wells and a centred medallion of stylised overlapping fruit, 29cm. square, 98 grams. (Christie's) **£1,925**

A William IV silver gilt vine leaf fruit dish. by John Watson, Sheffield 1834, 12in. wide, 29oz. **£2,376**

KOVSH

A circular silver-gilt and niello kovsh, Moscow, 1875, 16cm. long. **£715**

Russian 84 standard silver seven piece Kovsh form punch set, maker's mark *AK* (in oval), assay master's initials *AP*, circa 1899–1908, 62oz. 2dwts. (Butterfield & Butterfield) **£2,767**

A silver gilt and plique a jour enamel kovsh of wide boat form with flattened trefoil-shaped handle, Moscow, circa 1880, 14.7cm. long. **£1,255**

MEAT

Meat dishes were popular
from the Middle Ages for
serving meat or fish. Most
now extant date from the
17th century onwards. Early
examples have moulded rims
but after 1730 these became
shaped or gadrooned, with
beaded rims appearing from
circa 1775. Still later reed
and tie patterns and shaped
mouldings are found. They
are almost always oval in
form and are found in all
sizes from 10 to 30 inches.
Of these, the most popular
are either the very small, or
the very large (over 18
inches).

Many examples also had
domed covers to keep the
meat hot. They were
generally superseded in the
19th century by porcelain
dishes.

An oval meat dish and cover,
designed by H. Nielsen,
stamped marks Dessin HN
Georg Jensen 600S, 46.7cm.
wide, 129oz. **£8,470**

One of a pair of Sheffield
plated meat plates and covers
in sizes, the domed covers engraved with arms. (Lawrence
Fine Arts) **£638**

One of a pair of German meat
dishes, by Franz A. H. Nubell,
circa 1820, 18¼in. long, 123oz.
£18,750

An Old Sheffield Plate Tree
and Well carving dish, on four
bun feet, circa 1840, 68.6cm.
wide. (Bonhams) **£600**

One of a pair of Louis XV
meat dishes, by Barthelemy
Samson II, Toulouse, 1768,
13½in. long, 51oz. **£3,240**

A Regency Sheffield plate
oval meat dish and matching
cover, 18in. diam. **£350**

One of a pair of late Regency
Sheffield plate oval meat
dishes and matching covers,
16in. **£460**

A silver Martele meat dish,
maker's mark of Gorham Mfg.
Co., Providence, circa 1905, the
rim repoussé with flowers and
leaves, the centre engraved with
a monogram, 20½in. long, 66 oz.
(Christie's) **£3,696**

A pair of Old Sheffield Plate
shaped-oval, tree and well venison dishes, each on four lion's
paw and foliage feet, by Waterhouse and Co., circa 1835,
23in. and 22in. long.
(Christie's) **£1,375**

A set of four Victorian shaped-
oval meat dishes, each with
gadrooned border and engraved
with a crest, by J.C. Edington,
1838, 12in. long, 102 oz.
(Christie's) **£1,760**

MEAT

One of a pair of German meat dishes, by Johann C. Otersen, 1784-91, 18in. long, 119oz. **£8,525**

One of a pair of Dutch meat dishes, The Hague, 1756, maker's mark a head in a shield with coronet above, 22in. long, 199oz. **£7,245**

One of a set of four George III meat dishes, by J. Parker and E. Wakelin, 1761, 13½in. long, 108oz. **£6,535**

A pair of rare George II shaped-oval meat dishes, each with shell, foliage and reeded border, later engraved with a coat-of-arms, by Nicholas Sprimont, 1743, 13½in. long, 50oz.
(Christie's) **£9,900**

A good pair of meat dish covers of pleated domed form, by Joseph Cradock & William K. Reid, 1824, height overall 26.5cm.
(Phillips) **£900**

Two George I octagonal meat dishes, each with ovolo border, engraved with a coat-of-arms, by David Willaume I, 1725, Britannia Standard, 75oz.
(Christie's) **£3,080**

MUFFIN

An electroplated muffin dish, designed by C.R. Ashbee, the domed cover with a wirework finial set with abalone, 14cm. high. (Christie's) **£528**

A C.R. Ashbee silver muffin dish, set with three chrysoprase, the domed cover with a wirework finial set with another chrysoprase, with London hallmarks for 1900, 13cm. high, 650 grams. gross.
(Christie's) **£2,860**

A Guild of Handicraft Ltd muffin dish and cover, probably designed by C. R. Ashbee, circa 1900, 25cm. diam. (Henry Spencer) **£500**

SECOND COURSE

These are serving dishes
which look exactly the same
as large dinner plates, and
they can measure from eleven
to eighteen inches in
diameter, with value
increasing with size. They
were used throughout the
eighteenth and early
nineteenth centuries for
serving entremets and
puddings, and they conform
in style and pattern to the
meat dishes and plates of the
period.

One of a pair of French
second-course dishes, by
J. Chaumet, Paris, circa 1918,
14in. diam., 136oz.   £6,820

A Louis XV second-course
dish, by A. Pinel, Rodez,
circa 1750, 14¼in. diam.,
51oz.   £5,115

One of a set of four Russian
silver gilt second-course
dishes and covers, the covers
by J. W. Feurbach, 1766,
12⁵/₈in. diam. of dishes,
391oz.   £32,390

A set of four German second-
course dishes, by Franz A. H.
Nubell, circa 1820, 12¼in.
diam., 154oz.   £20,455

One of a pair of German silver
gilt second-course dishes, by
G. Menzel, 1717-18, 12¾in.
diam., the covers by C. Winter,
1729-30, 11³/₈in. diam.,
163oz.   £149,155

One of three George II
second-course dishes, by
P. Archambo I and Peter
Meure, London, 1753,
11⁷/₈in. diam., 79oz. £6,390

One of a pair of second-course
dishes, bearing probably spurious marks, D crowned possibly from Riom, 1781-85,
maker's mark SWB, 13½in.
diam., 68oz.   £1,020

One of three George IV
second-course dishes, by
Philip Rundell, London,
1822, 11⁷/₈in. diam., 87oz.
                £6,390

STRAWBERRY DISHES

This name was given to small, saucer-like dishes dating from the 17th and early 18th century. They tend to be scalloped, the earlier ones quite plain except for the fluted edges and armorials. Later examples are often quite elaborately flat chased. They range in size from about 6–10 inches. Not necessarily used for strawberries, many came in sets with an en suite serving dish.

SWEETMEAT DISHES

Less common than sweetmeat baskets, these dishes or bowls for serving sweets could be in the form of a dish or a bowl. They are usually quite ornate, as befitted display items which would be handed round among one's guests, and generally reflect the styles of the contemporary period. They sometimes came in pairs or even fours.

A George III Irish strawberry dish, of circular form with a scalloped rim, 24cm. diameter, by William Hughes, Dublin, 1772, 16oz.
(Phillips) £2,200

A George II circular strawberry dish, by Paul Crespin, 1735, 9½in. diam., 19oz. 5dwt. £3,090

A German parcel-gilt two-handled shaped oval sweetmeat dish, chased and embossed with a bird, fruit and foliage, maker's mark *H.B.*, Augsburg, late 17th/ early 18th century, 9in. wide overall, 7oz.
(Christie's) £1,725

An unusual Georg Jensen silver sweetmeat dish of shell shape, supported on an openwork foliate and beaded stem, 10.5cm. high.
(Phillips) £820

A Charles I shaped circular two-handled sweetmeat dish, 1634, maker's mark IP a bell between, 8½in. diam., 5oz. 10dwt. £3,145

A Continental sweetmeat dish, Dutch, 18th century, on an oval pedestal foot with similar lobed decoration, scrolled handles, import marks 1889, Chester, 21cm.
(Lawrence) £286

A Victorian shaped oval sweet meat dish heavily chased with flowers and scrolling foliage, 10½in. long, London 1898, 9.9oz.
(Bearne's) £260

VEGETABLE DISHES

These are very similar to entrée dishes, but usually have a domed cover and fixed handle. Few, if any, examples will be found from before 1760. They often come with a stand with lamp or iron for keeping food hot. This would be usually of Sheffield Plate, and then dishes themselves were made in this after 1800. The earliest types also had screw-in handles.

Sterling silver open vegetable dish by Durgin, applied floral border, monogrammed, 13³/₄in. wide, 16.8 troy oz. (Eldred's) **£140**

One of a pair of George III silver gilt kidney shaped vegetable dishes, by B. Smith, 1807, 11¾in. long, 66oz. **£11,285**

A French two-handled circular vegetable dish and cover, the slightly raised cover punched with a band of laurel foliage and with detachable flower finial, by J.B.C. Odiot, Paris, 1789–1809, 8in. diameter, 1,429grs. (Christie's) **£3,300**

A pair of German plain circular vegetable dishes and covers, with detachable wood handles, engraved with a coronet and initial W, by Christian Drentwett, Augsburg, 1795–97, 8³/₈in. diameter, 2,240 grs. (Christie's) **£4,400**

One of a pair of George III shaped circular vegetable dishes, by J. Parker and E. Wakelin, 1768, 11in. diam., 43oz. **£4,275**

A silver vegetable dish, maker's mark of Gorham Mfg. Co., Providence, circa 1870, with two stag-head handles, the domed cover with fawn finial, 13³/₄in. wide, 44 oz. 10 dwt. (Christie's) **£1,478**

A pair of silver vegetable dishes and covers, maker's mark of S. Kirk & Sons, Co., Baltimore, 1903–1924, 10¹/₂in. long, 64oz. (Christie's) **£5,194**

A silver covered vegetable dish, maker's mark of Gorham MFG, Co., Providence, 1916, with foliate scroll side handles, length over handles 12¹/₂in., 36 oz. 10 dwt. (Christie's) **£924**

DRESSING TABLE SETS

These were made of gold or silver for the fashionable ladies of the 17th and 18th centuries, and could contain over 50 pieces. Apart from silver-topped bottles, and pots, silver-backed brushes and so on, they could also include such items as bodkins and tongue scrapers! The dressing case, used mainly for travel purposes by men as much as women, saw many of these items neatly fitted into an elegant wooden box, in the 18th and 19th centuries.

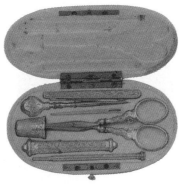

A 19th century French seven-piece silver-gilt nécessaire-à-coudre with engraved decoration in fitted and ivory case, circa 1870.
(Phillips) £400

A Victorian coromandel toilet box, having the complete fitted interior and assorted mother of pearl handled and silver mounted requisites.
(Locke & England) £700

A Victorian composite silver gilt dressing table set, by various silversmiths, 1885/89, 21-pieces including Dutch silver gilt coloured metal box.
£1,030

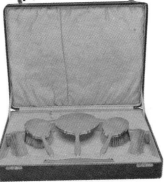

A late George V six piece dressing table set, with engine turned striped decoration and foliate chased borders, Birmingham 1929, in an apricot satin and velvet lined case.
(Spencer's) £200

A fine Victorian travelling toilet box, the veneered rectangular case with brass mounts, the lid with leather towel case and mirror, 12in., maker Frances Douglas 1854.
(Woolley & Wallis) £1,750

A Williams IV lady's rosewood dressing case, 1835 by Archibald Douglas, the small inkpot a replacement of 1836, 32.6cm.
(Lawrence) £484

A Victorian boulle dressing case with silver gilt fittings, with maker's name F. L. Hausburg, Liverpool, and the silver gilt mounts 1843, 32.3cm. wide.
(Lawrence Fine Arts) £990

An early Victorian gentleman's dressing case, the contents hall-marked, maker Thos. Diller, London, 1840, 11oz. weighable silver.
£680

DRESSING TABLE SETS

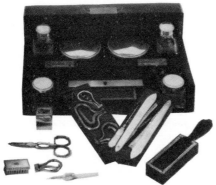

Early 19th century rosewood vanity box with fitted interior and plated tops.
(G. A. Key)   £125

A necessaire de voyage in a mahogany case, maker's mark, Paris, circa 1815, the case 30cm. wide.   £3,145

Good cased four piece silver and tortoiseshell backed dressing table set, Birmingham 1924.
(G. A. Key)   £240

An early 19th century French mahogany and gilt mounted nécessaire and musical box in the form of a piano, with extensively fitted velvet-lined interior, 30cm. wide.
(Phillips)   £600

An important Swiss necessaire with singing bird automaton and twin musical movements, by Frères Rochat, Geneva, circa 1825, the implements with restricted warranty mark for gold, Paris, 1819–1839.
(Christie's)   £99,000

A Victorian coromandel wood travelling dressing case, by Thomas Johnson, 1861, William Leuchars, 1886, Charles Asprey and George Asprey, 1899, 20$^{1}/_{2}$in. wide.
(Christie's)   £6,600

Fine Victorian rosewood and brass banded vanity box with several plated and glass interior fittings, 9 x 12in.
(G. A. Key)   £170

A very fine and attractive early George V five piece tortoiseshell and silver dressing table set, Birmingham 1914, 39.5cm. wide.
(Spencer's)   £500

A fine early Victorian toilet case, veneered in coromandel, brass bound and inlaid stringing, maker Francis Douglas London 1845/46.
(Woolley & Wallis)   £660

ÉPERGNES

This word derives from the French *épargner*, to save, and the item was intended to save the guest the trouble of passing dishes at table. It took the form of an elaborate centrepiece with such fittings as cake baskets, fruit and sweetmeat dishes and sometimes also candle sockets. It was in use in Britain from around 1730.

19th century examples can be quite massive, with cut glass dishes and baskets.

A George II épergne on four foliage, scroll and shell feet, and with four detachable scroll branches with openwork dish frames, maker's mark CM, 1759, 63oz. **£3,565**

A Sheffield plate épergne on reeded supports, fitted with six detachable reeded scroll branches, with cut-glass oblong central bowl and six smaller dishes ensuite, 12in. high. (Christie's) **£1,870**

Sheffield plated combination épergne candelabrum, unmarked, second quarter 19th century, supported by a shaped triangular plinth base, set on three scrolling feet, height 23in. (Butterfield & Butterfield) **£977**

A George III oval épergne, 1802, maker's mark IP, probably for Joseph Preedy, with cut glass bowl, 10in. high, 38oz. **£1,665**

A Victorian three-branch épergne, with acanthus leaf stem and three reed and foliage branches, by Robinson, Edkins and Aston, Birmingham, 1845, 15¹/₂in. high, 73oz. (Christie's) **£3,300**

A George III épergne, by Thos. Pitts, 1770, 51cm. high, 156oz. **£9,350**

Sheffield plate Regency épergne, unmarked, circa 1810–1820, supporting four oval glass dishes with scalloped borders and diapered sides, 12¹/₂in. high. (Butterfield & Butterfield) **£830**

A George III openwork épergne, by Francis Butty and Nicholas Dumee, 1769, 19in. high, 117oz. **£6,655**

A George III épergne and mirror plateau, the epergne on four fluted and foliage columns with lions' paw feet, by Matthew Boulton and Plate Company, Birmingham, 1810, the epergne 10½ in. high. weight of epergne 95oz.
(Christie's) £11,000

A Victorian four-branch épergne, the four scroll branches each terminating in a detachable circular dish and with similar larger central dish, by Walter and John Barnard, 1894, 8in. high, 75oz.
(Christie's) £3,300

A gilt Old Sheffield plate épergne with large central glass dish and four smaller dishes on mirror plateau, by Roberts, Cadman & Co., circa 1822, 13½in. high, 24in. wide.
£2,258

A George III six-branch épergne, with pierced circular frame hung with berried husk swags, by James Young, 1782, 16½in., 70oz.
(Christie's) £6,670

A George III épergne, 19in. overall length, on four leaf-chased scroll supports with pierced scroll feet, London, 1766, by John King, 86oz.
(Bonhams) £6,200

Victorian silver three branch épergne with leaded glass liners by John Harrison & Co., Ltd., Sheffield, 1870, 21in. high, 123oz. 12 dwts.
(Butterfield & Butterfield) £4,097

Victorian Sterling reproduction of a George III épergne by Thomas Bradbury, London, 1897, on four foliate scroll feet, 14in. high, 112oz. 10dwts.
(Butterfield & Butterfield) £5,189

Sorley silver épergne, Glasgow, central vase with four curved arms and attached collar suspending trumpet-shaped vases, 14in. high.
(Skinner) £141

An antique English Sheffield George III style plated silver épergne with five lead crystal liners, 14in. high.
(Selkirk's) £1,067

These were large jugs to carry water for mealtime ablutions, and were essential items of tableware in the later Middle Ages and 16th century. The most popular type was vase-shaped and had a grotesque handle. They were often matched with basins, but many of these have now disappeared. 16th and 17th century Spanish examples were rather smaller, and were mounted on short feet. Later they, and their French counterparts, became more helmet shaped. In the 17th century ewers would be profusely decorated with embossing and chasing. in the form of foliage and masks, or with cast relief ornament and fluting.

Ewers went out of use for their original purpose after the 17th century when eating with forks became widespread and thereafter were made mainly for ceremonial use.

Most of those found today will, however, date from the 18th and 19th centuries, when many fine examples were made as water jugs.

A presentation ewer, by Baldwin Gardiner, N.Y., circa 1835, 13½in. high, 45oz. 10dwt. £740

A George II oval shaving ewer by John Delmester, London, 1759, 8¼in. high, 19oz.11dwt. all in. £2,060

A Victorian plated lidded baluster ewer, with cast boar's head terminal, and domed hinged cover with cast rampant horse finial, 1885, 14¼in. (Christie's S. Ken) £1,078

A Danish oval ewer, with fluted knop and harp-shaped handle, the fluted body of shaped outline, by Silvert Thorsteinsson, Copenhagen, 1786, 9½in. high, 612grs. (Christie's) £1,650

An Italian fluted baluster ewer on a shaped circular domed foot, applied with a cast double scroll handle, Venice or Padua, 7¼in., 13.25oz. (Christie's S. Ken) £1,100

A Continental tapering circular ewer on a rising foot, and with an elaborate scroll handle, probably Spanish or South American, mid to late 19th century, 9¾in., 47.25oz. (Christie's) £1,925

A silver ewer by Edwin Stebbins & Company, New York, 1850-1856, with a scroll handle cast in the form of a branch, 15in. high, 30oz. £945

EWERS

A helmet-shaped ewer by Johann Breckerfelt, 21.9cm. high, maker's mark, Wesel, 1723-24, 620gr. £3,390

Italian silver ewer, 20th century, helmet form with relief vine design, 9¼in. high, approximately 16 troy oz. (Skinner) £597

A pyriform ewer with a flaring fluted neck, by Conrad Bard & Son, Phila., 1850-59, 29oz.10dwt. £1,210

A Spanish plain cylindrical ewer, the spout cast with a bearded mask, scrolls and foliage, 17th century, marked only *REISS*, 7¾in. high, 825grs. (Christie's) £11,000

A pair of silver presentation ewers, maker's mark of Forbes & Son, New York, circa 1836, with elaborate foliate scroll handles, 11¾in. high, 78 oz. (Christie's) £3,696

A Victorian parcel-gilt ewer, the vase-shaped body repoussé and chased with putti, hops and acanthus foliage, by Elkington & Co., Birmingham, 1864, in fitted wood case, 12in. high, 51oz. (Christie's) £3,960

Silver presentation ewer, maker's mark Shreve, Brown & Co., coin on base, 10½in. high, approx. 29 troy oz., circa 1857. £10,230

A small ewer, designed by J. Rohde, stamped marks JR Georg Jensen GJ 295 432A, circa 1928, 22.7cm. high, 17oz. £1,150

Silver ewer, Robert and William Wilson (active 1825–1846), Philadelphia, baluster form with foliate and acanthus decoration, 45 troy oz. (Skinner Inc.) £759

One of a pair of late 18th century Portuguese ewers, maker's mark G.I.P., 58oz. 14dwt., 10¼in. high. £6,290

A Queen Anne style ewer with caryatid handle, London, 1926, 8¾in. high, 20.25oz. £660

A vase-shaped silver ewer, by Thos. Fletcher, Phila., circa 1838, 13¼in. high, 39oz. £1,015

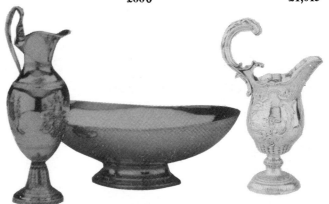

An impressive Victorian ewer, 14½in. high, with loop handle and domed hinged cover, London, 1871, by Stephen Smith, 27oz.
(Bonhams) £660

A silver gilt ewer and basin, by Johann Alois Seethaler, Augsburg, 1799, the ovoid jug applied with lyre and mythological ornament, total weight 2080gr.
(Finarte) £7,710

George II silver ewer, Philip Gardner, London, 1756, circular domed base with knopped stem supporting body with swelling belly, applied flying C-scroll handle, 14in. high, 41oz. 14dwt.
(Butterfield & Butterfield) £2,626

A helmet-shaped ewer in the style of the early 18th century, maker's mark T.C., 21.5cm. high, 22oz. £1,270

One of a pair of inverted, pyriform ewers, by F. Marquand, New York, 1826-39, 14½in. high, 38oz. 10dwt. £2,130

A silver vase shaped ewer, by Jones, Ball & Poor, Boston, circa 1846, 16¼in. high, 41oz. £835

A late 16th century Spanish tapering cylindrical ewer, 6¼in. high, 22oz. £4,990

One of a pair of baroque-style silver gilt ewers, London, circa 1900, C. & S. Co. Ltd., 13⅞in. high, 148 troy oz. £3,300

Silver ewer, Crosby, Morse & Foss, Boston, circa 1850, 14in. high, approximately 32 troy oz. (Skinner Inc.) £380

A Victorian Cellini pattern hot water ewer, 30cm. high, Stephen Smith, London 1880, 28.5oz. (Bearne's) £800

Pair of large vase-shaped ewers, by Messrs. Carrington, 1905 and 1906, height without plinth 17½in., 231oz. £11,880

An American silver ewer, Bailey & Co., Philadelphia, circa 1850, chased with chinoiserie buildings, a boat and birds, 64oz. 10dwt., height 19in. (Sotheby's) £3,783

A George II helmet shaped ewer, by David Willaume II, 1742, 10½in. high, 53oz. £49,895

A Victorian 'Cellini' pattern ewer, Charles Boyton, London, 1884, 11½in. high, 32oz.3dwt. £1,090

A large covered ewer, bearing spurious marks for Charles-Cesar Haudry, Paris, 1745, 11in. high, 55oz. £520

WINE

A Victorian plain vase-shaped wine ewer on spreading circular foot, by Thomas Rait & Sons, Glasgow, 1889, 13¹/₂in. high, 27oz.
(Christie's)   £575

A Victorian baluster wine ewer, by Elkington & Co., Ltd., Birmingham, 1893, 12¼in. high, 54oz.   £1,695

A George III wine ewer, 12¹/₂in. high, with beaded borders and leaf mounted wooden scroll handle, London, 1773, by Daniel Smith and Robert Sharp, 30 oz.
(Bonhams)   £2,000

A Victorian wine ewer, 12in. high, with scrolling borders and leaf-chased scrolling side handle on domed, circular base, London, 1856, by William Hattersley or William Hewit, 26.5oz. (Bonhams)   £850

A very attractive Victorian Aesthetic Movement wine ewer and two goblets en suite, in the Japanese style with cranes chasing butterflies amidst foliage and bamboo, by E.C. Brown, 1875, goblets 16.5cm. high, ewer, 29.5cm. high, 26.5 ozs.
(Phillips)   £1,550

A Cellini pattern vase-shaped wine ewer, after a model by Louis Briot, richly chased in the Renaissance manner with masks flora and fauna, by Mappin and Webb, 1903, 30oz., 30cm. high.
(Christie's)   £924

An American ovoid wine ewer, the body chased over-all in the Chinese style, by S. Kirk, Baltimore, circa 1830, 16¼in. high, 48oz.
                                      £2,060

A mid Victorian wine ewer and matching pair of goblets, the high curved lip with applied bacchanalian mask, London 1874, mark F.E., 1464 grammes total.
(Spencer's)   £2,000

A George III plain baluster wine ewer, the domed cover with flame finial and scroll handle, engraved with a crest, by Jacob Marsh, 1773, 11¹/₂in. high, 30oz.
(Christie's)   £660

An early Victorian fiddle pattern fish slice, with fish and seaweed pierced and engraved blade, London 1843, maker's mark *RW*, 164 grammes. (Spencer's) £100

An unusual Victorian fish slice and fork, modelled as a garden spade and fork, with ivory handles. (Christie's S. Ken) £330

A pair of engraved fish servers by Albert Coles, New York, circa 1850-1855, the slice with a scrolled blade elaborately engraved with scrolls and foliage, 12in. long, 8oz. (Christie's) £346

A pair of parcel-gilt silver fish servers, maker's mark of Gorham Mfg. Co., circa 1880, the ivory handles carved with swirling flutes, 12in. long. (Christie's) £739

A rare early period fish slice with a feather edge stem and a shaped oval blade, engraved with a fish and pierced with floral scrollwork, 33cm. long, circa 1780. (Phillips) £160

A silver fish slice, maker's mark of James Conning, Mobile, Alabama, 1842–1862, engraved with a fish amid foliate scroll decoration, 11³/₄in. long, 5 oz. (Christie's) £986

An attractive pair of early George V fish servers, with foliate pierced and engraved blade and tine, ivory handles with fluted silver pistol grips, Sheffield 1911. (Spencer's) £170

A good and attractive pair of late Victorian fish servers, the silver elliptical shaped blades centrally engraved with a fishing rod, net, creel and fish, Sheffield 1877, maker's mark *HA*. (Spencer's) £340

A silver fish slice with a faceted handle, by Hayden & Gregg, South Carolina, 1846/52, 12in. long, 6oz.10dwt. £540

A parcel gilt fish slice and fork, American, circa 1885, each engraved with two intertwined carp, 11½in. long, 8oz. (Christie's New York) £380

A Victorian pair of cast fish carvers, the heavy handles modelled as a stylised full length fish, assay marks for 1872, 1855, and the maker's mark HH for Hyam Hyams, 23oz. (Phillips) £800

A Dutch fish slice, pierced and engraved with flowers, foliage and trelliswork, the shaped handle with flower and foliage top, by Barend Swierink, Amsterdam, 1778, 15¹/₄in. long, 214 grs. (Christie's) £1,760

FLAGONS

Flagons, large vessels for serving wine, were popular in Europe from the 16th century. Silver or silver gilt examples were mainly for ceremonial use then, and after the Reformation they were used for Communion wine, often being made in pairs. Pear-shaped and cylindrical bodies existed contemporaneously in most periods. Except for ecclesiastical or ceremonial use flagons are rare after the mid-eighteenth century.

A large Victorian plated flagon, with embossed decoration. £570

Epping Forest Centenary flagon of tapering cylinder shape, London 1978, 41oz. £255

A Sir Edmund Berry Godfrey flagon, maker's mark IN mullet below, 1675, with short moulded lip added, circa 1720, 12³/₈in. high, 66oz. £47,520

English Sheffield silver plated covered flagon, 18th century, inscribed on base, *Green Dragon Tavern, 1760, Boston*, 10in. high. (Eldred's) £176

A George III plain cylindrical flagon, with scroll handle, corkscrew thumbpiece and hinged domed cover, by Thomas Whipham and Charles Wright, 1765, 12in. high, 42 oz. (Christie's) £2,200

A George I flagon, maker's mark of Richard Bayley overstriking another, 1717, 29.5cm. high, 40.5oz. £1,500

A German large tapering flagon, by Korner & Proll, Berlin, late 19th century, 15¼in. high, 3330gr. £3,500

A New York Yacht Club Trophy flagon, by Whiting Manuf. Co., circa 1892, 10in. high, 35oz.10dwt. £640

FLASKS

These are narrow-necked vessels usually for storing liquids particularly for use when travelling. They have remained popular to the present day under their modern appellation, hip flask, and are often used for presentation purposes.

As such they can range from the purely functional to the highly ornamental, extensively chased and ornamented.

A Chinese Export spirit flask, the body applied with a China-man playing a stringed instru-ment below an oak branch, silver coloured metal, 16.4cm. (Lawrence Fine Arts)   £165

An early George V silver pear shaped scent flask by Albert Edward Jones, Birmingham 1910, 9cm. high. (Spencer's)   £75

A curved shaped oblong silver spirit flask with detachable gilt lined cup and cover, by Omar Ramsden, 1924, 6½in. high, 18oz.   £1,310

A set of three Tiffany & Co. spirit flasks, the flattened rectangular bodies with screwed hinged covers, 20.6cm. high.   £1,575

An amusing flask, by Tiffany & Co., New York, 1891-1902 decorated with etched scenes of brownies frolicking and quarrelling and avoiding mos-quitoes, marked, 7¾in. high, 15oz. (Christie's New York)   £5,188

A baroque oval flask by Johan Daniel Planitz, 9.5cm. high, 110gr. (Herholdt Jensen)   £642

A silver flask by Whiting Manu-facturing Company, circa 1885, the front repousse and chased with a seahorse, 6in. long, 7½oz.   £1,689

A silver presentation flask by Gorham Mfg. Co., 1888, 7¾in. high, 19oz.10dwt.   £1,210

18TH CENTURY

This is the term used generically to describe table cutlery, knives, forks and spoons, and could fill a book in itself. Spoons in particular attract many collectors. Until the mid-17th century the spoon was wide-bowled with a straight stem ending in a solid knop, which could be shaped as an acorn, a diamond point pyramid or twisted or wrythen. In the 15th and 16th centuries apostle figures were popular as were the wildman or wodewose. Seal tops date often from the Elizabethan or early Stuart periods.

The first change in the knop style is the slipped-in-the-stalk stem, widening slightly and thickening towards the end, which then developed into the stump-end hexagonal stem, tapering sharply at the end, and the Puritan stem of 1660, widening at the end and cut straight across. The bowl by now was egg-shaped.

After the 1660s the stem assumed a curve from the lobed trifid end to the stem bowl junction, now strengthened with a V-shaped tongue which became known as a rat tail. By the 1700s the upcurved end, a plain semicircle, was given a tapering central ridge.

In the 1750s the main change was from the S-shaped stem to the single curve stem and decoration, such as feather edging, began to intrude down the front of the stem. Bright-cutting dates from the 1780s.

Forks appear in most countries from the later Middle Ages, but do not appear to have been used for eating meat. A folding version was often used in conjunction with a spoon.

A set of twelve Queen Anne dognose pattern table spoons, the reverse of the handles each engraved with a monogram, RSC, by Isaac Davenport, 1703, 24oz. £2,860

A large part service of George III Old English and thread pattern cutlery, by various silversmiths, circa 1780, 139oz. £3,025

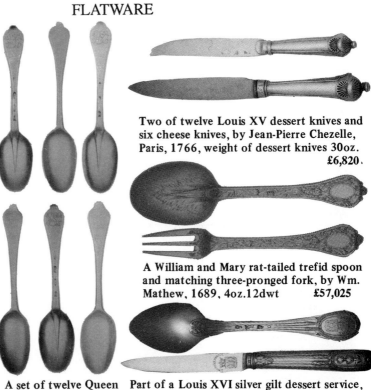

Two of twelve Louis XV dessert knives and six cheese knives, by Jean-Pierre Chezelle, Paris, 1766, weight of dessert knives 30oz. £6,820.

A William and Mary rat-tailed trefid spoon and matching three-pronged fork, by Wm. Mathew, 1689, 4oz.12dwt £57,025

Part of a Louis XVI silver gilt dessert service, the twelve dessert spoons and twelve dessert forks by J.-E. Langlois, Paris, 1782, the twelve dessert knives, Paris, 1779, 36 pieces. £13,640

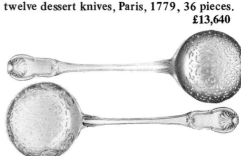

A Louis XV sugar sifter, Paris, 1744-50 and a silver gilt example, Paris, 1738-44, 8¼in. and 8 ⁵/₈in.long, 7oz. £725

Part of a Louis XV silver gilt dessert service, fiddle, thread and shell pattern, 70oz., 36 pieces. £5,965

18TH CENTURY

Forks for meat eating seem to have originated in 16th century Italy. The earliest forks were two-pronged, with three-pronged examples coming in only in the early 18th century, and these in turn were superseded by a four-prong version in the 1750s, after which they remain standard. Style and decoration follow spoon patterns throughout.

Silver-handled knives occur in all periods from the late 17th century onwards. From 1690 the handle is round or polygonal, followed by the pistol handle which became more highly decorated during the 18th century. Later, handles of thin, stamped sheet metal filled with resin became common and were made en suite with the main table service from about 1800.

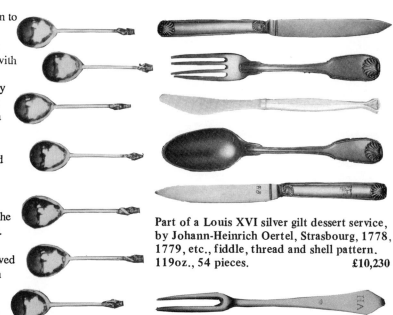

Part of a Louis XVI silver gilt dessert service, by Johann-Heinrich Oertel, Strasbourg, 1778, 1779, etc., fiddle, thread and shell pattern. 119oz., 54 pieces. £10,230

A set of seven James I silver apostle spoons by Daniel Carey, including one probably for a left-handed user.
(Academy Auctioneers) £1,500

An extremely rare American silver two prong dognose fork, John Noyes, Boston, circa 1700-1710, the terminal engraved with initials HA, 1oz. 8dwts, 7¾in. long. (Sotheby's) £15,586

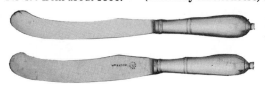

Two of a set of twelve Queen Anne cannon handled table knives, each engraved with a crest, two handles struck with indistinct maker's mark only, early 18th century.
(Christie's) (Twelve) £4,180

Two of a set of twelve William III dog-nose pattern table forks, each with three prongs and engraved with a coat-of-arms, by Isaac Davenport, 1701, 21oz.
(Christie's) (Twelve) £5,500

Part of a Louis XVI silver gilt dessert service, by Jean-Louis Kirstein, Strasbourg, 1778, 98oz., 54 pieces. £11,930

Part of a German silver gilt dessert service, by Phillip Jacob Jager I, Augsburg, 1732-33, 146oz., 66 pieces. £15,340

18TH CENTURY

Part of a set of twelve Louis XV silver gilt teaspoons, by Claude-Pierre Deville, Paris, 1769 and 1773, 13oz. **£8,095**

Part of a Louis XV silver gilt dessert service, Strasbourg, 1770 and 1771, thread and shell pattern, 78oz., 52 pieces. **£14,490**

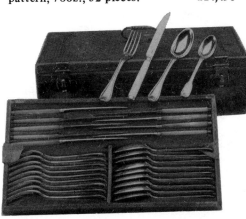

Part of a set of twenty-seven Louis XV table-spoons and twenty-seven table forks, by Nicolas Collier, Paris, 1768, fiddle, thread and shell pattern, 156oz. **£5,965**

A 72 piece canteen of cutlery by Johann Jakob Kirstein, Strasbourg 1785–93, the knives with mother of pearl handles, in original case. (Auktionsverket) **£15,050**

Part of a Louis XVI silver gilt dessert service, by Jean-Etienne Langlois, Paris, 1786, with the charge and discharge of Henri Clavel, 70 pieces, 130oz. **£5,965**

Part of a Louis XV silver gilt dessert service, by Edme-Pierre Balzac, Paris, 1768/69, with reeded fiddle pattern, together with a silver table fork, circa 1777, 69oz., 37 pieces. **£8,525**

Part of a Louis XV agate-handled dessert service, by Eloy Guerin, Paris, 1740, 24 pieces. **£11,930**

Part of a French silver gilt dessert service, by Francois-Daniel Imlin, Strasbourg, Warden's mark a five, for 1785 or 1796, fiddle and thread pattern, 37 pieces, 115oz. **£7,670**

A set of four George II silver-gilt dessert spoons, with shell-back bowls, the handles with shell terminals, each engraved with the royal cypher, garter motto and monogram, by Paul de Lamerie, circa 1730, 7oz.
(Christie's) **£3,960**

Part of a set of twelve George II fiddle and shell pattern dessert forks and six matching dessert spoons, by Paul de Lamerie, circa 1740, 27oz. **£15,730**

Part of a Louis XV silver gilt dessert service, by the Widow of Jean-Frederic Fritz, Strasbourg, 1773, one spoon and two knives Vienna, 1790, 150oz., 54 pieces. **£6,390**

Part of a set of eighteen Louis XV silver gilt dessert spoons and eighteen dessert forks, by Johann Heinrich Oertel, Strasbourg, circa 1773, 75oz. **£7,670**

19TH CENTURY

Empire silver gilt flatware service, Paris, early
19th century, maker *JPD* in lozenge, twelve
each: tablespoons and dinner forks, knives with
silver-gilt and steel blades, all mother-of-pearl
handles, 44 troy oz.
(Skinner Inc.) £1,306

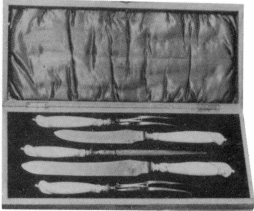

Five piece Victorian carving set, the bone
handles richly decorated with plated mounts, in
original oak box.
(G. A. Key) £130

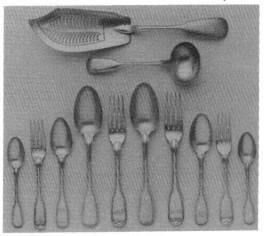

A fiddle and thread-table service, the majority
by William Eaton, 1826, 1834, 1837, etc.,
comprising 63 pieces, 131oz.
(Christie's) £4,180

A late Victorian fish service, comprising twelve
pairs of fish knives and forks with foliate
engraved blades and tines.
(Spencer's) £380

An American silver flatware set, Tiffany & Co.,
New York, circa 1890, chrysanthemum pattern,
196oz. 10dwt. weighable, 176 pieces.
(Sotheby's) £10,441

A set of thread edge Old English pattern cutlery,
makers Thomas Alfred & Walter Brinsley
Slater, London 1895/96, 85oz., sixty pieces.
(Woolley & Wallis) £1,500

19TH CENTURY

A serving fork and spoon, by Gorham Manuf.
Co., circa 1870, 11in. long, 6oz.10dwt.
£540

A French silver gilt dessert service, the
spoons and forks circa 1815, the knives
circa 1830, 2150gr. **£495**

Part of a German silver gilt dessert service, by
Abraham Warnberger IV, Augsburg, 1781-89,
eleven pieces by C.-H. Constant, Berlin, 1788-
1802, 36 pieces, 29oz.10dwt. **£2,555**

A pair of William IV cast naturalistic sugar
nips, oak bough decorated, William Theobalds,
London 1834.
(Woolley & Wallis) **£130**

An American silver wine syphon, Baldwin
Gardiner, Philadelphia or New York, circa
1820–30, of typical hooped form, 6oz. 10dwt.
gross, length 15in.
(Sotheby's) **£757**

Part of a set of seventeen silver gilt dessert-
spoons and seventeen dessert forks, all with
Belgian surcharge mark of 1814-1832, 61oz.
£2,130

A mid Victorian silver travelling apple corer,
the hollow handle of slightly tapering
cylindrical form with screw on corer,
Birmingham 1854, by John Tongue, 31
grammes.
(Spencer's) **£200**

A giant pair of silver-mounted carved ivory and
steel carvers, the mounts T. Rodgers, Sheffield,
1827, the ivory handles carved with busts of
George Washington, the American Eagle and
Seal, length of knife 37¹/₄in.
(Sotheby's) **£9,836**

An early Victorian Stilton scoop by Martin
Hall and Co., the silver cased handle stamped
with strapwork and beading, Sheffield 1854.
(Spencer's) **£300**

A George IV meat skewer, 11¹/₄in. long,
bevelled blade and pierced loop terminal,
London, 1825, 3 oz.
(Bonhams) **£120**

A pair of grape shears, by Tiffany & Co., circa
1880-85, of shaped scissor-form, 8in. long,
5oz. (Christie's) **£3,145**

A set of six teaspoons, maker's mark of Joseph
Lownes, Phila., circa 1785-1815, each with a
pointed oval bowl, 6¹/₈in. long, 3oz. **£685**

19TH CENTURY

Kirk Sterling flatware service, 1880-90, repoussé pattern, 104 pieces, monogrammed, approximately 93 troy oz. weighable silver. (Skinner Inc.) £899

Part of a 146-piece flatware service, by Tiffany & Co., New York, 1878-1900, in the original fitted oak box, 230oz. excluding knives. (Christie's) £5,660

A composite silver-gilt fiddle, thread and shell pattern dessert service, 1802, 1896 and modern, comprising, twenty-four dessert-spoons, dessert-forks and dessert-knives, weight without knives 88oz.. (Christie's) (Seventy-two) £2,750

Part of a 138-piece Elizabethan pattern composite table service, 1846, 1864, 1883 etc., some modern, weight without table and cheese knives 250oz. £6,655

Part of a silver gilt composite Kings pattern table service, 1815, 1819, etc. and modern, in fitted canteen with nine drawers, 377oz. £14,255

Part of an assembled flatware service, King's pattern, by R. & W. Wilson, Philadelphia, 1825-46, 175oz. excluding knives. £2,370

19TH CENTURY

Part of a composite silver gilt dessert service, the majority by C.-S. Mahler, Paris, 1824-38, the rest by P.-F. Queille, post 1838, the fruit knives by A. Touron, 1819-38, 49 pieces.

£3,750

Part of a 140-piece mixed metal flatware service, by Tiffany & Co., 1880–85, dinner fork, 8¹⁄₈in. long, ladle 13in. long, 201oz.10dwt., excluding knives. (Christie's)

£62,893

A 19th century canteen dinner service, flatware by Henin et Vivier, dishes by Puiforcat, Paris, circa 1870, weighable silver 341.5oz., 156 pieces.

£5,280

A set of six bright cut decorated taper end teaspoons, initialled by Edward Livingstone, Dundee, circa 1800, 2.5oz. **£165**

Five of twelve George III stag-hunt pattern table forks, by Paul Storr, 1816, 43oz.

£1,070

A William IV fiddle, thread and shell table service, by Samuel Hayne and Dudley Cater, 1836, 248oz. **£11,880**

Kirk Sterling flatware service, 1880-90, repoussé pattern, 104 pieces, monogrammed, approximately 93 troy oz. weighable silver. (Skinner Inc.) £772

A set of twelve pairs of Victorian silver gilt dessert knives and forks, the Continental porcelain handles painted with various exotic birds, George Adams, London, 1868. (Christie's S. Ken) £1,100

A part double-struck fiddle thread and shell pattern table service by Paul Storr, 1818, engraved with a crest, comprising: ten table forks, six table spoons (one 1815), seven dessert spoons, 61oz. (Christie's) £1,210

Three of seven parcel gilt condiment servers, by Tiffany & Co., circa 1880-85, serving spoon 9½in. long, sauce ladles each approx. 7in. long, 13oz. £5,000

Baltimore sterling rose pattern flatware service of 161 pieces, approximately 174 troy oz. weighable silver. (Skinner Inc.) £2,000

Part of a 24-piece set of parcel gilt dessert knives and forks, by Tiffany & Co., circa 1880-85, knives 8¼in. long, 48oz.10dwt. (Christie's) £4,000

20TH CENTURY

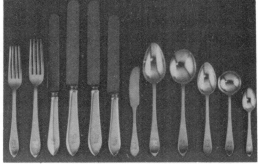

Georg Jensen sterling partial flatware service, cactus pattern, approximately 149 troy oz., 120 pieces.
(Skinner Inc.)   **£3,399**

An American silver flatware set, Tiffany & Co., New York, 20th century, Faneuil pattern, monogrammed, 151oz. excluding knives, 124 pieces.
(Sotheby's)   **£2,345**

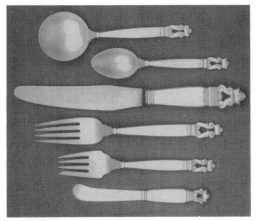

A set of King's pattern fish knives and forks having plated blades and embossed handles, also a matching pair of fish servers, Sheffield, 1928.   **£85**

Georg Jensen Sterling flatware service, Acorn pattern, twelve each: dinner forks, salad forks, soup spoons, dinner knives, butter knives, twenty four teaspoons, pair of salad servers, cake server, sauce ladle, two piece carving set, 107 troy oz.
(Skinner Inc.)   **£2,821**

A. D. W. Hislop set of four silver spoons and forks designed by Charles Rennie Mackintosh, stamped with maker's marks and Glasgow hallmarks for 1902. (Christie's London) **£22,000**

An oak canteen of cutlery, London 1929, viz: 24 table forks, 24 dessert forks, 24 dessert spoons, 18 table spoons, 2 sauce ladles, 11 teaspoons.
(Russell Baldwin & Bright)   **£2,700**

20TH CENTURY

Part of a Georg Jensen 36-piece 'Acorn'
pattern table service, designed by Johan Rohde.
(Christie's) £1,870

A Georg Jensen 64-piece 'chess pattern'
table service stamped Georg Jensen, Sterling,
Denmark, 50oz.12dwt. weight not including
knives. £2,020

Part of a Georg Jensen 75-piece 'Pyramid'
pattern table service, designed by Harald
Nielsen, 1926, stamped marks, 132oz.6dwt.
gross weight. (Christie's) £6,060

An 89-piece 'Cactus' pattern table service,
designed by Gundorph Albertus, stamped
marks, 102oz., weight not including items
that are part steel. £2,970

A 106-piece 'Cypress' pattern table service
designed by Tias Eckhoff, 112oz.2dwt.,
weight not including items that are part
steel. £2,735

20TH CENTURY

A Georg Jensen 180-piece 'Acorn' pattern table service, first designed in 1915 by Johan Rohde, 181oz. weight not including knives. **£22,570**

A Viners Studio fifty-one-piece stainless steel flatware service designed by Professor Gerald Benney, the handles with textured surface decoration.
(Christie's) **£374**

A 134-piece 'Pyramid' pattern table service designed by Harald Nielson, stamped marks, 181oz.5dwt., weight not including items that are part steel. **£7,128**

A Guild of Handicraft sixteen piece silver fruit service, comprising eight forks and eight knives, chrysoprase chamfered handles, with London hallmarks for 1905, in fitted case.
(Christie's) **£1,540**

Part of a service of fruiting vine design, also a pair of pierced and engraved fish carvers with bone handles, 1906, weighable silver 22oz., 68 pieces. **£1,210**

An E. Bingham & Co. 42-piece electroplated table service, designed by Charles Rennie Mackintosh, with flat trefoil finials, the knives with black bakelite handles and steel blades.
(Christie's) **£7,700**

LADLES

A George III Old English pattern soup ladle, by Hester Bateman, 1775, 4.7oz. £315

A George III Onslow pattern soup ladle, the cast terminal inscribed on the reverse with initials, maker Thomas Evans, London 1772, 4.5 oz. (Woolley & Wallis) £380

Silver ladle, Benjamin Burt, Boston, circa 1780, with tapered ivory tipped wooden handle, 14¾in. long. (Skinner Inc.) £428

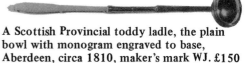

A Scottish Provincial toddy ladle, the plain bowl with monogram engraved to base, Aberdeen, circa 1810, maker's mark WJ. £150

A 19th century Russian enamelled silver ladle 8½in. long overall, maker's mark 84 standard mark, St. Petersburg, 95gms. (Bearne's) £500

A soup ladle with a circular bowl, by James Kendall, Delaware, 1795-1808, 11¾in. long, 5oz.10dwt. £635

A rare punch ladle, attributed to John Hastier, New York, 1725-1750, the circular bowl with a heart shaped join and an everted rim, marked (minor repair at handle join), 13½in. long. 3oz. (Christie's New York) £1,176

A silver ladle, maker's mark of Joseph Anthony, Philadelphia, 1785–1810, with downturned rounded-end handle, 10in. long, 3 oz. (Christie's) £739

A soup ladle, wave edge pattern, with a spirally-fluted oval bowl, by Tiffany & Co., N.Y., 1884-91, 10¾in. long, 5oz.10dwt. £320

A soup ladle, Persian pattern, by Tiffany & Co., N.Y., 1872–circa 1875, 12¾in. long, overall, 7oz.10dwt. £295

A rare George II soup ladle, the reverse of the deep circular bowl partly-fluted and with shaped handle terminating in a rococo shell, scroll and husk cartouche, by Paul Crespin, 1742, 15in. long, 16oz. (Christie's) £10,925

An Irish Provincial large soup ladle of Old English pattern, maker's mark *L.R.*, Cork, circa 1760, length 16in., 7.5oz. (Christie's) £747

An American silver soup ladle, Christian Wiltberger, Philadelphia, circa 1790, pointed end with wrigglework borders, 5oz. 10dwt., length 14½in. (Sotheby's) £605

A rare silver soup ladle, maker's mark of William & George Richardson, Richmond, Virginia, circa 1782–1795, with a downturned pointed-oval handle, 12¼in. high, 4 oz. 10 dwt. (Christie's) £1,047

SPOONS

A George III Old English feather edge pattern gravy spoon, by Wm. Fearn, 1775, 4.3oz. £255

A George IV hour glass pattern gravy spoon, by Wm. Eley and Wm. Fearn, 1823, 6.2oz. £110

A late Charles II trefid end rat tail pattern spoon, engraved *VH*, London 1680, maker's mark *IB* in shield, 51gr., 18.5cm. long. (Spencer's) £220

A Buddha knop spoon, English, the bowl back pricked with initials and the date 1638, 1oz.10dwt. £665

A Guild of Handicraft silver jam spoon, designed by C.R. Ashbee, set with abalone, with London hallmarks for 1906, 45 grams. gross. (Christie's) £198

A Dutch spoon with curved stem of diamond section and hoof finial, by E. Loesinck, Groningen 1656, together with another. £1,010

A 17th century trefid spoon, the stem of circular form, flattened and tapering to the terminal, 17cm. long. £485

An early 18th century dog nose or wavy end spoon with elongated rat tail bowl, engraved with initials, marker's mark *IH*, 59gr. (Spencer's) £200

A Guild of Handicraft silver jam spoon, designed by C. R. Ashbee, set with turquoise, engraved *Lorna*, 1904, 50 grams gross. (Christie's) £165

One of a pair of jam spoons designed by Georg Jensen, the hammered and cut bowls in the form of a leaf with curving handles. £235

A Henry VII apostle spoon, surmounted by the gilt figure of St. John, with rayed nimbus, 1508, maker's mark illegible. (Christie's) £4,620

A spoon with rat-tail bowl and embossed scroll work, the terminal with shell and scroll decoration and initials RC, circa 1700, 19.5cm. (Lawrence Fine Art) £418

An attractive Russian plique à jour sifter spoon, the circular bowl centred by a flowerhead, with wire work stem and triple flower finial, 15cm. long. (Spencer's) £280

A Charles II lace back trefid, punched in the bowl and punched twice on the stem with the letters TD and the T & Tun mark for Taunton, by T. Dare, Junior, circa 1680. (Phillips London) £1,100

SPOONS

A Guild of Handicraft Ltd. silver preserve spoon, stamped G. of H. Ltd. and London hallmarks for 1902. (Christie's)   £310

A Child & Child silver and shell spoon, the bowl formed by a thin scallop shell having subtle nacreous sheen, 26cm. long, 1903. (Phillips)   £320

A Royal silver serving spoon, Paris, circa 1815-20, 11in. long, 5 troy oz   £305

A George III Hanoverian pattern basting spoon, maker James Gilsland, Edinburgh 1771, 6oz.   £300

A Charles I seal top, of good gauge, with the initials RW for Robert Wade, Senior, circa 1640. (Phillips London)   £600

A George III Old English pattern gravy spoon, 1790 by Hester Bateman, 3.5oz. (Lawrence)   £242

A pair of George III Irish basting spoons, 12¼in. long, Old English pattern with crests engraved to terminals, Dublin, 1795, maker's mark *L&B*, 6 oz. (Bonhams)   £260

A rare pair of large silver ragout spoons made for Moses Michael Hays, maker's mark of Paul Revere, Boston, 1786, 12in. long, 8oz. (Christie's)   £27,000

A George II Hanoverian pattern basting spoon, the terminal engraved with presentation initials. 1742 by James Wilks, 5.8oz. (Lawrence)   £605

A Queen Anne Dog Nose pattern gravy spoon, the terminal engraved with a monogram, Britannia Standard bottom marks indistinct, probably 1707 maker's mark WD, 4.8oz. (Lawrence)   £665

A rare Mary I maidenhead spoon, the cast female terminal gilt, the bowl fig-shaped, 15.5cm. long, maker's mark, crescent enclosing a mullet, London, 1557. (Phillips)   £1,800

An Elizabeth I seal-top spoon, with a gilt elongated baluster fluted terminal, pricked with initials *EW*, pear-shaped bowl, 16.5cm. long, by W. Cawdell, London, 1589. (Phillips)   £800

An important Henry VII apostle spoon, the gilt finial formed as the figure of St. James the Greater, with deep fig-shaped bowl, 1490, maker's mark a gothic L, 7¼in. long. (Christie's)   £36,700

A Charles II trefid end rat tail pattern spoon, with prick-worked initials *F* over *IM*, London 1672, possibly by Joseph Simson, 45gr., 19cm. long. (Spencer's)   £300

Small pictures were sometimes mounted in silver frames during the 17th and 18th century. More impressive are the large cartagloria designed to stand on altars and hold cards inscribed with prayers, which are often richly embossed with rococo scrollwork. Many of these frames have since been converted for mirrors.

Silver mirrors too date mainly from the 17th century and originally formed part of a toilet service. They are mainly made of wood, sometimes with no more than a few silver strips on the side, silver leaf corner pieces to hold the sides in place and the crest at the top. Later mirrors from the George I and II periods were often made in one piece, with a shaped top and no separate crest.

In the Victorian and Art Nouveau periods, silver frames once again became hugely popular for dressing table mirrors and picture frames, many being made by Liberty and WMF.

An Edward VII shaped square photograph frame, chased and pierced with figs amongst scrolls and foliate festoons, 10in. high, London 1902.
(Bearne's)   £400

A Victorian heart-shaped photograph frame, decorated with cherubs faces amongst scrolling flowers and foliage, 7¹/₂in. high, William Comyns, London 1897.
(Bearne's)   £300

A silver repousse picture frame, shaped rectangular form, decorated in relief with flowers and insects, Birmingham hallmarks for 1907, 29.5cm. high. (Christie's London)   £715

A Liberty and Co. silver photograph frame, the top and base decorated with band of mistletoe, stamped maker's mark *L & Co.* and Birmingham hallmarks for 1892, 21.3cm. high. (Christie's)   £880

An Art Nouveau silver photograph frame, the shaped square frame with floral repoussé decoration, one corner with drape motif, Birmingham hallmarks for 1904, 15.8cm. high.
(Christie's)   £1,100

A William Hutton & Sons silver and enamel photograph frame, with applied decoration of stylised honesty on a panel of blue and green enamel, 1903, 30.5cm. high, 520 grams gross.
(Christie's)   £1,650

A William Hutton & Sons silver and enamelled picture frame, the top having interwoven tendrils picked out in green and violet enamels, 20.5cm. high.
(Phillips London)   £2,700

An Edward VII photograph frame in the Art Nouveau style, Birmingham 1902, 21cm. high. **£297**

Late 19th century Faberge heart-shaped silver and enamel frame, Moscow, 6.2cm. high. **£1,190**

A Wm. Hutton & Sons Arts & Crafts silver picture frame, London hallmarks for 1903, 20cm. high. **£1,575**

A William Hutton and Sons silver and enamel picture frame, with repoussé entrelac decoration, the top corners decorated with blue-green enamel, London hallmarks for 1903, 19.3cm. high. (Christie's) **£1,650**

A William Hutton & Sons silver picture frame, with pierced and repoussé stylised floral decoration with blue green enamel details, London hallmarks for 1904, 25.7cm. high, 330 grams gross. (Christie's) **£1,210**

An Art Nouveau shaped rectangular silver-mounted photograph frame, the mount stamped with flowers, foliage and a winged maiden, Birmingham 1907, 22cm. high. (Christie's) **£242**

One of a pair of silver coloured metal frames, each swivel mounted in angled open supports, 31cm. high, 1930's. **£220**

A William Hutton & Sons Art Nouveau silver and enamel photograph frame, decorated with stylised honesty and green and blue enamelling, 1904, 22.3cm. high. (Christie's) **£2,420**

An Art Nouveau silver shaped oval photograph frame with easel support, John and William Deakin, Birmingham 1904, 12in. high. (Christie's S. Ken) **£264**

FRAMES

A Liberty & Co. 'Cymric' silver and enamel frame, Birmingham, 1903, 23cm. high. £5,000

A late Victorian oblong photograph frame, by Wm. Comyns, London, 1904, 6¾in. high. £175

An Art Nouveau photograph frame, maker's marks W.N. and Chester hallmarks for 1903, 31cm. high. £2,060

A late Victorian shaped rectangular photograph frame, the body pierced with acorns and oak leaves and inlaid with tortoiseshell, H. A., London, 1894, 3¼in. (Christie's S. Ken) £880

A decorative Edwardian photograph frame, in the Art Nouveau style with ivy on a wood back, 1901, 24.8cm. high x 21.5cm. wide. (Phillips) £3,000

A silver and enanmel repoussé photograph frame, decorated in relief with stylised and green enamel flowers, Birmingham hallmarks for 1904, 21.5cm. high. (Christie's) £935

A William Hutton Art Nouveau silver frame, stamped in relief with entrelac medallions, Birmingham 1906, 18.5cm. high. (Christie's) £462

An Art Nouveau silver mounted photograph frame, by A. & J. Zimmerman, Birmingham, 1906, 28.8cm. high. £230

A Liberty silver and enamel picture frame, designed by Archibald Knox, with Birmingham hallmarks for 1904, 21.2cm. high. £4,275

An embossed and pierced shaped silver photograph frame, London, 1900, 8in. high **£200**

An Art Nouveau silver picture frame, 28cm. high, marked SB, Birmingham, 1903. **£290**

Late 19th century shaped silver photograph frame, 24.2cm. high. **£770**

An Edwardian Art Nouveau silver and enamel photograph frame, Wm. Hutton & Sons Ltd., London, 1904, 10.25in. high, also an Elkington & Co. vase, Birmingham, 1906. **£750**

A silver repoussé picture frame of shaped rectangular form, decorated in relief with a stylised foliate pattern, Chester hallmarks, 32.7cm. high. (Christie's) **£990**

A Liberty & Co. silver and enamelled picture frame, 19 x 14.50cm., with Art Nouveau hinged support, hallmarked L. & Co., Birmingham, 1899. **£2,035**

A late Victorian oblong photograph frame, Birmingham, 1895, 8½in. high. **£210**

An Art Nouveau silver picture frame, 35cm. high, marked WN and for Chester 1903. **£395**

A Ramsden & Carr silver picture frame, with London hallmarks for 1900, 15.5cm. high. **£1,045**

Silver goblets for individual rather than ceremonial use were made in large quantities between the late 16th and late 17th centuries. They come in various shapes of bowl and stem, such as a spherical or cylindrical bowl with a baluster or spool-shaped stem.

With regard to decoration, they could either be left plain or chased all over with foliage, grapes etc. Some examples with a bell-shaped bowl, usually plain but sometimes with semi-fluted, bright-cut or engraved ornament were produced in England from the mid 18th century.

A German silver gilt goblet, by Johann Cristoph Treffler, Augsburg, early 18th century 4½in. high, 3oz.5dwt. **£4,600**

A 17th century Flemish silver mounted glass goblet, unmarked, the bowl probably Liege, 8¼in. high. **£715**

Dutch silver goblet, Dordrecht, 17th century, chased with floral scrolls, 3¾in. high, approximately 3½ troy oz. (Skinner) **£240**

A pair of George III goblets and covers, the lower part of the bowl with applied acanthus leaves, the tapering covers with similarly chased acanthus leaves and with acorn finials, by D. Smith and R. Sharp, 1773, 9¼in. high, 32oz. (Christie's) **£4,400**

A Norwegian goblet, on octagonal foot and with cylindrical stem chased and engraved with scallop shells and stylised foliage, by Johannes Johannesen Reimers, Bergen, circa 1680, 4in. high. (Christie's) **£2,530**

A George III wine goblet, gilt interior, on a gadroon knopped and banded circular stem foot, 5in. maker Peter Gillois, London 1769, 5.5oz. (Wooley & Wallis) **£250**

A George III goblet, the ovoid body on a gadrooned trumpet shape pedestal foot, 1774 by Emick Romer, 15cm., 8.6oz. (Lawrence) **£330**

A George III goblet, engraved with a coat of arms, the circular foot with beaded border, by William Allen II, 1787, 15.5cm., 7.5oz. (Lawrence Fine Art) **£418**

18TH CENTURY

One of a pair of George III wine goblets, by Wm. Burch, London, 1791, 15.4cm. high, 15oz.6dwt. **£1,030**

William Grundy, a good pair of ovoid goblets, gilt lined with flared feet, 6¼in., London 1776, 17oz.
(Woolley & Wallis) **£1,100**

One of a pair of George III plain goblets, by John Wakelin and Wm. Taylor, 1779, 6in. high, 15oz. **£1,815**

Peter and Ann Bateman, a goblet, 6¼in. high, vase-form engraved with rosettes, husk swags and waved bands, London, 1796, 5.5oz.
(Bonhams) **£400**

A pair of George III goblets, each on a circular bead edge stem foot, 5.65in., one maker Charles Wright, London 1788, the other maker Stephen Adams, London 1808, 14oz.
(Woolley & Wallis) **£680**

A William III goblet, with cylindrical stem and tapering conical bowl, engraved with stylized strapwork, scrolls and foliage, by Robert Peake, 1701, 6¼in, 11oz.
(Christie's) **£2,200**

One of a pair of George III goblets, by R. Sharp, London, 1794, 6¼in. high, 17oz.17dwt. **£1,450**

A pair of George III gilt-lined goblets on beaded rising circular bases, Hester Bateman, London 1779, 6½in., 14.25oz.
(Christie's) **£825**

One of a rare set of five goblets, by J. Lownes, Phila., circa 1790-1820, 5½in. high, 38oz. **£13,720**

19TH CENTURY

A Victorian gilt-lined goblet on a rising circular foot and with a spherical knop, Messrs. Barnard, London 1887, 10¹/₂in., 22oz. (Christie's)   £385

A matched pair of Regency gilt-lined goblets on reeded rising hexagonal bases, I.B., London 1816 and T.R., London 1812, 6¹/₄in., 18oz. (Christie's S. Ken.)   £605

A Victorian gilt-lined and beaded goblet on a foliate, floral and thistle-chased rising circular foot, D. & C. Hands, London 1867, 7¹/₂in., 10.75 oz. (Christie's S. Ken)   £308

Sterling set of twelve chased water goblets, Heer-Schofield Co., Baltimore, Maryland, engraved with three letter script monogram within reserve, 6⁵/₈in. high, 76oz. 8dwt. (Butterfield & Butterfield) £2,251

A pair of goblets, the thistle shape bodies with a girdle moulding above fluting, 7¹/₂in., Peter and William Bateman, London 1806, and William Bateman, London 1818, 23.5oz. (Woolley & Wallis)   £850

A mid Victorian small goblet by Roberts & Briggs, the baluster bowl repoussé with lozenge shaped panels on a matt ground, London 1865, 150 grammes, 13cm. high. (Spencer's)   £180

A George III goblet, cylindrical body with half fluted decoration, on circular pedestal foot, by Samuel Hennell, 1816, 16.5cm., 11oz. (Lawrence Fine Art)   £352

A pair of George III campana-shaped goblets with reeded lower bodies on plain spreading bases, 6¹/₂in. high, John Edwards, London 1808, 22.7oz. (Bearne's)   £900

Paul Storr silver-gilt goblet, 4³/₄in. high, with an applied frieze of Classical females linked by floral swags, London, 1814, 5.5 oz. (Bonhams)   £1,800

19TH CENTURY

A China Trade goblet, by Leeching, probably Hong Kong, circa 1870, 7½in. high, 8oz.14dwt. **£545**

One of six George IV partly fluted thistle-shaped goblets, maker's mark WE for Wm. Eaton or Wm. Elliot, 1822, 5⁵/₈in. high, 65oz. **£4,990**

A 19th century Indian Colonial goblet, by Hamilton & Co., Calcutta, circa 1860, 19.6cm. high, 8.5oz. **£355**

A gilt-lined goblet on a beaded rim foot, the bowl engraved with an armorial and crest, possibly American circa 1860, 6in., 10.75oz. (Christie's S. Ken.) **£154**

Victorian silver goblet and beaker by William Hunter, London, 1870, and Henry John Lias & James Wakely, London 1881, 14oz. 8 dwts. (Butterfield & Butterfield) **£305**

A George IV gilt-lined part-fluted campana-shaped goblet on a rising circular foot, Langlands & Robertson, Newcastle, circa 1823, 7¹/₄in., 12.75oz. (Christie's S. Ken.) **£495**

One of six Victorian goblets, engraved with crest and initials, 1883, maker's mark overstruck with that of Frazer & Haws, 6½in. high, 109oz. **£3,565**

A George IV gilt lined part fluted campana shaped goblet, the bowl applied with a frieze of vines and engraved with a crest, Rebecca Emes and Edward Barnard, London, 1824, 6¾in., 14.25oz. (Christie's S. Ken) **£462**

An attractive Victorian silver gilt goblet, 6¹/₂in. high, chased with panels of cavorting putti, vines and masks, London, 1861, by George W. Adams, 7oz. (Bonhams) **£650**

GOBLETS

19TH CENTURY

A George IV goblet chased and embossed with a hunting scene, with reeded rim, by J. E. Terrey, 1821, 6¹/₂in. high, 8oz. (Christie's) £440

Victorian silver presentation goblet, foliate engraved, beaded circular foot, London 1875, 7¹/₂in. tall, 8oz. (G. A. Key) £70

American silver goblet with chased decoration, cast vintage design base, unmarked, 8in. high, 11.2 troy oz. (Eldred's) £176

A 19th century Chinese Export goblet, the sides chased in relief with arched panels, by Wang Hing & Co., Hong Kong, circa 1890, 21.4cm. high, 9.5oz. (Phillips London) £300

Coin silver goblet and a cup with handles and salt cellar, third quarter 19th century, by Peter L. Krider, Philadelphia, circa 1850–1860, 15oz. 14 dwts. (Butterfield & Butterfield) £245

Israeli silver Kaddish cup, Stanetzky, of goblet form, with applied filigree work on base, stem and lip, 5³/₄in. high, gross weight 3oz. 4 dwts. (Butterfield & Butterfield) £111

Fine antique American coin silver goblet, mid-19th century, with chased hunting decoration, marked *Pure Coin, Boston*, 8in. high, 11 troy oz. (Eldred's) £416

A C.R. Ashbee hammered silver goblet, the foot with a radiating repoussé pattern of stylised buds, London hallmarks for 1899, 12cm. high, 300 grams. (Christie's) £550

A presentation goblet; American, possibly Savannah, circa 1857, 7½in. high, 9oz.10dwt. £1,102

GOBLETS

19TH CENTURY

An American silver wine goblet, by Samuel Kirk, Baltimore, circa 1840, 6 1/8 in. high, and a beaker 4½in. high, 118oz. 10dwt. £755

An American silver wine goblet, a footed beaker and a cann, the first by Robert & Wm. Wilson, Phila., the second by W. W. Hannah, Hudson, New York, the third circa 1850. £535

One of two American silver wine goblets, by C. Bard & Son, one 5¾in. high, the other 6¼in. high, 9oz.10dwt. £472

20TH CENTURY

One of two Edwardian silver gilt goblets, by Edward Barnard & Sons Ltd., 1902 and 1903, 10¼in. high, 46oz. £1,090

An Arts and Crafts silver two handled goblet by Skinner & Co., the flared bowl with knopped base, with London hallmarks for 1907, 14.5cm. high, 309 grams. (Christie's) £242

One of three Desny electro-plated goblets, conical bowl and small conical foot connected by angled flange, 1920's, 12cm. high. £630

One of a pair of presentation Art Nouveau goblets, by Omar Ramsden and Alwyn Carr, London 1913, 5in. high. £905

A large goblet designed by H. Nielsen, stamped Dessin H.N. G.J. 535, circa 1928, 19.9cm. high, 25oz.15dwt. £1,900

An Omar Ramsden beaten silver goblet, the foot with inscription MCMXXI, 5in. high, London hallmarks for 1920. £200

A Sheffield plate 'Skep' honey pot, unmarked, circa 1800, 5in. high. £550

A George III honey pot formed as a bee skep, on circular stand with reed-and-tie borders, by Paul Storr, 1797, 4½in. high, 14oz.
(Christie's) £19,800

Late 19th century silver mounted cut glass beehive honeypot, unmarked, 8¾in. high. £5,940

HOT WATER URNS

An early 19th century Sheffield plate hot water urn, complete with burner, 14in. high. £440

George III silver plated hot water urn, late 18th century, with bell flower swags, on square base with ball feet, 21½in. high.
(Skinner Inc.) £261

A George III two-handled plain circular urn by George Eadon & Co., Sheffield, 1802, 19¾in. high, gross 142oz. £2,620

Gorham coin silver hot water urn, third quarter 19th century, Renaissance Revival style, monogrammed *M*, 14¼in., approx. 75 troy oz.
(Skinner) £2,828

Victorian silver plated hot water urn, 19th century, with stag's head handles, on a square base shaped by C-scrolls, 15½in. high. (Skinner Inc.) £169

Sheffield silver plated hot water urn with Federal-style high domed cover, England, circa 1810, 18⅞in. high. £250

INKSTANDS

18TH CENTURY

Inkstands, or standishes, as they were previously known, date from the 16th century, though the earliest surviving examples are usually 17th century. The 'Treasury' type consisted of an oblong casket with two centrally hinged lids.

Throughout the 18th century a tray form predominated, in the prevailing style of the period. These could be variously fitted with inkpots, sand and/ or pounceboxes, wafer boxes, sealing wax, bells and 'tapersticks'.

Glass bottles first appeared around 1765, as did pierced gallery sides. More often than not at least one of the bottles will have been replaced. How important this is to the value will depend on how well the replacement conforms with the whole.

Small, globe-shaped forms came in in the last years of the 18th century, and mahogany desk models with silver tops first made their appearance around 1800. Victorian examples were often highly ornamented and included many fanciful novelty designs such as cricketers, rowing boats with the pens as oars, etc. Usage declined after 1886, with the invention of the fountain pen.

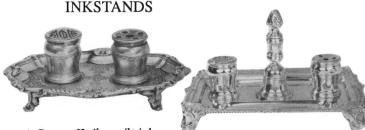

A George II silver-gilt inkstand by Edward Feline, London, 1734, 8½in. wide, 20oz.6dwt. **£1,090**

A George II shaped rectangular inkstand, by John Jacob, 1752, 11in. long, 43oz.   **£8,470**

A George II shaped rectangular inkstand, by Paul de Lamerie, 1730, Britannia Standard, 8¾in. long, 24oz.   **£18,150**

A George III rectangular inkstand, by Wm. Allen III, 1798, 30.3cm. long, 41oz.   **£1,450**

A Batavian silver writing tray comprising a pen box with hinged lid and finial handle and shaped trefoil tray, on three moulded animalistic feet, by Jurriaan van Kalker, circa 1725–1730, 24cm. wide, 38 oz. (Christie's)   **£11,000**

A George II inkstand, the shaped oblong sunk base with a moulded rim, decorated in the Baroque manner, by Paul de Lamerie, length overall 22cm., bell, 14cm. high, 1730, 25.5oz. (Phillips London)   **£26,000**

George II Sterling inkstand by William Cripps, London, 1749, set on four incurvate scrolled supports, the stand with a single penwell, 11½in. wide, 48oz. 2dwts.
(Butterfield & Butterfield) **£5,189**

Burradge Davenport, a George III oval galleried inkstand, with beaded serpentine edges to the pierced fret sides with swags, on claw and ball feet, 8in., London 1778, 12oz.
(Woolley & Wallis)   **£1,400**

A Venetian desk set on serpentine moulded oval tray on paw feet, two inkpots and covers a bell shaped pen holder, 1100gr., second half 18th century.
(Finarte)   **£3,214**

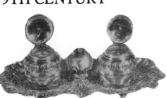

A Victorian rococo silver gilt shaped oval inkstand on bun feet, by G. Fox, London, 1875, 10in. long, 9.25oz. free. **£850**

Indian chased white metal inkstand with two glass bottles, ivory inlaid border to stand, 10½in. wide. **£110**

A late Victorian circular tortoiseshell inkstand with plated rococo scroll mounts, on bun feet, London, 1899, 5¼in. **£275**

A late Victorian double inkstand, by W. J. Barnard, London, 1894, 11in. long. 25oz. **£570**

An early Victorian shaped oblong inkstand, by R.F.A., Birmingham, 1838, 11½in. long, 20.75oz. **£1,575**

A George IV oblong inkstand, by Rebecca Emes and Edward Barnard, 1824, 25.7cm. long, 23oz. of weighable silver. **£1,270**

Richard Sibley, a fine early Victorian inkstand, the centre chased with leafy scrolls and engraved with the contemporary coat of arms of Butler, 13in. wide, London 1840, 26oz. (Woolley & Wallis) **£2,900**

A late Victorian ink stand, with beaded border and foliate engraved rim, the floriform stamped central panel supporting a diamond and slice cut globular glass ink well, 15.5cm. diameter. (Spencer's) **£170**

A Victorian ink stand, with pierced scrolled border to three sides, and two pierced divisions with two silver mounted cut glass bottles, by William & John Barnard, 1890, weighable silver 16oz. (Lawrence) **£825**

A Victorian ink stand, with inscription and oil lantern with snake motif handle, by Edward & John Barnard, 1858, 26cm., 33oz. (Lawrence) **£935**

An early 19th century inkstand with octagonal dishes in pierced silver coasters, the lids with pierced foliate decoration, on ball feet, Messina, 1180gr. (Finarte) **£234**

A George III inkstand, with gadroon rim, central taper holder and two cut glass silver mounted bottles, by Henry Nutting, 1811, 25cm., weighable silver 15½oz. (Lawrence) **£1,452**

19TH CENTURY

A William IV oblong ink-
stand, by Robinson,
Edkins & Aston, Birming-
ham, 1836, 13in. wide,
32oz.2dwt.   £2,060

A Victorian shell-shaped inkstand, by Elkington & Co.,
1851, 9¾in. long.   £665

A Victorian oblong ink-
stand fitted with two cut-
glass globular inkwells,
8in. wide, 8oz.   £165

A Victorian shaped oblong
inkstand on scroll feet, E. and J.
Barnard, London 1852, 9³/₄in.,
16.75oz. free.
(Christie's)   £748

A boat-shaped inkstand
on panel supports, maker's
mark, Cordoba, 1828,
25.3cm. wide, 565gr. £665

An Australian plate mounted
emu egg inkstand, 11in. wide,
circa 1870.   £465

A William IV shaped-oval
inkstand, the shaped sides and
bottle holders pierced with
foliate scrolls and gadrooned
rims, by Edward Farrell, 1836,
12³/₄in. long, 59oz.
(Christie's)   £3,080

An Old Sheffield plate globe
inkstand on a reeded rising
circular foot, applied with
paterae and drapery swags,
8¹/₂in. overall.
(Christie's S. Ken)   £385

An inkstand, with shell and
florally chased border, on four
scroll chased supports, the
inkwell Birmingham 1895,
25.5 x 17.8cm., 21oz.
(Bonhams)   £550

A George IV two-bottle oblong
inkstand, on four shell and scroll
feet with gadrooned borders, by
Messrs Barnard, 1832, 9in.
wide, 13oz.
(Christie's)   £1,955

A George III inkstand, 8³/₄ x
6in., with reeded borders and
two pen depressions, on four ball
feet, London, 1800, by John
Emes, 14oz.
(Bonhams)   £800

A late Victorian rectangular
inkstand with three quarter
gallery pierced with scroll
foliage, 1893 maker's mark of
William Gibson and John Lang-
man, 18.4oz. (Lawrence Fine
Arts)   £1,155

A late Victorian oblong inkstand, by Wm. Comyns, London, 1895, 12¼in. long, 16oz. **£700**

A George III inkstand, by Samuel and George Whitford, London, 1804, 10in. long, 29oz. weighable silver. **£1,735**

A Victorian inkstand, by Chas. Thomas and G. Fox, 24cm. diam., 1852, 27oz. **£1,320**

A Victorian rectangular inkstand with two receivers, London, 1884, the central taperstick London 1881, 8½in. long. (Tennants) **£1,300**

A Russian metal and marble desk set with three-quarter pierced gallery, 18½in. wide. **£3,800**

A Dutch 19th century beaded oblong gallery inkstand on bracket feet, 6in. long, 13oz. **£200**

A Victorian three-division rounded rectangular ink stand, on a stand with four tapering supports, 9in. long, Martin Hall and Co., London 1876, 466 gms, 14.9 oz.
(Bearne's) **£620**

A Victorian shaped oblong bright-cut inkstand, moulded with two pen rests and fitted with two silver-topped cut-glass inkwells, Messrs. Barnard, London 1868 and 1869, 9¾in., 16.75oz. free.
(Christie's S. Ken) **£968**

An inkstand by Antonio Maria Legnani, Milan, with ovoid pen holder surmounted by a figure of Mercury in the centre, 520gr., circa 1820.
(Finarte) **£3,364**

Silver-plated late Victorian desk set relief-carved and painted on three emu eggs. **£1,540**

Regency ebonised double ink stand, early 19th century, with ormolu beading, florettes, and centre ring handle, 13in. long.
(Skinner Inc.) **£510**

A George IV silver-gilt two-bottle inkstand, by P. Rundell, London, 1822, 16¾in. wide, 184oz.14dwt. **£24,200**

A George IV rectangular inkstand by M. Boulton, Birmingham, 1826, 11in. wide, 33oz.10dwt. £1,265

A George III inkstand, by Samuel and George Whitford, London, 1804, 9in. long, 17.75oz. free. £660

A William IV two-bottle inkstand, Sheffield, 1832 and 1835, 9in. wide, 17oz. £340

A Victorian shaped oblong large inkstand on scrolling feet, Elkington and Co., Birmingham 1893, 14¼in., 48.25oz. free. (Christie's) £1,540

A rectangular inkstand, fitted with a candleholder, by John and Thomas Settle, Sheffield, 1817, 15oz. £2,225

A William IV inkstand on shell and foliate feet, by Joseph and John Angell, London, 1836, 8in. long, 10oz. £605

A Victorian inkstand, with central taper holder and two cut ruby overlaid glass bottles, by Yapp and Woodward, Birmingham, 1850, 19cm., weight of taper holder and base 10 oz. (Lawrence Fine Art) £462

A Victorian oblong inkstand, surmounted by two pierced octagonal inkwells, each with hinged cover, and a similar hexagonal central wafer box, by Joseph Angell, 1855, 14¼in. long, 92oz. (Christie's) £3,080

A late Victorian small ink stand of lozenge form, set with a pair of slice cut glass ink wells of globular form, with silver mounts and pierced covers, Sheffield 1888, by Henry Wilkinson and Co., 261 grammes weighable silver. (Spencer's) £420

Victorian silver standish, London, 1848-49, Charles T Fox & George Fox, of pierced scrolling design, monogram, approx. 14 troy oz. weighable silver. (Skinner) £610

A George IV inkstand, with gadrooned borders, and scroll and shell corners, supporting foliate mounted paw feet, Sheffield, 1825, by John and Thomas Settle. (Bonhams) £950

A Victorian shaped rectangular ink stand with beaded edging, central rectangular reservoir with dog finial and two cut-glass wells, 10¼in. long, Birmingham 1890, 11.3oz. (Bearne's) £750

20TH CENTURY

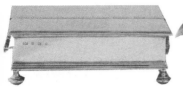

A Victorian treasury inkstand on four bun feet, by Elkington & Co., Birmingham, 1900, 10¾in. long, 90oz. **£2,260**

An Edwardian novelty inkstand in the form of an ear of maize, maker I.S.B., London, 1907, 9in. long, 9oz. **£880**

An Edwardian oblong inkstand in the Regency taste, W.K., London, 1910, 8½in. long, 17oz. free. **£725**

A silver-plated inkstand, the shaped rectangular tray top surmounted by a figure of a golfer, 9¹/₂in. wide. (Christie's) **£1,045**

An Edwardian gadrooned and foliate-pierced oblong gallery inkstand in the 18th century taste, Martin Hall and Co., Sheffield 1909, 8¹/₄in., 19oz. free. (Christie's S. Ken) **£682**

An Edwardian two-bottle inkstand in the George III manner on four paw feet, by C. S. Harris, 1909, 7in. wide. (Christie's) **£575**

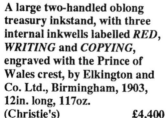

A commemorative inkstand by Tuttle Silversmiths, Boston, 1945-1949, marked with pine tree shilling mark and *HT1*, for President Truman's first term, 8in. high, 35oz. (Christie's New York) **£899**

A large two-handled oblong treasury inkstand, with three internal inkwells labelled *RED*, *WRITING* and *COPYING*, engraved with the Prince of Wales crest, by Elkington and Co. Ltd., Birmingham, 1903, 12in. long, 117oz. (Christie's) **£4,400**

A Scottish silver-mounted oak desk stand, of shaped oblong form, carved with thistles and foliage, maker's mark C.D., Inverness, hallmark Edinburgh, 1908, 12¹/₂in. wide. (Christie's) **£345**

A Victorian Britannia metal presentation two bottle inkstand the central dish formed as a ram's head, dated *1900*, by J. Dixon & Sons, 14in. wide. (Christie's) **£368**

An Edwardian presentation two-bottle ink stand on shaped oblong base with four Art Nouveau style shaped bracket supports, by Walker Hall, Sheffield, 1907, 14¹/₂in. wide, gross weight 52oz. (Christie's) **£3,300**

A parcel gilt two-bottle ink stand of shaped oval form, on four pierced scroll feet with pierced and engraved gallery, by Nathan and Hayes, Chester, 1913, 8in. wide, 10oz. (Christie's) **£572**

A commemorative silver
inkwell, circular with detachable
glass liner, London 1935,
Garrard & Co. Ltd.
(Bonhams)   £320

A silver inkwell, maker's mark
of Shiebler & Co., New York,
circa 1900, elaborately repoussé
with scrolls and rocaille, the
fitted silver-mounted glass
bottles with fluted swirls, 10in.
long, 19 oz. 10 dwt.
(Christie's)   £1,725

A plated elephant's-head inkwell
by Meriden Britannia Company,
last quarter 19th century, the
hinged cover with a cast figure of
a monkey, 6¹/₂in. long.
(Christie's)   £968

A good George VI silver
mounted heavy clear glass
inkwell, the silver mount with
hinged and swivelling watch
cover, Birmingham 1945,
possibly by J. Grinsell & Sons,
11.5cm. square.
(Spencer's)   £580

An unusual Continental
inkstand on a rising oval base,
the inkwell itself finely-modelled
and chased as the head of a wild
boar resting on scrolling oak
leaves, Berthold Muller, London
1910, 7in., 41 oz.
(Christie's S. Ken)   £1,705

Edwardian silver mounted
oversized glass inkwell and desk
clock combination by John
Gotliev Vander, London, 1902,
height 5¹/₂in.
(Butterfield & Butterfield)£1,127

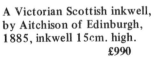

A Victorian Scottish inkwell,
by Aitchison of Edinburgh,
1885, inkwell 15cm. high.
                            £990

An unusual horn and plated
inkwell and bell, designed as two
dolphins, on a wooden plinth,
43cm.
(Lawrence Fine Art)   £572

A George III silver gilt shaped
circular inkpot and cover, by
B. Smith II and B. Smith, Jnr.,
1817, 6in. high, 32oz.   £3,025

Mount Washington Crown Milano biscuit jar, with shaded gold-amber colour handpainted with leafy brown and green stalks, 7¹/₂in. high. (Skinner Inc.) £346

An unusual silver and enamel powder jar, maker's mark of Gorham Mfg. Co., Providence, circa 1895, repoussé with foliate and drapery swags below a laurel band, 4¹/₂in. diameter, 6 oz. 10 dwt. (Christie's) £678

Cut glass and silver jar, brilliant hobstar and oval cut, with rose decorated flared silver rim, 9in. diameter. (Skinner Inc.) £381

GINGER

Sterling ginger jar by Howard & Co., New York, New York, 1885, the body and lid allover chased and embossed with scrolling foliage and various flowers, 6in. high, 10oz. (Butterfield & Butterfield) £299

A Victorian large ginger jar and cover and two similar trumpet-shaped vases, each chased with acanthus leaves and ribbon-tied fruit swags, by W.W. Williams, 1869, 224oz. (Christie's) £10,450

A silver and mixed-metal ginger jar, maker's mark of Whiting Mfg. Co., circa 1885, the matted surface applied with a copper fish and with silver and copper foliage, 5¹/₂in. high, 10 oz. 10 dwt. (Christie's) £1,109

TOBACCO

A George III barrel shaped tobacco jar and cover, engraved to simulate staves and with applied hoops, by John Emes, 1803, 4¾in. high, 13oz. (Christie's London) £3,740

Dutch silver-gilt and carved mother-of-pearl tobacco jar and cover, Barend van Mecklenburg, Amsterdam, 1786, with protruding gadroon edge rim fitted with a lift off lid with matching rim flaring a full shell, 5⁵/₈in. high, 21oz. 8dwts., all in. (Butterfield & Butterfield) £1,245

An unusual Victorian silver-mounted ebony tobacco jar modelled as a barrel with simulated staves and applied hoops, George Fox, London 1864, 6in. overall. (Christie's) £396

A whole host of vessels for various liquids come under this heading, and the earliest silver examples mainly date from the 16th century. The majority are pear-shaped, with plain or chased bodies, circular feet, and finely moulded scroll handles. Those for hot water or milk are, naturally, usually lidded. Wine jugs are distinct from claret jugs, the first being all of silver, whereas the latter are usually of glass with silver mounts.

Tigerware jugs are of German origin, a big-bellied stoneware type which appeared in England in the 16th century. English examples are silver mounted, with embossed and engraved covers, neckbands and footrings.

When determining value, whether or not a jug is lidded makes little difference, weight and size being more important. Also engraved jugs generally fetch considerably less than embossed examples.

A 19th century American cordial or water jug of baluster form, maker's mark of Jones, Ball & Poor, Boston, circa 1845, 28cm. high, 30oz. **£750**

A Spanish jug, by Antonio Fernandez Clemente, Salamanca, 1759, 23oz. 6dwt., 9½in. high. **£2,055**

Assembled and matching silver three piece presentation water set, pitcher marked *Vanderslice & Co., San Francisco, Cal.*; goblets unmarked, dated *1866*, 44oz. 2 dwts. (Butterfield & Butterfield) **£1,261**

A Liberty & Co. silver jug, the lightly hammered tapering cylindrical body with domed hinged cover, with Birmingham hallmarks for 1915, 22cm. high, 536 gr. gross. (Christie's London) **£440**

An early Scottish plain baluster-shaped jug on spreading rim foot, by Robert Keay of Perth, hallmark *Edinburgh, 1847*, weight 32oz., 11in. high. (Christie's) **£2,420**

A late Victorian beaded cylindrical jug applied with a foliate-cast scroll handle and with a shell-fluted cast spout, Chester 1897, 4½in., 10.75oz. (Christie's S. Ken) **£418**

A Continental toby jug with caryatid scroll handle, the bewigged figure wearing a frock coat and tricorn hat, import marks, 9in. (Christie's S. Ken) **£880**

A frosted silver kvass jug with reeded neck and scroll handle, Moscow, 1888, 10cm. high. **£200**

A Victorian 'ascos' jug, by Hunt & Roskell, 1844, 33.25oz. **£1,485**

A jug with ebony handle, stamped Georg Jensen 407A, 23.2cm. high, 35oz. 5dwt. gross weight. **£2,020**

A late George III jug by Edward Edwards, with everted gadrooned rim and hinged flat domed cover, with polished treen handle, London 1817, 737gm. gross. (Spencer's) **£400**

An Elizabeth I silver-mounted tigerware jug, chased with foliage and bead ornament, the cylindrical neck mount engraved with strapwork and foliage, by John Jones, Exeter, circa 1575, 8in. high. (Christie's) **£4,950**

A large Tiffany and Co. japanesque jug, the copper baluster body applied with three Sterling silver fish, stamped *Tiffany and Co.*, 21.5cm. high over frog. (Spencer's) **£11,000**

A rare Elizabeth I silver-gilt mounted tiger-ware jug, winged demi-cherub thumbpiece, 1561, maker's mark *GW*, 6½in. high. (Christie's) **£12,650**

A Regency jug, richly embossed with fruit and foliage, scrolls to the crested cartouche, 7½in., Alice & George Burroughs, London 1818, 27oz. (Woolley & Wallis) **£900**

A rare silver toby jug, maker's mark of A. E. Warner, Baltimore, 1840–1860, realistically formed as a man in contemporary dress, 14oz. (Christie's) **£10,980**

One of a pair of Queen Anne lidded jugs by Seth Lofthouse, London, 1713, 9½in. high, 61oz. **£9,900**

A Danish jug, the baluster body wrythen fluted, stamped *Christensen & Son, Copenhagen, 1902,* 9in., 16oz. (Lawrence Fine Art) **£209**

George II silver covered baluster jug by Pent Symonds, Exeter, 1739, 9½in. high, 27oz. **£3,850**

A late 19th century electroplated lidded jug in the style of an adapted 18th century tankard, 8¼in. high. (Bearne's) **£260**

A large pear shaped silver water jug, the body repousse and chased with rococo cartouche enriched with flowering blossoms, marked Faberge, with Imperial warrant, Moscow, 1891, 11in. high, 2208.4gr. (Christie's) **£3,850**

A late George III jug, with gadrooned border and hinged slightly domed cover with globular finial, London 1810, maker's mark *HN*, 695gm. gross, 19cm. high. (Spencer's) **£360**

A 19th century American 'ivy chased' jug, by Tiffany & Co., circa 1870, 23cm. high, 27.5oz. **£2,310**

A massive Victorian covered jug of baluster form, by George Fox, London 1861, 16in. high, 124oz. (Prudential) **£5,200**

An Elkington & Co. electroplated jug designed by Dr. C. Dresser, 19.3cm. high. **£1,425**

BEER

An Edward VII large beer jug with reed strap handle, London 1903, 24oz., maker Goldsmith & Co., London.
(Russell Baldwin & Bright) £360

A 19th century electrotype beer jug, the sides richly embossed with bacchante putti at the grape harvest, the base with a royal presentation inscription.
(Woolley & Wallis) £430

A George II plain silver pear-shaped beer jug, by Philip Elston, Exeter, the date letter probably for 1742, 7¾in. high, 22oz. £3,325

A Queen Anne plain pear-shaped beer jug, the body with applied moulded rib and with scroll handle, hinged waisted cover with button finial and openwork thumbpiece, by Simon Pantin, 1709, 11¾in. high, 45oz.
(Christie's) £9,775

George III silver barrel form beer jug, William Grundy, London, 1774, the body with applied reeded horizontal bands, hollow scroll handle, 7¾in. high, 36oz. 12dwt.
(Butterfield & Butterfield) £1,126

A George III plain pear-shaped beer jug, with leaf-capped scroll handle and moulded rim and spout, 1780, maker's mark erased, 7in. high, 21oz.
(Christie's) £2,420

A Victorian lidded beer jug, the sides embossed with foliage scrolls, maker Robert Harper, 11in., London 1864, 37oz.
(Woolley & Wallis) £1,050

A George II plain pear-shaped beer jug, with baluster drop to the curved lip and harp-shaped handle, by William Darker, 1729, 7½in. high, 24oz.
(Christie's) £4,950

A George II pear shaped beer jug with cast scroll handle and lip, maker Fuller White, London 1753, 23oz., 8¼in. high.
(Tennants) £2,400

BEER

A George II baluster beer jug by John Jacobs, London, 1740, 7in. high, 24oz. **£1,320**

A George III beer jug, of plain baluster form, on a pedestal foot, 25cm. high overall, by Thomas & Richard Payne, 1777, 24oz. (Phillips London) **£2,400**

A George II plain pear-shaped beer jug, with leaf-capped double scroll handle and moulded rim and spout, by Fuller White, 1748, 6¾in. high, 29oz. (Christie's) **£4,400**

HOT MILK

Fluted pear-shaped hot milk jug by Johann Georg Renner, Hannover, circa 1730, 8in. high, 20oz. **£5,700**

A Louis XVI hot milk jug, Paris, 1780, maker's mark indistinct, 5¼in. high, gross weight 6oz. **£1,280**

A milk pot on three scroll legs with pad feet, by T. Stoutenburgh, N.Y., circa 1735, 4¾in. high, 7oz.10dwt. **£3,195**

A silver covered hot-milk jug, maker's mark of Tiffany & Co., New York, 1891–1902, the spot-hammered surface etched with foliage and thistles, 7in. high, 20 oz. 10 dwt. (Christie's) **£1,848**

A Louis XVI hot milk jug, by Nicolas Canet, Paris, 1785, 6¼in. high, 9oz.10dwt. **£1,365**

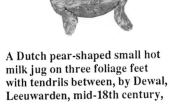

A Dutch pear-shaped small hot milk jug on three foliage feet with tendrils between, by Dewal, Leeuwarden, mid-18th century, 6½in. high, 10oz. (Christie's) **£2,300**

One of a matched pair of plain vase-shaped hot water jugs, 9in. high, 20.75oz. gross.   £290

A George IV baluster hot water jug on circular base with egg and dart border, by Emes & Barnard, 1827, 10¼in. high, 30oz.
(Christie's)   £690

A George III vase-shaped hot water jug, by Emick Romer, 1776, 12in. high, gross 30oz.   £3,390

A Louis XVI hot water jug, by Louis Clery, Paris, 1789, with the charge and discharge of Jean-Francois Kalandrin, 9¾in. high, gross weight 20oz.   £1,025

An American Aesthetic Movement white metal hot water jug, the oviform body extravagantly applied with pine-needles, 7in. high.
(Christie's S. Ken)   £629

A George III hot water jug, 11¼in. high, with fluted spout and wicker-bound scroll handle, London, 1768, by Augustin Le Sage, 26 oz.
(Bonhams)   £1,100

A 19th century French silver coloured metal hot water jug, the hinged gadrooned cover with applied pomegranate finial, Paris mark, 17cm. high.
(Spencer's)   £390

A silver hot water jug, of oval section, by Omar Ramsden, 1930, 27cm. high, 36.5oz.   £2,970

A George III Irish hot water or coffee jug of squat circular form, profusely chased with flowers and scrolls, maker's mark overstruck by that of James Le Bass, Dublin, 1819, 24cm. high, 33.5oz.
(Phillips London)   £680

HOT WATER

A George III neo-classical vase-shaped hot water jug by Thos. Wallis I, London 1775, 12in. high, 26oz.
£970

Fine late Victorian hot water jug of baluster design, treen handle, Edinburgh 1895, by Hamilton and Inches, 22oz. all in. (G. A. Key) £380

A George III vase-shaped hot water jug, maker's mark RG, possibly Richard Gardner, 1787, 12¾in. high, 25oz. gross. £1,665

An Edwardian plain vase-shaped hot water jug on a rising circular foot, with a reeded shoulder mount, Goldsmiths & Silversmiths Co. Ltd., London 1905, 11¾in.
(Christie's S. Ken) £264

A Victorian moulded oval hot water jug in the 18th century taste, on a rising foot, Richard Sibley, London 1871, 6¾in., 13 oz.
(Christie's S. Ken) £528

A plain tapering octagonal hot water jug in the George I manner with moulded borders, by Goldsmiths and Silversmiths Co. Ltd., 1929, weight 21oz., 10½in. high.
(Christie's) £451

A George III beaded vase-shaped hot water jug on a rising square base, possibly John Chapman, London 1773, 12¼in., 27.75oz. gross.
(Christie's) £858

A George III plain pear shaped hot water jug, with partly wicker covered foliate scroll handle, with gadrooned borders, 1770, maker's mark I. B. 9½in. high, gross 23oz.
(Christie's) £1,430

A George III gadrooned plain pear shaped hot water jug on a gadrooned rising circular foot, James Young & Orlando Jackson, London 1774, 10¾in., 21.50oz. gross.
(Christie's) £825

MILK

A Continental fluted pear-shape milk jug with an elaborate scroll handle, 6½in. high. £90

A William IV melon pattern milk jug, 4¼in. high, Jonathan Hayne, London 1792, 258 gms, 8.2 oz.
(Bearne's) £250

An American 19th century inverted pear-shaped large milk jug, B. Gardiner & Co., New York, circa 1840, 8in., 20oz.
(Christie's) £286

A Victorian beaded and fluted tapering oval gilt-lined milk jug, Henry Holland, London 1874, 4½in., 7.25oz.
(Christie's) £176

A late Victorian novelty milk jug modelled as a bedroom hot water jug with wicker-covered handle, Heath and Middleton, Birmingham 1895, 7¼in., 13.50oz. gross.
(Christie's) £550

A Dutch pear-shaped milk jug, with beaded leaf-capped scroll handle and shaped rim, by Wijnand Warneke, Amsterdam, 1792, 5½in. high, 266grs.
(Christie's) £1,540

E. E. J. & W. Barnard, a naturalistic milk jug, melon panelled with foliage entwined root spout, rim and handle, London 1837, 7¹/₂₀oz.
(Woolley & Wallis) £380

A highly unusual milk jug, by Charles Fox, 4⁷/₈in. high, the body chased with hare coursing scenes, London, 1830, 12.5oz.
(Bonhams) £1,900

George III vase shaped milk jug with reeded loop handle, makers mark rubbed, London 1794 (loaded)
(Phillips) £110

George III silver covered wine jug, Peter and Ann Bateman, London 1795, bright cut decoration, approximately 31 troy oz. (Skinner Inc.) **£1,080**

A German parcel gilt wine jug, the cover with bayonet fitting, formed as the head of a sphinx, with foliage finial, by Jacques Louis Clement, Kassel, 1793, 11¾in. high, gross 915gm. (Christie's) **£4,180**

A Victorian Scottish wine jug, by Wm. Marshall, Edinburgh, 1866, 15in. high, the handle altered for hot water and reassayed H.W.C., London, 1866, 27oz. **£825**

A good George III wine jug, the domed cover with pineapple finial, scroll handle and square pedestal base with ball feet, maker's mark *Morson & Stephenson*, 1772, 33cm., 36 oz. (Lawrence Fine Art) **£3,740**

A Victorian wine jug, the elongated baluster body engraved with panels of strapwork, shaped cover with turned finial and scroll handle, by Robert Hennell, 1863, 25cm., 16 oz. (Lawrence Fine Art) **£418**

A George III wine jug, the body of elongated baluster form, engraved with a coat of arms and on pedestal foot, by Boulton & Fothergill, Birmingham, 1775, 34cm., 20 oz. (Lawrence Fine Art) **£1,100**

A Victorian wine jug, the body engraved with panels of fruit and an inscription dated 1867 surrounded by scrollwork, by Henry Holland, 1867, 35cm., 26oz. (Lawrence Fine Art) **£1,100**

A fine Victorian Scottish jug, the frosted neck embossed with grape vines and a branch handle, 14in. high, maker J. Murray 1858, 35oz. (Woolley & Wallis) **£1,550**

A good Victorian wine jug of baroque design, the silver mounts repoussé with shells and flowers, female caryatid handle, 1898 (maker's mark obscured), 35cm. (Lawrence Fine Art) **£1,210**

The letter rack was another Victorian development, consisting of two silver plates attached to opposite sides of a flat base, the space between used to file letters. Most examples were electroplated and some were quite ornate with openwork or pierced designs. The size usually did not exceed 8in. long by 5in. high.

MENU HOLDERS

The menu holder took various forms – either two plates with a small gap between to hold the card, or a small frame, like a photograph frame, sometimes fitted with frosted white glass so the menu could be written. Stand types were also varied, in the form of animals or birds, for example, and they usually came in sets.

Menu holders date from the mid-Victorian period and were produced both in silver and electroplate.

MINAUDIERES

These were ladies' fashion accessories during the 1930s, the first designed by van Cleef & Arpels, though later Cartier, Asprey and other jewellers followed their lead. The minaudière was a metal box with separate compartments for everything the wealthy emancipated woman might require, cigarettes, cosmetics, money etc. The finish was usually expensive and highly decorative, lacquer, gold and silver being especially popular.

Curiously, the word itself means a simpering, affected woman!

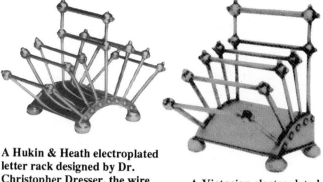

A Hukin & Heath electroplated letter rack designed by Dr. Christopher Dresser, the wire frame with seven adjustable supports joined by small spheres, with date lozenge for *9 May 1881*, 12.5cm. high. (Christie's) **£495**

A Victorian electroplated letter rack in the style of Christopher Dresser, by Hukin & Heath, 12.9cm. high. **£125**

A cased set of four silver gilt menu holders, depicting putti in a scrolling and floral decoration, Chester 1911. (Bonhams) **£180**

A set of six Edwardian silver menu holders, the double discs passed with a De Dion Bouton automobile, Chester 1907, 166 grammes total. (Spencer's) **£200**

An amusing German minaudiere, embossed on the front with two cats and a kitten in a wicker basket, 9.50 x 6.50cm., bearing marks for Louis Kuppenheim of Pforzheim, and '900'. (Phillips) **£600**

A Lacloche Freres patterned silver and red gold minaudiere set with five sapphires, stamped with import marks for 1935, 13oz.14dwt., 13 x 8.6cm. **£1,188**

Plated lady's dressing table mirror with easel back, late 19th century, with wire easel back, 13½in. high.
(Butterfield & Butterfield) £275

Silver plated dressing mirror, 26½in. high.
(Skinner) £646

A Charles II toilet mirror, the border and cresting chased with chinoiserie figures, by Anthony Nelme, 1684, 23in. high. £21,385

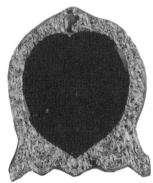

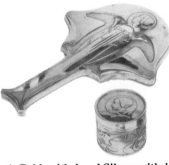

A late Victorian heart-shaped easel mirror, with richly pierced and embossed frame, by William Comyns, 1899, 20in. high.
(Christie's) £1,045

A Goldsmiths' and Silversmiths' Co. silver handmirror, designed by Kate Harris, and a Goldsmiths' and Silversmiths' Co. silver box and cover, London hallmarks for 1890.
(Christie's) £1,100

A Victorian silver mounted dressing glass, on a ebonised base with easel supports, 1885 by William Comyns, 32.3cm.
(Lawrence) £660

A white metal and coloured enamel dressing mirror in the Art Nouveau style, attributed to the March Bros., 50cm. high. £220

Late 19th century Howard & Co. rococo-style sterling silver dressing mirror, New York, 33in. high. £6,710

A cartouche-shaped easel dressing table mirror frame, makers T. May & Co., Birmingham, 1904, 17½ x 18in. overall. £990

A George III driving plate by W. Pitts and J. Preedy, 1792 and 1793, 12in. long, gross 53oz. **£3,090**

A George IV nipple shield, plain, of usual form, by T. & I. Phipps, 1821. (Phillips) **£260**

An early George V silver novelty pin cushion in the form of a boot, Birmingham 1912, by S. Blanskensee and Son Ltd., 12.5cm. long. (Spencer's) **£150**

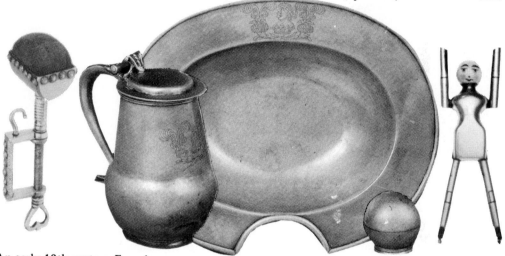

An early 19th century French silver metal needlework clamp, with netting hook and pin cushions. (Phillips West Two) **£100**

A Charles II shaving jug, dish and soap box, the jug circa 1680, 52oz. **£27,500**

An unusual pair of sugar nips formed as a Dutch doll, the head enamelled with a face and hair, London 1911, 3½in. (Christie's S. Ken) **£495**

An Edwardian novelty pin cushion as a chick in an egg, by Samsons Morden and Co., Chester 1908, 2in. high. (Spencer's) **£115**

A George III oval jardinière and stand, the sides pierced and applied with folded acanthus leaves and ribbon-tied oval cartouches, by John Wakelin and William Taylor, 1779, 15in. long, 91oz. (Christie's) **£12,650**

One of a pair of Liberty & Co. three-branch silver wall sconces, with Birmingham hallmarks for 1901, 29oz., 20cm. high. **£1,305**

A composite set of six napkin rings, each cast and applied with the figure of a dog, Birmingham 1935/6/7, 96gm. total.
(Spencer's) £200

An American silver-plated tilt-top tea table, Tiffany & Co., New York, circa 1893, length of top 28^{1}/$_{2}$in.
(Sotheby's) £19,671

A large charger, possibly German in plated metal with a naval scene within an ornate foliate border, 19th century, 73.5cm. wide.
(Finarte) £1,285

An important and rare Indian-trade silver armband, maker's mark of Joseph Richardson, Jr., Philadelphia, circa 1795, 3in. high, 4^{1}/$_{8}$in. overall length, 2oz. 10dwt.
(Christie's) £17,806

A French large wine barrel and stand, the stand with X-shaped frame and stretcher, the barrel with two dolphins mask spouts, the stand stamped *C. Bayard*, late 19th century, 27^{1}/$_{2}$in. high overall.
(Christie's) £5,500

An Art Nouveau circular plaque stamped in high relief with a classical maiden seated in a garden, stamped with Sheffield hallmarks, 11^{1}/$_{2}$in. diameter, 11oz.
(Christie's S. Ken) £374

A George III dish-cross, on three openwork sliding shell feet and with similar supports and vase-shaped lamp with detachable beaded cover, by John Swift, 1768, 14in. long, 29 oz.
(Christie's) £1,760

Elkington silver plated circular charger, circa 1876, depicting a classical beauty and her attendants in a courtyard, designed by Morel, 20^{1}/$_{4}$in. diam.
(Skinner) £287

A pair of silver-gilt Queen Anne brushes, each baluster shaped handle engraved with a crest, maker's mark only, Benjamin Payne, 10cm.
(Lawrence) £2,695

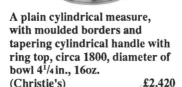

A George V silver cased perpetual desk calendar of rounded horizontal rectangular form with black painted ivorine markers, Birmingham, 1929, 9cm. wide, and a pair of Carlton china small roundels, with silver rims, Birmingham 1910.
(Spencer's) £70

A plain cylindrical measure, with moulded borders and tapering cylindrical handle with ring top, circa 1800, diameter of bowl 4¼in., 16oz.
(Christie's) £2,420

Smith-Corona sterling typewriter, Gorham Mfg. Co, Providence, Rhode Island, made by Gorham for L. C. Smith and Corona Typewriters, Inc., with original carrying case, 4½in. high.
(Butterfield & Butterfield) £3,002

A cylindrical parcel-gilt trompe l'oeil caviar cooler, with simulated wood cover and bracket handle, by P. Ovchinnikov, Moscow, 19th century, containing stand and glass liner, 6½in. high, 714grs.
(Christie's) £2,090

Pair of English silver-plated cache-pots with cobalt blue glass liners, unmarked, circa 1900, large goblet shape with pierced domed base of overlapping tongues supporting a stem, height 16¼in.
(Butterfield & Butterfield) £977

A set of six Georgian 'picture-back' silver teaspoons in case, London, mid-18th century, maker's mark *WT*, possibly for William Trenholme, height of case 6⅜in., 1oz. 10dwt.
(Christie's) £2,242

A spirit barrel, the cut glass body with silver mounts, including bung, spigot and on a stand of trestle design, Birmingham, 1927, 24cm.
(Lawrence Fine Art) £825

A Belgian altar cruet, comprising shaped oval tray and two ewers and covers, by Johannes Moermans, Antwerp, circa 1660, the tray 15½in. wide.
(Christie's) £18,700

German silver bun warmer, 19th century, tripartite globular form, with figures of Bacchic putti, 800 fine, 9½in. high, approximately 62 troy oz.
(Skinner Inc.) £1,360

A Continental silver bottle and stopper, decorated with cameo heads and swags, false gadroons around the base, 8.2cm.
(Phillips) £320

Sterling Smith Corona typewriter by Gorham Mfg. Co., Providence, Rhode Island, 1930, 10³/₄in. wide.
(Butterfield & Butterfield) £4,888

A Victorian electroplated meat press, by Elkington & Co., 44cm. high, excluding wood base. £1,575

An early 19th century South German silver celestial globe, unsigned, the 3 inch diameter globe divided at the equator into two hemispheres, the interiors gilded, supported by figure of a Turk wearing turban and tunic, 7³/₄in. high.
(Christie's) £12,100

Pair of German silver cornucopia, each side with a cartouche depicting courting couples, mounted on other end with a female putto holding a floral garland, 22oz. 12dwt.
(Butterfield & Butterfield) £1,201

An important Queen Anne two-handled vase-shaped wine fountain, applied with bands of strapwork, scrolls, rosettes and shells on a matted ground and with cast swing handles, by Pierre Platel, 1713, height overall 30in.
(Christie's) £89,500

A George III gilt-lined tapering swing-handled cream pail decorated with friezes of horizontal fluting, maker's initials W. and A. L., London 1769, 4¹/₂in.
(Christie's) £440

A French circular chamber pot, with scroll handle applied with fruit and foliage and with everted moulded rim, by Veyrat, Paris, circa 1880, 9¹/₄in. diameter, 1,126grs.
(Christie's) £1,650

A 19th century French silver incense burner as a vase and cover of panelled baluster form, cast with putti within cartouche, the domed cover with urn finial, 4in. high.
(Spencer's) £200

One of a pair of pounce pots, by John McKay, Edinburgh, 1798, 3oz. £255

Polish silver Torah pointer, maker's mark: *W.S.*, circa 1840, of heavy gauge, 84 standard, the upper section applied with filigree panels, 10¹/₂in. long, gross weight 7oz. 6dwts. (Butterfield & Butterfield) £968

A George IV fireman's arm badge, by R. Emes and E. Barnard, 1823, 6in. high, 9oz.5dwt. £1,695

A silver koro, the pierced spherical body worked in coloured shippo and gilt with a continuous decoration of insects amongst a dense mass of mixed flowers and plants, late 19th century, 15.4cm. high. (Christie's) £3,080

A pair of rare William IV circular silver-gilt spittoons, the detachable spreading rims with lobed borders, by Paul Storr, 1834, 7in. diameter, 32oz. (Christie's) £3,850

A spherical bezoar stone holder and stand, the holder pierced overall with foliage and with gilt liner and stone, the stand by Adey Bellamy Savory, 1826, the holder probably Middle Eastern, 18th century, 5in. high. (Christie's) £5,720

Continental silver religious crown, unmarked, a tooled band and openwork base of scrolls and palmettes, finial of a cast bird surmounting a sphere, 6³/₄in. diameter, 10oz. 18dwt. (Butterfield & Butterfield) £600

A WMF plated corkholder, each cork surmounted by a sculptural figure, 15.5cm. high. £605

A German silver-gilt mounted nautilus shell, chased and applied with flowers and foliage, the stem formed as a standing wood figure of a blackamoor, by Paul Solanier, Augsburg, 1690–1695, 14in. high. (Christie's) £4,950

A silver horse bell, the bulbous body applied with silvered copper strapwork, 2¾in. high.
£1,090

Baltic silver Scroll of Esther case with amethyst stones, late 19th century, boldly embossed and chased with rocaille work, 13½in. long.
(Butterfield & Butterfield) **£2,248**

A textured and beaded plated oval watering can with scroll handle and hinged cover, 7½in.
(Christie's S. Ken.) **£104**

An unusual cased pair of silver gilt ear trumpets with ivory earpieces, the trumpets engraved F. C. Rein & Son, London, in leather covered case with velvet lining, case 4¾in. wide.
(Lawrence Fine Arts) **£363**

A pair of fine George IV silver-gilt double wine decanter trolleys, by Benjamin Smith, 1827, each stamped *LEWIS ST JAMES'S STREET*, 19½in. long, gross 226oz.
(Christie's) **£25,300**

A rare George IV tapering cylindrical ear trumpet, engraved with a coat of arms, by Mary Ann and Charles Reily, 1828, 13in. long, 5oz.
(Christie's London) **£3,080**

A parcel-gilt, mixed-metal and silver chatelaine, maker's mark of Tiffany & Co., New York, circa 1875, 9in. overall length, gross weight 7oz.
(Christie's) **£1,039**

A late Victorian trump marker, the silver fascia stamped with scrolls and foliage, the colour decorated ivorine marker with silver slides, Birmingham mark, 3in. wide.
(Spencer's) **£175**

Russian silver-gilt and shaded enamel Easter egg, Khlebnikov & Co., Moscow, 1908–1917, 4¾in. high.
(Skinner Inc) **£1,785**

A George III two handled oval verriere, with applied ram's mask, by John Wakelin and William Taylor, 1790, 13½in. long, overall, 49ozs. (Christie's) £9,350

Sterling silver cuff, circa 1950, of abstract sculptural design, signed *Lobel*.
(Skinner) £1,568

A crocodile travelling dressing case opening to reveal silver mounted fitted interior, 8in. wide.
(Hy Duke & Son) £220

A William IV hollow, heart-shaped badge chased on either side with two Biblical shepherds and their flocks, by James Dixon & Son, Sheffield, 1830. (Phillips) £140

A rare 18th century German Hannukah lamp, of small size, the rectangular body with foliate chased cover opening to reveal eight oil compartments, by Rotger Herfurth, Frankfurt-on-Main, circa 1765, 13cm. long, 9oz. (Phillips) £5,800

A good Continental silver-gilt and enamel aide-memoire, enamelled with a rower in student's cap, probably German, circa 1895. (Phillips) £580

A parcel gilt punch service, with repousse and chased view of the Kremlin, by Antip Kuzmichev, Moscow, 1882, the tray 12½in. wide, 3486.4gr. (Christie's) £3,850

An early Victorian castle top aide-mémoire, with ivory slips for each day bar Sunday, by Nathaniel Mills, Birmingham, 1844.
(Phillips) £620

A set of six Art Nouveau silver buttons, cast with a portrait of a girl, Chester 1902.
(Spencer's) £120

A silver bell push in the form of a bear by Faberge, Moscow, 1899-1908, 9.5cm. high.   £4,620

A Victorian figure of a donkey and cart, the silver gilt two wheeled cart with spindle sides, 1891, 16 oz.
(Lawrence Fine Art)   £2,090

A Victorian cigar lighter, formed as a deer-hound, by J.S. Hunt, 1851, 5¼in. high, 18oz.17dwt.   £1,425

The Royal Hunt Cup 1845 - A Victorian Racing Trophy, by John S. Hunt of Hunt and Roskell, London 1844, on wood plinth applied with gothic lettering, 24in. high overall. (Prudential) £18,000

A Continental model of a pig, the detachable head with an appealing quizzical expression, Berthold Muller, bearing import marks for Chester 1899, 5¼in., 7.75oz.
(Christie's S. Ken)   £660

A WMF figure of a blacksmith, 10½in. high, the well modelled figure pictured by his anvil with a hammer in hand, on ebonised rectangular plinth.
(Bonhams)   £200

A Victorian model of an equestrian knight in armour, by Stephen Smith, 1870, 9in. high, 28oz.   £1,130

A late 19th century English silvered bronze group of a jockey on horseback, signed and dated J. Willis Good, 1875, 27cm. high.   £2,750

A silver-plate figure of an elephant, the howdah in the form of a gu-shaped vase, 10in. high.   £220

A Victorian model of a thoroughbred stallion, by Robert Garrard, London, 1860, 8in. high, 38oz. 15dwt. **£2,420**

A Victorian trophy, by E. Barnard & Sons, London, 1894, 88oz.10dwt. excluding the ebonised wood plinth, 18in. wide. **£3,630**

A Continental silver model of a grouse, by B. Muller, import marks for 1902, 10½in. high, 26oz. **£1,250**

A German silver model of a fiddler seated on a stool with a cat beneath, on domed oval base by Berthold Muller, Chester import hallmarks for 1909, 5½in. high, 9oz. (Christie's) **£575**

A late 19th century English silvered bronze group of a jockey on horseback, signed and dated J. Willis Good, 1875, 32.5cm. high. **£2,200**

A Victorian model group of two girls, wearing windswept diaphanous garments, one holding a basket of flowers, by Elkington & Co. Ltd., 1891, 16½in. high. (Christie's) **£3,300**

A model leopard, realistically chased with fur and engraved with spots and with detachable head revealing a gilt-lined well, 1928, 10½in. long overall, 33 ozs. (Christie's) **£1,980**

An inlaid silver ox and ceremonial cart, the ox standing foursquare with head raised, chased with foliate scrolls in relief, the hooves and harness gilt, late Qing Dynasty, 47cm. long. (Christie's) **£4,400**

A silver cast model of a Clydesdale horse, the sculptor G. Halliday, made by Elkington & Co., Birmingham, 1911, 21in. high, 309oz. **£10,700**

A table bell in the form of a tortoise, maker's mark JB, London, 1897, 6¼in. long. **£535**

A His Master's Voice silver model of the famous trademark, 3⅛in. wide, with Jubilee hall marks for 1935 (Mappin & Webb), on wood plinth. (Christie's) **£715**

An Edwardian crouching rabbit pin cushion, by Adie & Lovekin Ltd., Birmingham, 1907. (Phillips) **£140**

'Vestal' a silvered bronze figure by Le Faguays, on stepped square shaped marble base, 14½in. high. **£1,210**

Two Victorian model figures of Mr Punch, by Charles and George Fox, 1844 and 1845, 7¾in high overall, gross 19ozs. (Christie's) **£1,870**

'Nude Girl with Shawl', a silvered bronze figure cast from a model by Lorenzl, decorated by Crejo, 37.5cm. high. **£1,425**

A German decorative silver carriage, import marks for 1901, sponsor's mark of John George Piddington, 12.7cm. (Lawrence Fine Arts) **£286**

A Victorian cast model of a whippet, after Jiji by Jules-Pierre Mene, Sheffield, circa 1860, maker's mark WB, 6¼in. high overall. **£1,100**

A Victorian model of a knight in armour, by John Samuel Hunt, 1841, height overall 15in., 42ozs. (Christie's) **£1,870**

MUGS

17TH CENTURY

Generally speaking mugs and tankards can be distinguished by the fact that the latter have covers, while the former do not. However, one does occasionally find covered mugs, just to confuse the issue! Mugs were made in silver from the mid 17th century, and the earliest usually had baluster bodies and cylindrical necks rather like the pottery of the period. Cylindrical forms followed in the early 18th century, to be superseded by bellied bodies in the middle of the century and later by hooped barrel forms. Shaped forms returned in the 19th century. In the 18th and 19th century Sheffield plate mounts are also applied to stoneware mugs.

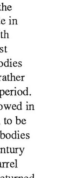

One of a pair of William and Mary baluster mugs, probably by J. Chadwick, London, 1691, 3¼in. high, 7oz.11dwt. **£2,785**

A William and Mary small mug with bulbous body, by Thos. Havers, Norwich, 1689, 2in. high, 10z. 5dwt. **£1,190**

One of a pair of James II baluster mugs, by G. Garthorne, London, 1688, 4in. high, 19oz.2dwt. **£2,660**

A Charles II globular mug, the body flat chased with Chinoiserie figures and foliage, by George Garlthorne, 1683, 4¹/₄in. high, 8oz. (Christie's) £5,500

James II plain cylindrical mug by Thomas Havers, 1688, 2¼in. high, 2oz. 3dwt. **£2,500**

A rare Charles I plain cylindrical mug and domed cover with scroll handle, the cover with reeded rim and ring handle, both engraved with the initials *TEP*, 1628, 5in. high, 7oz. (Christie's) **£5,980**

A late 17th century tapering mug with a moulded rim and applied fluted scroll handle, the body engraved with two reeded bands, possibly Norwich, 3³/₄in. (Christie's S. Ken) £440

A William and Mary mug of tapered cylindrical form, maker's mark IC over a star, London, 1691, 4½in. high, 419gr. **£2,300**

18TH CENTURY

A George II plain baluster mug, by Robert Albin Cox, London, 1758, 15cm. high, 17oz. **£485**

An 18th century Irish gilt-lined tapering mug with moulded rim 3¹/₂in., 9oz. (Christie's) **£308**

An early George III baluster mug, by T. Whipham and C. Wright, London, 1760, 8.5oz. **£520**

A George II baluster mug later-chased with rococo flowers and scrolling foliage and on a rising circular base, Humphrey Payne, London 1744, 4¹/₂in., 11.75oz. (Christie's S. Ken) **£495**

A mug, the tapering cylindrical body plain, apart from an engraved reeded band and moulded rim foot, by Timothy Ley, William III or Queen Anne, possibly 1701, 9cm., 6 oz. (Lawrence Fine Art) **£715**

A George II plain baluster mug on a spreading foot, with a moulded rim and double scroll handle, maker's initials *R.C.*, London 1754, 5in., 11.75oz. (Christie's) **£440**

A George III plain baluster mug with leaf-capped scroll handle and spreading foot, probably by John Deacon, 1774, 12.3cm. high, 10.5 ozs. (Phillips) **£450**

A Queen Anne mug of tapering form, with a reeded band and plain thumbpiece to scroll handle, 10cm. high, by Humphrey Payne, 1710, 6.7 ozs. (Phillips) **£650**

A George II plain baluster pint mug, with a moulded rim and double scroll handle, Robert Albin Cox, London 1752, 4³/₄in., 7.75oz. (Christie's S. Ken) **£682**

A George I mug with scroll handle, by George Wickes, London, 1726, 8.9oz. £505

A George III baluster pint mug with leaf-capped double scroll handle, W.T., London 1776, 5$\frac{1}{2}$in., 12.75oz.
(Christie's)   £495

A George III silver baluster shaped mug, maker's mark B.C., 4$\frac{7}{8}$in. high, London 1776, 6oz.18dwt.   £350

A George III plain baluster mug, with a scroll handle and spreading circular foot, engraved with a monogram, 13cm. high, maker's mark *WF* in Gothic script, 1765, 12.25 ozs.
(Phillips)   £450

A late George II mug by Isaac Cookson, on a skirt foot, the scrolling and rescrolling handle with heart shaped terminal, Newcastle 1750, 577 grams, 16cm. high over handle.
(Spencer's)   £680

A large George III plain mug of tapering shape with flared lip, applied girdle and leaf-capped scroll handle, by Peter & Anne Bateman, 1791, 16cm. high, 20.5 ozs.
(Phillips)   £1,100

A George I mug with moulded foot, scroll handle of tapering semi-circular section, maker's mark *C* enclosing *R*, London 1717, 9$\frac{1}{2}$oz., 4$\frac{1}{4}$in. high.
(Tennants)   £420

A George II mug of circular baluster form with engraved inscription on spreading base, 4$\frac{1}{2}$in. high, maker's mark *R.B.*, London 1738, 360 gms, 11.7 oz.
(Bearne's)   £580

A George III plain baluster mug with leaf-capped scroll handle and spreading foot, by Francis Crump, 1762, 10.25cm. high, 6.75 ozs.
(Phillips)   £350

18TH CENTURY

A George III plain mug of baluster form by P. & J. Bateman, 1790, 5¹/₈in. high, 11oz.2dwt. **£605**

A Queen Anne mug, Britannia Standard 1706 by M. E. Lofthouse, 12.4cm. high, 13.2oz. **£410**

A George II Provincial mug with leaf-capped scroll handle, by Langlands & Goodrick, Newcastle, 1756, 9cm. high, 7.25oz. **£420**

Silver mug, George Hanners, Boston, circa 1740, tapering cylindrical form with moulded mid-band and base band, scroll handle, 10 troy oz. (Skinner Inc.) **£3,293**

A George III mug, with a leaf capped scroll handle, all on a domed foot rim, 1764 by Louis Black, 11.9cm., 10.4oz. (Lawrence) **£572**

A George III tapering cylindrical mug on a flaring foot and with a moulded body band and rim, probably Jacob Marsh or John Moore, London 1774, 6¹/₄in., 17.25oz. (Christie's) **£825**

An early George II mug, by Francis Spilsbury I, 1735, 11cm. high. **£555**

A pint mug with moulded lip and foot, the scroll handle of tapering semi-circular section, by Langlands and Robertson, Newcastle, 1778, 10oz., 5in. high. (Tennants) **£380**

A George II plain baluster mug, London, 1733, 13cm. high, 11oz. **£305**

Joseph Angell, a George IV mug, campana shape repoussé with dancing maidens, London 1830, 8³/₄oz. (Woolley & Wallis) £410

Antique American .900 fine silver mug by Wood & Hughes of New York City, chased and applied decoration, gilt interior, dated 1872, 3³/₄in. high, 6 troy oz. (Eldred's) £210

A medallion mug by Gorham, Providence, circa 1865, with a squared handle and beaded borders, applied with two medallions, 3in. high, 4 oz. (Christie's) £277

A Victorian Aesthetic Movement mug, the body finely engraved with Japanese style swallows, foliage, half-circular and geometric patterns, 10cm. high, Edward Charles Brown, 1879, 6 ozs. (Phillips) £300

A fine early Victorian campana shape half pint mug, chased and embossed with a cow and sheep in pastoral landscape, 5¹/₄in., John Evans II, London 1839, 6.5 oz. (Woolley & Wallis) £440

A silver mug, maker's mark of Tiffany & Co., New York, 1875–1891, baluster form on spreading rim foot, elaborately repoussé with flowers, 6in. high, 18 oz. (Christie's) £1,232

A mug by William B. Durgin Co., Concord, New Hampshire, circa 1880, with a curved handle, the spot-hammered surface repoussé and finely-chased, 3⁵/₈in. high, 7 oz.(Christie's) £654

A William IV child's mug, the scrolling campana shape body engraved with initials, by Charles Reily and George Storer, London 1833, 4oz. (Woolley & Wallis) £300

A Mexican silver plain baluster mug with reeded rim and leaf-capped scroll handle, engraved with initial M, Mexico City, 19th century, 3³/₄in. high, 10oz. (Christie's) £352

18TH CENTURY

Until well into the 18th century, mustard was taken dry from unpierced or 'blind' casters (on which the piercing design was nevertheless marked) and mixed on the plate.

Mustard pots appeared only after 1760. Unless they are pierced, or cut-out underneath, Georgian examples were gilded inside and liners were not required. Neo-classic vases for mustard date from the 1770s onward, and have tall reeded handles, a tall lid and a tall pedestal foot on a square base. Also in the late 18th century, legs appeared on mustard pots, and pots became solid and cylindrical, with flat lids. Oval examples, often dipping slightly towards the centre of each side, were also made at this time, before convex sides and barrel styles came in around 1800. In the 1820s forms became heavier and more elaborate.

By and large, oblong mustard pots seem less popular than other shapes. Extra-large drum-shaped examples on the other hand often do extremely well, as they are considered highly desirable as marmalade pots!

John Denziloe, pierced drum shape mustard pot, with gothic fret sides, blue glass liner, London 1773.
(Woolley & Wallis)   £480

George III silver drum mustard engraved with a band of flowers and leaves, plus liner, Dubin 1779, by Joshua Jackson.
(G. A. Key)   £270

A French vase-shaped mustard pot, the bowl chased with a band of foliage and with double serpent scroll handle, Lille, circa 1755, maker's mark *I.B.H.*, $5\frac{1}{4}$in., 274grs.
(Christie's)   £2,860

A George III mustard pot, with bands of bright cut decoration, domed cover, by Crispin Fuller, 1792 (with a salt spoon of 1808), 9cm.
(Lawrence Fine Art)   £682

A George III mustard pot, $3\frac{3}{4}$in. high, with beaded borders and scroll handle, the hinged domed cover with urn finial, detachable blue glass liner, London, 1786, by Thomas Shepherd.
(Bonhams)   £900

A George III gadrooned drum mustard pot pierced with birds on flowering branches and with a blue glass liner, London 1767, 3in. high.
(Christie's)   £308

A George III beaded drum mustard pot bright-cut with paterae and swags, Hester Bateman, London 1781, 4in.; and a George III Old English pattern salt spoon.
(Christie's)   £616

19TH CENTURY

A mid Victorian drum mustard pot of shaped circular form, London 1862, by George Fox, approximate weight 4oz.
(Bonhams) £300

A fine George IV mustard pot, the melon panelled body and hinged cover chased and embossed with foliage, William Elliott, London 1823, 5 oz.
(Woolley & Wallis) £350

A Victorian mustard pot, 3in. high, with leaf-capped scroll handle and domed fluted hinged cover, Sheffield 1875, by Henry Wilkinson, 4oz.
(Bonhams) £190

A Victorian mustard pot, 3½in. high, on rim foot with scroll handle, the raised hinged cover with baluster finial revealing detachable blue glass liner, London, 1844, by Hayne and Carter, 5 ozs.
(Bonhams) £240

A Regency oval mustard pot, with a clear glass liner, artichoke finial and domed hinged cover engraved with a crest and motto, Philip Rundell, London 1820, 3¼in.
(Christie's S. Ken) £660

A Victorian barrel-shaped mustard pot realistically decorated with simulated staves and hoops and with an engraved bung hole, George Fox, London 1864, 3¼in. high.
(Christie's) £308

A large Regency mustard pot, the hinged cover with a cast flower finial, cast satyr mask scroll handle, John Wakefield, London 1819, 9.5 oz.
(Woolley & Wallis) £580

Fine large George Fox silver mustard of circular shape with blue glass liner, the body embossed with flowers and leaves, London 1827.
(G. A. Key) £320

A Victorian unusual mustard pot, the cauldron-shaped body finely embossed and matted with a desert oasis scene, 10cm. high, by A. Sibley, 1857, 7oz.
(Phillips) £450

A French 19th century openwork mustard pot on a laurel leaf and berry-decorated shaped triangular base with foliate feet, 5¹/₂in., 13oz.
(Christie's) £935

A Victorian circular mustard pot with hinged cover, plain, engraved crests, 5.72oz., with blue glass liner.
(Phillips) £110

A Victorian gilt-lined baluster mustard pot on applied Chinaman and shell feet, William Cooper, London 1851, 4¹/₄in., 8oz.
(Christie's) £935

A late Victorian moulded circular mustard pot in the mid 19th century taste, chased with flowers and foliage, George Adams, London 1891, 2³/₄in. high.
(Christie's) £187

An unusual Victorian novelty mustard pot in the form of a pineapple standing on a scrolling foliate base, E.H. Stockwell, London 1876, 3³/₄in., 5.25oz.
(Christie's) £660

A late George II large mustard pot by the Barnards, of squat baluster form, repoussé with acanthus leaves and flowerheads and with a rococo scroll cartouche, London 1810, 131 grammes.
(Spencer's) £180

A George IV gilt-lined part-fluted compressed vase-shaped mustard pot on a spreading circular foot, Philip Rundell, London 1822, 3³/₄in., 9.25oz.
(Christie's) £1,155

A Victorian novelty mustard pot modelled as a swing-handled cauldron, with a blue glass liner, Henry Stockwell, London 1859, 4in. overall.
(Christie's) £660

A mid Victorian mustard pot, London, 1844, by Edward, Edward Junior, John and William Barnard, approximate weight 5oz.
(Bonhams) £300

19TH CENTURY

A Victorian drum mustard pot with green glass liner with star-cut base, Reily and Storer, London 1847, 3¼in.
(Christie's) £440

A mixed-metal mustard pot and spoon by Dominick & Haff, New York, 1880, with a circular low-domed hinged cover with a ball finial, 2½in. high, gross weight 4 oz. 10 dwt.
(Christie's) £1,383

A Victorian gilt-lined pear-shaped mustard pot on floral and foliate feet, Henry Holland, London 1852, 3½in.
(Christie's) £418

An unusual Victorian mustard pot, 3½in. high, the flat hinged cover engraved with a crest and with an applied frog thumbpiece, London, 1850, by Charles and George Fox, 7 ozs.
(Bonhams) £680

A Victorian novelty spool-shaped mustard pot modelled from woven wire and with ropework borders and scroll handle, B. & C. or B. & G., Birmingham 1858, 3in.
(Christie's) £968

A George III mustard pot, 3¾in. high, with shell and 'C'-scroll border leaf-capped strap handle on three scroll supports, London, 1819, by Sarah and John William Blake, 7 oz.
(Bonhams) £200

A George III mustard pot, 3¼in. high, the domed hinged cover with shell thumbpiece and urn finial, London, 1810, by Emes and Barnard, 5 oz.
(Bonhams) £200

An early Victorian mustard pot of shaped circular form, by John and Henry Lias, plus a spoon, with blue glass liner, approximate weight 5.5oz.
(Bonhams) £200

A silver mustard pot and spoon, maker's mark of Eoff & Shepherd, for Ball, Black & Co., New York, circa 1840, 4oz. 10dwt.
(Christie's) £254

An early 19th century Scottish mustard pot of oval form, maker F. Howden, circa 1815, approximate weight 3.5oz. (Bonhams) £200

A Victorian mustard pot, gourd-shaped, engraved in panels with scrollwork, Birmingham 1847, by Yapp and Woodward. (Bonhams) £350

Good quality Victorian silver drum mustard with gadrooned rim, London 1842, by John and Henry Lias. (G. A. Key) £240

A good George IV gilt-lined moulded circular mustard pot the body cast and chased with game birds in a mountainous landscape, Charles Price, London 1823, overall length 4³/₄in., 10oz. (Christie's S. Ken) £935

A Victorian mustard pot, 2³/₄in. high, with moulded borders, double scroll handle, the flat cover with pierced thumbpiece and engraved monogram, *London, 1853, by Martin Hall and Company*, 5 ozs. (Bonhams) £240

An early Victorian gilt-lined moulded circular mustard pot on mask and lion's paw feet and with elaborate bead and foliate-decorated scroll handle, William Brown, London 1838, 3¹/₂in. high. (Christie's) £484

A George IV mustard pot, 3¹/₂in. high, circular, with gadrooned border and double scroll handle on raised circular foot, London, 1822, by Joseph Biggs, 5 oz. (Bonhams) £120

A Regency tapering circular mustard pot chased with a frieze of foliage and standing on leaf-capped lion's paw feet, Paul Storr, London 1801, 3¹/₂in. high. (Christie's) £495

A Victorian gilt-lined compressed pear-shaped mustard pot on figural scroll feet, John S. Hunt, London 1851. (Christie's) £638

A William Hutton & Sons
silver mustard pot, of drum
shape with vertical ribs and
set with garnet cabochons,
7cm. high, maker's marks
for Birmingham 1905.
(Phillips) £400

A C.R. Ashbee hammered silver
mustard pot, set with three
amber cabochons, original clear
glass liner, stamped *C R A* with
London hallmarks for 1900,
6.5cm. high, 100 grams. gross.
(Christie's) £880

A mustard pot, 2³/₄ in. high,
cylindrical bar pierced sides
engraved with leaves and scrolls,
London 1936, by A. & F.
Parsons, 3oz.
(Bonhams) £180

A C. R. Ashbee silver mustard
pot, set with six turquoise
cabochons, London hallmarks
for 1900, 8cm. high. £950

A pair of Ramsden and Carr
silver mustard-pots, supported
on four pad feet, cylindrical blue
glass liners, stamped maker's
mark RN & CR and London
hallmarks for 1903, 7cm. high.
(Christie's) £330

A rare example of a Bates
improved mustard pot, the
plain cylindrical body with
spread base, by Arnold Neale
Baily and Thomas House
Bates, 1914, gross weight
2.5oz. (Phillips) £575

A novelty mustard pot modelled
as an owl with yellow and black
glass boot button eyes and
detachable liner, 3¹/₄ in. high.
(Christie's) £198

Crichton Brothers, a pair of
mustard pots, 4in. diam., with
moulded borders, scroll handles
and detachable blue glass liners,
London, 1913, 10.5oz.
(Bonhams) £360

A Guild of Handicrafts silver
mustard pot, designed by C.
R. Ashbee, with London
hallmarks for 1902, 8.5cm.
high, 4oz.11dwt. gross weight.
£1,010

NEFS

The nef, an elaborate silver vessel shaped like a ship, was used in the Middle Ages to hold the lord's napkin, knife and spoon. Many were very detailed models, richly enamelled and peopled with little figures of sailors. Many were made in the 19th century for display, or adapted for use as wine servers or bottle coasters.

NUTMEG GRATERS

Though they were already in use in the late 17th century, most nutmeg graters found today date between the 1770s and 1830s, when hot toddy was popular. They consist of a tiny silver box large enough to contain a nutmeg and a steel grater, hinged at the top for using the grater and at the bottom for removing the grated spice. They were made in many attractive shapes, such as acorns, hearts, and barrels. Also, as the outer covering of the nutmeg was sold as mace, some were shaped as ceremonial maces. The grater itself sometimes helps to date the item; this was usually of silver until 1739, with irregular holes, then of hammered sheet steel, silver framed, until the 1770s, then of tinned rolled steel, and from the 1790s, of blued steel with symmetrical perforations in concentric circles in the best examples.

PAP BOATS

The pap boat was a particularly British device, a small, shallow, oval bowl with a tapering spout at one end, used in the 18th and 19th centuries for feeding pap (semi-liquid food such as bread and milk) to infants. Some had an ornamental rim, and many were later converted to cream boats by adding a handle and feet.

A Continental model of a two masted nef, the hull chased with panels of Mercury and Europa, the prow formed as a dolphin, Chester import marks for 1909, 26³/₄in. high, 96oz. (Christie's) **£3,080**

Late 19th century Dutch or German nef, modelled as a galleon with putti and dolphin chased hull, 23¹/₂in. high, 114oz.16dwt. of silver-coloured metal. **£2,750**

A 19th century Continental silver nutmeg grater, with two hinged ends, 2⁷/₈in. long. **£195**

A George IV silver-gilt nutmeg grater, with hinged rasp and container, engraved with Garter Motto, by Philip Rundell, 1823, 7in. long, 5oz. (Christie's) **£4,620**

A George IV kitchen nutmeg grater with tongue and dart borders, by Charles Rawlings, 1824. **£460**

An English silver nutmeg grater, maker's marks for T. Phipps and E. Robinson, circa 1800/1, 2³/₈in. long. **£270**

George III oval silver pap boat with reeded edge and off set pourer, London 1798 by Andrew Fogelberg. (G. A. Key) **£120**

A George III silver-gilt pap-boat, with gadrooned shell, acorn, oak leaf and flower rim, 1814, 5¹/₂in. long, 3oz. (Christie's) **£368**

An emerald pearl Parker vacumatic standard pen and pencil set with three narrow cap bands and original Canadian arrow nib, circa 1933–36. (Christie's S. Ken)   £154

A dark green vacumatic filling Parker 51 with 'Icicle' pink and gold caps inscribed 14K and a matching propelling pencil, circa 1944. (Christie's S. Ken)   £715

A gold filled scrolled and twisted design overlay eyedropper Swan pen with over/under feed nib, circa 1908–12. (Christie's S. Ken)   £550

A fine lacquered Dunhill Namiki lever fill pen, with maki-e design of a Japanese fisherman wearing large hat, carrying rod and bait basket on the barrel, with original Dunhill Namiki no. 20 nib. (Christie's S. Ken)   £2,420

A Pelican self feeding reservoir pen by Thomas de la Rue, hallmarked *London 1897*. (Bonhams)   £5,500

A heavily chased and scrolled sterling silver eyedropper Swan over fed pen, in original presentation box with red velvet lining, circa 1900–1908. (Christie's S. Ken)   £605

A sterling silver 'filigree' design overlay eyedropper Waterman's 12 pen, circa 1900–03. (Christie's S. Ken)   £286

A sterling silver 'Gothic' design overlaid Waterman's lever filled pen, circa 1926. (Christie's S. Ken)   £143

Dunhill-Namiki: a taka maki-e lacquer pen, decorated with three carp swimming amongst green aquatic plants, signed by the lever, circa 1937. (Bonhams)   £1,250

A gold filled Hick's 'Detachable' pen, with telescopic barrel fitting into barleycorn decorated casing with ribbon ring, in original box with instructions in the base. (Christie's S. Ken)   £66

In their earliest form, pepper casters came as small, round pierced balls attached to 16th and 17th century bell salts, though they later adopted conventional caster form. In the early 18th century bun and kitchen peppers became popular. These were about 3in. high, the bun pepper of the same shape as larger casters, while the kitchen pepper, though having a similar cover, invariably has a cylindrical body and a simple loop handle. Kitchen peppers are fairly rare and now command high prices.

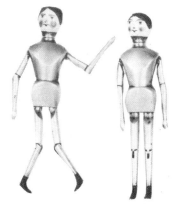

A pair of Edwardian novelty peppers, the articulated bodies with porcelain heads, 13.5cm. long, 1905. **£1,430**

A George I kitchen pepperette on a spreading foot and with an applied scroll handle, probably James Goodwin, London 1717, 2³/₄in.
(Christie's) **£528**

A silver and mixed-metal pepper mill, maker's mark of Tiffany & Co., New York, circa 1889, inlaid with niello and copper tear drops and flowers, with bud finial, 3³/₄in. high, 5 oz.
(Christie's) **£1,232**

A pair of novelty pepperettes in the form of busts in suits of armour, the hinged visor opening to reveal hollow interior, Birmingham, 1906, by George Unite.
(Bonhams) **£320**

A caster, marked *HM*, probably New York, circa 1700, the domed and pierced cover with bayonet mounts and a turned finial, 3½in. high, 3oz.
(Christie's New York) **£2,767**

A fine octagonal silver pepper box, maker's mark of Andrew Oliver, Boston, circa 1740, of octagonal form on moulded base, 4¹/₄in. high, 3oz. 10dwt.
(Christie's) **£5,935**

Pair of Victorian peppers, with detachable heads, by Frederick Edmonds of Johnson, Sons & Edmonds, 6cm. high.
(Lawrence Fine Art) **£605**

An Edwardian novelty pepperette as a golf ball, on a swept circular foot supported by three curved arms, 40 grams 7.5cm. high
(Spencer's) **£30**

PITCHERS

It was Paul Revere who, in the early 19th century, adapted in silver the Liverpool pottery pitchers favoured by sea-captains, and he left three sizes of them in his own inventory. They were much copied as water pitchers, with smaller examples serving as milk jugs, and most found today are of American origin. The form of course exists equally elsewhere, but it is most usually referred to as a jug.

A baluster-shaped silver pitcher by Dominick & Haff, Newark, 1884, 8 ¹/₈in. high, 27oz.10dwt.
£810

Fine Sterling silver and cut and engraved crystal pitcher by Gorham, ornate leaf and berry decoration, 14¹/₂in. high. (Eldred's)
£1,151

A fine silver and mixed-metal pitcher, maker's mark of Gorham Mfg. Co., Providence, 1880, the spot-hammered surface applied with a brass turkey, bamboo leaves, and a bronze fruit-tree branch, 7³/₄in. high, 30 oz.
(Christie's)
£5,544

Sterling hand chased pitcher, S. Kirk & Son Co., Baltimore, 1903–1907, repoussé with an urn shaped body swelling to a cylindrical neck with a helmet spout, height 11¹/₂in., 44oz. 6dwts.
(Butterfield & Butterfield)
£2,067

A fine silver and mixed-metal pitcher, maker's mark of Tiffany & Co., New York, circa 1880, the spot-hammered sides and handle applied with a dragonfly and butterflies amid a trailing vine of gold and copper, 7³/₄in. high, 26 oz. 10 dwt.
(Christie's)
£16,800

A pitcher of baluster form with an open handle, by Gorham Manuf. Co., 1897, 8³/₄in. high, gross weight 31oz.
£1,435

Silver milk pitcher, maker's mark Hayden & Gregg, 1846–52, 6⁵/₈in. high, approx. 14 troy oz.
£550

A silver pitcher, maker's mark of Tiffany & Co., New York, 1878–1891, in the Japanese taste, 8¹/₄in. high, 34oz. 10dwt.
(Christie's)
£10,387

Kirk repoussé silver covered pitcher, Baltimore, 1846–61, recumbent deer finial, chased floral and village landscape decoration, 9in. high, aproximately 33 troy oz. (Skinner Inc.) £972

Georg Jensen sterling pitcher, Denmark, with openwork grapevine decoration, 9in. high, approx. 30 troy oz. (Skinner Inc.) £1,840

A pitcher, by Edwin Stebbins, New York, 1828-1835, the foliate scroll handle with a cast helmet thumbpiece, marked, 13¾in. high, 45oz. (Christie's New York) £657

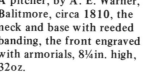

A pitcher, by Tiffany & Co., New York, 1869-1891, the cast handle in the form of stylised leafage above classical mask handle join, marked, 22cm. high, 36oz. (Christie's) £2,213

A pitcher, by A. E. Warner, Balitmore, circa 1810, the neck and base with reeded banding, the front engraved with armorials, 8¼in. high, 32oz. (Christie's) £5,534

American Arts and Crafts hand beaten silver pitcher by LeBolt, Chicago, Illinois, circa 1915–1920, applied with cypher monogram on the side, 8¼in. high, 22oz. 6dwts. (Butterfield & Butterfield) £969

Dominick and Haff Sterling pitcher, late 19th century, chased vintage decoration, retailed by Bigelow Kennard and Company, 13¾in. high, 44 troy oz. (Skinner Inc.) £713

American silver octagonal pitcher by Whiting Mfg. Co., Providence, Rhode Island, 1921, on four cushion feet, hollow harp handle, 6¾in. high, 21oz. 8dwts. (Butterfield & Butterfield) £277

A pitcher, by William Gale for Tiffany & Company, New York, 1856-1859, the neck and foot with repousse acanthus leaf borders, marked, 11½in. high, 29oz. (Christie's) £1,314

A silver covered pitcher, maker's mark of Bassett and Warford, Albany, New York, 1800–1805, 13³/₈in. high, 36oz. (Christie's) £5,445

A pitcher of baluster form, with a curved spout and S-scroll handle, by Jones, Ball & Poor, Boston, circa 1852, 11¼in. high, 29oz. £725

A silver-mounted 'craquelé' glass ice pitcher, maker's mark of Gorham Mfg. Co., Providence, circa 1880, with glass rope-twist handle and silver collar, 12¼in. high. (Christie's) £1,047

A plated pitcher, by Meriden Britannia Co., circa 1885, the entire surface spot hammered, the sides repousse and chased with a dragonfly, waterlilies and flowers, marked, 26cm. high. (Christie's) £691

A pitcher, by Haddock, Lincoln & Foss, Boston, circa 1855, with a rustic handle and a leaf form spout, marked (bruises), 9¾in. high, 33oz. (Christie's New York) £588

A vase-shaped pitcher, in the Japanese taste, by Gorham Manuf. Co., Providence, 1885, 9in. high, 40oz.10dwt. (Christie's) £4,618

A vase-shaped pitcher, American, with unidentified eagle touch mark, circa 1825-35, 12in. high, 35oz. £1,000

A silver vase-shaped pitcher, with double scroll handle, by Samuel Kirk & Son, 1846-61, or 1880-90, 10in. high, 25oz. £845

A presentation pitcher, by Newell Harding & Co., Boston, circa 1854, with a cast rustic handle and a cast grapevine spout, marked, 13in. high, 39oz. (Christie's New York) £1,037

WATER

Whiting Sterling and mixed metal water pitcher, 1881, bird and floral decoration, 8¹/₂in. high, approximately 33 troy oz. (Skinner)   £2,357

Bigelow, Kennard & Co. repoussé sterling water pitcher, circa 1863, globular form with cylindrical neck, 8¹/₂in. high, approx. 39 troy oz. (Skinner)   £1,220

Georg Jensen Sterling water pitcher, 1922, marks of Copenhagen, Jensen, London import mark of 1922, 9in. high, approximately 18 troy oz. (Skinner)   £1,131

Sterling hand chased Art Nouveau water pitcher, Dominick & Haff, New York, dated *1902*, baluster form body on domed base, height 9³/₄in., 29oz. 2dwts.
(Butterfield & Butterfield) £1,278

American silver hand wrought water pitcher by Herbert Taylor for Arthur Stone, Gardner, Massachusetts, circa 1935, with mild harp thumbrest, helmet brim spout, 40oz. 4dwts.
(Butterfield & Butterfield) £830

Sterling hand chased water pitcher, S. Kirk & Son Co., Baltimore, Maryland, circa 1903–1924, repoussé, engraved with three initial script monogram on underside, 7¹/₄in. high, 18oz. 6dwt.
(Butterfield & Butterfield) £1,051

Tiffany & Co. sterling silver water pitcher, of spherical form with a cylinder shaped neck, with bands of stylised foliate and geometric motifs, 9in. high, approximately 37oz.
(William Doyle Galleries) £1,656

A silver water pitcher, maker's mark of Whiting Mfg. & Co., circa 1885, elaborately repoussé with flowers on a matted ground, 7¹/₈in. high, 23 oz. 10 dwt.
(Christie's)   £1,047

A silver water pitcher, maker's mark of S. Kirk & Son., Baltimore, 1846–1861, elaborately repoussé with architectural landscapes amid flowers and foliage, 12in. high, 30 oz. 10 dwt.
(Christie's)   £862

Howard sterling water pitcher, retailed by Bigelow and Kennard, octagonal-form with ovolo border at lip, 9¼in. high, approx. 34 troy oz.
(Skinner) £431

An American silver and other metals 'Japanese style' water pitcher, Tiffany & Co., New York, circa 1875–80, 26oz. 15dwt. gross, height 7¾in.
(Sotheby's) £27,993

A silver water pitcher, maker's mark of John W. Forbes, New York, circa 1830, with foliate scroll handle and gadrooned rim, 12in. high, 31 oz. 10 dwt.
(Christie's) £862

Sterling hand chased water pitcher, Shreve & Co., San Francisco, circa 1909–1922, engraved with fruiting vine monogram at the front, on a stepped circular pedestal base and knopped stem, 13½in. high, 44oz.
(Butterfield & Butterfield) £1,051

Sterling water pitcher, S. Kirk & Son, Baltimore, Maryland, circa 1903–1907, repoussé, spherical body with cylindrical neck with applied band at mouth and hollow harp handle, 7¾in. high.
(Butterfield & Butterfield) £1,051

Sterling presentation water pitcher, Gorham Mfg. Co., Providence, Rhode Island, 1905, domed circular base supporting an inverted pyriform body with horizontal shoulder and helmet shaped spout, height 10⅝in., 30oz. 8dwts.
(Butterfield & Butterfield) £639

A silver water pitcher, maker's mark of Krider & Co., Philadelphia, circa 1851, elaborately repoussé with flowers enclosing a presentation inscription, with foliate scroll handle, 11in. high, 29 oz. 10 dwt.
(Christie's) £554

Mexican silver water pitcher by William Spratling, Taxco, circa 1931–1945, fitted with a carved wooden handle with an abstracted bird mask design, 6⅝in. high, 19oz., all in.
(Butterfield & Butterfield) £1,902

A silver water pitcher, maker's mark of S. Kirk & Sons, Co., Baltimore, 1903–1907, eleborately repoussé with architectural landscapes amid flowers and foliage, 12in. high, 43 oz. (Christie's) £1,848

WATER

Bailey & Kitchen coin silver
water pitcher, monogram,
approximately 38 troy oz.
(Skinner) £511

French silver water pitcher,
Boucheron, Paris, 19th century,
barrel-form, 10¼in. high,
approximately 46 troy oz.
(Skinner) £1,938

Sterling silver water pitcher by
Durgin, pedestal base, circa
1913, monogrammed, 28.4 troy
oz.
(Eldred's) £298

Gorham sterling water pitcher,
baluster form on a spreading
foot, monogram, 10⅜ in. high,
approx. 33 troy oz.
(Skinner) £679

Tiffany repousse sterling water
pitcher, 1891-1902, chased
overall with flowers and leaves,
7¾in. high, approx. 28 troy oz.
(Skinner) £1,659

W. Adams coin water pitcher,
New York, mid 19th century, of
panelled pear form, 9¾in. high,
approx. 37 troy oz.
(Skinner) £980

William Gale & Son coin silver
water pitcher, New York, circa
1852, decorated with chased
grapes and leaves, 11½in. high,
approx. 30 troy oz.
(Skinner) £603

Georg Jensen sterling water
pitcher, Denmark, 1925-30,
with beaded base and ebony
handle, 9½in. high, approx.
27 troy oz.
(Skinner Inc.) £1,227

A water pitcher, American,
circa 1815, with a squared
handle and a broadly reeded
body, unmarked, 8¼in. high,
26oz. £755

Dinner plates are the round flat dishes off which you actually eat your food. They have varied very little over 400 years, and then only in decoration and width of rim. Most come by the dozen, and a lower number is worth less pro rata, though eight is considered quite a good number. It is always worth checking that they are all by the same maker and of the same date.

One of a set of six Austrian dinner plates, by Ferdinand Ebenwimer, 1776, 9⁷/₈in. diam., 98oz.   **£4,260**

Twelve Austrian dinner plates, seven 1761, and five 1763, maker's mark IS, 9¾in. diam., 203oz.   **£7,670**

Twelve Old Sheffield plate shaped-circular dinner plates, with moulded gadrooned borders, engraved with a coat-of-arms and later initials M & S, circa 1780, 9¹/₂in. diameter. (Christie's)   £1,650

German silver Pidyon Haben plate, mid 19th century, in the late 17th century style, the oval dish embossed and chased, struck with pseudo-Augsburg and other marks, 13³/₄in. wide, 18oz. 10dwts. (Butterfield & Butterfield)   £2,594

Twelve George III shaped circular dinner plates, with moulded gadrooned borders, engraved with two coats-of-arms and a Ducal coronet, by Andrew Fogelberg, 1773, 9¹/₂in. diameter, 203oz. (Christie's)   £10,450

Twelve George II shaped-circular dinner plates, with reed-and-tie borders, by George Hindmarsh, 1740, 9¹/₂in. diameter, 238oz. (Christie's)   £11,000

One of six German dinner plates, 1784-91, five with maker's mark IFF, and one by J. P. Crutzenberg, 9½in. diam., 76oz.   £5,965

A set of twelve George III silver gilt dinner plates, by John Wakelin and Wm. Taylor, London, six 1787 and six 1788, 9¼in. diam., 181oz.   £20,455

18TH CENTURY

A George III silver plate, makers Fras. Butty and N. Dumee, London 1769.
£330

A set of twelve Spanish dinner plates, by Larranaga, San Sebastian, mid 18th century, 9½in. diam., 185oz. £10,230

One of ten Louis XV dinner plates, by various makers, 10⅛in. diam., 184oz.
£3,410

One of a pair of Louis XV silver gilt dinner plates, by Nicolas Outrebon, Paris, 1738, 10in. diam., 50oz. 10dwt. £3,410

One of twelve George III plain shaped circular dinner plates, by Robt. Calderwood, Dublin, circa 1760, 9½in. diam., 210oz. £4,515

One of twelve George II shaped circular dinner plates, by Paul De Lamerie, 1741, 9½in. diam., 233oz. £33,265

One of twelve George II shaped circular dinner plates, by Wm. Grundy, 1753, 9¾in. diam, 215oz. £8,315

A set of six George III silver gilt dinner plates, by Eliz. Godfrey, London, 1761, in the George I style, 9½in. diam., 89oz. £5,965

One of twelve George III shaped circular dinner plates, by J. Young and O. Jackson, 1774, 9⅝in. diam., 237oz. £6,890

Set of eight J. E. Caldwell Sterling dinner plates, reticulated borders and engraved interiors, 12in., approximately 204 troy oz. (Skinner) £3,746

Eighteen German dinner plates, by Joachim C. Neuss, seven 1801 and eleven 1804, 10in. diam., 345oz. £20,425

A set of twelve William IV shaped-circular soup plates, by William Eaton, 1832, 9¾in. diameter, 255oz. (Christie's) £6,050

Fourteen shaped-circular soup plates, each with gadrooned border, thirteen by William Brown, twelve 1835, one 1834; and one by John S. Hunt, 1860, 10in. diameter, 310oz. (Christie's) £6,600

A parcel-gilt silver wheat-pattern serving plate and cake knife, maker's mark of Gorham Mfg. Co., Providence, 1871, the rim applied and chased with gilt wheat sheaves amid foliage, 10¼in. diameter, 22 oz. 10 dwt. (Christie's) £1,602

A set of twelve William IV shaped-circular dinner plates, each with a gadrooned and foliage border, by William Eaton, 1832, 9¾in. diameter, 229oz. (Christie's) £10,450

Twelve George III shaped-circular dinner plates, with gadrooned shell and foliage borders, by William Bennett, 1816 and 1817, 10½in. diameter, 332 oz. (Christie's) £8,800

Sterling soup plate from the Mackay Service, Tiffany & Co., New York, circa 1878, Indian, of shaped circular form with chased floral panel sides, diameter 9in., 21oz. 10dwts. (Butterfield & Butterfield) £1,692

A set of twelve George III dinner plates, by Thomas and Joseph Guest and Joseph Craddock, 1810, 9¾in. diameter, 220oz. (Christie's) £7,700

20TH CENTURY

One of a set of four French silver gilt cake plates, by J. Chaumet, Paris, circa 1918, 10½in. square, 104oz.
£5,540

Set of five Black, Starr & Frost Sterling plates, neoclassical design, approximately 107 troy oz.
(Skinner) £749

Twelve American Sterling service plates by International Silver Co., Meriden, Connecticut, Trianon, 10½in. diameter, 234oz.
(Butterfield & Butterfield)
£2,421

A set of twelve silver dinner plates, maker's mark of Graff, Washbourne & Dunn, New York, 1899–1941, each of shaped circular form, 10¼in. diameter, 171oz.
(Christie's) £3,413

One of a set of twelve plates, by Gorham Manuf. Co., 1907, 10¼in. diam., 204oz. £3,195

A set of twelve silver dinner plates, maker's mark of Howard & Co., New York, dated 1907, the centre engraved with a coat-of-arms and crest, 10in. diameter, 292 oz.
(Christie's) £3,696

Set of Twelve Schofield Co. Sterling dinner plates, Baltimore, 20th century, in the Baltimore Rose pattern, 10½in. diam, approximately 242 troy oz.
(Skinner Inc) £5,194

Charles Stuart Harris, set of twelve Edwardian silver gilt dessert plates, the matt borders embossed with foliate scrolls and birds, 9¼in. diameter, London 1902–09, 217 oz.
(Woolley & Wallis) £4,500

Eight American octagonal dessert plates, each with fluted shaped border, by Black Starr & Frost, stamped *Sterling, 817,* 7in. wide, 54oz.
(Christie's) £368

17TH CENTURY

These were two handled bowls with or without cover, for porridge and spoon meat, and silver examples began to appear in the 17th century. Until circa 1650 the sides were straight, slanting inwards to a flat base, but later rounded sides and a baluster shape became popular. The ears were often strengthened by an additional wedge or ring. French porringers sometimes have cast relief ornament, while Dutch examples may have rose decoration. It was a particularly popular form in America. American porringers may either be quite simple, with a solid handle, or pierced with the handle also elaborately pierced. Cupping or bleeding bowls are also known as porringers in America.

Many of the larger examples can be confused with cups. The difference is simple; cups have a foot, porringers do not. Miniature forms also became highly popular during the Britannia silver period. This standard was compulsory between 1697 and 1720 (and optional thereafter) and decreed that silver must be 928 parts per thousand pure.

An early Charles II two-handled porringer and cover, on three cast gilt spread scallop feet, circa 1670, 23ozs.
(Phillips)   £40,000

A Charles II two-handled porringer and cover, 1674, maker's mark CM, 7in. high.
£21,385

A Charles II two-handled porringer, with beaded scroll handles and chased with a band of foliage and with a vacant oval cartouche, 1660, 3¹/₂in. wide, 7oz.
(Christie's)   £2,090

A James II silvergilt two-handled porringer and cover, on flattened reeded foot, with scroll handles and domed cover with acorn finial on a gadrooned rosette, by Robert Cooper, 1688, 7¹/₂in. high, 32oz.
(Christie's)   £4,620

A William and Mary part spiral-fluted porringer applied with scroll handles and with a rope-twist body band, maker's initials W.G., London 1691, 7¹/₂in. overall, 9.50oz.
(Christie's S. Ken)   £1,210

A Charles II two-handled porringer, flat chased with European figures, exotic birds and flowering trees, probably by Samuel Dell, 1684, 3³/₄in. high, 8 oz.
(Christie's)   £5,500

A Charles II two-handled plain circular porringer and cover, with scroll handles, the base engraved with initials E.S., 1677, maker's mark T.K., the cover with maker's mark only, 4¹/₄in. high, 12oz.
(Christie's)   £2,750

A James II two-handled porringer, maker's mark PR in monogram, 1685, 3¹/₈in. high, 6oz.10dwt. **£1,780**

A James II small two-handled porringer with half fluted body, London, 1685, 3½oz. **£480**

A Commonwealth two-handled porringer, by Gilbert Shepherd, 1658, 2½in. high, 4oz.14dwt. **£1,935**

A Charles II two-handled porringer, engraved 'Little Canfield Church', 1675, 2¾in. high, 4oz.2dwt. **£910**

A Charles II silver gilt two-handled porringer and cover, 1676, maker's mark TC, a fish above, a trefoil below, 5¾in. high, 21oz. **£4,160**

A Charles II two-handled porringer, 1679, maker's mark IR, between rosettes, probably for John Ruslen, 3¼in. high, 4oz.17dwt. **£1,695**

A Charles II two-handled porringer and cover, 1663, maker's mark AC or CA in monogram, 7¼in. high, **£7,865**

A Charles II plain two-handled porringer, with scroll handles, pricked with initials *EK*, 1681, maker's mark indistinct, 3¼in. high, 5oz. (Christie's) **£1,500**

A Charles II two-handled porringer and cover, on waisted rim foot, chased in the Chinoiserie style, 1683, maker's mark F.S., 5¹/₂in. high, 13oz. (Christie's) **£3,300**

A two-handled porringer, with beaded and mask scroll handles, engraved beneath the foot with the initials *WWW* and the date *1688*, unmarked, circa 1684, 2³/₄in. high, 4oz. (Christie's) **£1,500**

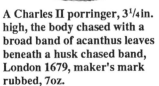

A Charles II porringer, 3¹/₄in. high, the body chased with a broad band of acanthus leaves beneath a husk chased band, London 1679, maker's mark rubbed, 7oz. (Bonhams) **£1,000**

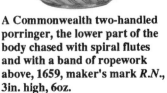

A Commonwealth two-handled porringer, the lower part of the body chased with spiral flutes and with a band of ropework above, 1659, maker's mark *R.N.*, 3in. high, 6oz. (Christie's) **£1,100**

18TH CENTURY

A Queen Anne gilt-lined part spiral-fluted porringer with beaded scroll handles and rope twist body band, Nathaniel Lock, London, 4¹/₄in., 9.25oz.
(Christie's)   £825

Late 18th century Boston-style silver porringer, 5in. diam., 8 troy oz.   £340

A Queen Anne Provincial two-handled porringer, the campana-shaped body chased with upper beaded girdle, by Richard Freeman, Exeter, 1706, 2¹/₂oz. (Phillips)   £850

A silver porringer, maker's mark of Charles Le Roux, New York, circa 1740, 7⁵/₈in. long, 8oz.
(Christie's)   £1,452

An early 18th century porringer, possibly by Wm. Gibson, London, circa 1705, 7¾in., 13.25oz.   £485

A silver porringer, maker's mark of Thauvet Besley, New York, circa 1740, 7⁷/₈in. long, 8oz. 10dwt.
(Christie's)   £1,888

A Queen Anne porringer, chased in typical style with a vacant scrolling cartouche, the handles beaded, maker probably John Cowsey, London 1706, 11oz., 5¹/₂in. diameter.
(Tennants)   £1,200

A Queen Anne part spiral-fluted two-handled tapering circular porringer, maker's initials possibly T.E., London 1704, 8.25oz.
(Christie's)   £935

A twin handled half fluted porringer with bands of stamped flower heads and crescents, probably by Thomas Waterhouse, London 1704, 1³/₄in. diameter.
(David Lay)   £230

A George III porringer, 3in. high, with ropetwist band and two double-scroll handles, London, 1769, by Thomas Cooke II and Richard Gurney, 4 oz.
(Bonhams)   £780

A silver porringer, maker's mark of Benjamin Burt, Boston, 1760–1800, with a pierced keyhole handle engraved *WMc to FH*, 8in. high, 7 oz.
(Christie's)   £986

Fine George II silver two handled porringer with fluted decoration to base, marked for London 1755, maker Henry Brind, 5in. tall, 16oz.
(G. A. Key)   £800

Silver porringer, Samuel Casey maker, South Kingston, Rhode Island, mid-18th century, 5in. diam., approx. 8 troy oz. (Skinner Inc.) £1,923

A circular silver porringer, by Daniel Russell, Rhode Island, circa 1740-71, 7¾in. long, overall, 8oz. £1,440

A porringer by John Hancock, Boston, circa 1750–1765, with a pierced keyhole handle, 8¼in. long, 8 oz. (Christie's) £1,522

A porringer by William Simpkins, Boston, 1730–1770, with a pierced keyhole handle engraved with block initials, 8in. long, 7 oz. 10 dwt. (Christie's) £1,245

A porringer by Jonathan Otis, Newport, circa 1750–1765, with a pierced keyhole handle engraved 'S. Coggeshall', 8in. long, 8 oz. 10 dwt. (Christie's) £1,799

An American silver porringer, Edward Webb, Boston, circa 1700, of typical form with double arch handle, 5oz. 10dwt., 4¾in. diameter. (Sotheby's) £6,294

A silver porringer, maker's mark of Joseph Loring, Boston, 1770–1810, with pierced keyhole handle engraved with initials *ET*, 8⅛in. high, 8 oz. 10 dwt. (Christie's) £1,355

Silver porringer by Thomas Dane, Boston, Massachusetts, circa 1760, with slightly domed base and bombé sides, cast pierced 'keyhole' handle, 7½in. long, 6oz. 2 dwts. (Butterfield & Butterfield) £672

A silver porringer by Thomas Edwards, Boston, circa 1750, with a pierced keyhole handle engraved with script initials, 5¼in. diam. 9½oz. with cover. (Christie's) £1,540

18TH CENTURY

Late 18th century Boston-style silver porringer, 5in. diam., 8 troy oz.   £600

A Queen Anne small silver bleeding bowl or porringer, Britannia standard 1706 , maker's mark rubbed, 7.4cm.   £800

A silver porringer, by Benjamin Burt, Boston, 1750-1800, with a pierced keyhole handle, 5¼in. diam. 8oz.   £1,250

19TH CENTURY

A porringer with a pierced keyhole handle, marked 'Davis', early 19th century, 5½in. diam., 8oz.   £1,040

A Victorian porringer and cover in Charles II style, with chased and repoussé decoration of a lion, unicorn and flowerheads, maker's mark *WC/JL*, 1897, 16cm., 22.5oz.
(Lawrence Fine Art)   £770

American silver porringer by Wm. Smith Pelletreau, New York, circa 1815, 5¼in. diam., 8 troy oz.   £1,000

A Gorham sterling silver porringer of circular form with two side mounted 'C' scroll handles, 4½in. diam., 7 troy oz.   £300

A Kirk sterling silver porringer with reticulated handle, 4¼in. diam., 8 troy oz.   £300

A Victorian two-handled porringer with leaf capped scroll handles, 19cm. high, Britannia Standard 1884.   £990

A Guild of Handicraft twin-handled silver porringer and cover with spoon, the cover with turquoise and wirework finial set with mother of pearl, with London hallmarks for 1903, 340 grams. gross.
(Christie's)   £3,300

A Guild of Handicraft twin-handled hammered silver porringer, the wirework handles set with a triangular panel with repoussé decoration of stylised leaves and each set with an amber cabochon, with London hallmarks for 1900, 210 grams. gross.
(Christie's)   £1,430

A Guild of Handicraft silver porringer, shallow bowl with single strap handle set with cabochon chrysoprase, with London hallmarks for 1901, 18.5cm. long, 175gr. gross.
(Christie's)   £600

A good reproduction Charles II two handled porringer and cover, engraved with chinoiserie birds and foliage, 22.5cm. high overall, by Messrs. D. & J. Welby, 1912, 42oz. (Phillips London) £800

A Carolean style compressed pear-shaped porringer and cover chased with a lion and a unicorn surrounded by elaborate rococo flowers and foliage, George Fox, London 1905, Britannia Standard, 5in. overall, 12oz.
(Christie's S. Ken)   £198

A lidded porringer, in Restoration style, decorated with a repoussé lion and unicorn with flowers, the lid with a pomegranate finial, 6^1/$_2$in., by Harry Brasted, London 1900, 20oz.
(Woolley & Wallis)   £440

A porringer, 7^1/$_8$in. wide, double scroll handles and cut cardwork to base, London, 1905 by D. & J. Welby, 14oz.
(Bonhams)   £120

A large porringer and cover, 7^1/$_2$in. high, in late 17th century style, with two cast scroll side handles, London, 1908, by the Crichtons, 33oz.
(Bonhams)   £670

A porringer, 5^1/$_2$in. diameter, spiral fluted to lower body, beaded double-scroll handles and stylised foliate chasing to base, London, 1908, 5.5oz.
(Bonhams)   £170

POT POURRI

An attractive pot pourri vase and cover, the slightly domed cover pierced and engraved with foliage and with cast dove finial, London 1914, 181 grammes. (Spencer's) £150

An early 19th century French baluster form censer with repoussé and chased decoration of rosettes and acanthus leaves and flame finial, by A. Renauld, Paris, 30cm. high, 670gr. (Kunsthaus am Museum) £938

An attractive Edwardian pot pourri vase and cover, the high swept cover with flammiform finial and with foliate piercing, Chester 1909, 184 grammes total, 14.5cm. high. (Spencer's) £240

POWDER COMPACTS

An Art Deco enamelled silver compact signed and dated 1937. £95

Art Deco gold and silver compact with French-cut sapphire and gold mounts, housing a lighter and a lipstick. £275

A Boucheron powder compact and two lipstick holders, Made in France. £240

PRAYER BOOKS

A Book of Common Prayer, the applied silver fascia stamped with the *Good Shepherd*, Birmingham 1910, 9.5 x 6cm. (Spencer's) £70

A small silver mounted prayer-book, the interior printed in German and with date 1652, 3in. long. £1,030

Bezelel silver bound prayer book, 20th century, one side etched with symbols of the Twelve Tribes and four filigree rondels, 7in. high. (Butterfield & Butterfield) £1,384

17TH CENTURY

The importance of salt in medieval times is reflected by the fact that the standing, or master salt was the most prominent item of tableware, placed in front of the host, with other, smaller salts placed centrally for less important diners. We have the phrase 'above or below the salt'; one's status was reflected by where one sat in relation to this vital item. And does the word 'standing', in the sense of status, come in fact from the standing salt?

The earliest salt dishes which are commonly available now are of the trencher variety, made of one piece, usually before 1700, with a central depression for the salt, then continuing in a skirt to the table. After 1700, the commonest form is the octagonal trencher salt, the sides often made separately from the top, and the best ones were cast. These were in use up to 1735. The circular, three legged type is by far the most commonly found from the period 1735–85, though from circa 1760 pierced, oval salt dishes with blue glass liners began to appear. After 1785 boat-shaped salts became popular, and after 1800 oblong tub salts in various patterns were used. Shell types were also popular in the late 18th century, and were much copied for the next 100 years.

The corrosive nature of the contents took a heavy toll of silver salt cellars, and the bowls of early trenchers are often almost eaten away. In the 18th century salts, unless pierced, did not have glass liners, but after 1740 the insides were usually gilded, which would protect them from attack as long as the gilding remained sound.

One of a pair of William and Mary trencher salt cellars, London, 1690, diam. 7cm., with a pair of 18th century spoons, 7oz. £785

Charles II octagonal trencher salt, London, 1680, 1oz.14dwt., 3in. diam. £600

A German silver gilt salt, maker's mark F. above a wheel (Rosenberg no. 498), Augsburg, 1600-10, 3oz., 2¼in. high. £700

A parcel gilt hexagonal trencher salt by Georg Wilhelm Fesenmayr, circa 1650, 166gr. £5,565

An Austro-Hungarian silver gilt-mounted horn salt cellar of cylindrical form, carved with a shepherd and herdsmen, maker's mark M.V. conjoined, Salzburg, late 17th/early 18th century. (Christie's) £1,035

A rare trencher salt, maker's mark of Richard Conyers, Boston, circa 1700, with gadrooned rim and foot rim, 2⅛in. high, 1 oz. 10 dwt. (Christie's) £10,472

A German circular salt, maker's mark I.E., Nuremberg, circa 1600, 8cm. diam., 55gr. £1,275

One of a pair of mid 17th century trencher salts of hexagonal form, 10oz.14dwt. £700

18TH CENTURY

One of a pair of George I plain octagonal trencher salts by Henry Daniell, Dublin, 1715, 5oz. 18dwt. £2,000

Two of a set of four 18th century American oval salts on pedestal bases, by Lewis Fueter, N.Y., circa 1785, 13.75oz. £1,980

One of a set of six George II salt cellars, by Paul Crespin, London, 1734, 3⅝in. diam., 60oz. £7,865

One of four George II circular salt cellars, by Paul de Lamerie, two 1730, two 1731, Britannia Standard, 27oz. £8,910

One of a pair of George II/III salts, by David Hennell I, 1760, 7cm. diam., and J. Pasley, Dublin, 1770, and a pair of Russian salt spoons, 1861, 10oz. £265

One of a set of four George III plain circular salt cellars, by Paul Storr, 1798, 15oz. 5dwt. £1,425

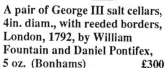

A good pair of George II salts, on cast knurled appliques, scroll legs to hoof feet, maker Henry Herbert, London 1738, 10oz. (Woolley & Wallis) £350

A set of four George II salt cellars, by Paul de Lamerie, London, 1733, scratch weight 32oz.19dwt. £3,300

A pair of George III salt cellars, 4in. diam., with reeded borders, London, 1792, by William Fountain and Daniel Pontifex, 5 oz. (Bonhams) £300

One of a pair of German silver gilt trencher salts, by Paul Solanier, Augsburg, apparently 1710-12, 1¾in. long, 8oz.10dwt. £2,215

A Louis XV covered double salt cellar and two single examples, by J. T. Van Cauwenbergh, Paris, 1771 and 1773, the double 6in. long. £2,385

One of a pair of Queen Anne trencher salt cellars, by Wm. Pearson, London, 1710, 2½in. wide, together with a pair of salt spoons, 4oz.14dwt. £755

18TH CENTURY

A set of four George II silver gilt salt cellars, by George Wickes, London, 1754, 3¹/₈in. diam., 31oz. £11,080

A matched pair of 18th century double lipped salts, on shaped oval bases, gilt interiors, one London, 1756, the other with rubbed marks, possibly by David Hennell.
(Bonhams) £360

David Hennell, set of four early George III oval salts, on shell applique legs, with hoof feet, London 1762, 12 oz.
(Woolley & Wallis) £420

A fine and rare pair of silver salt cellars, maker's mark of Simeon Coley, New York, 1767–1769, on four scroll feet with scallop-shell knees and stepped pad feet, 3¹/₄in. wide, 6 oz.
(Christie's) £1,725

A set of four George II salts, on spreading moulded foot, maker probably I. Wood, London 1759, 12¹/₂oz.
(Woolley & Wallis) £1,500

A pair of French shaped-oval trencher salts, each on scroll base and with quatrefoil rims, Arles, 1750, 130 grs.
(Christie's) £1,478

Pair of George III oval silver salts with pierced sides, complete with blue glass liners, London 1784.
(G.A. Key) £210

A pair of George III basket-shaped double salt cellars with central woven wirework handles, probably Thomas Pitts, London 1763, 3¹/₂in., 9oz.
(Christie's) £990

Pair of George III boat shaped silver pedestal salts, gilt lined, London 1796 by Henry Chawner and John Emes.
(G. A. Key) £190

Two of a set of four Victorian cast salts, fashioned as shells supported by stylised dolphins, 8cm. wide, circa 1860.   £640

Two of a set of four Hukin & Heath silver salts with salt spoons, Birmingham hallmarks for 1879, 6oz. 4dwt, each 3.4cm. high. £950

A pair of George III silver plain oval boat-shaped salt-cellars, each on four bracket feet and with reeded rim, by John Emes, 1802, 3¼in. long, 2oz. (Christie's)   £299

Four Victorian salt cellars each formed as a standing peasant figure, by R. Garrard, 1863, 1865 and 1866, 62oz.   £15,730

A good pair of early Victorian large salts by Henry Wilkinson & Co., of octagonal form, pierced and engraved with lobed oval panels enclosing leaves, Sheffield 1841. (Spencer's)   £190

A pair of Victorian parcel-gilt shell-shaped salts, the shells chased with flutes and with rococo borders, by Robert Garrard, 1861, 4¼in. long, 17oz. (Christie's)   £2,860

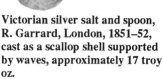

A pair of salts by Tiffany & Co., New York, 1870–1875, with a die-rolled guilloche border and three cast ram's-head feet, 3in. diam, 4 oz. (Christie's)   £458

Five Victorian salt cellars with matching spoons, London 1869, 6½oz., in case.   £175

Victorian silver salt and spoon, R. Garrard, London, 1851–52, cast as a scallop shell supported by waves, approximately 17 troy oz. (Skinner Inc.)   £1,298

A pair of George III silver oval salt-cellars, each on four ball feet and with gadrooned, shell and foliage border, 1809, 9¹/₂in. long, 4oz.
(Christie's)   £322

A pair of Victorian figure salt cellars by Robert Garrard, London 1855, 6in. high.   £4,235

A pair of George III silver circular salts, maker possibly S. C. Young & Co., Sheffield, 1813, 3½in. diam., and a pair of salt spoons.   £340

A pair of Victorian salt cellars, 3¹/₂in., oval with waved gadrooned borders and ovolo pierced sides, London 1853, by W.R. Smily, 5oz.
(Bonhams)   £320

Set of four Victorian silver-gilt figural salts by Walter, John, Michael & Stanley Barnard, London, 1898, 6¹/₂in. high, 59oz. 13 dwts.
(Butterfield & Butterfield) £3,360

A set of four salts by Daniel Fueter, New York, 1786-1806, on a spreading oval stem on a rectangular foot, 5.4cm. high, 12½oz. (Christie's) £2,214

A pair of early Victorian salt cellars, each cast in the form of a scallop shell on three dolphin feet, 1837, maker's mark overstruck with that of Joseph and Albert Savory, 3¹/₄in. wide, 14oz.
(Christie's)   £3,520

A George III good set of four cauldron salts, the bellied circular bodies finely chased with sprays of flowers and leaves, by Thomas Holland II, 1808, 34 ozs.
(Phillips)   £2,530

A pair of Victorian octagonal salts, each applied with a coat-of-arms and Royal monogram, the detachable tapering cover with beaded finial, by James Garrard, 1897, 5in. high, 12oz.
(Christie's)   £3,300

One of a pair of George IV silver gilt shell-shaped salt cellars, by Edward Farrell, 1824, 8¾in. high, 70oz.
£12,475

A set of four George IV silver salt cellars of oval tub shape, London 1802 and 1821, maker Richard Cooke, 16oz. (Phillips) **£1,100**

Four plated nautilus shaped salts, complete with spoons in original case, marked *E. Sanderson, London*, late 19th century. (G. A. Key) **£75**

A pair of Regency gadrooned and gilt lined cauldron salt cellars, by R. Garrard, London, 1808, 4in., 24.25oz. **£1,375**

A set of four George III large circular salt cellars, each on dished circular stand with three bracket feet chased with anthemion ornament, by Benjamin and James Smith, 1810, 4½in. diameter, 74oz. (Christie's) **£11,550**

A pair of Victorian circular salt cellars in the rococo manner, each on three mermaid supports, maker's mark *E.D.*, possibly for Emma Dear, 1846, 3½in. diameter, 16oz. (Christie's) **£1,380**

A pair of Victorian salt cellars, each on cast simulated coral and seaweed base, by John Mortimer and John S. Hunt, 1845, 3¾in. wide, 22oz.
(Christie's) £3,850

Heavy pair of late Victorian cast silver salt frames of ornate pierced and draped design, complete with blue glass liners, Sheffield 1892, 5oz. free. (G. A. Key) **£220**

A French silver gilt double compartment salt cellar and a mustard pot, maker's mark apparently F.A.T., Paris, circa 1860, 4in. high, 1289gr. **£2,310**

One of a set of four George III silver gilt octagonal salt cellar stands, by Robert and Samuel Hennell, 1805, 5¼in. long, 28oz. **£3,325**

Four Victorian silver salt cellars, each formed as a standing figure, by E. & J. Barnard, 7¾in. high, 70oz. **£20,195**

One of a pair of Elkington & Co. Victorian salts, with blue glass liners, Birmingham 1852, 8 oz. (Woolley & Wallis) **£200**

A salt cellar by Gorham, Providence, 1872, with a bail handle attached to angular handles, on four flaring cylindrical raking legs, 3in. high, 2 oz. (Christie's) **£415**

A pair of Victorian circular salts cast and pierced with scrolls, festoons and acanthus with blue glass liners, 3¼in. diameter, John and Henry Lias, London 1840. (Bearne's) **£350**

One of a set of six silver gilt Victorian swing handled salts, 9cm. long, 1872, by George Fox, also one of six cast gilt salt spoons, by G. Adams, 1880, 16oz. **£1,540**

Pair of Russian salt boxes with shaped back plates and stud feet, gilt lined, Moscow, 1876, 5in. high. **£715**

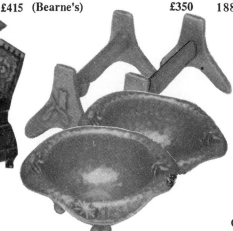

A pair of knife rests and open salts, by Tiffany & Co., 1878-91. **£1,000**

One of a pair of silver octagonal salts, by Wm. Forbes for Ball, Tompkins & Black, N.Y., 1839-51, 2½in. high, 7oz. **£460**

20TH CENTURY

A Faberge silver salt in the form of an elephant, circa 1900, 3.2cm.
£2,500

A Guild of Handicraft lidded hammered silver salt dish, set with a cabochon amethyst, with green Powell glass liner, with London hallmarks for 1904, 5.5cm. high, 50 grams. gross. (Christie's) £308

An Edwardian novelty silver salt caster as a pear, Chester marks, 3in. high. (Spencer's) £110

Whimsical Georg Jensen sterling figural salts, modelled as owls, with hardstone eyes, 2½ in. high. (Skinner) £287

One of a pair of Guild of Handicraft Ltd. silver salts, the design attributed to C. R. Ashbee, the bowls embossed and pierced with fish, 4cm. high, marks for G of H Ltd. 1907. (Phillips) £2,000

A C.R. Ashbee hammered silver salt stand, the vertical supports with openwork design of stylised trees set with heart-shaped amber cabochons, London hallmarks for 1900, 5cm. high, 50 grams. gross. (Christie's) £462

A set of four Arts and Crafts oblong salt cellars of shallow boat-shaped form, on four shaped bracket supports, by Omar Ramsden, 1932, 2¾in. wide. (Christie's) £770

Set of six Georg Jensen Sterling salts and spoons, Acorn pattern, approximately 5 troy oz. (Skinner) £545

A pair of Guild of Handicraft Ltd. silver salts, designed by C. R. Ashbee, 5.70cm. high, London hallmarks for 1900, with green glass liners. (Phillips) £1,500

18TH CENTURY

SALVERS

Salvers, known as waiters in the trade (they were used by servants when waiting upon you) can be oval, round or rectangular, but they only become trays when they have handles. The earliest surviving examples date from the 17th century and have a central spreading foot. They are often called tazze (q.v.). From about 1725 small feet were applied at the circumference.

In the 18th century square and octagonal shapes with cast, chased or pierced ornamentation became fashionable. Armorials were a particularly popular form of decoration, while early borders had plain mouldings, followed by shell and scroll, pierced, beaded and gadrooned patterns. Salvers were made in various sizes, and many formed part of a toilet service.

After 1760 salvers were also made in Sheffield Plate. Salvers were much used, not to say abused, items, and many, therefore, tend to be in poor condition. The feet in particular are apt to be pushed through or torn out.

A George II shaped circular salver on scroll feet, by John Swift, 1751, 22¾in. diam., 136oz. £5,810

One of a pair of George I plain circular salvers, by R. Timbrell & J. Bell I, 1714, 9¾in. diam., 33oz. £6,535

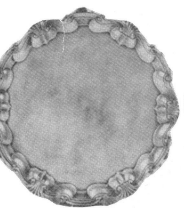

A George II shaped circular salver, with an applied shell and scroll rim and plain ground, Hugh Mills, London, 1748, 12¼in., 33oz. (Christie's S. Ken) £1,210

A George III shaped circular salver, 8in. diameter, maker's mark *E.C.*, probably that of Ebenezer Coker, London 1771, 396 gms, 12.7 oz. (Bearne's) £360

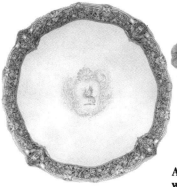

A large silver gilt shaped circular salver, on four curved openwork vine tendril feet, by Wm. Cripps, 1750, 22½in. diam., 157oz. £21,385

A Danish shaped-circular salver, with foliage border and the centre engraved with a paterae, Copenhagen, circa 1740, maker's mark illegible, assaymaster Peter Nicolai von Haven, 11½in. diameter, 831grs. (Christie's) £1,760

A mid 18th century style shaped circular salver on hoof feet, with a moulded rim and plain ground, Elkington & Co., 12in. 26oz. (Christie's S. Ken) £385

A George II shaped circular salver, by George Wickes, 1739, 13in. diam., 43oz. £2,615

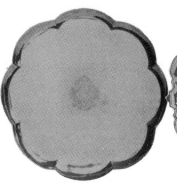

A George II plain octafoil salver, by John Robinson II, 1738, 13½in. diam., 30oz. £2,375

A George II shaped circular salver, by Sarah Holaday, 1740, 16³/₈in. diam., 70oz. £3,445

One of a pair of George II shaped circular salvers, by David Willaume II, 1743, 13¼in. diam., 118oz. £61,775

A George II shaped circular salver, of exceptional quality and gauge, 32cm. diam., by Thomas Gilpin, 1748, 45oz. (Phillips London) £5,500

A large George III shaped circular salver with plain centre, 1776 by John Carter II, 43.7cm., 61oz. (Lawrence) £1,540

An early George III circular salver, 1763, maker's mark script WT., possibly for William Turner, 35.5cm., 38.5oz. (Lawrence Fine Arts) £1,980

A George III plain oval salver, on four scroll feet, with reeded border, later engraved with a coat-of-arms, 1781, maker's mark over-struck with that of Thomas Daniell, 15¼in. wide, 48 oz. (Christie's) £1,870

An Adam circular salver, the centre engraved with the coat-of-arms of the Purchas Family, maker probably Wm. Chawner, London 1778, 15in. diam., 51oz. £1,430

SALVERS

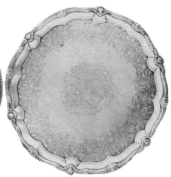

A George III salver with raised shaped shell pattern border, maker Thos. Hannan, London 1763, 12in. diam, 29oz.   £825

A George III gadrooned and shell-decorated octafoil salver on scroll feet, probably David Bell, London 1763, 14in., 47 oz. (Christie's S. Ken)   £990

One of two George II salvers in sizes, 38cm. and 24cm. diam., by George Wickes, London 1746, 74oz.1dwt.   £3,510

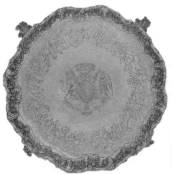

A George II silver-gilt shaped-circular salver, the border cast and chased with Bacchanalian masks and applied with trailing vines, by Charles Frederick Kandler, 1738, 13½in. diameter, 50 oz.
(Christie's)   £2,860

A George I shaped-square salver, on four bracket feet and with shaped corners and rosette moulded border, with a vacant baroque cartouche, by David Willaume, 1728, 8in. wide, 20oz. (Christie's)   £3,680

A George II shaped circular salver with shell motifs around the border, on three hoof feet, by John Tuite, 1738, 16cm. diameter, 8 ozs.
(Phillips)   £700

Irish George II silver footed salver, Charles Fox, Dublin, 1746, the circular salver with applied shaped border of scrolls and rocaille, supported by four claw and ball feet, diameter 15in., 40oz. 2dwts.
(Butterfield & Butterfield)   £1,563

A George III circular salver, the raised moulded border with leaf tied bead edge, 8in. diameter, maker Timothy Renou, London 1792, 13oz.
(Woolley & Wallis)   £700

A George II salver, with pie crust border, cast with shells, the centre engraved with a coat of arms, by James Morison, 1755, 12¾in., 28oz.
(Lawrence Fine Art)   £605

18TH CENTURY

A George I silver gilt fifteen sided salver, by A. Courtauld, 1723, 11¼in. wide, 35oz.
£33,265

A George III shaped circular salver with shell border, London 1763, 12¼in. diam., 26½oz. (Tennants) £750

An early George III shaped circular salver, by R. Rew or Rugg, London 1762, 10¼in. diam., 20oz.17dwt. £485

A George II shaped circular salver on three leaf-capped volute feet, flat chased and engraved with initials *KS* and an Earl's coronet, by John Tuite, 1755, 10in. diameter, 18oz. (Christie's) £440

A George III shaped circular salver with bead borders, on ball and claw feet, by Makepeace & Carter, 1777, 25cm. diameter, 19 ozs. (Phillips) £750

A Portuguese shaped-circular salver, engraved with a band of flowers and shell ornament and with chased shell and scroll border, Lisbon, circa 1780, 11½in. diameter, 605grs. (Christie's) £1,430

A George III circular salver, the raised rim with a reeded border and on three similar splayed supports, 1796, by Peter and Ann Bateman, 41.1cm., 42oz. (Lawrence Fine Arts) £1,705

A circular silver salver with finely moulded edge punctuated with acanthus leaves in repoussé, and on four feet, 1040gr., probably Italian and late 18th century. (Duran) £889

A George II shaped circular salver, on four scroll feet, with moulded border, engraved with a coat-of-arms and motto, by John Tuite, 1733, 12¾in. diameter, 30oz. (Christie's) £2,090

A William IV silver-gilt
shaped circular salver, by
Paul Storr, London 1836,
10in. diam., 24oz.11dwt.
£1,815

A Regency rectangular salver
by Rebecca Emes & Edward
Barnard, London 1817, 12in.,
32oz. £835

A Victorian salver, of
hexagonal form, Sheffield
1854, by Henry Wilkinson
and Co., 817 grammes, 32cm.
wide. (Henry Spencer) £520

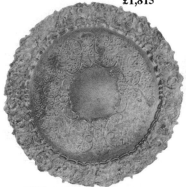

A William IV large shaped-
circular salver, on four eagle,
shell and foliage feet, chased
with birds, flowers and foliage,
by J.E. Terrey, 1831, 24¼in.
diameter, 172oz.
(Christie's) £4,180

A fine silver and mixed-metal
salver, maker's mark of Tiffany
& Co., New York, circa 1880,
the spot-hammered surface
inlaid with three butterflies of
copper, gold, platinum, and
brass, 11in. diameter, 26 oz.
10 dwt.
(Christie's) £7,392

A Victorian shaped circular
salver, the diaper flat chased
rim with a scroll and matted
leaf border, 1862 by Stephen
Smith and William Nicholson,
26.6cm., 19.6oz. (Lawrence
Fine Arts) £440

A Victorian circular salver, with
beaded edging on three tapering
feet, 14in. diameter, Frederick
Elkington, Birmingham 1879,
1035 gms, 33.2 oz.
(Bearne's) £700

A Victorian large shaped-
circular salver, the openwork
border cast and chased with
Bacchanalian masks, by Robert
Garrard, 1856, 25in. diameter,
210 oz.
(Christie's) £5,280

A Victorian shaped circular
salver, the centre engraved with
a crest, 1871, by Henry Holland
of Holland, Aldwinckle and
Slater, 41.3cm., 55.5oz. (Lawrence Fine Arts) £990

A silver salver, the centre with hunting scene, surrounded by a dedication to Count von der Schulenberg, 59.5cm. long, 1600gr.
(Arnold) £606

Mixed metal salver in the Persian taste by Tiffany & Co., New York, New York, circa 1880, of shaped octagonal form, 12in. wide, 26oz. 14 dwts.
(Butterfield & Butterfield) £5,358

Tiffany sterling and mixed metal salver, circa 1880, decorated in the Japanese taste with a dragonfly and maple branch on a hammered ground, $11^{3}/_{4}$in. wide, approximately 19 troy oz.
(Skinner Inc.) £7,817

A Victorian shaped circular salver, crested within a surround of scrolling acanthus and strapwork, $12^{1}/_{2}$in. diameter, R. Garrard, London 1865, 1105 gms, 35.5 oz.
(Bearne's) £1,100

An early Victorian small salver by the Barnards, the pie-crust rim with cast and pierced escallop shell flower head and scroll border, London 1840, 460 grammes, 25cm. diameter.
(Spencer's) £460

A William IV Scottish shaped circular salver on foliate and shell feet and with an applied foliate, shell and floral rim, J. McKay, Edinburgh 1830, 12in., 29.75 oz.
(Christie's S. Ken) £495

A George III shaped circular salver, engraved with shells, scrolls and scalework, $10^{1}/_{4}$in. diameter, Paul Storr, London, 1817, 885 gms, 28.4 oz.
(Bearne's) £1,350

A George III circular salver engraved at the centre with crest and motto above a coat-of-arms, 20in. diameter, W. and P. Cunningham, Edinburgh 1802, 3240 gms, 104.1 oz.
(Bearne's) £1,650

Victorian silver salver, Storr, Mortimer and Hunt, London 1852, chased and reticulated vintage pattern rim, approximately 88 troy oz.
(Skinner Inc.) £1,836

A spot hammered circular salver on leafy pad feet, with flower capped wavy border, 21.5cm. diam., 1925, 11.75oz. (Phillips London)   £900

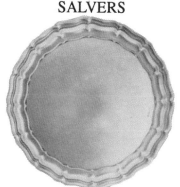

An attractive salver, with moulded border, on three scroll chased bracket feet, Sheffield 1939, by Gladwin Ltd., 35.6cm. diam., 51oz. (Bonhams)   £520

Attractive late Victorian shaped circular silver salver having applied foliate and scrolled border, Birmingham 1900, 12in. diameter, 15oz. (G. A. Key)   £200

An Edwardian small salver, the central circular panel flat chased with scrolling foliage within a shell, scroll and acanthus leaf cast pie-crust border, Birmingham 1905, 845 grammes, 32.5cm. diameter. (Spencer's)   £400

A large circular salver, 18in. diameter, with raised scroll and shell border, commemorative inscription engraved to centre, London, 1911, by Thomas Bradbury & Sons, 80 ozs. (Bonhams)   £1,000

A good and attractive early George V salver by Mappin & Webb, of lobed circular form, the central panel bright cut engraved in the neo-classic style, Sheffield 1916, 1146 grammes, 40cm. diameter. (Spencer's)   £600

Sterling hand chased salver, S. Kirk & Son, Baltimore, circa 1932–1961, the border chased in repoussé with flowers on a stippled ground, with plain face, 24oz. 2dwts. (Butterfield & Butterfield) £301

An attractive salver, 16in., shaped circular with scroll border, on four shell-chased scroll supports, Sheffield, 1929, 58 ozs. (Bonhams)   £640

A salver, with a Chippendale style shaped rim, on three scrolled feet, engraved with crest to centre, by S. Blanckensee & Son Ltd., 1939, 32cm., 26oz. (Lawrence)   £187

18TH CENTURY

Sauceboats for the newly fashionable pouring sauces first appeared in the Georgian England of the early 18th century. The first examples were of a canoe design, with a lip at each end and a handle at each side, the sides soon becoming higher than the lips. Many double-lipped sauce boats with florid relief decoration are, however, 19th century copies.

In the 1720s the sauceboat assumed its final, single-spouted form, with the handle at the other end. The wide, upcurving spout is balanced by a high, double-scroll handle, and the vessel is mounted on a wide oval foot. In the 1730s three and four-footed designs appeared, the feet joining the body with wide lion masks and sometimes also with further applied ornament. Shell shapes, often with scalloped foot rings, usually date from the 1740s–1760s, but again one finds heavier, cast ornamented 19th century copies.

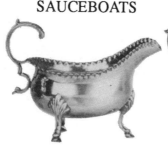

A George III sauce-boat on shell and hoof feet, with a punch-beaded rim and leaf-capped double scroll handle, maker's mark probably *W.S.*, London 1771, 5³/₄in. (Christie's) £308

A George III Irish sauceboat with repoussé decoration of a dog, bird and squirrel among scrollwork, Dublin, circa 1765 (maker's mark poorly struck), 7.5oz.
(Lawrence Fine Art) **£528**

A pair of George II shaped-oval sauceboats, each with quilted double-scroll handle and gadrooned rim, by William Cripps, 1750, 8¹/₄in. long, 29oz. (Christie's) £4,180

A pair of George II large gadrooned sauce boats on knurled scroll and shell feet, George Metheun, London 1751, 8³/₄in., 28.75oz. (Christie's) £1,595

A pair of fine George I plain two-handled double-lipped sauceboats, each on spreading oval foot and with moulded rim, by George Wickes, 1725, 7¹/₂in. long, 26oz.
(Christie's) **£22,000**

A pair of George III Irish plain shaped-oval sauceboats, each on cast spreading foot and with leaf-capped scroll handle, by Robert Calderwood, Dublin, circa 1760, 8in. long, 33oz. (Christie's) £7,150

A pair of fine George II plain double-lipped sauceboats, each with moulded shaped rim and faceted double scroll handles, by Peter Archambo, 1729, 8¹/₂in. long, 37oz.
(Christie's) **£24,200**

French solid silver sauceboat, Paris, 1793-94, 8in.
long, approx. 14 troy oz.
£405

One of a pair of George II oval-
shaped sauceboats, by Wm.
Skeen, London, 1755, 16oz.
4dwt., 6¾in. high.   **£555**

One of a pair of George II
sauceboats in the rococo
style, London 1759, 19cm.
high, 37.6oz.   **£1,540**

One of a pair of George II
plain sauceboats with serpent scroll handle, by Robt.
Brown, 1743, 24oz. **£2,375**

One of a pair of George III
sauceboats, by Abraham
Portal, 1763, 42oz. **£4,160**

One of a pair of oval sauceboats
by J.A.G. L'Herminotte,
Maastricht, 1768–70, 16.5cm.,
745gr.   **£3,965**

George II silver sauce boat with
bold card cut rim, flying scrolled
handle, standing on three
animal feet, London 1737.
(G. A. Key)   **£400**

A George II Irish shaped-oval
sauceboat, on moulded base with
leaf-capped scroll handle,
Dublin, circa 1735, maker's
mark probably that of John
Williamson, 9in. long, 22oz.
(Christie's)   **£1,980**

One of a pair of George III
two-handled double-lipped
sauceboats, by Thos.
Heming, 1761, 38oz.
      £4,160

One of a pair of George III
Irish oval sauceboats, by
Matthew West, Dublin,
1775, 23oz.17dwt., 8¾in.
long.   **£1,575**

One of a pair of Belgian
double-lipped sauceboats,
Mons, 1778, maker's mark
CL crowned, 7¼in. long,
19oz.10dwt.   **£4,260**

One of a matching pair of
George III sauceboats, by
D. Smith and R. Sharp,
1760/62, 22cm. long, 27oz.
      £1,430

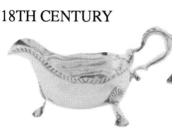

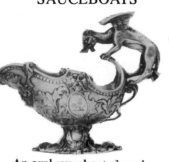

A George III sauceboat with shaped gadroon border and shell pad feet, London 1761, 13oz. (Tennants) **£620**

An oval sauceboat chased with foliage, unmarked, circa 1740, 7in., 15oz.11dwt. **£3,750**

One of a pair of George III oval sauceboats, by Wm. Skeen, London, 1767, 6¾in. high, 16oz.15dwt. **£1,185**

One of a pair of George III oval ogee sauceboats, possibly by W. Vincent, 1771, 8¼in. long, 27oz. **£925**

One of a pair of George III plain oval sauceboats, by Wm. Skeen, 1763, 5¾in. high, 35oz. **£2,785**

One of a pair of George II Irish shaped oval sauceboats, by J. Hamilton, Dublin, circa 1745, 33oz. **£2,375**

An elegant George III sauce boat, the oval boat with high looped spur handle, London 1790, probably by Hester Bateman, 224 grammes. (Spencer's) **£250**

One of a pair of George III sauceboats, by Wm. Skeen, London, 1767, 6½in. high, 15oz.5dwt. **£995**

One of a pair of George III sauce boats on shell and hoof feet, maker's initials *W.F.*, London 1766, 7¹/₂in., 18.50oz. (Christie's) **£715**

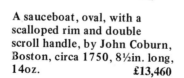

One of a pair of George II sauceboats on three rococo scroll and shell feet, by J. Kirkup, Newcastle, 1754, 46oz. **£2,375**

A sauceboat, oval, with a scalloped rim and double scroll handle, by John Coburn, Boston, circa 1750, 8½in. long, 14oz. **£13,460**

One of a pair of George II plain sauceboats with rising dolphin handles, by Francis Crump, 1742, 29oz. **£4,990**

18TH CENTURY

A good quality George I sauce-boat, the sides flat chased with C-scrolls, scalework and leaves, London 1718, by Robert Pilkington, 20.4cm., 14.5oz. (Bonhams) £580

A George II fluted and moulded sauce boat on lion's mask, paw and serpent feet, Edward Feline, London 1737, 7¹/₂in., 13.75oz. (Christie's) £990

An Irish Provincial sauce boat of plain oval form on three lion's mask and paw feet, by Jonathan Buck, Limerick, circa 1740, 8in. wide, 12oz. (Christie's) £4,025

A pair of George II fluted shaped-oval sauceboats, each with leaf-capped scroll handle and reeded rim, by John Jacobs, 1739, 7¹/₄in. long, 29oz. (Christie's) £6,050

Two plain oval sauceboats, with shaped rims and upcurved scroll handle engraved with acanthus foliage, 18th century, marks not identified, 1137grs. (Christie's) £3,740

A pair of George II silver sauce-boats, each on three shell and scroll feet and with double scroll handle, by John Barbe, 1748, 9¹/₄in. long, 26oz. (Christie's) £2,070

A pair of George II large sauce boats on shell and scroll feet, Thomas Whipham, London 1749, 8¹/₂in., 32oz. (Christie's) £1,540

A pair of silver sauce boats, maker's mark of Joseph Anthony, Jr., Philadelphia, circa 1785, 7¹/₂in. long, 28oz. 10dwt. (Christie's) £13,794

A pair of George III oval sauce boats, each on three pad feet, 7in. long, maker's mark W.S. possibly that of William Skeen, London 1768, 20.1oz. (Bearne's) £920

19TH CENTURY

One of a pair of George IV oval ogee sided sauceboats, by I.H. and G. Lias, London, 1824, 28oz. £1,375

A George III sauceboat, makers probably WF for Wm. Fountain, 1809, 15oz. 13dwt. £1,900

One of a pair of late Victorian cast shell-shape sauceboats, by Charles S. Harris, London, 1897. £505

A pair of silver sauceboats and pair of sauce ladles, maker's mark of Jones, Ball & Poor, Boston, 1847–1854, height of sauceboat 6in., 32oz. (Christie's) £2,597

Pair of French silver sauce boats, late 19th century, helmet form with mythical beast handle, 8³/₈in. high, approximately 52 troy oz. (Skinner Inc.) £2,780

A pair of George III large shaped-oval sauceboats, each body applied with a similar band and with leaf-capped scroll handle and gadrooned rim, by Thomas Robins, 1811, 9¹/₂in. long, 48oz. (Christie's) £6,050

A pair of silver sauce boats, on three hoof feet, foliate capped scroll handles, Sheffield 1892, weight 17oz. (Bonhams) £340

Two Victorian sauce boats of George III design, the boat shape bodies with floral repoussé decoration, maker's mark *J.A.*, 1854/1859, 16.5cm., 14.5 oz. (Lawrence Fine Art) £572

A pair of George IV gadrooned sauce boats on shell and scroll feet, Richard Sibley, London 1825, 8in., 32oz. (Christie's S. Ken.) £2,640

19TH CENTURY

One of a pair of George IV oval sauceboats, by Edward Farrell, London, 1829, 8¾in. high, 29oz.10dwt.
£1,695

A French late 19th century two-handled double lipped oval sauce boat with shaped reeded border and fitted oval stand, 10in. wide. (Christie's S. Ken)   £308

An Austro-Hungarian 19th century gilt lined double-lipped sauceboat on an oval stand, 9¾in. wide, 23.25oz.
£265

A pair of silver Victorian large plain oval sauceboats each on three shell and scroll feet, by James Garrard, 1895, 8½in. long, 32oz.
(Christie's)   £862

A pair of silver sauce boats, maker's mark of Marquand & Co., New York, 1833–1839, 9½in. long, 34oz.
(Christie's)   £2,033

A pair of Victorian sauceboats, each on oval moulded foot, by John S. Hunt, 1865, stamped Hunt & Roskell Late Storr & Mortimer, 48oz. (Christie's London)   £6,600

A silver-gilt mounted agate sauceboat, Charles Rawlings & William Summers, London, 1848, the handle formed as a wriggling snake, 6¼in. long.
(Sotheby's)   £880

Swedish silver sauceboat, Bengt Fredrik Tellander, Jonkoping, early 19th century, with applied classical medallions on the sides, 5¾in. high, 5oz. 12 dwts.
(Butterfield & Butterfield) £410

One of a pair of William IV sauceboats by J. D. Edington, London, circa 1830, 8in., 40oz.8dwt.
£970

20TH CENTURY

Pair of Kirk repousse sterling sauce boats, Baltimore, 1903, chased floral design, 8¾in. long, approximately 18 troy oz. (Skinner) **£600**

One of a pair of Regency-style scallop shell bowl sauceboats, makers Carrington & Co., London 1907. **£705**

A pair of George V oval sauce boats, each on three shell capped feet, 8in. long, Goldsmiths and Silversmiths Company Ltd., London 1932, 750 gms, 24.1 oz. (Bearne's) **£520**

A fine pair of George II style shaped oval sauceboats and ladles, by D. & J. Welby, 1959 and 1960, 7¾in. long, 41oz. (Christie's) **£1,760**

A pair of plain helmet-shaped sauce boats, each on rectangular base with reeded borders and scroll handles, by Hawkesworth Eyre & Co. Ltd., 1911, weight 20oz.(Christie's) **£715**

Pair of Edwardian silver sauceboats of Georgian style, London 1905, 6¼in. wide, 17oz. **£550**

Danish Sterling sauceboat, Georg Jensen, Copenhagen, circa 1925–1930, plain long oval vessel with twisted flat wire handle, 6½in. high, 14oz. 8 dwts. (Butterfield & Butterfield) **£1,009**

Arthur Stone sterling silver gravy boat with undertray, circa 1918, Arthur L. Hartwell and David Carlson, impressed marks. (Skinner) **£521**

A George V large sauce boat in the early Georgian style, of baluster form with acanthus leaf sheathed high scrolling and re-scrolling handle, London 1935, 302 grammes. (Spencer's) **£190**

SAUCEPANS

A Christofle white metal saucepan designed by Lino Sabattini, the almond shaped pan with curving sides, 18.9cm. wide. **£300**

A circular silver brazier by Myer Myers, New York, circa 1760, 4¹/₈in. diam., 6oz.4dwt. **£13,715**

A shallow saucepan designed by H. Nielsen, stamped Dessin H.N. Georg Jensen G.J. 925S 644, circa 1920, 5.3 cm. high, 11oz.12dwt. gross weight. **£415**

An Old Sheffield plate plain tapering brandy saucepan and cover with ebonised turned wood side handle, 11in. overall. (Christie's S. Ken) **£176**

A late 17th century saucepan, circa 1690, 3½in. high, 12oz.4dwt. **£790**

George III saucepan and cover of slightly bombe form, by J. Wakelin & W. Taylor, 1780, gross 9oz. 16dwt. **£890**

A George III saucepan, marked James Le Bass, also struck Hamy, Dublin, 1814, 6¹/₄in. high, 33oz.3dwt. **£1,815**

An Indian Colonial plain circular saucepan and cover with two detachable turned wood handles, Twentyman & Co., Calcutta, probably circa 1830, 8³/₄in. overall, 29oz. gross. (Christie's) **£418**

A silver saucepan, maker's mark of Abraham Carlile, Philadelphia, 1791–1794, overall length 8³/₄in., gross weight 12oz. (Christie's) **£2,904**

SHAVING POTS

Rare solid silver shaving mug, circular shaped on a stepped base with beaded edges, Birmingham 1905, 3¹/₂in. tall, 6oz.
(G. A. Key) **£270**

George IV shaving pot on stand, by Archibald Douglas, London, 1829, 17oz.15dwt., 7½in. high. **£605**

An unusual late Victorian shaving mug, the hinged cover engraved with a monogram, London 1899, by Alex Clark, 251 grammes gross. (Henry Spencer) **£290**

SMOKING ITEMS

'Zeppelin' a white metal cigarette
and match holder, 22.8cm. long.
£205

A composite three piece smoking
set, comprising a small cigarette
box, a small ashtray and a
cigarette case, Birmingham
1951, 113 grammes weighable
silver.
(Spencer's)   £110

MG Magic Midget George
Eyston's Record Breaking
Car, modelled as a silver
petrol lighter, Birmingham,
1931, 7½in. long.   £1,210

A Victorian novelty conical cigar
lighter modelled as a candle
snuffer, applied with a scroll
handle and engraved with an
initial and coronet, L.D., London
1883, 6¼in.
(Christie's S. Ken)   £418

A rare elephant tusk humidor
by Tiffany & Company, New
York, the body formed by an
oval shaped section of an elephant's tusk, repousse and
chased in stylized floral motifs
in the Indian taste, 10½in. high.
£6,752

A cigarette case and lighter
given to Sam K. Winston by
Marlene Dietrich, French, 1931,
in silver- and gold-coloured
metal, black enamel outer with
red, black and white rectangles/
squares. (Sotheby's)   £2,200

A large white metal petrol-
burning table lighter with clock
mounted to the front, the matt
gilt dial with stepped bezel,
10 x 8cm.
(Christie's S. Ken)   £165

A figural cigar stand, Tiffany &
Company, New York,
1865–1870, supported by three
cast fully-modelled putti, on a
shaped plinth base, 8³/₈in. high,
29 oz. 10 dwt. (Christie's) £1,245

A Russian table lighter of urn
or tureen shape by Karl Faberge,
decorated with swags and bead
borders, circa 1910, 9.8cm.
high. (Phillips)   £700

An ivory and silver cigar
holder on six flattened
ball feet, by Tiffany &
Co., N.Y., 1881, 6½in.
high.   £4,065

18TH CENTURY

Snuff is powdered tobacco for inhaling, and the habit of 'taking snuff' was first adopted by both sexes in 17th century France, quickly spreading to the rest of Europe. Louis XIV, however, disliked the habit, so his courtiers used little boîtes à portrait as secret snuff containers. Thus the snuff box was born.

Because the boxes had to be tightly closed, a hinged lid was most common, with an integral hinge being introduced after 1730. Boxes became prized gifts, and were made in precious metals, often set with enamelling or precious stones. They lent themselves too to novelty shapes.

A French cartouche-shaped snuff box, 7.9cm. wide, Paris, 1738. £990

A late 17th/early 18th century oval tortoiseshell snuff box, the cover inlaid with chinoiserie scene. £135

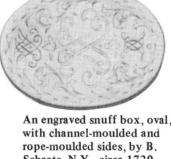

An engraved snuff box, oval, with channel-moulded and rope-moulded sides, by B. Schaats, N.Y., circa 1720, 2¹/₁₆in. wide, 2oz. £13,550

A large German hardstone snuff box of cartouche form, after the manner of the designs of M. Engelbrecht of Augsburg, circa 1740-50, 12cm. wide. £1,915

American silver snuff box, Daniel Henchman, Boston, circa 1750–1775, disc shaped, the lid engraved with a border of repeating scored leaves centering a stylised flower, diameter 2³/₈in., 1oz. 14dwts. (Butterfield & Butterfield) £714

A Louis XV cartouche-shaped silver-mounted tortoiseshell snuff-box, the hinged cover inlaid in mother-of-pearl and repoussè, Paris, 1738-44, 3in. wide (Christie's) £550

A German circular amethystine quartz snuff-box, the cover applied with a chased and engraved openwork vine entwined with shell, scroll and foliage border, probably Dresden, mid-18th century, 2³/₄in. diameter. (Christie's) £7,475

A gilt metal and mother-of-pearl snuff box, probably German, 2¾in. wide, circa 1740. £460

A good and rare George III fox head snuff box, by Phipps & Robinson, 1795, 9.5cm. high, 5.25oz. (Phillips London) £2,200

A George II cartouche-shaped silver snuff box, circa 1740, unmarked, 3in. long. £830

19TH CENTURY

A Victorian shaped rectangular pocket snuff box, Birmingham 1844 by Nathaniel Mills, 5.5.cm. (Lawrence) £242

A Continental silver and tortoiseshell snuff box, unmarked probably French, circa 1820. £125

A Victorian rectangular silver snuff box, maker's mark F.M., Birmingham, 1854, 3½ x 2½in., 4½oz. £225

An early Victorian gilt lined, engine-turned box with applied cast floral thumbpiece, possibly by E. Edwards, London, 1839, 4¾in. long. £495

A William IV cartouche shaped gilt lined snuff box, applied with an engraved tortoiseshell plaque, Nathaniel Mills, 1833, 3¼in. (Christie's S. Ken) £572

A George IV oblong snuff box, the cover engraved with the Nassau Balloon rising over Norwich, by T. Shaw, Birmingham, 1824, 7.9cm. long. £530

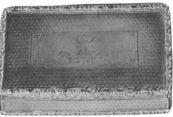

A Victorian silver snuff box engraved on the cover with a view of Wricklemarsh, Blackheath, Kent, by Yapp & Woodward, Birmingham, 1845, 4¾in. long. £1,485

A George IV silver-gilt oblong snuffbox, the cover engraved with a crest and motto within a rectangular cartouche, by Edward Smith, Birmingham, 1831, 3¹/₂in. long, 4oz. (Christie's) £517

A George IV rectangular snuff box, the cover chased with a view of Newstead Abbey, by Joseph Willmore, Birmingham, 1825, 7.2cm. long, 3.75oz. (Phillips London) £320

An early Victorian Castle Top snuff box by Nathaniel Mills, with a view of Newstead Abbey, Birmingham 1837, 6cm. wide. (Henry Spencer) £625

A George IV Scottish gilt lined oblong snuff box, the hinged cover with a plaque of Pegasus, maker's or retailer's mark Home, Edinburgh, 1824, 3¼in. long. £830

A Victorian table snuff box, the cover engraved with a view of St Michael's Mount, Penzance, by Edward Edwards, 1846, 7.25oz. (Phillips London) £620

A George III oval silver snuff box, by Joseph Angell, London, 1817, 4¼in. wide. £990

An early Victorian silver snuff box by Nathaniel Mills, of plain rectangular form, Birmingham 1846, 75 grammes, 7.5cm. wide. (Spencer's) £340

An oblong snuff box by Bernt Christopher Kelberlade, the base dated 1772, 7.3cm. wide. £765

A Russian rectangular gilt lined snuff box, the lid nielloed with figures on a gilt matted ground, 3in. (Christie's S. Ken) £605

An early Victorian casket-shape snuff box, with an engine turned base, Joseph Willmore, Birmingham 1842, 4oz. (Woolley & Wallis) £400

A Chinese export silver gilt oblong snuff box, chased overall with fruiting vine on a matted ground, 19th century, 10.4cm. (Lawrence) £319

An oval parcel gilt and niello snuff box, maker's mark D. L., Moscow, 1836, 7.1cm. wide. £1,320

A 19th century small silver snuff box modelled as a skull with articulated jaw, 1 ⅝in. long. £580

A silver-mounted carapace snuff box with reeded borders and shell thumbpiece, with Dutch control mark, 3in. long. (Christie's) £506

A Russian rectangular snuff box, one side nielloed with scrolling foliage, 3.1in. (Christie's S. Ken) £286

An early Victorian rectangular snuff box, engraved overall, 1841 by Edward Edwards, 7.8cm. (Lawrence) £418

A George III oblong silver gilt snuff box, marked Linnit & Atkinson, London, 1812, 3in. wide. £1,735

A Scottish silver mounted cowrie shell snuff box, circa 1810. **£120**

A 19th century Swiss gilt metal singing bird box, 10.5cm. wide. **£795**

A silver and niello snuff box of rectangular form, maker's mark N.M., Moscow, mid 19th century, 9.2cm. wide. **£430**

A Victorian oblong engine-turned snuff box, inscribed 'Coronation 1841 the Derby Winner', by F. Clarke, Birmingham, 1841, 8.3cm. long. **£330**

An early Victorian oblong snuff box, engine turned, by Rawlings & Sumner, London, 1837, 8.6cm. wide. **£910**

A William IV oblong table snuff box with hinged cover, by Chas. Reily and George Storer, 1835, 4in. long, 10oz.12dwt. **£730**

An early Victorian castle top snuff box, by N. Mills, Birmingham, 1838, 7.2cm. long. **£435**

A George III silver gilt fox mask snuff box, by T. Phipps & E. Robinson, 1807, 3¼in., 3oz. 10dwt. **£2,375**

A George IV silver gilt oblong table snuff box with double hinged cover, by Thos. Edwards, 1820, 3¾in. long, 9oz.4dwt. **£970**

A silver gilt and niello snuff box, maker's mark O.B., Moscow, 1834, 6.6cm. wide. **£395**

A Continental silver gilt and enamel snuff box, decorated after C. Spitzweg. **£220**

A George III snuff box in the form of a purse, maker's mark RB incuse, 1814, 6.3cm. **£245**

A Scottish cartouche-shaped silver and agate snuff-box, gilt interior, by Graham and Anderson, Edinburgh, 1834–35, 3⅝in. long.
(Christie's) £920

A George III silver-gilt shaped-oblong snuffbox, the cover applied with a cast oval cartouche of winged putti within a foliage border, by William Snook Hall, 1818, 3¾in. long, 4oz.
(Christie's) £690

A George III oval snuff box, the hinged cover with a cast panel depicting a tavern scene within gadrooned border, maker probably Joseph Hayward, 1802, 3½in. wide.
(Christie's) £418

A Victorian rectangular gilt lined snuff box, with a cast view in high relief of the Burns Memorial within a heavy scroll work border, F.M., Birmingham, 1861, 3¼in.
(Christie's S. Ken) £528

A two-air musical snuff box, French/Swiss, first quarter 19th century, unsigned, the Sur-Plateau movement with two sets of separate teeth, 8.5cm wide.
(Bonham's) £2,800

A George III snuff box, of curved rectangular form, the hinged cover engraved *Souvenir* within a rectangular cartouche, Birmingham 1814, maker John Shaw, 2½ x 1½in., approximate weight 1oz.
(Bonhams) £280

A French shaped-rectangular gold, silver, diamond and enamel snuff-box, chased and applied with a central silver and gold plaque with diamond set star and crescent in a diamond border, late 19th century, 3⅜in. long.
(Christie's) £5,750

A French shallow octagonal ivory snuff-box, the hinged cover carved with a profile medallion of Louis XIV, circa 1715, probably Dieppe, 3½ in. wide.
(Christie's) £483

A William IV Scottish presentation oblong snuff box, the hinged cover with presentation inscription within cast border of thistles, shamrocks and roses, by A. G. Wigton, Edinburgh 1835, 3½in. wide, 6.5oz.
(Christie's) £715

A ram's horn snuff mull with plain silver rim and stand-off butterfly hinge, unmarked. **£55**

An English hallmarked silver and horn presentation snuff mull, Sheffield, 1901-02, by Walker & Hall, 20½in. wide. **£895**

A George III Scottish snuff mull with engraved silver mounts, the hinged cover with initials having original chain with tools, circa 1800. (Woolley & Wallis) **£300**

A gold-mounted tortoiseshell smeeching-mull, the oval hinged cover with fluted thumbpiece, probably Scottish, mid 18th century, 2³/₈in. high. (Christie's) **£935 $1,842**

A Victorian ram's head snuff mull fitted with four various snuff containers, three decorated with thistles, the fourth decorated with thistles and also engraved with an armorial, crest and motto, 15¹/₂in. overall. (Christie's) **£1,210**

A Scottish silver-mounted ebony and ivory-banded capstan snuff mull with 'butterfly' hinge and oval initial disc, circa 1745, 2¹/₂in. in. high. (Christie's) **£704**

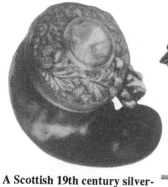

A Scottish 19th century silver-mounted horn snuff mull applied with a shield-shaped cartouche engraved with a crest and initials, unmarked, probably circa 1850, 3¹/₂in. (Christie's S. Ken) **£330 $648**

A silver mounted stag's horn snuff mull with chained pricker and perforated stopper, circa 1700, 4¾in. wide. **£355**

A 19th century silver mounted ram's horn tobacco mull, the lid with the badge and inscription *The Royal Scots.* (Finarte) **£607**

SNUFFERS

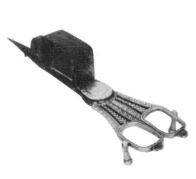

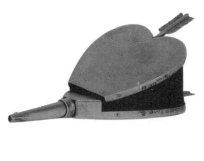

A pair of George III candle snuffers with steel cutter and box, indistinct maker's mark only, c.1800, 18.2cm. (Lawrence) £154

A Queen Anne snuffers-stand and a pair of snuffers, by Matthew Cooper, 1704, 11oz.18dwt. £8,080

An unusual late Victorian candle snuffer modelled as a pair of bellows, by James Bell & Louis Wilmott, 1900 and inscribed with retailer's name *H. Wells, Shrewsbury.* (Phillips) £299

SNUFFER TRAYS

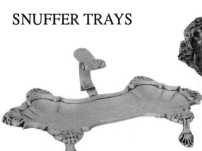

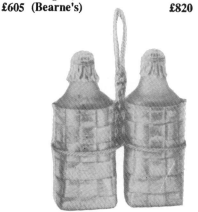

A George II snuffer's tray, the angles with projecting shells, scroll side handle, on shell pattern feet, by John Priest, 1754, 21cm., 9oz. (Lawrence Fine Art) £605

A pair of William IV shaped rectangular snuffers trays, with gadroon, acanthus and foliate edging, 9¾in. long, maker's mark *W.E.* possibly that of William Eaton, London 1830, 798 gms, 25.6 oz. (Bearne's) £820

Fine George II silver snuffers tray of waisted rectangular shape, London 1751, maker *I.P.*, 9oz. (G. A. Key) £520

SPIRIT BOTTLES

A late 19th century Russian vodka set, maker's mark IIN (Cyrillics), St. Petersburg, circa 1890, 7oz. £825

Pair of silver and glass spirit bottles, the trompe-l'oeil basketwork covers tied with a silver rope, St. Petersburg, 1880, 29cm. £2,245

A glass and silver trompe-l'oeil spirit bottle, with rope-bound wicker holder, St. Petersburg, 1884, 23cm. high. £1,650

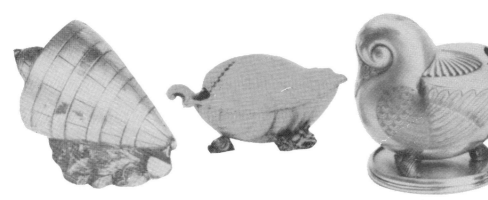

A Victorian plated spoon
warmer, in the form of a ship's
buoy, 21cm. long, circa 1870.
£190

An electroplated spoon
warmer by Elkington,
Mason & Co., Birming-
ham, 1862, 8¼in. long.
£220

A Victorian novelty plated
spoon warmer modelled as a
stylised duck on periwinkle
feet, 6in. (Christie's S. Ken)
£286

A Hukin & Heath plated
spoon-warmer with ebony
handle, the design attributed to Dr. C. Dresser, stamped H & H 2857, 14.4cm.
high.   **£285**

An electroplated spoon warmer
in the form of a nautilus shell
with bright-cut decoration on
rocky base with shell handle,
5³/4in. high.
(Bearne's)   **£80**

A Hukin & Heath electroplated
metal spoon-warmer, supported
on four spike feet, oval body,
angular bar handle, the bar of
ebonised wood, 14.5cm. high.
(Christie's)   **£935**

STANDS
BOTTLE

A Victorian electroplate decanter
stand, by Elkington & Co., with
design registration mark for 2nd
October 1868, 29.4cm. high
overall.   **£365**

Mauser Co. Sterling bottle
carrier, New York, c. 1900, in
the form of a wine bottle with
repoussé vine decoration,
11¹/₂in. high, approximately 27.5
troy oz.
(Skinner Inc)   **£909**

Victorian three bottle plated
decanter stand, registration
marks for 1870, with three cut
glass pear shaped bottles, 16in.
(G.A. Key)   **£300**

CAKE

STANDS

An Arts & Crafts fluted circular cake stand on a rising foot, J.S.B., London, 1915, 12¼in. high, 26.75oz. **£390**

An unusual George V cake stand, of three tiers with scroll supports, Sheffield 1910, makers mark *R.R.*, 764 grammes, 43cm. high.
(Spencer's) **£260**

An Edwardian foliate pierced shaped circular pedestal cake stand, G.H., London, 1910, 11¼in., 24.25oz. (Christie's S. Ken) **£352**

DESSERT

Continental style silver plateau, 20th century, shaped rising sides of parallel bracketed grooved and floral bands, mounted with a mask of a sylvan deity on front and back, 18in. long, 66oz. 14dwt.
(Butterfield & Butterfield) **£1,126**

A Victorian dessert stand, cast in high relief with entwined scaly dolphins and putti holding reins, by Frederick Elkington, 1875, 12½in. high, 84oz. (Christie's) **£5,280**

A Victorian parcel gilt dessert stand, the vine tendril stem flanked by bacchanti, the openwork frame above with applied pendant grapes and vine leaves, by J.S. Hunt, 1858, 12½in. high, 62oz. (Christie's) **£3,080**

KETTLE

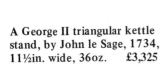

A George II triangular kettle stand, by John le Sage, 1734, 11½in. wide, 36oz. **£3,325**

A George II shaped-triangular kettle stand wind shield, on three scroll feet engraved with a crest and a cypher, by Edward Wakelin, 1757, 5in. high, 21ozs. (Christie's) **£1,265**

A George II triangular kettle stand, on three lion's paw feet and with moulded foliate scroll border, by William Peaston, 1752, 10½in. wide, 22oz. (Christie's) **£1,760**

STRAINERS

Strainers were at their height of popularity in the late 17th and early 18th century. Early examples had almost hemispherical bowls, which became shallower in subsequent designs. Two handles are generally more common than one, and both should be marked. The piercing is often done in ornamental or geometric designs. Strainers were used for straining particles, such as orange or lemon pips, particularly from punch.

A strainer with ring handle, by John Brevoort, N.Y., 1742 75, 3½in. diam., 1oz.10dwt. **£1,300**

A George III orange or lemon strainer, the pierced shallow circular body, 1799 by Henry Nutting. 19.7cm. across handles. (Lawrence Fine Arts) **£275**

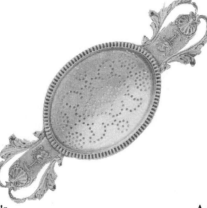

A silver punch strainer, maker's mark of John David, Jr., Philadelphia, circa 1785, with pierced scrollwork handle engraved with initials *TSC* on front, 4¹/₂in. high, 1 oz. (Christie's) **£4,620**

A George III Scottish silver two-handled punch strainer, by Robt. Gray & Sons, Edinburgh, 1811, 11¾in. long, 8oz. **£2,500**

A rare Irish Provincial orange strainer with simply pierced circular bowl and shaped lug handles, with maker's mark for William Newenham, Cork, circa 1730, 7¹/₄in. wide overall, 3oz. (Christie's) **£2,875**

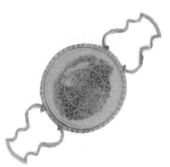

George III silver wine strainer, London, circa 1764-65, maker's mark S.H. over B.S., 9¼in. long, 4 troy oz. **£600**

A George II oval mazzarine, pierced and engraved with scrolls and shells, by Paul De Lamerie, 1745, 17¹/₂ in. long, 26ozs. (Christie's) **£2,300**

A George I lemon strainer, London, 1722, 6½in. wide over handles, 1oz.13dwt. **£510**

A sugar urn with a pierced gallery and a tapering conical lid with an urn finial, circa 1785-1810, 9½in. high, 15oz. £680

A silver covered sugar urn, maker's mark of Samuel Williamson, Philadelphia, circa 1800, 11¼in. high, 15oz. (Christie's) £1,742

Silver sugar urn, by Joseph Lownes, Phila., 1758–1820, 10in. high. £1,258

Silver covered sugar urn, Philadelphia, 1790–1800, on square pedestal base, beaded border, bright cut with festoons and shields, 9in. high, 9¾ troy oz.
(Skinner Inc.) £494

A pair of George III beaded and gilt-lined sugar vases and covers, maker's initials *H. A.*, with a pellet between, London 1801, 6¾in., 21.25oz. (Christie's) £660

A sugar urn, by Joseph Richardson, Jr., Philadelphia, circa 1790-1810, the cover and foot with beaded borders, marked, 9½in. high, 17oz. (Christie's New York) £1,798

SUGAR VASES

A George III beaded, pierced and bright-cut swing-handled pedestal sugar vase with blue glass liner, Hester Bateman, London 1779, 6¼in. overall. (Christie's S. Ken) £462

A French 19th century silver-gilt openwork sugar vase and cover, fitted with a blue glass liner, 10¼in., 25.25oz. free. (Christie's) £770

A George III pierced and engraved wing-handled sugar vase with blue glass liner and corded rim, William Plummer, London circa 1780, 7in. overall. (Christie's S. Ken) £286

17TH CENTURY

Tankards seem to have been among the most popular silver vessels in northern Europe and particularly in Scandinavia, in the 17th and 18th centuries. In Germany, those which first appeared in the 16th century were small and tapering, but later they increased in size and became more ornate. Many were made in the 17th and early 18th centuries inset with coins.

Tall, cylindrical models were favoured in the late 16th and 17th centuries in Scandinavia, while later Swedish examples have shorter, downward-tapering bodies, and broader covers and larger thumbpieces. In the Baltic states on the other hand, heavy squat tankards on ball feet were the norm in the later 17th century.

In England, embossed tankards are found dating from the 16th century, but from the 17th century, a very functional, unadorned form with cylindrical tapering barrel was preferred. The only adornment was usually a moulded rim at the junction of body and foot, or sometimes an engraved coat of arms.

A German parcel gilt tankard, possibly by Marx Schaller II, Augsburg, circa 1655, 14.3cm. high, 440gr. £2,645

A silver gilt tankard by H. C. Lau(e)r, 15cm. high, Nuremberg, circa 1610, 290gr. £2,810

A Scandinavian plain parcel-gilt cylindrical tankard, with scroll handle, ball thumbpiece and hinged, slightly domed cover, possibly by Henrik Moller of Stockholm, circa 1660, 5³/₄in., 796grs.
(Christie's) £3,300

A Charles II plain tapering cylindrical tankard, the handle pricked with initials, the body later engraved with a coat-of-arms within plume mantling, by John Sutton, 1672, 6in. high, 22oz. (Christie's) £5,500

A Charles II plain tankard, circa 1670, letter G a coronet above and three fleur-de-lys below, 8in. high, 37oz. £6,050

A Swedish gilt-lined lidded tankard in the 17th century taste, on ball feet, 8¹/₂in.
(Christie's) £935

A William III Irish plain tapering cylindrical tankard, by Joseph Walker, Dublin, 1699, 7½in. high, 28oz. £2,495

17TH CENTURY

A German silver tankard and cover, Augsburg, circa 1690, maker's mark PS, 4½in. high, 8oz.11dwt. **£2,850**

A Charles II tankard and cover engraved with scenes of the Plague and Fire of London, 1675, maker's mark IN mullet below, 7¾in. high, 38oz. **£65,340**

A Charles II plain cylindrical tankard and cover, 1671, maker's mark EG, 6½in. high, 21oz. **£3,900**

A rare Charles I Provincial silver-mounted slightly-tapering serpentine tankard, on reeded foot and with scroll handle, by Robert Mathew, Barnstable, circa 1640, 5in. high. (Christie's) **£3,910**

A German cylindrical tankard, on domed circular foot and with scroll handle, the body chased with a Bacchanalian procession, by Abraham Wilde, Köningsberg, circa 1680, 7½in. high, 849gr. (Christie's) **£3,450**

A Charles II tapering cylindrical tankard and cover, the lower part of the body chased with acanthus leaves and with a similar narrow band above, 1680, maker's mark C over W, 8¼in. high, 38oz. (Christie's) **£5,280**

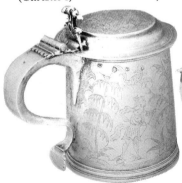

A James II slightly tapering cylindrical tankard, 1686, maker's mark SD, pellet below, possibly for Samuel Dell, 7in. high, 24oz.17dwt. **£23,760**

A parcel gilt tankard by N. Schlaugitz, Danzig, circa 1685, 16.4cm. high, 655gr. **£2,150**

A Charles II silver gilt tankard and cover, maker's mark MK in a lozenge, mullet above and below, 1683, 7½in. high, 34oz. **£2,730**

18TH CENTURY

In the 18th century bodies had become bulbous, with a boldly moulded foot, double scroll handle and also sometimes a domed lid. Broadly speaking, they passed out of fashion around the middle of the 18th century in England, with the few that were made of Sheffield plate copying silver styles. In the 19th century old tankards were often heavily embossed and sometimes converted into jugs by adding a short spout.

In the United States, in non-Conformist New England, tankards were used rather than flagons for the Communion service. Heavier forms were made in New York; in the early days these were tapering and cylindrical and the flat top persisted there, though Boston adopted a domed cover about 1715 and used a midband on the body. The New York tankard can be distinguished by an applied foliate band at the bottom, and often, also, by a corkscrew thumbpiece. Boston silversmiths preferred a dolphin, and many American makers also used a cast cherub's head for ornament on the handle.

A fine silver tankard, maker's mark of Myer Myers, New York, circa 1760, with double scroll handle, 6⁷/₈in. high, 31oz. (Christie's) £15,972

George II silver tankard, J. Kentenber, London, 1759, with later chased scrolls, approximately 24 troy oz. (Skinner) £1,294

German parcel gilt silver tankard by Dominikus Saler, Augsburg, circa 1700, with domed cover set on collet base, applied cast scrolling handle with bifurcated thumbpiece, 8¹/₄in. high. (Butterfield & Butterfield) £4,151

George III Sterling tankard by Sutton & Bult, London, 1768, the domed lid set with chair back thumb piece, fully marked on base and lid, 8¹/₄in. high, 29oz. 8dwts. (Butterfield & Butterfield) £2,075

A silver tankard, maker's mark of William Cowell, Sr. or Jr., Boston, 1725–1740, the scroll handle with moulded drop, 7⁷/₈in. high, 29oz. (Christie's) £5,082

A George II lidded tankard of plain tapering shape with angular ring, maker Samuel Wood, London 1750, 7¹/₂in., 30oz. (Tennants) £1,300

George III silver tankard, London, 1766-67, probably Jacob Marsh, engraved monogram on handle, 7¹/₄in. high, approx. 22 troy oz. (Skinner) £754

A George II plain tapering cylindrical tankard with moulded borders and girdle, engraved with a crest, maker's mark I?, 1736, 7¹/₂in. high, 26oz. (Christie's) £1,540

Early George III silver baluster pint tankard, later chased and embossed with flowers, scrolls and cartouches, London 1761 by Robert Lucas, 11 ozs. (G.A. Key) £280

A George III plain tapering cylindrical tankard, on moulded foot with plain girdle, by John Younghusband, Newcastle, 1712, 6¹/₂in. high, 18oz. (Christie's) £1,495

A Queen Anne plain tapering cylindrical tankard, with scroll handle, hinged domed cover and bifurcated thumbpiece, by Seth Lofthouse, 1705, 7¹/₄in. high, 27oz. (Christie's) £3,300

A George II lidded baluster quart tankard on a rising circular foot, with a moulded body band, probably Richard Bayley, London 1750, 7³/₄in., 25 oz. (Christie's S. Ken) £1,595

A George II plain tapering cylindrical tankard with moulded borders and girdle, the domed cover with corkscrew thumbpiece, maker's mark I?, 1736, 7¹/₂in. high, 26oz. (Christie's) £1,380

A George II plain tankard and cover, with scroll handle and domed cover with openwork thumbpiece, by Francis Spilsbury, 1741, 7¹/₂in. high, 28 oz. (Christie's) £2,860

A fine silver tankard, maker's mark of John Moulinar, New York, circa 1750, applied with a band of cut-card leaves above the moulded foot rim, 7¹/₄in. long, 35oz. (Christie's) £25,410

A George II quart lidded tankard, on a spreading moulded foot, 8in., makers William Shaw II and William Priest London 1753, 25oz. (Woolley & Wallis) £1,400

344

18TH CENTURY

A late George II tankard by William Shaw and William Priest, the hinged stepped domed cover with volute thumb piece, London 1757, 731 grams. (Spencer's) **£1,300**

An early George III tankard by W & J Priest, of single girdled tapering cylindrical form, London 1772, 846 grammes, 19.5cm. high overall. (Spencer's) **£820**

An American silver small tankard, Benjamin Burt, Boston, circa 1799, of typical New England form, 18oz. 10dwt., height 7⁷/₈in. (Sotheby's) **£6,809**

An early George I Britannia standard tankard by John Wisdome, of slightly tapering cylindrical form with applied girdle, London 1718, 663 grammes, 17cm. high. (Spencer's) **£2,300**

A George III baluster tankard chased and embossed at a later date with foliage and scrolls, by Thomas Law, Sheffield, 1793, 9in. high, 25oz. (Christie's) **£747**

A Queen Anne tankard, possibly Irish, the body finely engraved with armorials, the cover stepped domed and with a cast scroll thumbpiece, 19cm. high overall, apparently unmarked, circa 1705, 24 ozs. (Phillips) **£900**

A rare silver tankard, maker's mark of Eleazer Baker, Ashford, Connecticut, circa 1785, with an applied midband and a moulded circular base, 8in. high, 29 oz. 10 dwt. (Christie's) **£22,000**

A Queen Anne small tapering tankard with scroll handle and spreading foot, maker Thomas Holland, London 1709, 6oz., 3¹/₂in. high. (Tennants) **£650**

A George II plain tapering cylindrical tankard and cover, with a moulded rib around the body with scroll handle, by Robert Williams, 1728, 7¹/₄in. high, 24oz. (Christie's) **£2,200**

18TH CENTURY

A George II tankard, with thumbpiece and domed cover engraved with coat of arms within a rococo cartouche, by John Macbride, 1747, 18cm., 29oz. (Lawrence) £1,980

Silver tankard, Nicholas Roosevelt, New York, circa 1740, with moulded base band, scrolled thumbpiece with oval shield terminal, 7in. high, 39 troy oz. (Skinner Inc.) £527

A silver tankard, maker's mark of John Hastier, New York, circa 1740, with a flat-domed cover and a corkscrew thumbpiece, 7in. high, 29 oz. 10 dwt. (Christie's) £8,624

A George II plain baluster tankard, with scroll handle, hinged domed cover and openwork scroll thumbpiece, by John Payne, 1754, 7³/₄in. high, 30oz. (Christie's) £2,640

An American silver tankard, maker's mark of George Hanners, Boston, circa 1720, the tubular scroll handle with moulded top and terminating in a George I coin, 7³/₄in. high., 23oz. 10dwt. (Christie's) £5,325

A late George II baluster lidded tankard later chased with rising foliage, lion's masks and laurel swags, William Shaw and William Priest, London 1757, 7½in., 23.50oz. (Christie's S. Ken) £1,705

A George III, lidded tapering quart tankard on a skirted foot, Langlands and Robertson, Newcastle, 1785, 29oz. (Christie's S. Ken) £2,200

A George III plain tapering tankard on a skirted foot, with a moulded body band, John Langlands, Newcastle, 1772, 5½in., 14.75oz. (Christie's S. Ken) £858

A George I tapering cylindrical lidded quart tankard on a skirted foot, Richard Green, London 1715, Britannia Standard, 6³/₄in., 23³/₄oz. (Christie's) £1,540

A silver tankard, maker's mark of Nathaniel Hurd, Boston, 1758–1780, 8⅝in. high, 29oz. 10dwt.
(Christie's)   £11,129

A Continental lidded tankard on leaf-capped berry feet, with presentation inscription and date 1771, 6¼in. high, 20.25oz.   £1,760

A Queen Anne double quart lidded tankard, by John Downes, London 1708, 8in. high, 32oz.   £1,120

A George III small plain baluster tankard, on spreading circular foot, engraved with a coat-of-arms within a rococo cartouche, by William and John Priest, 1768, 6in. high, 15oz.
(Christie's)   £5,060

A George II plain baluster tankard, the body with applied rib and with scroll handle, hinged domed cover and scroll thumbpiece, by John Langlands, Newcastle, 1757, 7½in. high, 25oz. (Christie's)   £2,090

A silver tankard, maker's mark of Josiah Austin, Charleston and Boston, Massachusetts, circa 1765, with a scroll handle applied with a moulded drop, 8⅝in. high, 28 oz. 10 dwt.
(Christie's)   £4,928

A George III gilt lined baluster pint tankard on a chased spreading circular foot, T. W., London, 1770, 4½in., 10.25oz.
(Christie's S. Ken)   £440

An Austro-Hungarian silver-gilt and ivory tankard of tapering cylindrical form, on domed oval base chased with a band of fruit on a matted ground, 9¾in. high.
(Christie's)   £4,370

A James II plain cylindrical tankard and cover, York, 1686, maker's mark IO, perhaps for John Oliver, 6¾in. high, 21oz.   £3,565

347

18TH CENTURY

George III silver tankard, London, 1771–1772, probably John Kentenber, monogram, approximately 25 troy oz. (Skinner) £933

A late George II plain baluster pint tankard on a rising circular foot, John Langlands, Newcastle, 1757, 5in., 10oz. (Christie's S. Ken) £440

Silver tankard, circa 1770, James Butler, Boston, marked at base and to left of handle, 8¹/₂in. high, 30 troy oz. (Skinner) £2,512

A George III plain baluster tankard with applied girdle, domed cover, chair-back thumbpiece, the handle terminating in a heart motif, by Jacob Marsh or John Moore I, 1764, 21.5cm. high, 27.5 ozs. (Phillips) £2,200

A George III plain tapering cylindrical tankard, the body with applied rib and with scroll handle, hinged domed cover and corkscrew thumbpiece, by Charles Wright, 1772, 7³/₄in. high, 24oz. (Christie's) £2,090

An early George III quart lidded tankard, the baluster body with a girdle moulding, 7¹/₂in. high, makers Thomas Cooke II and Richard Gurney, London 1760, 23¹/₂oz. (Woolley & Wallis) £1,450

A George III plain tapering cylindrical tankard, on spreading base with moulded girdle, maker's mark probably that of John Dutton, 1772, 7³/₄in. high, 24oz. (Christie's) £977

A George I plain tapering cylindrical tankard, with scroll handle, hinged domed cover and corkscrew thumbpiece, the handle engraved with initials, by Henry Jay, 1718, 7in. high, 27oz. (Christie's) £3,740

A George III baluster tankard, on spreading circular base, openwork thumbpiece and scroll handle, engraved with a crest, by John Payne, 1766, 8¹/₄in. high, 32oz. (Christie's) £1,265

19TH CENTURY

A 19th century Continental parcel gilt peg tankard and cover, 8½in. high, 38oz.

£1,665

A massive plated-on-copper tankard of tapering cylindrical form with crimped borders, the body richly embossed with a cavalry skirmish, 14in. high overall.
(Christie's)   £638

A massive Continental tankard in the Scandinavian manner, on three foliage ball feet, London import hallmarks for 1892, 12½in. high, 88oz.
(Christie's)   £2,415

A Victorian cylindrical flagon, hinged domed cover with seated boar finial, chased and applied with masks, boars, dogs, fruits and strapwork, with inscription dated *1867*, by James Charles Edington, 1866, 10¾in. high, 47oz.
(Christie's)   £1,955

A Hukin & Heath electroplated tankard designed by Dr. Christopher Dresser, tapering cylindrical form with ebonised bar handle, 21.5cm. high.
(Christie's)   £418

Peter, Anne & William Bateman, a George III quart baluster tankard, with reeded girdle moulding, engraved with a picture of a prize bull in a field, 8½in., London 1804, 26.5oz.
(Woolley & Wallis)   £1,200

A late Victorian early Georgian style tankard, of single girdled baluster form, London 1823, makers mark *H.S.*, 915 grammes, 20cm. high.
(Spencer's)   £660

A repoussé tankard, by Tiffany & Co., N.Y. finished March 10, 1893, for the World's Columbian Exposition, Chicago, 1893, 10in. high, 52oz. 10dwt.   £17,987

A Victorian spouted lidded plain tapering quart tankard in the mid-18th century taste, Daniel and Charles Houle, London, 1877, 7in., 27¼oz.
(Christie's S. Ken)   £1,100

A Continental large cylindrical three-handled tankard and cover, the body and cover inset with various thalers of Saxony, Austria, etc., London import marks for 1892, 15in. high, 104oz. (Christie's) £2,970

Late 19th century Dutch silver-coloured metal tankard, 5¾in., 8oz. £500

An antique American silver tankard by Thomas Fletcher and Sidney Gardiner of Boston and Philadelphia, circa 1812, 10½in. high, 43.6 troy oz. (Selkirk's) £5,197

A George III tankard, the slightly tapering cylindrical body applied with a reeded girdle, monogrammed, Samuel Godbehere, Ed Wigan & J. Bult, 1802, base weighted, 7½in. high. (Lawrence Fine Art) £902

Regency silver quart tankard, William Bateman, London, 1815, set on a wide flaring collet base with applied ribbed band on centre, 6½in. high, 28oz. 4dwt. (Butterfield & Butterfield) £1,689

An unusual George III tankard, 9in. high, with a broad band of vines, leaves and 'C'-scrolls chased against a stippled ground, London, 1818, by William Bateman I, 44 oz. (Bonhams) £1,400

A trophy tankard by Tiffany & Co., New York, circa 1890, with a low circular cover and scrolled handle, 10¼in. high, 47 oz. (Christie's) £2,618

A George III tapering cylindrical tankard, by J. W. Storey and W. Elliot, 1813, 7¾in. high, 57oz. £4,280

An unusual mid-19th century China Trades topographical tapering pint tankard with applied sinuous dragon scroll handle and moulded rim, circa 1850, 5in. (Christie's S. Ken) £550

20TH CENTURY

A Liberty & Co. 'Cymric' silver tankard designed by Archibald Knox, 1901, 19.25cm. high. £4,355

An Omar Ramsden hammered silver tankard, London hall-marks for 1914, 16oz., 12.5cm. high. £1,000

A late Victorian baluster tankard with moulded girdle, by J. Round, Sheffield 1900, 21.5cm. high, 25oz. £1,000

A good Queen Anne-style tankard, the flat cover with inscription and twist thumbpiece, Carrington & Co., London 1920, 27.5 oz.
(Woolley & Wallis) £560

A good Charles II-style tankard, 'C' scroll thumbpiece, scroll handle and moulded foot rim, Robert Frederick Fox, London 1915, 27oz.
(Woolley & Wallis) £600

Scandinavian white metal tankard, decorated with mask mounts and embossed band of fruit and foliage, 44oz. (of white metal).
(G. A. Key) £220

TAPERSTICKS

A Victorian fluted and foliate-stamped taperstick on a rising shaped circular base, Henry Wilkinson and Co., Sheffield 1850, 5³/₄in.
(Christie's S. Ken.) £660

A matched pair of Victorian taper holders, each on a shaped circular base with foliage borders, by H. Wilkinson and Co. Sheffield, 1838 and 1844, 5¹/₂in. high.
(Christie's) £715

An early Victorian taperstick, of lobed flared cylindrical form with acanthus leaf sheathed double 'C' scroll handle, Sheffield 1841, by Henry Wilkinson & Co., 13.5cm. high.
(Spencer's) £220

TAZZE

The word 'tazza' has the same root as the French *tasse* or Scottish *tassie*, and, strictly speaking, means a wine cup with round, shallow bowl. It was first applied to vessels of this type dating from the 16th and 17th centuries.

Many early examples were made of Venetian glass, but silver forms appeared in Britain and Europe from the early 16th century. Dutch examples can be extremely ornate, embossed with Biblical, mythological or genre scenes, the interior set with an embossed circular plaque. 17th century examples more often had a plain bowl and a baluster stem. The form was revived in Britain in the mid 19th century as being suitable for racing cups and other presentation items.

The term has since come erroneously to mean a flat dish or salver on a circular foot.

In this form they usually followed typical salver styles as far as decoration was concerned, mainly plain, or with a central armorial and a beaded or gadrooned rim. In their later revived form they are often much more ornate.

Attractive Guild of Handicraft Ltd. silver and enamel tazza, London, 1905, 15.25cm. high.　£2,500

Dominick & Haff sterling tazza, with a reticulated shaped rim and bell-form base, monogram. (Skinner)　£302

A Queen Anne tazza, of good gauge, the plain circular surface engraved with a finely executed contemporary coat-of-arms, by David Willaume I, 1702, 34oz.
(Phillips London)　£20,000

A large tazza designed by G. Jensen, stamped marks Georg Jensen GI925, 264, 26.7cm. high, 35oz.12dwt.　£4,750

A late Victorian part gilt tazza, by George Fox, in the Renaissance manner, 16.5cm. high, 1872, 19oz. (Phillips) £650

A pair of pierced and engraved circular tazze with applied stylised foliate rims, 8½in. diam., 19.75oz.　£165

A covered tazza designed by J. Rohde, stamped Dessin J.R. Georg Jensen 43, circa 1920, 15.5cm. high, 14oz. 9dwt.　£1,190

A Jensen coupe, 12.5cm., stamped 'Sterling Denmark', 1930's. **£330**

A good Edwardian gilt tazza, the incurved sides finely embossed with Bacchanalian masks, trophies and cartouches, by Christian Leopold Reid, London 1909, 37oz. (Tennants) **£850**

A tazza with two scrolling strapwork handles, by Tiffany & Co., 1870-75, 6½in. high, 12⅝in. wide, overall, 23oz.10dwt. **£1,015**

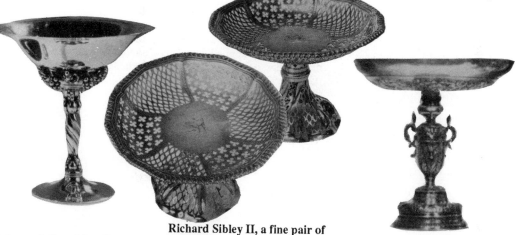

A tazza designed by Georg Jensen, stamped 1921, G J 830 S 263, 18.8cm. high, 16oz. 5dwt. **£1,070**

Richard Sibley II, a fine pair of Victorian tazze, pierced fret, interspersed with bright cutting, 9in. diameter, London 1870, 46¹/₂oz. (Woolley & Wallis) **£1,800**

A Continental 19th century parcel gilt tazza with three applied caryatid handles, 8¾in. high. **£330**

A late Victorian small tazza, of circular form with crimped rim, richly repoussé with pineapples, fruits and acanthus leaves, London 1894, 19cm. diameter. (Spencer's) **£250**

A silver tazza on circular foot, by Gorham Mfg. Co., bearing the mark of Kennard & Jenks, Boston, circa 1880, 10½in. diam., 19oz. **£10,015**

A Georg Jensen silver tazza, stamped with maker's marks, Georg Jensen, Denmark, Sterling, 263B and London import marks for 1928, 18.5cm. high, 18oz. **£1,190**

19TH CENTURY

A tea set comprises a teapot, sugar basin and cream jug, and a tea and coffee service obviously the same with the addition of a coffee pot. The idea of making them as one unit seems to have occurred to some genius around 1785, and quickly caught on in Britain, Europe and America. Sometimes a hot water jug was also added, as was a tea kettle and stand with spirit lamp. Sets came in many different designs according to the taste of the day. Many 19th century examples were massive with highly ornate decoration in the rococo taste.

A Victorian three piece tea service, circular with raised floral and wreath frosted panels, all on cast decorative panel feet, circa 1860.
(Woolley & Wallis)   £170

A three-piece Chinese export silver tea service, maker's mark *WHL*, late 19th/early 20th century, the bodies repoussé as bamboo stalks applied with foliate bamboo branches and dragonflies, height of teapot 5^{7}/8in. high, 34oz.
(Christie's)   £1,047

Victorian silver four-piece tea set, London, 1888-95, Barnard, fluted oval stand, fluted oval form with chased ribbon and floral band, approx. 49 troy oz.
(Skinner)   £574

Three-piece silver tea set, John Vernon, New York, circa 1800–10, each of bulbous oval form engraved with herringbone border and shields, 44 troy oz.
(Skinner Inc.)   £1,712

An early Victorian four-piece tea and coffee service of baluster form with angular loop handles, the bodies decorated with a frieze of applied classical female figures, by J. & J. Angel, 1840, 71oz.
(Phillips)   £1,500

A late George III four piece tea service by Dorothy Langlands, of lobed rounded rectangular baluster form, with prickwork engraved leaf and rosette band, Newcastle 1803/4, 1513 grammes total.
(Spencer's)   £800

19TH CENTURY

Mexican sterling five piece tea and coffee set with tray, comprising: hot water kettle on stand, coffee pot, teapot, creamer and covered sugar with tray, in the neoclassical taste, 286oz.
(Butterfield & Butterfield)   £1,876

Assembled and matching four piece Regency style silver tea and coffee set by Messrs. Barnard, London, 1891 and 1904, gross weight 80oz. 2 dwts.
(Butterfield & Butterfield)   £1,009

Assembled and matching English Victorian Sterling tea and coffee set together with a plated kettle on lampstand by William Hunter, London, 1854/5, embossed with flowers and diaper panels, and melon finial, 63oz. 12dwts.
(Butterfield & Butterfield)   £2,421

Sterling five piece tea and coffee set with matching tray, Reed & Barton, Taunton, Massachusetts, comprising: coffee pot, teapot, sugar bowl with cover, cream pitcher and waste bowl, pedestal base oval urn forms, 139oz. 6dwts.
(Butterfield & Butterfield)   £1,278

Continental silver four-piece tea set, lobed ovoid from with chased panels, scrolling feet, handles, and finials, marked *800* and *Fui Peruzzi*, approx. 101 troy oz. (Skinner)   £682

An American silver assembled four piece tea set, Ball, Tompkins & Black, Ball, Black & Co., New York, circa 1840 and 1850, 85oz. 10dwt., height of teapot 10^{3}/4in.   £908

A fine composite Victorian three piece tea service by Stephen Smith, each piece cast and applied with a 'Cellini' type band of fruiting vine, masks and animals, London 1876, 1686gr. total gross.
(Spencer's)   £1,250

Sterling five piece hand chased tea and coffee set, Peter L. Krider Co., Philadelphia, Pennsylvania, comprising: coffee pot, teapot, covered sugar bowl, cream pitcher and waste bowl, height of coffee pot 12^{1}/2in., 107oz. 2dwt.
(Butterfield & Butterfield)   £1,689

19TH CENTURY

A composite Victorian four piece tea and coffee service, of lobed baluster form bright cut engraved with scrolls, London 1877 by Steven Smith, 2311 grammes total gross.
(Spencer's) £1,450

An early 19th century three-piece circular tea service, with chased foliate and scroll decoration above reeded girdles, Joseph and John Angel, London 1835, 1836 and 1839, 33.9oz.
(Bearne's) £500

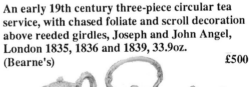

A composite late Victorian/Edwardian three piece tea service by W & G Sissons, comprising teapot with prow and hinged domed cover, with ebony handle, two handled sugar basin and milk jug, London 1899/1901, 1126 grammes total
(Spencer's) £540

Sterling six piece tea and coffee service, Mermod & Jaccard, St. Louis, Missouri, 1891, comprising: hot water kettle on stand, coffee pot, teapot, covered sugar, creamer and waste bowl, height coffee pot 7³/₄in., 123oz. 16dwts.
(Butterfield & Butterfield) £2,255

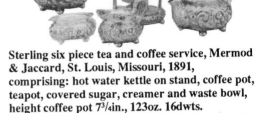

A Victorian circular tea service, comprising, teapot, sugar-basin and cream-jug, each on four acorn and foliage feet, by John Tapley, 1843, gross 53oz.
(Christie's) £1,650

A William IV tea and coffee service, chased with flowers and acanthus leaves on a matted ground, with curved spouts, by Jonathan Haynes, 1831 and 1833, gross 82oz.
(Christie's) £1,870

A Victorian four piece tea and coffee service, the pear shaped panelled body repoussé with foliage and scrolls, makers Josiah Williams & Co., 1878, 72oz.
(Woolley & Wallis) £1,700

A good and attractive early Victorian four piece tea and coffee service by Richard Pearce and George Burrows, London 1840, 2189 grammes total gross.
(Spencer's) £2,000

19TH CENTURY

A George III Scottish three piece tea service of partly-fluted squat circular form with foliage and gadrooned borders, marks of JH and JWH, Edinburgh, 1817, 48oz.
(Christie's) £1,045

American Empire silver three piece tea service by F. Marquand, New York, 1830–1840, comprising: teapot, creamer and covered sugar, height teapot 10in., 73oz. 18dwts.
(Butterfield & Butterfield) £977

Victorian four piece associated silver tea snd coffee service, coffee pot S. LeBass, Dublin, 1869; teapot London, 1890, creamer London, 1893, and sugar Sheffield 1898, each by R.Martin & E. Hall, 83 troy oz.
(Skinner Inc.) £1,188

George III silver three piece tea set by Duncan Urquhart and Naphtali Hart, London, 1802 and 1803, comprising: teapot and creamer (1804) and open sugar (1803), in neoclassical design, height teapot 6⅝in., gross weight 28oz. 2dwts.
(Butterfield & Butterfield) £752

Tiffany sterling three piece tête à tête, circa 1864, pear form, pineapple finial, chased ivy decoration, together with a pair of small Whiting sugar tongs, approximately 28 troy oz.
(Skinner Inc.) £1,483

Shreve Stanwood & Co. sterling five-piece tea set, circa 1860, urn form with ram's heads, beaded borders and openwork finials, engraved monogram, approx. 89 troy oz.
(Skinner) £2,153

A Victorian four piece tea and coffee service, each on spreading circular foot and chased overall with scrolls, foliage and scalework, by George Richard Elkington, 1856, gross 84oz.
(Christie's) £2,860

An unusual Victorian silver-gilt tea service, in the German taste, each chased with broad flutes and engraved with panels of scrolls, by William Cooper, 1842, height of teapot 5in., gross 25oz.
(Christie's) £1,650

19TH CENTURY

Mexican Sterling five-piece tea and coffee service, Taxco, approximately 105 troy oz. (Skinner) £511

American coin silver tea set, early 19th century, with chased C-scrolls, impressed *N.A. Freeman*, approximately 68 troy oz. (Skinner) £1,158

A silver coloured metal four piece tea set and tray, with foliate and scrolled repoussé decoration, German, late 19th century, tray length 64cm, tea pot height 24cm., 125oz. (Lawrence Fine Art) £1,430

An electroplated four-piece tea and coffee service engraved with scrolling acanthus and with scroll handles on spreading bases, the teapot and coffee pot with strawberry finials. (Bearne's) £370

A silver four-piece tea and coffee set, Elkington & Co., Birmingham, 1861, the decagonal bodies linear engraved with geometric motifs, the coffee pot further engraved with armorials, 84oz., 17dwt. all in. (Sotheby's) £2,970

Tea service by Wm. Wilson & Son, Philadelphia, comprising tea and hot water pots, sugar basin, milk jug and sweetmeat dish, the pots with swirled baluster finials, 2190gr., 19th/20th century. (Finarte) £1,308

A fine George IV three piece tea service, chased and repoussé with a band of fruit and flowers enclosing two rococo cartouches engraved with a crest and motto *Libertas et Plenitas*, London 1823, by William Hattersley or William Hewit. (Spencer's) £1,200

A composite three piece tea service, of squat globular form, comprising teapot (Dublin 1827 by Edward Power); two handled sugar basin and milk jug (London 1910 by The Goldsmiths and Silversmiths Co), 1837 grammes total gross. (Spencer's) £1,050

19TH CENTURY

An American silver three piece tea set, Charles Louis Boehme, Baltimore, circa 1804, 40oz. gross, height of teapot 6³/₄in.
(Sotheby's)   £3,216

A Chinese three-piece teaset, the sides chased with bamboo fronds against a stippled ground, the teapot with flat hinged cover.
(Bonhams)   £410

Mexican sterling five piece tea and coffee service with matching tray, Sanborn's, Mexico City, comprising: coffee pot, teapot, covered sugar, creamer, waste bowl and tray, 187oz. 6dwts.
(Butterfield & Butterfield)   £1,052

Sterling five piece tea and coffee set, Frank Smith Silver Co., Gardner, Massachusetts, comprising: coffee pot, teapot, covered sugar, creamer and waste bowl, 98oz. 6dwts.
(Butterfield & Butterfield)   £827

A Hukin & Heath electroplated metal three-piece tea-set, designed by Dr. Christopher Dresser, comprising: a tea-pot, milk jug and two-handled bowl, each piece on four short curly feet, registration lozenge for 1878, 8.5cm. height of teapot.
(Christie's)   £4,905

A James Dixon & Son three-piece electroplated metal tea-set, designed by Dr. Christopher Dresser, the globular bodies supported on three curving feet, with angular spout, curving handles, registration lozenge for 1880, 10.5cm. height of teapot.
(Christie's)   £8,250

A George IV three piece tea service by Charles Fox, of squat globular form with everted stiff leaf cast borders, richly chased with flowerheads and leaves, London 1827, 1453 grammes total gross.
(Spencer's)   £1,260

A composite late Victorian morning tea service, the upper sections chased and repoussé with flowerheads, acanthus leaves and scrolls beneath everted crimped borders, London 1893/4, 499 grammes total gross.
(Spencer's)   £330

19TH CENTURY

Victorian silver four piece tea set in the neoclassical taste by Samuel Green, London, 1873, comprising: teapot, hot water jug, cream pitcher and open sugar bowl, rounded urn forms, gross weight 74oz. 14dwts.
(Butterfield & Butterfield) £1,691

Silver five piece tea and coffee set by Gorham Mfg Co., Providence, Rhode Island, circa 1863–1865, the set comprising: coffee pot, teapot, sugar bowl with cover, cream pitcher and waste bowl, oval urn forms with wide collars, 92oz.
(Butterfield & Butterfield) £2,255

A George IV Irish three piece tea service by James Fray, each piece of cushioned circular form, richly repoussé with birds of prey amongst heavy foliage and flowerheads, Dublin 1826, 1543 grammes total gross.
(Spencer's) £1,100

A late Victorian four-piece tea and coffee service of tapering oblong form engraved in the Aesthetic manner with exotic birds, insects and foliage, by Walker and Hall, Sheffield, 1894/5, 70oz.
(Christie's) £1,760

Indian silver six-piece tea and coffee service, each repoussé with scrolling vines, approximately 175 troy oz.
(Skinner) £1,022

An American silver four piece tea and coffee set, Ball, Black & Co., New York, circa 1870, 97oz. 10dwt., height of coffee pot 11½in.
(Sotheby's) £1,437

Sterling six piece tea and coffee set, Goodnow & Jenks, Boston, Massachusetts, comprising: kettle on lampstand, coffee pot, teapot, cream pitcher, sugar bowl with cover and waste bowl, gross weight 132oz. 14dwt.
(Butterfield & Butterfield) £1,201

Sterling hand chased six piece tea and coffee set, Watson Company, Attleboro, Massachusetts, comprising: tea kettle on lampstand, coffee pot, teapot, covered sugar bowl, cream pitcher and waste bowl, height of kettle 13in., 112oz.
(Butterfield & Butterfield) £1,426

20TH CENTURY

Tiffany & Co. sterling silver tea and coffee service, comprising a coffee pot, teapot, covered sugar, creamer and waste bowl; each of simple ovoid form with a reeded rim, total approximately 99oz. all in.
(William Doyle Galleries) £2,860

Gorham sterling five-piece coffee and tea service and plated silver waiter, circa 1928, Plymouth pattern, coffee and tea pots, covered sugar, creamer and waste bowl, monogrammed, approximately 71 troy oz.
(Skinner) £538

Five piece sterling tea and coffee service with an associated plated tray, Reed & Barton, Taunton, Massachusetts, 1948, comprising: coffee pot, teapot, covered sugar, creamer and waste bowl, 83oz. 12dwts.
(Butterfield & Butterfield) £1,128

Sterling hand chased six piece tea and coffee set, S. Kirk & Son Co., Baltimore, circa 1903–1924, comprising: kettle on lampstand, coffee pot, teapot, covered sugar bowl, cream pitcher and waste bowl, 192oz. 12dwts.
(Butterfield & Butterfield) £4,886

An Art Deco tea service comprising two teapots, a sugar basin and a milk jug, the squat bodies with gadrooned ornament, 890gr.
(Finarte) £963

Lino Sabattini for Christofle, five piece tea and coffee service, 'Como', 1960, electroplated metal, cane covered handles, 5⅝in. height of teapot.
(Sotheby's) £2,860

Composite tea and coffee service by Elkington & Co., of tapering oval form, engraved with the initials *JM* and *JBB*, comprising teapot and cover, coffee pot and cover, two sugar basins, two cream jugs, and hot water jug and cover.
(Spencer's) £560

A Victorian four-piece tea and coffee service and somewhat similar teapot, richly chased and embossed with diaper work and matted foliage, by Martin and Hall, 1888, teapot by Walker and Hall, Sheffield 1929, 122oz.
(Christie's) £1,815

20TH CENTURY

An Edward VII three-piece tea service with applied decoration and with scroll handles on spreading bases, London 1904, 41.6oz.
(Bearne's)   £420

A fine five piece tea and coffee service, in Regency style, makers The Goldsmiths and Silversmiths Co., London 1905, 116^{1}/$_{2}$oz.
(Woolley & Wallis)   £1,500

Important silver gilt three-piece tea set by Mauser Manufacturing Company, chased floral and acanthus decoration, inscribed on base, *From the first run of the Mill of the 'Eleventh Hour' Gold Mining Co., April 1906,* 32.8 troy oz.
(Eldred's)   £703

Messrs. Barnard, a late Victorian four piece tea and coffee service, the pear shaped bodies with shaped flanges, chased and embossed with rococo foliage and vacant cartouches, London 1900/01, 40oz. in an oak fitted box.
(Woolley & Wallis)   £940

A four-piece part spiral-fluted moulded oblong tea service, the teapot and hot water jug with ebonised wood bracket handles, Viners, Sheffield 1925, 61 oz. gross.
(Christie's S. Ken)   £825

An Arts and Crafts style spot-hammered four-piece tea service on curved feet, possibly Charles Edwards, London 1919, height of hot water jug 8in., 51.75 oz. gross.
(Christie's S. Ken)   £990

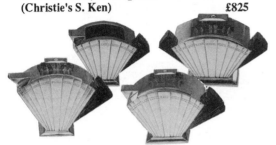

A Boulenger electroplated four-piece tea and coffee service, of fan-shaped design with similarly decorated handles and finials, 16.8cm. high.
(Christie's)   £770

A Walker & Hall four-piece electroplated tea-service, designed by David Mellor, the teapot of ovoid form with concave cover and ebonised handle and finial, 16cm. high.
(Christie's)   £495

20TH CENTURY

A good late George V four piece tea service, Sheffield 1934, by Mappin & Webb, 1177 grams total gross, and a matching circular tray. (Spencer's)
£1,950

German tea and coffee service comprising tea and coffee pots, cream jug and sugar basin, on shallow tray, circa 1920, 3520gr. (Galerie Koller Zürich)
£9,009

A Georgian style three piece tea service, of semi-fluted rounded rectangular cushioned form with acanthus leaf sheathed handles, comprising teapot, two handled sugar basin and milk jug. (Spencer's)
£160

A composite three piece tea service, the teapot repoussé with vacant cartouche and flower filled cartouche with acanthus leaf scrolling, London 1929, by T. Cox Savory, 1311 grammes total gross. (Spencer's)
£820

A Puiforcat four-piece white metal and ivory tea and coffee service, comprising: a coffee-pot with lid, a teapot with lid, a sugar basin with lid and a cream jug, 15.5cm. height of coffee-pot. (Christie's)
£7,150

Three piece Austrian silver tea set on matching tray designed by Josef Hoffmann for the Wiener Werkstätte, Vienna, early 20th century, 900 standard silver, gross weight 81oz. (Butterfield & Butterfield)
£5,043

Dominick and Haff sterling five-piece coffee set, retailed by Shreve, Crump & Low Co., early 20th century, chased scroll and floral decoration, approximately 91 troy oz. (Skinner Inc.)
£1,112

An attractive composite George V three piece boat shaped tea service, with swept shoulders and bobbin cast borders, Sheffield 1923/4, 1024 grammes total gross. (Spencer's)
£500

Danish Sterling four piece tea and coffee set designed by Johan Rohde for Georg Jensen, Copenhagen, circa 1925–1930, gross weight 49oz. 4 dwts.
(Butterfield & Butterfield) £1,576

A five piece Art Deco coffee service with handles in Macassar ebony, 5500gr.
(Galerie Moderne) £1,692

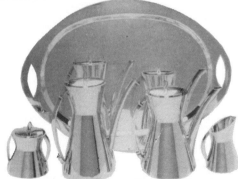

Sterling five piece tea and coffee set with matching tray by Shreve & Co., San Francisco, California, circa 1909–1922, adapted from early George III plain forms, 255oz. 16 dwts.
(Butterfield & Butterfield) £2,994

Sterling hand chased six piece tea and coffee set, Reed & Barton, Taunton, Massachusetts, 1936, comprising: kettle on lampstand, coffee pot, teapot, covered sugar bowl, cream pitcher and waste bowl, height of kettle 15³/₄in., 197oz.
(Butterfield & Butterfield) £2,439

German hand wrought sterling four piece tea and coffee set with matching tray, Hanau, circa 1956, comprising: coffee pot, teapot, covered sugar bowl and cream pitcher, plain contemporary design, 118oz. 4dwt.
(Butterfield & Butterfield) £1,501

Hand wrought sterling six piece tea and coffee set with matching tray, Barbour Silver Co., Hartford, Connecticut, circa 1910–1920, in modified Arts and Crafts style with octagonal panelled sides, 251oz. 10dwt.
(Butterfield & Butterfield) £2,626

Thomas Bradbury & Sons, a four piece tea and coffee service, the octagonal pear shaped bodies with girdle mouldings, London 1911, 67¹/₂oz. all in.
(Woolley & Wallis) £820

A George V five-piece tea and coffee service of plain circular form, crested, with everted rims, scroll handles and rim bases, D. & F. Welby, London 1915/16, 118.5oz.
(Bearne's) £1,200

TEA CADDIES

18TH CENTURY

Tea was an extremely expensive commodity in the early 18th century and the Western counterpart of the 'tea ceremony' achieved a degree of importance in fashionable drawing rooms rivalling even that of the Japanese original! The hostess herself would preside over the preparation of the beverage, so required the leaves to be brought to her in an elegant container, to which she alone would hold the key. Tea containers were made in silver from the late 17th century, and were known as canisters for the next hundred years. They were then more usually called caddies, from the Malay *kati*, meaning a weight of about 1¹/₂lb.

Early examples have small domed lids used for measuring the tea, but by 1710 the whole canister top, including the lid, would lift off for refilling. Hinged and lockable lids in a stepped design covering the whole canister top came in about ten years later, and by the 1740s roundly curving forms were being introduced. By the 1730s the fashion was to have three matching canisters in the box, but by the later 18th century two matching canisters and a wide mouthed sugar box were the norm.

In the 1760s the canisters became much larger, and were being produced in the shape of vases and urns. Those with tall, arching handles very often date from the last twenty years of the century, by which time too designs were becoming sturdier. Many canisters of this time are square or rectangular, and many were also made to conform with teapots of both the straight-sided or elliptical varieties.

A pair of George III vase-shaped tea caddies, the detachable covers with urn-shaped finials, 6¹/₂in. high, Peter Gillois, London 1777, 14.8oz. (Bearne's) £1,400

A George I silver tea caddy, William Fawdery, London, 1714, engraved with armorials below a foliate mantling, 11oz. 10dwt, 4in. high. (Sotheby's) £1,207

A pair of George II tea caddies and sugar bowl, each on spreading moulded base chased overall with flowers, foliage and scrolls, by Samuel Taylor, 1754, with shagreen casket, 12cm., 30oz.
(Lawrence) £3,025

A Queen Anne octagonal baluster tea caddy and cover, the detachable cover with shaped finial, the base engraved with initials, by Ebenezer Roe, 1711, 4³/₄in. high, 6oz.
(Christie's) £1,870

A pair of George III gadrooned and part spiral-fluted inverted pear-shaped tea caddies, Samuel Taylor, London 1765, 5¹/₄in., 14oz.
(Christie's) £935

A pair of George III octagonal tea caddies, by James Phipps, 1775, contained in contemporary gilt painted lacquer case, 4in. high, gross 27oz.
(Christie's) £6,600

18TH CENTURY

A George III cylindrical tea caddy, by J. Parker and E. Wakelin, circa 1765, 5¼in. high, 19oz. **£3,090**

A set of three George III rectangular tea caddies, 1774, maker's mark IP, in ivory case with silver handle, 40oz. **£6,535**

A tea caddy by Jacobus Potholt, Middleburgh, 1734, 13.8cm. high, 174gr. **£665**

A good George II rectangular tea caddy, the moulded rectangular lid with circular finial, 4in. high, probably by John Newton, London 1731, weight 7oz. (Canterbury) **£620**

A pair of George II vase-shaped tea caddies and sugar box, chased with flowers and foliage between swirling fluting, by Samuel Taylor, 1753, in fitted silver mounted wood case, 31oz. (Christie's) **£4,400**

One of a set of three George III tea caddies by D. Smith and R. Sharp, London, 1763, 5½in. high, 27oz. 2dwt., with a fitted shagreen case. **£2,120**

A George III tea caddy, by Robt. Hennell I, London, 1788, of shaped oval form, 10oz.18dwt., 5¾in. high. **£1,150**

A set of three oblong tea caddies, maker's mark of John Newton, circa 1739, 30oz. **£1,425**

A George III oval tea caddy engraved with an armorial within a drapery cartouche, Daniel Smith and Robert Sharp, London 1782, 5¹/₄in., 12.25oz. (Christie's) **£1,870**

A George III plain, oval tea caddy, by Hester Bateman, London, 1785, 12.5cm. wide, 10oz. **£1,430**

A set of three George III oval tea caddies, 1777, maker's mark IP, in silver mounted case, 32oz. **£5,195**

A George II silver-gilt rectangular tea caddy by E. Wakelin, 1747, 14oz. 19dwt. **£3,210**

A George III plain oval tea caddy, with domed cover and foliage and ball finial, engraved with a coat-of-arms and presentation inscription, by Robert Sharp, 1796, 14 oz. (Christie's) **£1,430**

A fine set of three George III tea caddies, chased with vertical sprays of flowers and similar looped cartouches, in the original tortoiseshell case, by W. Vincent, London 1770, the case relined by Lambert in the 19th century, 28oz. (Tennants) **£5,800**

One of a set of three George II tea caddies and sugar boxes, by Isabel Pero, 1741, the caddies each with a pewter liner, and a George III Old English pattern caddy spoon, 68oz. **£16,630**

One of a set of three George II silver gilt, vase-shaped tea caddies, by Samuel Taylor, 1752, 31oz. **£5,940**

A good set of three early George III tea caddies in a fitted and silver mounted mahogany case, with chequer stringing and ball and claw feet, by Thomas Pitts, 1762, 32$^{1}/_{2}$oz. (Phillips) **£7,000**

A rectangular tea caddy by Anthony Conker, 13.4cm. high, 1700, 284gr. **£730**

A George III silver tea caddy, the flat cover with beaded urn finial, by Robt. Hennell, 1781, 12oz.12dwt.
£1,425

A George III shaped oval tea caddy, by Robt. Hennell, London, 1782, 4.75in. high, 14oz. £2,750

A George III octagonal tea caddy, by Henry Chawner, 1791, 13oz. 8dwt. £1,935

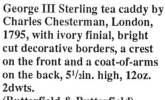

Fine George III Sterling tea caddy by Robert Hennell, London, 1793, the body and lid with tooled decoration retaining original crispness, 6¼in. high, 11oz. 8dwts.
(Butterfield & Butterfield)
£2,421

A pair of George II oblong tea caddies and a matching square sugar box, the caddies each with sliding base and cover, 1756, maker's mark W.A., contained in a silver-mounted shagreen case, height of caddies, 4¾in., 43oz.
(Christie's) £12,100

George III Sterling tea caddy by Charles Chesterman, London, 1795, with ivory finial, bright cut decorative borders, a crest on the front and a coat-of-arms on the back, 5½in. high, 12oz. 2dwts.
(Butterfield & Butterfield)
£1,729

A George II oval tea caddy fitted with a lock and with a flat hinged cover with foliate and acorn finial, William Vincent, London 1776, 4½in., 11oz.
(Christie's S. Ken) £1,760

A Dutch oblong tea caddy, Sneek 1737, maker's mark illegible, probably FE for Feddeiedes Edema, 6oz. 5dwt. £830

A George III oval engraved tea caddy with swags and crested motifs, maker J. Hampston and J. Prince, York, circa 1790, 5½in. long.
(Tennants) £2,500

A George III shaped oval tea caddy, by Wm. Plummer, 1784, 14oz. 15dwt. **£1,575**

A George III oblong tea caddy by D. Smith & R. Sharp, 1762, gross 16oz. 5dwt. **£2,735**

A George III oval tea caddy, by Thos. Phipps and Edward Robinson II, 1784, 12.4cm. high, 12.4oz. **£1,090**

A George III fluted moulded oval divided tea caddy on a reeded spreading foot, Charles Aldridge, London 1797, 7in., 16.75oz. (Christie's) **£880**

George II Sterling tea caddy set by Thomas Blake, Exeter, 1741, each box engraved with a coat-of-arms on one side and a crest on the shoulder, 5in. high, 33oz. (Butterfield & Butterfield) **£5,535**

A George III oval tea caddy with domed cover and leaf finial, engraved with two bands of starbursts and leaves, 14cm. high, by Peter and Anne Bateman, 1788, 14oz. (Phillips London) **£1,200**

A George III oval tea caddy, engraved with bright-cut flowers and foliage, with domed cover and cone finial, engraved with a crest, by Robert Hennell, 1788, 12 oz. (Christie's) **£2,530**

George III Sterling tea caddy by Thomas Heming, London, 1779, the straight sided oval form with flat hinged lid centred with a stirrup handle, 4in. high, 11oz. 18dwts. (Butterfield & Butterfield) **£1,038**

A George III shaped-oval tea caddy, the sides bright-cut engraved with festoons of flowers within stylised borders, by Thomas Chawner, 1786, 5¾in. high, gross 12oz. (Christie's) **£1,650**

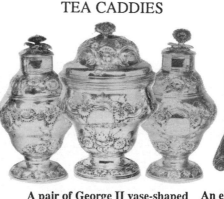

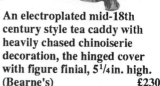

A George III tea caddy, of plain rectangular form, engraved with a shield of arms, 1770 maker's mark ED in script, 12.5cm., 11.1oz. (Lawrence) £2,090

A pair of George II vase-shaped tea caddies and circular bowl and cover, chased overall with flowers, foliage and scrolls, by Samuel Taylor, 1751, 27oz. (Christie's) £3,080

An electroplated mid-18th century style tea caddy with heavily chased chinoiserie decoration, the hinged cover with figure finial, 5¼in. high. (Bearne's) £230

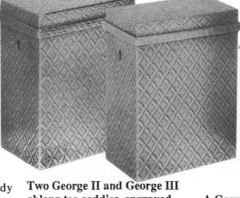

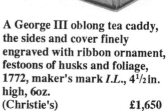

A George II chinoiserie caddy decorated in relief with a woman and boy boiling a pot of tea, maker's mark apparently overstruck by that of Abraham Portal, 1754, 14cm. high, 15.75oz. (Phillips) £3,800

Two George II and George III oblong tea caddies, engraved with a foliage and trelliswork design, the covers with similar scroll borders, one by Edward Wakelin, circa 1755, the other by J. Langford and J. Sebille, 1764, 28oz. (Christie's) £3,850

A George III oblong tea caddy, the sides and cover finely engraved with ribbon ornament, festoons of husks and foliage, 1772, maker's mark *I.L.*, 4½in. high, 6oz. (Christie's) £1,650

A George III rectangular tea caddy on rim foot, with blue glass liner, unmarked, circa 1775. £3,565

A pair of George II oblong tea caddies, each chased with bands of scrolls, foliage and rocaille ornament and engraved with initials, by William Soloman, 1758, 4½in. high, gross 46oz. (Christie's) £4,840

A Queen Anne plain oblong tea caddy, maker's mark overstruck with another, perhaps that of Thos. Farren, 10oz. £1,935

370

A French 19th century shaped oblong tea caddy on stylised shell feet, decorated with two friezes of foliage and berries, 5¹/₄in., 18oz.
(Christie's)   £495

Late 19th century Faberge silver tea caddy in the form of a large tea packet, Moscow, 13cm. wide.   £8,580

A Victorian tea caddy, repousse with mythological figures, London, 1875, 3½in. high, 5oz.   £205

A Victorian tea caddy in Indian taste, the engraved borders including a band of figures, animals and fish, by Richard Sibley, 1867, 9.5cm., 8.5oz.
(Lawrence Fine Art)   £418

A pair of silver-gilt tea caddies, rectangular, die-struck, with amorini and leafage, by Gorham, circa 1890, 14.5cm., 18oz.
(Phillips)   £763

A good George IV Irish tea caddy, the body of bombé shape with repoussé and chased decoration of flowers and scrolls, by W. Nolan, Dublin, 1828, 17cm., 16oz.
(Lawrence Fine Art)   £1,155

A tea caddy, the hammered body chased and embossed with tulips, signed *Gilbert Marks 1898*, 4¹/₄in., London 1897, 10oz.
(Woolley & Wallis)   £1,350

A Victorian shaped oblong tea caddy on openwork mask and scroll feet joined by elaborate openwork aprons, Joseph Angell, London 1853, 6in., 26oz.
(Christie's)   £1,045

A silver tea caddy, maker's mark of Tiffany & Co., New York, 1879–1891, the shoulder and slip on cap chased with scrolls, 8¹/₈in. high, 9 oz.
(Christie's)   £739

A silver tea caddy, maker's mark of Eoff & Shepherd, for Ball, Black & Co., New York, circa 1855, 5¼in. long, 13oz. 10dwt.
(Christie's) £1,016

A George III oval double tea caddy, engraved at the shoulder with a band of stylised foliage, with centrally hinged cover and reeded loop handle, by John Emes, 1800, 17 oz.
(Christie's) £2,200

A Japanese tea caddy of panelled baluster form on rim foot, the sides engraved with flowering prunus and bamboo, the engraving signed *Ganshu*, 5½in. high, 9oz.
(Christie's) £528

A silver tea caddy, maker's mark of Tiffany & Co., New York, 1891–1902, elaborately repoussé with flowers on a matted ground, 4½in. high, 7 oz. 10 dwt.
(Christie's) £524

A pair of George III oblong tea caddies, the sides chased with panels of scrolls enclosing Chinese figures and pagodas, by Robert Garrard, 1819, in a fitted silver-mounted and ivory case inlaid with flowers and foliage, 35oz. (Christie's) £9,350

Aesthetic Movement sterling tea caddy, Gorham Mfg. Co., Providence, Rhode Island, circa 1880, flat based bombé domed vessel with pull off flat lid, height 4¼in., 8oz. 2dwts.
(Butterfield & Butterfield) £4,134

A rare silver tea caddy, maker's mark of S. Kirk & Son, Baltimore, 1846–1890, of flaring cylindrical form, 7¾in. high, 42oz.
(Christie's) £1,855

A late Victorian fluted bombé-shaped moulded oval tea caddy on leaf-capped stylised paw feet, T R and Co., Sheffield 1897, 3¾in., 8oz.
(Christie's) £308

A silver tea caddy, rectangular with cut corners, melon fluted circular pull-off cover with fruit finial, London 1897, by William Comyns.
(Bonhams) £160

TEA CADDIES

An oval tea caddy, the plain body with reeded rims, Chester 1929 Stokes and Ireland Ltd., 9.4cm.
(Lawrence)   £330

An Edwardian tea caddy in the form of a Georgian knife box, Birmingham 1905 by William Hutton and Sons Ltd., 8.8cm.
(Lawrence)   £330

An Edwardian tea caddy, Sheffield 1903 by Richard Martin and Ebenezer Hall of Martin, Hall and Co., 9.3cm.
(Lawrence)   £264

A late Victorian tea caddy, Birmingham 1900 by T. Hayes, the cap Birmingham 1896, 10.6cm.
(Lawrence)   £220

Russian silver set of a tea caddy and a sugar box, with initials: *W.T.S.* (in Cyrillic), Moscow, circa 1899–1908, the boxes engraved similarly with chinoiserie figures, flowers, rococo scrolls and insects, 20oz. 6dwts.
(Butterfield & Butterfield)
                            £2,067

A George V tea caddy, with gadroon edging and chased with foliate festoons, 13cm. high, London 1911, 11.5oz.
(Bearne's)   £440

An Edwardian tea caddy in the form of a Georgian knife box, Chester 1907 by S. Blanckensee and Sons Ltd., the caddy spoon by Benoni Stephens, 8.8cm.
(Lawrence)   £352

A Ramsden & Carr silver tea-caddy and spoon, London hallmarks for 1931, 10.9cm. high, 13oz.7dwt. gross wt.
                          £1,815

A Liberty & Co. silver and enamel tea caddy of oval section, Birmingham hallmarks for 1907, 9.3cm. high, 5oz.2dwt. gross weight.   £245

18TH CENTURY

Tea kettles were much à la mode from about 1690 until the mid 18th century. Essentially they are a large vessel for hot water, resembling a teapot, with either a fixed or swing handle, with wood inset. A common early form was of a flattened globular or octagonal shape, usually flamboyantly decorated with rococo embossing. Similarly embossed pear shapes became more popular towards the middle of the century.

Tea kettles came first with brazier-like stands for charcoal or spirit lamps, and some late 18th century examples have a tap instead of a spout. This taste may be significant, as they were soon to be largely superseded, after circa 1760, by tea urns.

The form was revived in the early 19th century, and most of the examples dating from this time also have taps. Some upmarket models also came with their own silver tripod table to accommodate both kettle and stand, but these are rare and consequently extremely valuable.

A George III plain circular tea kettle, stand and lamp, by John Scofield, 1787, 12½in. high, gross 55oz. **£1,815**

A George II tea kettle stand and lamp, by Ayme Videau, London, 1733, 35cm. high, 70oz. **£1,630**

A Dutch melon-fluted tea kettle, stand and lamp, the kettle with curved spout, hinged foliate cover and partly ivory swing handle, Cornelis de Haan, The Hague, 1770, gross 1,817gr. (Christie's) **£5,750**

A Queen Anne plain pear-shaped tea kettle, stand and lamp, the kettle by John Jackson, 1708, the stand and lamp, circa 1710, maker's mark only, probably that of William Fawdery, 11in. high overall, gross 51oz. (Christie's) **£6,600**

A good George I tea kettle-on-stand, 12in. high, compressed pear-shape with faceted spout, fully hallmarked for London, 1723, by Thomas Farrer, 70 ozs. all in. (Bonhams) **£17,500**

A George III plain circular tea kettle, stand and burner, the kettle by H. Bateman, 1783, the stand and burner by Chas. S. Harris, 1881, 63oz. **£1,190**

A George II silver inverted pear-shaped tea-kettle, stand, lamp and triangular stand, by Hugh Mills, 1746, 15³⁄₄in. high, gross 90 oz. (Christie's) **£5,280**

374

A George I plain octagonal tea-kettle, stand and lamp, the stand by Wm. Fleming, 1717, 15½in. high, 105oz.   £12,474

A George II inverted pear-shaped tea kettle, stand and lamp, by Wm. Cripps, 1744, gross 84oz.   £2,140

An early George II tea kettle and lampstand, marked Abraham Buteux, London, 1727, 10¼in. high, 40oz.11dwt. £1,450

A George II tea kettle, stand and lamp, partly wicker-covered swing handle and domed cover with wrythen finial, by Thomas Heming, 1758, 15in. high, gross 82oz.
(Christie's)   £2,415

A George II spherical tea kettle, stand and lamp, the stand on three leaf-capped shell and scroll feet and with openwork apron, the kettle by Paul de Lamerie, 1736, the stand by Lewis Pantin, 1736, 13¼in. high, gross 61oz.
(Christie's)   £4,950

A Scottish inverted pear-shaped tea kettle, stand and lamp, richly chased and embossed with fruiting vines, by Dougal Ged, Edinburgh, 1760, weight 78oz., 14½in. high.
(Christie's)   £2,860

A Portuguese tea kettle, apparently Lisbon, circa 1750, and an English stand, Lewis Herne & Francis Butty, London, 1760, 99oz. 10dwt., 17in. high.   £1,695

A George II inverted pear-shaped tea kettle, stand and lamp, by John Jacobs, 1754, 15¼in. high, gross 76oz.
(Christie's)   £2,750

Russian tea kettle and stand, bone inlaid swing handle and finial, St. Petersburg 1759, 1700gr.
(Galerie Koller Zürich)   £9,009

An F. Minsfiberg kettle-on-stand with ivory handle and ivory finial, 29.2cm. high.
£1,815

An electroplated kettle, the design attributed to Dr. Christopher Dresser, 15cm. high.
£140

Large Victorian plated spirit kettle of reverse pear form, with ornate handle and lid finial.
(G.A. Key)
£450

A Victorian plain tapering tea kettle with rising curved spout, scroll handle and flattened rising hinged cover, Hunt and Roskell, London 1869, 12³/₄in., 46oz.
(Christie's S. Ken)
£748

An early Victorian Scottish tea kettle on stand, in George II style with scroll and presentation engraved pear-shaped body and ivory swing handle, Edinburgh 1842, maker's mark *RK*, 70oz, 40cm.
(Bristol Auction Rooms) £1,000

A German 19th century spiral-fluted compressed pear-shaped swing-handled tea kettle with fluted rising curved spout, Friedlander, 16in., 56.25oz. gross. (Christie's S. Ken) £715

A large Victorian Louis Quatorze pattern tea kettle, with central burner, Sheffield, 1854, by Martin, Hall and Co., 43.5cm., 81.5oz. (Lawrence Fine Arts)
£4,070

A Georgian style tea kettle on stand with burner, chased with scrolling foliage and raised upon three double 'C' scroll supports and scroll trefoil pad feet.
(Spencer's)
£330

George III tea kettle on stand by Joseph Angell, 1817, the front hinge a later addition with marks for 1858, 38cm. high.
£2,120

Tiffany sterling hot water kettle on stand, circa 1850, pear-form with chased leafy decoration, 3¼in. high, approx. 62 troy oz. (Skinner) £1,507

A Victorian inverted pear-shaped tea-kettle, stand and lamp, by D. & C. Hands, 1856, 15½in. high, 72oz. £1,815

A Victorian tea kettle on stand, 15¾in., in early 18th century style, Sheffield, 1862, Martin Hall and Company, 82oz. (Bonhams) £1,500

A silver kettle on stand, maker's mark of *Gorham Mfg. Co., Providence, 1885–1895*, the sides elaborately repoussé and chased with flowers on a matted ground, 12in. high, gross weight 66oz.
(Christie's) £772

Italian silver kettle on lampstand, Venice, 19th century, bombé oval form with fluted sides, hinged domed lid with floral finial, 16½in. high, gross weight 76oz. 16dwt.
(Butterfield & Butterfield) £1,351

An imposing silver plate kettle on stand of later Georgian design with bright cut motifs, supported on Greek inspired base, 18in. high.
(Locke & England) £260

An American silver Japanese-style tea kettle on stand, Gorham Mfg. Co., Providence, RI, 1883, 57oz., height 12in.
(Sotheby's) £908

A teapot and burner, of squat baluster form with elaborate foliate repoussé decoration, signed *Schott*, 38cm. high, total weight 1770gr.
(Arnold) £1,277

An attractive Chinese white metal tea kettle on stand with burner, of baluster form repoussé with flowers on a matt ground, stamped *Shancha*.
(Spencer's) £420

19TH CENTURY

A tea kettle on lampstand, the kettle Sheffield 1837, the stand and burner London, 15¾in. high, 82oz. 2dwt.   £1,390

Silver tea kettle on stand by William Forbes, New York, 1839-51, 14in. high. £840

A pyriform kettle on stand, by Grosjean & Woodward for Tiffany & Co., 1854–65, 11⅝in. high, 30oz.   £760

Dominick and Haff sterling kettle and lamp stand, circa 1880, the hammered globular body decorated in the Japanese taste, 11½in. high, approximately 37 troy oz.(Skinner Inc.)   £2,806

A Dutch 19th century reeded tapering boat-shaped tea kettle with rising curved spout, ebonised wood swing handle and domed detachable cover, 15¾in. overall, 48oz. gross. (Christie's S. Ken)   £715

A Victorian tea kettle in the George II style, on a stand with central burner and three scroll supports, 1879 by Robert Harper, 35cm. overall height, 46.1oz.(Lawrence)   £1,155

A Hukin & Heath electroplated picnic kettle with folding tripod stand and spirit burner, designed by Dr. C. Dresser. 14.5cm. high.   £190

An early Victorian circular panelled kettle on stand by J. & G. Angell, London, 1841, 86oz.   £1,540

A late Victorian tea kettle, burner and stand, the oval stand on four 'S' scrolling supports, Sheffield 1899, maker's mark H.S., 1068 gr. total gross.   £275

A late 19th century spirit kettle, richly chased allover à rocaille, part ivory handle, Vienna, 34.5cm., 1710gr.
(Finarte) £1,542

A Hukin & Heath electro-plated tea kettle with stand and burner, designed by C. Dresser, 1868, 21.5cm. high. £850

Late 19th century sterling silver hot water kettle on stand, by Dominick & Haff, New York, 11½in. high.
£790

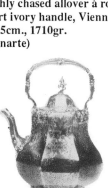

A good Victorian large silver tea kettle, stand and burner, 16½in., fully marked, London 1851, maker George John Richards, 75½oz.
(Phillips) £1,550

An Austro-Hungarian, mid 19th century, compressed swing handled tea kettle, on a trefoil stand, fitted with a burner, 14½in. high, 55oz. free. £750

A kettle on stand and a teapot, by Tiffany & Co., New York, 1876-1891, each globular, kettle 13in. high, gross weight 85oz. (Christie's New York)
£1,176

Continental silver kettle on stand, 19th century, probably German, of pear form with chased scrolls and flowers, 12½in. high, approx. 74 troy oz.
(Skinner) £641

A fine tea kettle and stand by Tiffany & Co., New York, 1881–1891, in the Japanese taste, 12¾in. high, 467 oz.
(Christie's) £7,198

Victorian electro-plated kettle-drum form hot water kettle on stand, maker T.H, last quarter 19th century, 7½in. high.
(Butterfield & Butterfield)
£336

20TH CENTURY

Early 20th century Crichton Bros., English hallmarked silver kettle on stand, kettle 46 troy oz. **£720**

A tea kettle and stand by The Goldsmiths & Silversmiths Co. Ltd., 1930, 31 cm. high, 66oz. all in. **£790**

A tea kettle in George III style, on stand with spirit burner, Sheffield, 1936, 12in. high, 43½oz. **£430**

A Regency style part-fluted moulded oblong tea kettle applied with a gadroon, shell, foliate and floral rim, by William Hutton & Sons Ltd., Sheffield 1911, 12¼in., 42.25oz. gross. (Christie's S. Ken) **£572**

An Edwardian part-fluted compressed globular tea kettle with rising curved spout, everted rim, ebonised wood handle and domed hinged cover, Heath & Middleton, London 1902, 10½in., 34.75oz. gross. (Christie's S. Ken) **£418**

A kettle and stand, in a Queen Anne style, plain pear shaped body with domed cover and scrolled spout, by Charles Reynolds & Co. Ltd., 1926, 28cm., 65oz. (Lawrence) **£792**

A Victorian tea kettle on stand, complete with spirit burner, on reeded scroll supports and scallop feet, Sheffield 1900, 34oz. all in. (Russell Baldwin & Bright) **£355**

An Edwardian part fluted compressed tea kettle applied with a shell and foliate rim, James Dixon & Son, Sheffield, 1908, 12in., 48oz. gross. (Christie's S. Ken) **£605**

A beaded and foliate chased, part fluted tea kettle with mother-of-pearl finial, on a naturalistic crossed branch stand fitted with a burner, 13¼in. high. **£110**

20TH CENTURY

A tea kettle on stand, retailed by Starr and Marcus, N.Y., circa 1910, 14½in. high, 53oz. 10dwt. **£880**

An Edwardian tapering circular tea kettle in the Georgian taste, D. & J. Wellby, London 1910, 11¾in., 57.75oz. gross. (Christie's) **£484**

George V silver kettle on stand, Hunt and Roskell Ltd., London, 1933–34, stand with shell feet, 13in. high, 44 troy oz. (Skinner Inc.) **£475**

A William Hutton & Sons silver kettle and stand, the design probably by Kate Harris, of broad cylindrical shape embellished with abstract ivy and swirls, 30.50cm. London 1901. (Phillips) **£1,200**

An Edwardian tapering moulded oval tea kettle with foliate-decorated rising curved spout, Goldsmiths & Silversmiths Co. Limited, London 1902, 14¼in., 62oz. (Christie's) **£638**

American style silver hot water kettle on stand, marked *Old Friend*, 20th century, similar to Gorham's Plymouth, possibly Chinese, the kettle with swing handle over urn form body, 11¾in. high, 60oz. 10dwts. (Butterfield & Butterfield) **£553**

An early George V small tea kettle on stand with burner, with swept shoulders and hinged domed cover, London 1913, 1302gm. total gross. (Spencer's) **£420**

A plated tea kettle with fluted decoration by Orvit AG, Cologne, with swing handle, circa 1905–10. (Kunsthaus am Museum) **£352**

A plain oval tea kettle stand and lamp in the George III manner, the kettle of plain oval bombé form with reeded borders, 1916, 13½in. high, 40oz. (Christie's) **£440**

18TH CENTURY

Urns replaced tea kettles in popularity in the 1760s, though a few earlier Scottish examples are found. The earliest have a pear-shaped body on four feet or a square base with four feet, a spigot and tap at the bottom of the body, two handles and a domed cover with finial. The body was fitted with a compartment at the base or suspended in the mouth for a red-hot heating iron. Classical vase shapes were also made later in the century.

A Victorian two-handled ovoid pedestal tea urn in the 18th century taste, Elkington & Co., 22¼in. overall.
(Christie's) £660

An Old Sheffield plate melon-fluted pear-shaped tea urn on shell and foliate-capped fluted column and lions' paw supports, 13½in. high.
(Christie's) £418

A George III Irish tea urn, with cast rococo handles and gadroon borders, the spool shape cover with pineapple finial, by John Loughlin, Dublin, circa 1770, 48cm., 89 oz.
(Lawrence Fine Art) £1,320

George III silver tea urn by Jacob Marsh or John Moore, London, 1769, with spiral fluting on waisted stem and square form base with cast scroll supports, 22in. high, 99oz. 12 dwts.
(Butterfield & Butterfield) £2,521

A George III two-handled vase-shaped tea urn, with foliage rosettes and with reeded, foliate scroll handles, by Daniel Smith and Robert Sharp, 1771, 19¾in. high overall, gross weight excluding wood base 107oz.
(Christie's) £3,300

A George III two-handled vase-shaped tea urn, on four ball feet and square base, the urn chased with drapery swags and foliage, by Thomas Heming, 1777, 20in. high, gross 102oz.
(Christie's) £2,300

A George III tea urn, the body with embossed ribbon tied floral swags, beaded edges and fluted neck, 21in., Charles Hougham, London 1770, 98.5oz.
(Woolley & Wallis) £2,100

A George III two-handled vase-shaped tea urn, on square base and four curved bracket feet, by John Scofield, 1785, 21½in. high, gross 110oz.
(Christie's) £1,760

19TH CENTURY

A tea urn by Eoff & Shepherd for Ball, Black & Co., N.Y., 1839–51, 18in. high, 15in. wide, 112oz.10dwt. **£2,513**

An Old Sheffield plate tea urn and cover, of melon fluted globular form engraved with a crest, 16in. high over finial. (Spencer's) **£500**

A Victorian plated tea urn of fluted urn shape, makers James Dixon & Son, 17in. high. **£110**

A rare silver tea urn by Stephen Richard, New York, circa 1812, with a domed rectangular cover, a knop finial, a curved spigot and two cylindrical open handles, 14¾in. high, 104oz. (Christie's) **£24,214**

A plated tea urn, by Gorham, Providence, 2nd half 19th century, on four angular supports each surmounted by a figure of a seated Chinese man, marked, 14¾in. high. (Christie's New York) **£1,037**

Sheffield plate tea urn, first third 19th century, with flattened top, pinched neck above and domed lid with leafy knop finial, 17½in. high. (Butterfield & Butterfield) **£277**

Large Sheffield plate tea urn on shaped square base, 18in. high, circa 1815. **£440**

A George III two-handled oval tea urn, by Samuel Hennell and James Taylor, 1814, 13¾in. high, gross 143oz. **£3,270**

A George III oval tea urn on stand, by John Emes, London, 1805, 9in. across, 97oz. all in. **£1,375**

A Victorian two-handled vase-shaped tea urn with foliate decoration and on scrolling foliate feet, 20½in. high. (Christie's S. Ken) £616

A plated two handled spherical tea-urn, on square base and four ball feet, 13¼in. high. (Christie's) £80

A 19th century Adam style tea urn, the square tiered platform base on four ball supports, 18in. high. (Greenslade Hunt) £300

A silver tea urn, New York, circa 1810; maker's mark indistinct, probably those of John and Peter Targee, with a domed cover, ball finial, two ring handles, faceted spout, and flaring stem with square base, 15¾in. high, 68 oz. (Christie's) £2,341

A rare tea urn, attributed to Edward and Samuel S. Rockwell, New York, circa 1825, on a shaped square base with four lion's paw feet, the spigot in the form of a dolphin, 16in. high, 139oz. (Christie's New York) £3,459

A George III two-handled circular tea urn, the lower part of the body chased with vertical fluting, with reeded and foliage handles and fluted spigot, by John Edwards III, 1810, 15in. high, 133oz. (Christie's) £3,740

A Russian silver two-handled samovar, by Adolf Sper, 1847, 15¼in. high, gross 129oz. £4,515

A William IV melon-fluted two-handled tea urn on a square base, by J. W. & E. H., Sheffield, 1837, 18in. high, 145oz. £2,540

A Belgian fluted, pear-shaped tea urn, on an ebonised trefoil base fitted with a burner, hallmarked in London, 1899, 14¼in. high, 53.25oz. gross. £1,650

George III silver tea urn, John Parker and Edward Wakelin, London, gadrooned oviform body, approx. 74 troy oz. (Skinner) £1,794

A Sheffield plate two-handled circular tea urn, on foliage and paw feet and shaped square base, circa 1815, 17in. high. (Christie's) £825

Continental silver tea urn, the vasiform body surmounted by a swan finial, 16¹/₂in. high, approx. 127 troy oz. (Skinner) £3,230

A George III two-handled circular tea urn, the plain body on fluted and foliage supports terminating in shells and sprays of fruit and acanthus foliage, by Benjamin Smith, 1819, the spirit lamp by Paul Storr, 1812, 15¹/₂in. high, gross 181oz. (Christie's) £3,850

A George III part-fluted vase-shaped tea urn on a foliate-decorated and reeded shaped square base with ball feet, by John Emes, London 1801, 18¹/₄in. overall, 92.50oz. gross. (Christie's S. Ken) £2,200

Scottish Victorian silver tea urn, William Mortimer, Edinburgh, 1841, inverted ovoid vessel, melon fluted, the panels embossed with scrollwork, on a stepped pedestal base, 19in. high, 198oz. 16dwt. (Butterfield & Butterfield) £4,127

A large and impressive tea urn and cover, the high domed cover with bud finial, all over chased and repoussé with scrolling foliage, 50cm. high. (Spencer's) £440

An American silver tea urn, R. & W. Wilson, Philadelphia, circa 1840, of bulbous urn form with die-rolled borders of grapevine, 100oz., 15⁷/₈in. high. (Sotheby's) £3,597

Fine Sheffield plated tea urn, second quarter 19th century, a plain stem supporting the urn shaped body with fluted sides, height 18¹/₄in. (Butterfield & Butterfield) £451

18TH CENTURY

Silver teapots were modelled on ceramic examples imported from China and were produced in most European countries from the 18th century onwards. The earliest teapots commonly seen today date from the reign of Queen Anne and tend to be small and rather squat with a melon-shaped body and domed lid. Sometimes too they can be pear-shaped and octagonal. Until circa 1710 they would have D-handles, but then recurving scrolls are often found, and the swan-neck spout was also introduced around 1705.

In the Georgian period, teapots became wider, and globular, bullet shapes became popular, decorated with chasing, either flat or in high relief. In Scotland, a stemmed bullet pot found favour at this time. An inverted pear-shape with a wide foot and often a bird-headed spout achieved brief popularity around the mid 18th century, but was soon superseded by the neo-classical urn shape with smoothly curving spout and handle.

The huge general demand for teapots led to research into how less expensive examples could be produced and this was achieved by adopting styles that could be shaped from rolled sheet silver, resulting in vertical-sided and either round, oval or polygonal styles.

In the late 18th century the teapot acquired ball feet, or a flaring footrim characteristic of George IV style. Ornamentation too became more restrained, before blossoming once more in the neo-rococo revival of the 1820s and 30s.

Edward Cornelius Farrell, ogee teapot, in Britannia standard, chased in high relief with gun dogs, fowling pieces and game birds, London 1817, 24 oz. all in. (Woolley & Wallis)   **£860**

A George I plain pear-shaped teapot, on circular rim foot and with decagonal curved spout, by Humphrey Payne, 1714, 6in. high, gross 13 oz. (Christie's)   **£5,500**

A Queen Anne plain pear-shaped teapot, stand and lamp, with octagonal curved spout and hinged flap, the domed cover with baluster wood and silver finial, by Simon Pantin, 1709, the stand and lamp by Nathaniel Lock, 1713, 8in. high, gross 22oz. (Christie's)   **£16,500**

A George I plain octagonal teapot, on narrow rim foot and with curved spout, hinged domed cover and baluster finial, by Joseph Clare, 1715, 6in. high, gross 14oz. (Christie's)   **£11,000**

A George I plain pear-shaped teapot, on circular rim foot and with curved decagonal spout, hinged domed cover and baluster finial, engraved with a crest, by John Gorsuch, 1726, 6in. high, gross 19oz. (Christie's)   **£10,450**

A George I plain pear-shaped octagonal teapot, with curved octagonal spout and domed cover with baluster finial, by Joseph Ward, 1717, 6in. high, gross 16oz. (Christie's)   **£14,300**

A George II Scottish bullet-shaped teapot, on spreading foot, chased around the rim and cover with shells, scrolls and foliage, by Hugh Gordon, Edinburgh, 1745, 6in. high, 19oz.
(Christie's) £977

A teapot and stand en suite by Henry Chawner, London 1795/6, the undulating body with incised decoration and foliate cartouches, pot 17cm. high, 660gr. all in.
(Finarte) £1,308

A German decagonal pear-shaped teapot, with curved spout and shaped domed cover, probably by Heinrich Bohlens II, Bremen, circa 1735, 5³/₄in. high, 433grs.
(Christie's) £4,180

A teapot by William Ball, Baltimore, 1790–1800, with a conical cover, and a carved wood handle, 11¹/₂ in. high, gross weight 28oz.
(Christie's) £4,769

A silver teapot and caddy by Robert Hennell, London 1778–9 and 1783–4, the urn shaped bodies richly chased with foliate motifs and festoons, 21 and 21.5cm. high, 1450gr.
(Finarte) £4,206

A teapot, urn-shaped, the conical cover with a pineapple finial, by Charles Westphal, Phila., circa 1790-1800, 11in. high, gross weight 25oz. £6,600

George II silver teapot of pear form with turned finial on squat domed cover, London 1740-1, 5 ⁷/₈in. high.
£380

A teapot, pyriform, with a high domed cover, marked 'HM', N.Y., 1715-25, 5³/₄in. high, gross weight 16oz. 10dwt. £25,272

A rare teapot, New York, circa 1740–1760, the domed hinged cover with gadrooning and a turned finial, 8¹/₄ in. high, 24 oz. 10 dwt.
(Christie's) £10,377

18TH CENTURY

A George III teapot, by
Cornelius Bland, London,
1789, 13oz.6dwt., 6in.
high.   £850

A George II bullet shaped
teapot with straight tapering
hexagonal spout, by Gabriel
Sleath, 1728, gross 15oz.
3dwt.   £4,040

A George III oval teapot on
stand, 1796, the stand 1795,
by Henry Chawner, 26cm.
across, 19.2oz. all in.   £850

A George III tea pot, with
beaded borders, straight
tapering spout and wood handle,
the flat cover with pineapple
finial, maker's mark SW, 1778,
15.5oz.
(Lawrence Fine Art)   £902

A George III cylindrical teapot with crested flush-hinged
cover, by Charles Wright,
1772, 4.75in. high, 13oz.
gross.   £505

A George I Irish plain bullet
teapot, on rim foot and with
tapering angular spout, by
Phillip Kinnersly, Dublin, 1719,
5in. high, gross 17oz.
(Christie's London)   £13,200

A George III fluted tapering
oval teapot with tapering square
spout, polished wood scroll
handle, James and Elizabeth
Bland, London, 1796, 6¼in.,
15.75oz.
(Christie's)   £418

George III oval silver teapot of
plain design, London 1790 by
James Young, together with a
contemporary plain oval stand,
London 1791 by Elizabeth
Jones.
(G. A. Key)   £480

Aldridge & Green, a George III
oval tea pot, the sides engraved
with a coat of arms in swagged
cartouche, the cover with
mother-of-pearl fluted finial,
London 1779, 18oz.
(Woolley & Wallis)   £800

A George III teapot, 5½in. high,
with 'bat-wing' fluted sides,
angled spout and wooden scroll
handle, London, 1792, by Henry
Chawner, 14 oz.
(Bonhams)   £1,000

A George III beaded drum
teapot with tapering angular
spout, possibly Samuel Wood or
Samuel White, London 1777,
4¾in., 14.75oz. gross.
(Christie's S. Ken)   £770

A George III bright-cut fluted
oval teapot with tapering
angular spout, Robert Hennell,
London 1790, height of teapot
5¾in., 18oz. gross.
(Christie's)   £1,210

18TH CENTURY

A George III teapot on stand by Robert and David Hennell 1797, 28cm. across teapot, 17.7oz. all in. **£485**

A French provincial tea-pot, maker's mark of Pierre Brun, circa 1740, 14.9cm. high, 605gr. **£3,390**

An inverted pear-shaped teapot by A. Grasimov, Moscow, circa 1760, 12.4cm. high, 285gr. **£655**

A George III tea pot, the straight sided oval body engraved with script initials within a shield, 1780 by Thomas Daniell, 25.5cm. across, 13oz. all in. (Lawrence) **£1,045**

A late George III teapot and stand by Robertson and Darling, the teapot of slightly tapering oval form, Newcastle 1795, 548 grams total gross. (Spencer's) **£1,000**

A George III small oval teapot engraved with swags and crested cartouche, maker J. Hampston and J. Prince, York, circa 1790, 14oz., 8¹/₂in. long. (Tennants) **£1,750**

A George III beaded oval teapot, the body applied with two oval vignettes decorated with putti, Andrew Fogelberg & Stephen Gilbert, London 1784, 5¹/₂in., 17 oz. gross. (Christie's S. Ken) **£660**

A George III teapot, with bright cut engraved bands and contemporary initials, straight tapering spout and domed cover, by Peter & Ann Bateman, 1794, 14.5 oz. (Lawrence Fine Art) **£660**

A George III tea pot and stand, with bright cut engraved bands and beaded borders, the stand with conforming borders, by John Mitchison, Newcastle, 1784/1786, 19 oz. (Lawrence Fine Art) **£1,595**

George III silver teapot by Robert Hennell I, London, 1793, the oval body with vertical fluted ribbed sides, 6in. high, gross weight 14oz. 10 dwts. (Butterfield & Butterfield) **£946**

George III teapot, Peter, Anne & William Bateman, London, 1789–9, with bright-cut banded borders, (minor repairs, dents), 6¹/₂in. high, approximately 230 troy oz. (Skinner Inc) **£630**

George III silver teapot by Joseph Scammel, London, 1791, with ebony pineapple finial on a silver leafy calyx, 6in. high, gross weight 14oz. 6 dwts. (Butterfield & Butterfield) **£630**

18TH CENTURY

A George II Scottish bullet-shaped teapot, by Wm. Aytoun, Edinburgh, 1736, assaymaster Archibald Ure, gross 22oz. £1,980

A George II compressed circular teapot, by A. Videau, London, 1747, 4¾in. high, 26oz.9dwt. all in. £2,180

A silver teapot with an S-shaped spout, by Samuel Williamson, Phila., 1794/1813, 7¾in. high, gross weight 28oz. £920

A George III oval serpentine panelled teapot on a matching oval stand, by M. Plummer, London 1795, teapot 18oz. all in. £1,035

Silver teapot, 18th century, pear form with median moulding, double scrolled ebony handle, 7¾in. high, 24 troy oz. (Skinner Inc.) £1,186

George III teapot and associated stand, Peter and Ann Bateman, London, 1792–93, approximately 15 troy oz. (Skinner Inc.) £601

A George II Scottish plain compressed spherical tea or punch pot, the base engraved with Latin inscription dated *1761*, by Robert Gordon, Edinburgh, 1741, 6¼in. high, 30oz. (Christie's) £2,860

A George III shaped oblong teapot with tapering angular spout, polished wood scroll handle and domed hinged cover, Duncan Urquahart and Napthaii Hart, London 1791, 6¼in., 17.75oz., gross. (Christie's S. Ken) £990

A George III teapot and stand, the concave panelled and oval body with an upper and lower bright cut draped frieze, 18cm. high, by Peter & Anne Bateman, 1791, 21oz. (Phillips London) £1,400

A rare silver teapot, maker's mark of Asa Blansett, Dumfries, Virginia, 1795–1820, of oval form, 6½in. high, gross weight 17oz. 10dwt. (Christie's) £10,387

A George II plain bullet teapot on a rim foot, with a faceted tapering angular spout, Thomas Mason, London 1735, 4in., 11.75oz. gross. (Christie's) £1,650

A George III plain oval teapot, with straight spout, beaded border and hinged domed cover, by Hester Bateman, 1786, 5½in. high, gross 14ozs. (Christie's) £1,092

18TH CENTURY

A George III silver teapot of oblong form, London 1791, maker Robert Hennell, 15³/₄oz. all-in. (Phillips) £560

A fine silver teapot, maker's mark of Samuel Johnson, New York, circa 1765, 10in. long, gross weight 24oz. 10dwt. (Christie's) £30,492

A pear-shaped teapot by J.C. Girschner, 12cm. high, Augsburg, 1763–65, 300gr. (all in). £2,480

A silver teapot, maker's mark of Elias Pelletreau, Southampton, New York, circa 1765, 9³/₄in. long, gross weight 19oz. (Christie's) £7,986

A George III Irish teapot, with prick engraved and bright-cut borders, and wooden loop handle, Dublin, circa 1780. (Bonhams) £480

German-made silver teapot, 18th century, with floral engraving, French import marks, 5¹/₂in. high, 13 troy oz. (Eldred's) £120

A George I bullet-shaped teapot, with partly octagonal curved spout, the shoulder and almost flush cover engraved with masks, foliage and strapwork, by William Darker, 1731, 4in. high, gross 13oz. (Christie's) £3,850

Fine George III Sterling teapot by Andrew Fogelberg, London, 1795, with straight sides, stepped domed cover, straight spout, ivory C-form handle and finial, 12 oz. 6 dwts., all in. (Butterfield & Butterfield) £1,729

A George III tea pot and stand, with bright cut engraved decoration, the tea pot with domed cover and straight tapering spout, by Henry Chawner, 1788, 19.5oz. all in. (Lawrence Fine Art) £1,100

A George I bullet tea pot, with tapering nine-sided spout, upon moulded collet foot, maker possibly Thomas Burridge, circa 1720, 4¹/₂in. to finial, 16oz. (Tennants) £1,400

A George III teapot of concave oval form with finely engraved design, London 1797, by George Smith and Thomas Hayter. (Russell, Baldwin & Bright) £800

A silver teapot, maker's mark of Isaac Hutton, Albany, 1790–1810, with straight spout, hinged domed cover, and urn finial, 6¹/₄in. high, 19 oz. (Christie's) £2,772

Robert and Samuel Hennell, an oval boat shape teapot, with oval wood finial, London 1804, 20oz.
(Woolley & Wallis)   £350

A silver teapot, Boston, dated *1801*, the sides with panels of vertical flutes, 12in. long, 21oz.
(Christie's)   £2,178

Large Victorian circular silver teapot on cast four footed base, London, 1840, 22oz.
(G.A. Key)   £230

A George III circular teapot, with a band of anthemion ornament at the shoulder and curved spout, by Paul Storr, 1814, gross 26oz.
(Christie's)   £2,640

George III silver teapot, Peter, Anne and Wm. Bateman, London, 1803–04, 7in. high., approximately 15 troy oz.
(Skinner Inc.)   £610

A Victorian Irish tea pot, the body with reeded girdle, scroll handle, by R.S., Dublin, 1870, 23.5oz.
(Lawrence Fine Art)   £572

A Regency compressed circular teapot, embossed and chased with foliage, shells and scrolls to a scale ground, makers Rebecca Emes & Edward Barnard, London 1818, 24oz. all in.
(Woolley & Wallis)   £380

An Irish George III teapot, 6½in. high, on domed circular base chased with a floral band, the mask mounted spout formed as an eagle's head and neck, Dublin 1818, by James Le Bass, 31 oz.
(Bonhams)   £660

A George III oblong teapot and stand with incurved, canted corners, the sides half-fluted below a wide engraved band of flowers and berries, by John Robbins, 1802, 21.25 ozs.
(Phillips)   £1,600

A George III bright-cut moulded oblong teapot with rising curved spout, Dorothy Langlands, Newcastle, probably 1805, height of teapot 5½in., 19.75oz. gross.
(Christie's S. Ken.)   £935

A Victorian compressed pear shaped teapot on scrolling foliate feet, E. & J. Barnard, London, 1856, 6¾in., 23.25oz.
(Christie's S. Ken)   £462

A George IV silver teapot of compressed circular form, with florette finial, foliate claw and ball panel feet, London 1823, 25¾oz.
(Phillips)   £360

19TH CENTURY

A Victorian silver oval drum teapot in 18th century style, London 1858, makers Hands & Son, 19½oz. **£230**

A George III circular teapot with ivory finial and scroll handle, by Paul Storr, 1809, '6¼in. high, gross 40oz.**£2,970**

A George III compressed circular teapot, by R. & S. Hennell, London, 1806, 25.5oz. **£395**

A George III oblong silver teapot, part fluted and with bands of anthemions, London 1812, marks rubbed, 21¹/₄oz. (Phillips) **£250**

A George IV teapot, 6¹/₄in. high, with leaf-capped reeded scroll handle and spout, London, 1821, by Emes and Barnard, 22oz. (Bonhams) **£360**

A George III oblong silver teapot with wooden handle and finial, Sheffield 1806, maker Thomas Law, 16¹/₂oz. (Phillips) **£320**

A George III Irish tea pot, with a band of rose, shamrock and thistle decoration, the shoulders with gadroon and foliate border, by James Scott, Dublin, 1818, 29.5oz. (Lawrence Fine Art) **£638**

A Regency part spiral-fluted and gadrooned moulded rounded oblong teapot on ball feet, Thomas Wallis & Jonathan Hayne, London 1819, 5¹/₂in., 20oz. gross. (Christie's) **£418**

A George IV bullet shaped teapot by Garrards, the flat hinged cover and shoulders later engraved and chased with scrolls, London 1824, 681 grams gross. (Spencer's) **£540**

A George III oval teapot, the domed hinged cover with an oval ivory finial, makers Alice & George Burroughs, London 1804, 16¹/₂oz. all in. (Woolley & Wallis) **£340**

A Victorian teapot, the sides chased with scrolls and foliage, on shaped circular skirt foot, London, 1839, by Charles Gordon, 19¹/₂ ozs. (Bonhams) **£580**

A George III teapot, with ivory finial and angular handle on four ball feet, 6³/₄in. high, Thomas Robins, London 1805, 19.2oz. (Bearne's) **£330**

A silver teapot, maker's mark of Gerardus Boyce, New York, circa 1830, 7⅞in. high, gross weight 21oz.
(Christie's) £690

A Victorian squat circular teapot engraved with armorials, the elaborate spout with blackamoor mask, by Robert Garrard, 1859, 40¼oz.
(Phillips) £1,300

An urn-shaped teapot with a domed cover, by Bailey & Co., Phila., circa 1848-65, 10¾in. high, gross weight 37oz. £800

Silver teapot, Fletcher and Gardner, Philadelphia, circa 1810, applied mid band of grapevine on a pedestal base, 8½in. high, 28 troy oz.
(Skinner Inc.) £428

An electroplated teapot on stand, the design attributed to Dr. Christopher Dresser, the circular cover with cylindrical ebonised finial, on tripod stand, with spirit burner, 19.7cm. high.
(Christie's) £418

Silver teapot, Joseph Lownes, Philadelphia, circa 1800, engraved with foliate monogram on circular pedestal foot with square base, 11in. high, 26 troy oz.
(Skinner Inc.) £1,383

E. E. J. & W. Barnard, a naturalistic teapot, melon panelled with foliate entwined root spout and handle, London 1837, 24oz.
(Woolley & Wallis) £720

A Victorian Scottish bullet teapot chased with arabesques and with two vacant scrolling foliate cartouches, Marshall & Summers, Edinburgh 1844, 6¼in., 21.75oz.
(Christie's S. Ken) £528

C. R. Ashbee, a Guild of Handicrafts bachelor teapot, the hammered ogee body with tapering spout, on a spreading foot, London 1899, 12oz.
(Woolley & Wallis) £2,100

19TH CENTURY

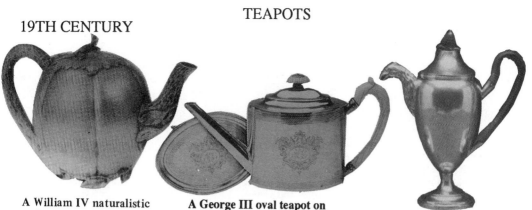

A William IV naturalistic melon-shaped teapot, by E. J. & W. Barnard, 6in. high, Portcullis crest, London, 1835, 17oz. all in. £420

A George III oval teapot on matching stand, the pot of straight sided oval section, 6¾in. long, Andrew Fogelberg, London 1799, 578 gms, 18.5 oz. (Bearne's) £1,100

German silver teapot, Seethaler, Augsburg, 1804, with eagle spout, approximately 15 troy oz. (Skinner) £1,022

Round silver teapot, moulded with floral medallions and knopped lid and black wooden handle on round base with shell relief and ball feet, lower Saxony, Hamburg, mid-19th century, 22cm. high. (Kunsthaus am Museum) £435

A German oval teapot and pear-shaped cream jug, each on moulded foot with stylised leaf border, by J.C.W.P. Hessler, Hanau, circa 1825, 1,266grs. (Christie's) £1,650

An Elkington & Co. electro-plated barrel-shaped metal teapot, designed by Dr. Christopher Dresser, with ebonized curving wooden handle, stamped with a variety of Elkington & Co., 17cm. high. (Christie's) £3,300

A William IV plain pear shaped teapot, with partly fluted curved spout and domed cover, by Paul Storr, 1831, stamped *Storr & Mortimer*, gross 30oz. (Christie's London) £1,430

Japanese silver teapot, Arthur & Bond, Yokohama, late 19th century, globular body with long neck modelled in high relief with two dragons, approximately 15½ troy oz. (Skinner Inc) £621

A square teapot, the hinged cover with a green stone finial, by Tiffany & Co., N.Y., 1877-91, 5in. high, gross weight 15oz. £11,975

19TH CENTURY

An English silver teapot, Sheffield, maker's mark of Thos. Law, 1804/5, 4¾in. high, 15oz. **£215**

European repousse silver teapot with curled snake handle, 4¾in. high, 13.5 troy oz. **£240**

George III silver teapot, Wm. Plummer, London, 1809, 5in. high, approximately 17 troy oz. (Skinner) **£511**

A George III teapot with an oblong boat-shaped body and foliate chased borders, on four ball feet, by Samuel Hennell, London 1813, 11¾in., 20oz. (Hy. Duke & Son) **£250**

A George III teapot, 6in. high, with gadrooned border and long shaped handle on four ball feet, London, 1812, by Thomas Wallis and Jonathan Hayne, 19 oz. (Bonhams) **£500**

Emes & Barnard, a fine Regency compressed circular teapot, partly ribbed with a reeded band, London 1814, 25¹/₂oz. (Woolley & Wallis) **£440**

George III silver teapot and matching stand, London, 1801, with incurvate shoulder and domed hinged lid fitted with an ivory finial, 6¾in. high, 17oz. 14 dwts. (Butterfield & Butterfield) **£819**

George IV Scottish silver teapot by John McKay, Edinburgh, 1827, with a knopped leaf-wrapped berry finial, the body chased in repoussé with rocaille, scrolls, flowers and a scroll framed cartouche, 27oz. 10dwts. (Butterfield & Butterfield) **£484**

A George IV compressed circular teapot, the body heavily chased with sea-scrolls, foliage and rocaille on a scale-work ground, Michael Starkey, London 1827, 4¹/₄in., 18.50oz. gross. (Christie's S. Ken) **£605**

An early Victorian bachelor's teapot of bullet shape, with engraved shoulders and scroll cartouches, crested, London 1856, maker Henry Holland, approximate weight 8oz. (Bonhams) **£220**

A George III foliate and floral bright-cut moulded oval teapot with rising curved spout, Andrew Fogelberg, London 1802, 6¹/₂in., 17oz. gross. (Christie's S. Ken) **£660**

A Regency part spiral-fluted and gadrooned compressed moulded circular teapot with foliate-decorated rising curved spout, Thomas Robins, London 1815, 5¹/₄in., 23oz. gross. (Christie's) **£605**

19TH CENTURY

A George III teapot with beech scroll handle and finial, by J. Emes, 1801, 27cm. across, 16.7oz. all in. **£180**

A George IV silver gilt hexagonal teapot by Paul Storr, London 1825, 5¼in. high, 25oz. 3dwt. **£7,865**

An Indian oval teapot on rim foot, by Hamilton & Co., Calcutta, circa 1822, 6¾in. high, gross 29oz. **£1,900**

A George III oval teapot, 6¼in. high, Charles Fox, London 1804, and a matching oval teapot stand, 6½in. long, Peter, Anne and William Bateman, London 1803, 563 gms, 18.1 oz. (Bearne's) **£580**

A William IV teapot by Charles Fox, of melon fluted squat globular form, London 1831, 793 grammes gross. (Spencer's) **£500**

A Victorian silver teapot of compressed circular form, London 1841, makers Charles Thomas Fox and George Fox, 23¼oz. (Phillips) **£230**

An early Victorian teapot, chased and repoussé with flowerheads, acanthus leaves and rococo scrolls, with cast and applied flower knop, London 1853, maker's mark *W.M.*, 497 grammes gross. (Spencer's) **£360**

Russian parcel-gilt silver trompe l'oeil teapot, A. N. Sokolov, Moscow, dated *1880*, designed and chased to simulate a plain baluster form ceramic pot with lift-off lid wrapped in a birchwood basket frame, 5½in. high, 21oz. 4dwt. (Butterfield & Butterfield) **£750**

A Hukin & Heath electroplated teapot designed by Dr. Christopher Dresser, the circular cover with ebonised finial, stamped maker's marks, *Designed by Dr. C. Dresser*, 14.5cm. high. (Christie's) **£418**

A late George III teapot, of rounded rectangular cushioned form, the everted rim with cast gadrooned border, London 1811, by T. Robins, 498 grammes gross. (Spencer's) **£300**

A George III hexagonal teapot, on rim foot and with angular handle and spout and detachable cover with seated Chinaman finial, 5in. high, gross 26 ozs. (Christie's) **£1,650**

A silver teapot and cover modelled as a pomegranate, the chased details realistically rendered, its leafy branches forming a handle rendered in ivory, late 19th century, 12.8cm. long. (Christie's London) **£2,420**

20TH CENTURY

An Edwardian part-fluted and gadrooned tapering moulded oblong teapot on ball feet, James Dixon & Son, Sheffield 1901, 5³⁄₄in., 17.75oz. gross. (Christie's) £286

A Liberty & Co. silver teapot, Birmingham, 1900, designed by Archibald Knox, 4³⁄₄in. high, Birmingham, 1900. (Bonhams) £1,000

WMF hammered silver clad ceramic tea pot, Germany, felt interior liner, cream glazed porcelain pot with low relief concentric rings. 6³⁄₄in. high. (Skinner) £241

A Charles Boyton hammered silver teapot, London hallmarks for 1933, 21oz. 19dwt., 12.5cm. high. £1,000

A reeded fluted oval teapot in the George III taste, with a fluted rising curved spout, Elkington and Co., Birmingham 1916, 5³⁄₄in., 16oz. gross.

American silver teapot, 'Fletcher and Gardiner Phila', 9¹⁄₂in. high, approx. 32 troy oz. £275

An unusual part fluted tapering teapot with rising curved spout, the base engraved: "Patent Trade S.Y.P. Mark Teapot", James Dixon & Son, Sheffield 1912, 9¹⁄₄in., 42oz. gross. (Christie's) £528

A. W. M. Hutton & Sons electroplated teapot and hot-water jug, designed by H. Stabler, 15.7cm. high. £350

A teapot on stand after Paul Revere by George C. Gebelein, Boston, circa 1930, with a straight spout, a hinged domed oval cover, and a carved wood handle, 11¹⁄₄in. wide, gross weight 28oz. (Christie's) £1,066

Fine quality Queen Anne style silver teapot with domed lid and treen handle, London 1908, 25oz. all in. (G. A. Key) £350

A Napper & Davenport silver 'cube' teapot, Birmingham, 1922, 13.25cm. £2,000

A Hutton & Sons silver teapot, of broad cylindrical shape with angular spout, wickered loop handle and flat cover, Sheffield 1909, 16.5cm. high. (Phillips) £340

THIMBLES

Thimbles, the protective covers for the finger used for needlework, are a very old invention, and examples survive from Roman times. Most were made of metal, and silver lent itself particularly well to the purpose. Some very attractively decorated examples from the Victorian period can readily be found. Thimbles were also treated as novelty items, and collecting commemorative thimbles is a very popular hobby.

Silver 'stone top' thimble, circa 1890. **£35**

Plated thimble with patterned border. **£5**

Silver and turquoise thimble, circa 1890. **£45**

Plated 'Just a thimble full' measure. **£20**

Plated thimble 'Prest-wick' **£20**

Cable bottom silver thimble, circa 1870. **£45**

Silver thimble with leaf border, circa 1890. **£25**

Elizabeth II coronation thimble. **£85**

Charles Horner silver thimble. **£75**

Mrs. Thatcher re-election thimble. **£25**

French silver thimble with gilt border. **£30**

A fine filigree silver thimble, circa 1800. **£275**

Dorcas silver thimble size 8, circa 1890. **£15**

Silver thimble containing a bottle, circa 1800. **£330**

Great Exhibition 1862 thimble. **£190**

TOAST RACKS

18TH CENTURY

Toast racks were first introduced about 1770, early examples having detachable wires on an oval base. Most have seven wires or bars to separate six slices of toast. Boat shaped forms became popular around 1790, followed by an oblong style. They remained popular throughout the 19th century, in the latter years of which the designer Dr Christopher Dresser produced many highly original examples, which command good prices today.

A George III lyre-shaped toast rack with scroll ends and ring handle, maker Nathaniel Smith & Co., Sheffield, 1798, 5oz.
£250

A George III seven bar toastrack, the arched wirework divisions supported on oval base, London, 1799, possibly by John Fountain.
(Bonhams)   £200

An unusual George III wirework shaped oblong toast rack of cage form, on baluster feet, Henry Chawner, London 1792, 4½in.
(Christie's S. Ken)   £418

A George III toast tray, 10in. long, the oval body with moulded border and scroll end grips, the four triple hooped bars detachable, London 1785, possibly by John Tweedie, 7oz.
(Bonhams)   £300

A George III oval six-division toast rack, the base with reeded rim, London 1792, by Peter and Ann Bateman.
(Greenslade Hunt)   £400

19TH CENTURY

One of a pair of George III six-compartment toast racks by Paul Storr, London, 1818, 6⅞in. wide, 33oz.   £1,210

A Victorian silver toast rack, the seven reeded scroll divisions on a chased shell and scroll base on four foliate scroll feet, London 1839, 12oz.
(Bonhams)   £300

A good William IV seven bar toast rack, on four anthemion and scroll supports, 1835, by Joseph and John Angell, 18.7cm., 14.2oz. (Lawrence Fine Arts)   £418

A Hukin & Heath plated toastrack, attributed to Christopher Dresser with open rectangular base supported on block feet, 11.5cm. high. (Phillips)   £560

A Hukin and Heath electroplated toast rack, the wirework frame with seven supports, on a convex base, stamped *H & H*, 12cm. high. (Christie's London)   £220

A Hukin & Heath electroplated toast rack designed by Dr. Christopher Dresser, on pad feet, the arch base with seven supports, 14cm. high. (Christie's)   £352

A Hukin & Heath electroplated toast rack designed by Dr. Christopher Dresser, the central support raised to a handle, stamped *H&H 2556* with dated lozenge for May 1881, 13cm. high. (Christie's)   £330

A rare James Dixon & Sons electroplated toastrack designed by Dr Christopher Dresser, the rectangular frame with seven triangular supports, each with angular wire decoration, on four spike feet and with a raised vertical handle, stamped with maker's marks and facsimile signature Chr. Dresser, 16.4cm. high. (Christie's)   £14,300

A rare James Dixon & Sons electroplated toast rack designed by Dr. Christopher Dresser, on four pin feet supporting seven parallel hexagonal sections, 16.7cm. long. (Christie's)   £3,300

A Victorian toastrack, designed as openwork fans of foliate design on four bun feet, by Yapp & Woodward, Birmingham, 1850, 16cm. (Lawrence)   £160

A George III seven-arch toastrack, the circular wirework divisions with arched side supports, London, 1801. (Bonhams)   £220

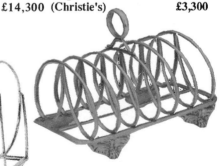

A George IV seven bar butterfly toast rack, of plain rounded rectangular form with central spade handle, by James Barber, George Cattle and William North, 308 grammes, 16cm. long, 1828. (Spencer's)   £350

Large and heavy Victorian silver toast rack of seven hoop design, on four ball feet, London 1874, 9oz.
(G. A. Key) £115

Late 19th century silver plated on brass **toast rack** with pierced base. £35

A rare silver toast rack, maker's mark of A. E. Warner, Baltimore, 1818, 8³/₄in. long, 7oz. 10dwt.
(Christie's) £4,356

A rare James Dixon & Sons electroplated toast rack, designed by Dr. Christopher Dresser, divisions with lunette shaped designs, central loop handle, 8.5cm. high.
(Christie's) £4,400

An Elkington & Co. electroplated toast rack, designed by Dr. Christopher Dresser, with a tall central 'T' base and three low triangular shaped supports on either side of it, 13.5cm. high.
(Christie's) £7,150

A Hukin & Heath plated toastrack, designed by Christopher Dresser, the arched base on four bun feet supporting six pronged divisions, 12.50cm. high.
(Phillips) £220

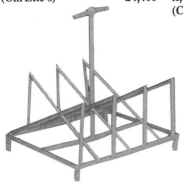

A James Dixon & Sons electroplated toast rack designed by Dr. Christopher Dresser, with seven triangular supports, on four spike feet and with raised vertical handles, 13.5cm. high.
(Christie's) £1,980

An electroplate toastrack designed by Dr. Christopher Dresser, the rectangular footed base surmounted by five rods on each side, 5¹/₄in. high.
(Christie's) £2,970

A late George III seven bar toast rack, with acanthus leaf sheathed ring handle, London 1817, by Rebecca Emes and Edward Barnard, 335 grammes, 17cm. wide.
(Spencer's) £190

A 6½in. golf club pattern seven-bar toast rack, with ball and ring carrying handle.
(Anderson & Garland) £120

A late Victorian small five bar toast rack, the arched upright on a wrythen fluted 'shell' base, Sheffield 1900, 103 grammes, 5in. long.
(Spencer's) £70

A Charles Boynton silver toast-rack of oval, almost boat shape, 9.5cm. high, 5.5oz., marked CB for London 1936.
£500

A Guild of Handicraft silver toast rack, on bun feet, with repoussé decoration of stylised fish and cabochon turquoises, London hallmarks for 1904, 12.5cm. high, 230 grams.
(Christie's) £1,430

An unusual silver-gilt toastrack, the five divisions formed from crossed apostle spoons, and surmounted by a coronet handle, London, 1910.
(Bonhams) £140

A Guild of Handicraft toast rack, designed by C.R. Ashbee, the end panels with repoussé decoration of stylised trees, London hallmarks for 1906, 13cm. high, 220 grams.
(Christie's) £1,430

A six-division toast-rack, on four bun feet and with central bracket handle, by Omar Ramsden, 1928, 4in. long, 7oz.
(Christie's) £600

An Edwardian novelty five bar toast rack by Heath & Middleton, the wire work rack forming the letters 'Toast', Birmingham 1906, 94 grammes, 12.5cm. wide.
(Spencer's) £160

Fine large late Victorian silver toast rack in Gothic taste, standing on four ball feet, Sheffield 1901, 10oz.
(G.A. Key) £115

18TH CENTURY

The terms 'tray' and 'waiter' are often interchanged indiscriminately, though, to be strictly accurate, trays really should have handles. The smaller examples are coffee trays, the larger ones tea trays. These last came into general use in the late 1780s, and it is unusual to see any before this date. They are always oval, with a threaded or beaded border, usually with bright-cut engraving, and can be anything from 16in. or, more usually, 20–22in. across, excluding handles. They may or may not have feet. By 1805, gadrooned borders were coming in, and about 1810, trays become oblong, (as, indeed, do teasets).

In Victorian times, tea trays were usually flat chased during the early period, with engraving coming back into fashion around 1850.
In the 19th century many were made in Sheffield Plate – indeed, between 1800–1840 more trays were produced in this medium than any other single item. Plate examples usually have elaborate silver rims, chased designs and engraved shields.

A George III oval gallery tray, on four claw and ball feet, by John Crouch and Thomas Hannam, 1792, 24½in. wide, gross 290 ozs. (Christie's) £7,150

An 18th century Maltese shaped oval tray, embossed with shells and foliage, maker's mark MX, probably Michele Xicluna, circa 1770, 27.7cm. long, 7oz. (Phillips London) £750

An early George III waiter, engraved with a crest and foliage, within a shallow pie-crust border with gadrooned rim, London 1772, by John Carter, 276 grammes, 7in. diameter. (Spencer's) £280

An attractive early George III waiter by Hugh Mills, the piecrust border with escallop shell angles, London 1750, 281 grammes. (Spencer's) £300

A small waiter, square, with cusped corners and a moulded rim, by Jacob Hurd, Boston, circa 1740-50, 5¾in. square, 5oz. £6,500

A George II shaped square waiter, by Lewis Pantin I, 1735, 12½in. wide, 52oz. £7,000

A George I shaped square waiter, probably by E. Cornock, 1725, 5.7 ⁷/₈in. square, 6oz.4dwt. £1,250

A Tiffany sterling silver sealing wax set, N.Y., circa 1891-1902, 8½in. sq., wt. approx. 20 troy oz. **£500**

A George III two handled tray, with reeded borders, the centre engraved with a coat of arms within a bright cut surround, by John Cotton and Thomas Head, 60cm., approximately 81 oz. (Lawrence Fine Art) **£4,620**

An inlaid waiter with an everted brim, on four cast feet, by Tiffany & Co., 1878-91, 9½in. diam., gross weight 10oz. **£12,500**

A waiter, by Gorham, Providence, 1881, the surface engraved with swallows and cattails, above a raised and chased folded damask napkin, marked, 6in. diam., 5oz. (Christie's New York) **£899**

An American silver rectangular tray, Gorham Mfg. Co., Providence, RI, 1899, Martelé, .950 standard, 42oz. 10dwt., length 15in. (Sotheby's) **£4,161**

Victorian silver tray, Sheffield, 1839–40, maker S.W. & Co., with chased interior and armorial featuring three fleurs-de-lys, 20in. diameter, approximately 102 troy oz. (Skinner Inc.) **£1,563**

A late Victorian dressing table tray, with a rococo scroll cartouche flanked by birds, a dog and house within a foliate and scroll border, Birmingham probably 1893, by S. Walton-Smith, 248 grammes, 10in. wide. (Spencer's) **£150**

An impressive late Victorian two handled tray by Thomas Bradbury and Sons, of oval form, the central panel with presentation inscription, *Presented to Miss Steward by the Parishioners and the Choir of Whitton ... February 1893*, 77.5cm. wide over handle. (Spencer's) **£190**

A good Victorian tray, the centre engraved with a coat of arms within elaborate borders of entwined roses, butterflies and peacocks, by the Fenton Brothers, Sheffield 1891, 67cm., 199oz. (Lawrence Fine Art) **£4,950**

Sterling silver asparagus tray in "Virginia Carvel" pattern, by Towle, pierced liner, applied border, 10 x 15in., 34.4 troy oz. (Eldred's) £352

Victorian Sterling galleried and footed tea tray by Bradbury & Henderson, Sheffield, 1887, with scrolled cast bracket handles applied at ends, the face tooled with decorative borders, 24in. long, 157oz.
(Butterfield & Butterfield) £5,189

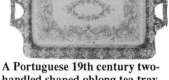

A Portuguese 19th century two-handled shaped oblong tea tray on open-work vine feet, 28¹/₂in. overall, 161.25oz.
(Christie's) £3,080

A good quality tea tray, the centre engraved with strap-work oval roundels, by Barnards, London 1845, 76.2cm. diam., 168oz.
(Bonhams) £3,700

A Victorian two-handled octagonal tray, with foliate pierced rim and bracket handles, by Martin Hall & Co. Ltd., Sheffield, 1899, 23¹/₂in. long, 99oz.
(Christie's) £1,870

A George IV two handled tray, with gadroon, shell and foliate border and leafy scroll handles, by William Bateman I, 1826, 66cm., approximately 114oz.
(Lawrence Fine Art) £2,750

Coin silver tray, Newel Harding & Co., Boston, circa 1855, engraved with the arms of the Bates family, 21in. wide, 103 troy oz.
(Skinner Inc.) £2,569

Sterling tray for an extinguisher from the Mackay Service, Tiffany & Co., New York, circa 1878, Indian, applied armorial and monogram, of shaped rectangular form, length 10³/₄in., 19oz. 10dwts.
(Butterfield & Butterfield) £2,443

A Victorian two-handled oval tea tray with central presentation inscription and bright-cut decoration, 27¹/₂in. over handles, Frederick Elkington, London 1872, 3721 gms, 119 oz.
(Bearne's) £2,600

A George III two-handled oval tray, with fluted border and gadrooned rim, by Thomas Hannam and John Crouch, 1801, 22in. long, 68ozs.
(Christie's) £2,875

A George IV shaped-rectangular two-handled tray, with shell, foliage and gadrooned border and similar detachable handles, by Samuel Hennell, 1823, 28¹/₂in. long, 165oz.
(Christie's) £4,620

Austrian Art Nouveau silver tray, late 19th century, 23in. wide, approx. 57 troy oz.
(Skinner) £1,734

Tiffany sterling silver butler's tray, rectangular, stylised foliate border, 21in. wide. (Skinner Inc.) £8,280

A Russian Art Nouveau rectangular pen tray, by O. Kurlyukov, 26cm. wide. £1,000

A George V shaped rectangular two-handled tea tray, 27¹/₄in. over handles, London 1918, 3866 gms, 124.3 oz. (Bearne's) £1,200

Tiffany & Co. Sterling tray, New York, early 20th century, 20in. long., approximately 74 troy oz. (Skinner Inc) £1,233

Elizabeth II silver waiter, Garrard Bros., Sheffield, 1967, oval with scroll handles, 25in. long, approximately 90 troy oz. (Skinner) £1,077

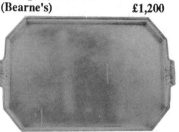

A large fine quality plated tray, with leaf-capped scroll handles, gadrooned borders and bun feet, 27in. over handles. (Woolley & Wallis) £460

A two handled tray, the centre with an engraved initial and bright cut band, on bun feet, by Walker & Hall, Sheffield, 1938, 60cm., approximately 82oz. (Lawrence Fine Art) £1,265

Sterling hand chased waiter, en suite, S. Kirk & Son Co., Baltimore, circa 1903–1924, centred with a three initial script monogram, 182oz. 6dwts. (Butterfield & Butterfield) £4,510

Louis XVI style silver tray, maker SK, 20th century, navette shaped with fluted sides, applied scrolling gadrooned border, 27¹/₄in. long, 79oz. 10dwt. (Butterfield & Butterfield) £1,201

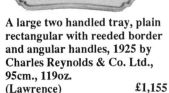

A large two handled tray, plain rectangular with reeded border and angular handles, 1925 by Charles Reynolds & Co. Ltd., 95cm., 119oz. (Lawrence) £1,155

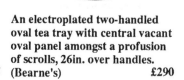

An electroplated two-handled oval tea tray with central vacant oval panel amongst a profusion of scrolls, 26in. over handles. (Bearne's) £290

A rectangular tea tray, the raised gadroon rim with shell motifs at the angles, Sheffield, 1936 by Emile Viner of Viner and Co., 62cm., 89.4oz. (Lawrence Fine Arts) £1,155

20TH CENTURY

Sterling silver footed tray by Meriden Britannia Co., monogrammed, 9in. diameter, 7.6 troy oz.
(Eldred's)   £53

An Edwardian dressing table tray, with stamped and pierced scroll and flower work folded border, Birmingham 1907, 284 grammes, 12in. wide.
(Spencer's)   £250

A Georg Jensen circular tray, designed by Johan Rohde, the handles cast with interlocking scrolls, 13in. diam.
(Christie's S. Ken)   £660

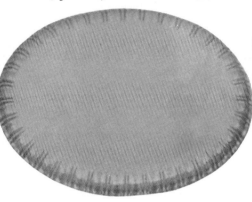

An Edwardian dressing table tray of rectangular form, Chester 1901, by John and William Deakin of James Deakin and Sons., 30.5cm., 12.4oz.
(Lawrence)   £374

A Wiener Werkstatte plated oval tray, designed by Josef Hoffmann, embellished with vertical lobes and fluting, 34cm. wide. (Phillips)   £800

An Edwardian shaped oblong trinket tray die-stamped with rococo shells, flowers and scrolling foliage, William Hutton and Sons Limited, Birmingham 1905, $11^{1}/_{2}$in., 9.75oz.
(Christie's S. Ken)   £341

A fine silver chrysanthemum-pattern tea tray, maker's mark of Tiffany & Co., New York, 1902–1907, with cast chrysanthemum border, 29in. long, 270 oz. 10 dwt.
(Christie's)   £12,320

Art Nouveau sterling waiter, Mauser Manufacturing Co., New York, 1900–1910, applied with chased stylised flower stalks, crescent shaped handles, length $28^{1}/_{2}$in., 139oz.
(Butterfield & Butterfield)
                                          £2,631

Japanese sterling two handled tray, early 20th century, impressed *Arthur & Bond Yoko-hama,* applied with irises in relief, 30in. long to handles, approx. 118 troy oz.
(Skinner Inc.)   £2,454

A good Regency Sheffield plate tureen, engraved tower crest, having acanthus applique paw feet, the cover with a foliate handle, 16½in. across handles. (Woolley & Wallis) **£900**

Regency Sheffield silver plated tureen, circa 1820, domed cover with gadrooned rim, with paw feet and foliate handles, 10in. high. (Skinner Inc.) **£782**

A French covered tureen, with two scroll foliate loop handles, post-1838, guarantee and purity marks for .950, maker's mark EP, 25.5cm. across handles, 1189g. (Lawrence Fine Arts) **£935**

A Hukin & Heath electroplated metal tureen, designed by Dr. Christopher Dresser, with bone finial and cylindrical bar handle, on three spike feet, with registration lozenge for 1880, 25.5cm. high. (Christie's) **£6,600**

A Sybil Dunlop hammered silver tureen and cover, on circular foot the spherical body chased in relief with two bands of scrolling foliage, flanked either side with scrolled handles, London 1922, 4½in. high. (Christie's) **£600**

A fine tureen and cover, designed by Georg Jensen, the bombé bowl with curved leaf and bud handles on four scroll feet with stem and flower head decoration, 31.5cm. long, 1980 grams. (Christie's) **£13,200**

A silver covered tureen, maker's mark of Tiffany & Co., New York, 1875–1891, the foot and lower body repoussé with spiral flutes, 11in. wide, 41 oz. (Christie's) **£2,156**

A covered tureen, by Samuel Kirk & Son, Baltimore, 1880-1890, the low domed cover with a pineapple finial, marked 10in. high, 57oz. (Christie's New York) **£1,383**

S. Kirk and Son repoussé silver covered tureen, circa 1885, round with pineapple finial, 10½in. high, approximately 49 troy oz. (Skinner Inc.) **£2,410**

SAUCE

Sauce tureens followed soup tureens into existence around 1760, and were essentially smaller versions of a matching design, made in sets of two or four as an alternative to the sauce boat. They are quite difficult to find in good condition, but a pair still tends to cost less than one soup tureen.

One of a pair of George III sauce tureens and covers, by Robt. Sharp, London, 1802, 54oz.13dwt., 9¾in. wide.   **£2,360**

One of a pair of George III Regency two-handled oval sauce tureens and covers, by Thos. Robins, 1810, 9in. long, 74oz.   **£3,565**

A Regency gadrooned compressed sauce tureen, with eagle crest finial, William Bruce, London, 1818, 8¼in., 31oz. (Christie's S. Ken) **£770**

Hester Bateman, a pair of sauce tureens and covers, the plain oval or boat-shaped bodies on pedestal bases, 19cm. high, 1784, 42¹/₂oz.
(Phillips)   **£2,600**

A silver covered sauce tureen, maker's mark of Ball, Black & Co., New York, circa 1860, length over handles 8⁵/₈in., 27oz. (Christie's)   **£799**

A George III sauce tureen, on pedestal base, the domed part-fluted cover with leaf mounted loop handle, London 1804, by Richard Sibley I, 23.5cm. diam., 26oz. (Bonhams) **£900**

A pair of Sheffield plate sauce tureens, having detachable liners, the covers with leaf shell corners and detachable handles, 8¹/₂in., circa 1805.
(Woolley & Wallis)   **£380**

Paul Schofield, oval sauce tureen, with two loop handles, the cover with an urn finial, London 1789, 20 oz.
(Woolley & Wallis)   **£1,100**

SAUCE

A Continental 19th century moulded circular sauce tureen and cover chased with arabesques, 9in. overall, 19¼oz. (Christie's S. Ken) £495

A pair of small sauce tureens and covers on stand, the tureens of two handled wrythen fluted globular form, 25cm. long. (Henry Spencer) £200

A George II two-handled oval sauce tureen and cover, Sebastian and James Crespell, London 1768, 19.6oz. (Bearne's) £880

A silver covered sauce tureen, maker's mark of Gorham Mfg. Co., Providence, 1868, the angular handles surmounted by alligators and terminating in a flowerhead and ribbon, 7¼in. wide, 15 oz. 10 dwt. (Christie's) £1,725

A pair of George III sauce tureens and covers, of boat shape with beaded borders, the covers with leafy urn finials, by Thomas Evans, 1777, 42 oz. (Lawrence Fine Art) £3,410

One of a pair of silver sauce tureens, maker's mark of Edward Lownes, Philadelphia, circa 1825, the sides applied with cast vintage decoration and two cast handles, 48 oz. (Christie's) £9,856

One of a pair of George III boat-shaped sauce tureens and covers, by Peter, Ann & William Bateman, London, 1802, 9½in. wide over handles, 36oz.4dwt. £3,390

A pair of George III two-handled oval sauce tureens and covers, with partly-fluted lower body, shell-capped foliage reeded ring handles issuing from lions' masks, by Phillip Rundell, 1819, 9¾in. wide, 69oz. (Christie's) £3,300

A George III large two-handled shaped-oval soup tureen and cover, gadrooned waved borders and slightly domed cover with detachable pomegranate finial, by Sebastian and James Crespell, 1767, 19in. long, 155oz. (Christie's) £26,450

SOUP

These were circular or oval bowls and covers for soup and were introduced in the early 18th century. In the rococo period they were suitably ornate, but later passed through a period of plain classical vase form, before becoming elaborate again in the 19th century. Stands are very common with Continental tureens, but are rare in England, and can almost double the value of a piece.

A George III soup tureen and cover, of oval bellied shape, by Smith, Tate, Hoult and Tate, Sheffield 1820, length over handles 19in., 133oz.
(Tennants) £4,000

A Regency partly-fluted oval soup tureen and cover on richly chased acanthus foliage and scroll supports, by Paul Storr, 1811, weight 180oz., 18in. wide.
(Christie's) £18,700

A George IV two-handled shaped-oval bombe soup tureen and cover, with vine tendril and leaf handles and gadrooned, shell and foliage border, by William Ker Reid, 1826, 13in. wide, 162oz.
(Christie's) £7,700

A French plain oval two-handled soup tureen, cover and stand, the stand on four lion's paw feet and with a foliage and beaded frieze, by Jean-Nicolas Boulanger, Paris, 1798–1809, 14in., 6,950grs.
(Christie's) £8,250

A George III two-handled circular partly-fluted soup tureen and cover, the bombé body with reeded and foliage handles, by John Edwards III, 1807, with plated liner, 11in. diameter, 109oz.
(Christie's) £8,800

An American silver circular two-handled soup tureen and cover, S. Kirk & Son, Baltimore, circa 1860, 48oz. 10dwt., length over handles 11⁵/₈in.
(Sotheby's) £1,816

A George II quilted two-handled shaped-oval soup tureen and cover, with leaf-capped gadrooned scroll handles, the domed cover with similar handle, by Peter Archambo and Peter Meure, 1756, 15¹/₂in. long, 100oz.
(Christie's) £8,800

A South American soup-tureen and cover, chased with bands of fluting and engraved with rosettes, Guatemala, circa 1800, 10³/₄in. long.
(Christie's) £2,185

SOUP

A Victorian soup tureen, cover and liner, of bellied oval form, 39cm. long, by John Mortimer & John Samuel Hunt, 1840, 126.5oz.
(Phillips London) £4,000

A Victorian silver two-handled shaped oval soup tureen and cover, by B. Smith II, 1838, 17½in. long, 179oz. £4,750

Early Victorian plated covered soup tureen by Elkington & Co., Birmingham, circa 1868, with a crown finial on a cushion with tassels, 12in. wide.
(Butterfield & Butterfield) £259

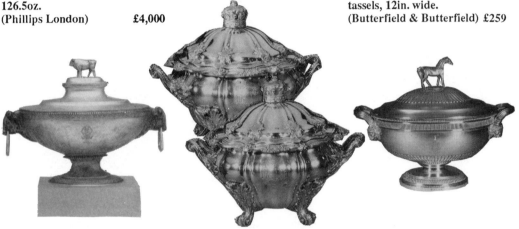

A covered soup tureen by William Gale, Jr., New York; retailed by Ford & Tupper, circa 1860, with a cast steer finial above repoussé and chased grass, 11¾in. high, 90 oz.
(Christie's) £5,188

A pair of Victorian two-handled melon-fluted soup tureens, covers and liners, by Robert Garrard, 1843, the base of each tureen stamped *GARRARDS PANTON STREET LONDON*, 14¾in. wide, 288oz.
(Christie's) £16,500

A George III oval two-handled soup tureen and cover, engraved with inscription and coat-of-arms, by Paul Storr, 1804, the finial by Benjamin Smith, 17in. long, 141oz.
(Christie's) £15,400

Sheffield plated soup tureen, circa 1830, the rectangular body on four paw feet with fluted sides spreading in a sunburst, with an everted neck, height 10in.
(Butterfield & Butterfield) £564

Victorian plated covered soup tureen by Elkington & Co., Birmingham, circa 1850, the pinched neck with everted lip applied with scrolling foliage and flowers, 15½in. wide.
(Butterfield & Butterfield) £484

Sheffield plated soup tureen, first third 19th century, oval body set on four boldly scrolling feet with acanthus leaf terminals, 10½in. high.
(Butterfield & Butterfield) £825

A Victorian soup tureen and cover, by T. W. H. & H. Dobson, 1880, 30cm. across handles, 46.5oz. **£1,150**

A George III circular soup tureen, stand and cover, by Paul Storr, 1805, 11¾in. high, 267oz. **£49,895**

A George II two-handled oval bombe soup tureen and cover, by Wm. Cripps, 1751, 14½in. long, gross 117oz. **£8,080**

Italian silver soup tureen with cover in the mid 18th century taste, 20th century, bombé oval form vessel with panelled sides, on domed pedestal base, length (over handles) 15¾in., 69oz. 16dwt.
(Butterfield & Butterfield) **£1,126**

An Old Sheffield plate two-handled oval soup tureen and cover, with foliage handles and gadrooned border, the domed cover with similar detachable foliage ring handle, circa 1820, 16½in. wide.
(Christie's) **£1,210**

Sterling floral chased soup tureen with cover, Whiting Mfg. Co., Providence, Rhode Island, circa 1880, bombé round form body set on four ball supports, length (over handles) 11¼in., 42oz. 12dwt.
(Butterfield & Butterfield) **£1,689**

A George III partly-fluted oval soup tureen and cover, by Peter, Ann and William Bateman, 1802, 15in. long, 90oz.
(Christie's) **£6,050**

A covered soup tureen, with domed oval lid, by Bailey & Kitchen, Phila., 1833-46, 15½in. high, 16in. wide, 127oz. **£2,555**

A George III two-handled oval soup tureen and cover, by Wm. Fountain, 1806, with liner by R. Garrard, 1862, 11¼in. long, 138oz. **£5,710**

SOUP

A two-handled shaped oval soup tureen and cover, by Elkington & Co., Birmingham, 1909, 126oz. £3,565

A Regency two-handled oval soup tureen, cover and stand, by Thos. Robins, 1811, the liner 1812, 20¾in., 387oz. £21,385

A George II two-handled shaped oval soup tureen and cover, by F. Kandler, 1753, 11¼in. long, 132oz. £10,695

'Japanese Movement' Sterling soup tureen with cover and associated ladle by Tiffany & Co., New York, New York, circa 1881, 13in. wide, together with a Tiffany & Co. soup ladle. (Butterfield & Butterfield) £7,333

A silver soup tureen and cover of historical interest, maker's mark of George B. Sharp for Bailey & Co., Philadelphia, circa 1857, length over handles 15½in., 64oz. 10dwt. (Christie's) £2,904

A George III partly-fluted two-handled oval soup tureen and cover, the slightly domed cover with detachable entwined snake and foliage handle with beaded surround, by Paul Storr, 1808, 17½in. wide, 164oz. (Christie's) £26,400

A Victorian two-handled shaped oval silver soup tureen and cover, by S. Hayne and D. Cater, 1845, 14½in. long, 111oz. £4,990

A Regency pierced Sheffield plate rectangular soup tureen, the part fluted lid with reeded leaf tie ring handle, 11.5in. £615

An Old Sheffield plate shaped oval, two handled soup tureen and cover, on four foliate scroll feet, circa 1820, 16¾in. long overall. (Christie's London) £990

One of a pair of George III neo-classical sugar urns by John Carter, London 1774, 6.5in. high, 16.5oz. **£815**

A silver plated Art Nouveau covered urn, circa 1900, 16¼in. high. **£150**

Silver gilt urn, by Howard & Co., New York, circa 1900, 14in. high, 45 troy oz. **£620**

Sterling covered presentation urn, Tiffany & Co., New York, 1897–1902, cup shaped body with double scrolled handles on either side, height 10¼in., 43oz. 18dwts.
(Butterfield & Butterfield) **£752**

A pair of silver plated metal and perspex urns, each of hexagonal bucket form on tubular stem and square base, 20¼in. high.
(Bonhams) **£800**

A Puiforcat silver urn, of shouldered ovoid form, tapering to an everted scalloped rim, with domed cover and carved ivory finial, 34.5cm. high. (Christie's London) **£880**

A two-compartment caviar container of urn-shaped form, by Omar Ramsden and Alwyn Carr, 1903, 25.5cm. high, 27.75oz. **£1,650**

A Victorian cylindrical commemorative urn, formed as the Choragic monument of Lysicrates in Athens, 1888, 8in. high, 50oz. **£850**

George III silver two-handled urn, J. Robins, London, 1808–09, chased decoration, approximately 46 troy oz. (Skinner) **£1,226**

19TH CENTURY

A silver gilt two-handled 'Trafalgar Vase', by B. Smith, 1807, the finial by C. Gordon, circa 1835, 15¾in. high, 104oz. £3,630

A George IV replica of the Warwick vase and cover, by The Boulton Plate Co., Birmingham, 1827, 13in. high, 163oz. £9,505

Repoussé sterling two-handled vase, sold by Theodore B. Starr, with chased grapevines, on a moulded spreading foot, 10½in. high, approx. 44 troy oz. (Skinner) £790

A rare presentation vase by W. K. Vanderslice, San Francisco, circa 1876, with a flaring rim and two scrolling handles enclosing pierced and chased oak leaves and acorns, 11⅝in. high, 31 oz. 10 dwt. (Christie's) £2,145

A pair of Continental vases, 7in. high, on floral and scroll pierced oval bases with leaf-chased bracket feet, circa 1880, Bertholdt Müller. (Bonhams) £460

A Victorian two-handled campana-shaped vase, body and handles formed as entwined grape-laden vine tendrils, by John S. Hunt, 1852, fitted with frosted glass liner, 21in. high, 225 oz. (Christie's) £8,250

A quartz cup and cover, the vase shaped body collet-set with oval shaped faceted and cabochon amethyst, 25cm. high. (Lawrence) £1,320

A William IV two-handled silver-gilt vase, the body of shaped outline with applied horses' heads and foliage, by Paul Storr, 1837, 9¼in. high, 96oz. (Christie's) £9,680

An urn-shaped vase with two cast mask handles, by Shreve, Stanwood & Co., Boston, 1860-69, 13in. high, 24oz. £550

19TH CENTURY

An attractive vase, part gilt Classical form, by Frederick Elkington, Birmingham 1875, 29.8cm. high, 23oz. (Bonhams) £620

A WMF Ikora patinated metal vase, shouldered ovoid shape with short cylindrical neck, 23.6cm. high. (Christie's) £302

An Art Nouveau baluster vase chased with lilies of the valley, the base impressed with a date 1896, 7¼in., 14.75oz. (Christie's) £275

A Chinese export silver vase, maker's mark of Wang Hing & Co., Hong Kong, late 19th/early 20th century, elaborately chased with Chinese figures at battle within an architectural landscape, 15in. high, 59 oz. 10 dwt.
(Christie's) £1,232

A pair of late 19th century electroplated vases of amphora shape, the body decorated in high relief with a procession of allegorical figures above a band of vine leaves and grapes, 28in. high.
(Christie's S. Ken) £880

A trophy vase by Whiting Manufacturing Co., New York, 1887, with a flaring scalloped rim, the sides etched with mermaids riding seahorses, 15½in. high, 37 oz. 10 dwt.
(Christie's) £2,945

Gorham Sterling vase, circa 1878, repoussé decoration, chased stag's head handles, 9½in. high, approximately 19 troy oz.
(Skinner Inc.) £386

An ovoid vase, by Tiffany & Co., N.Y., 1878–90, 6⅝in. high, 14oz.
(Christie's) £4,322

A fine silver-mounted ivory vase, maker's mark of *Tiffany & Co., New York 1889–1891*, 17¾in. high.
(Christie's) £15,220

19TH CENTURY

A late 19th/early 20th century Arts & Crafts sterling silver vase, America, 22 troy oz. £315

A WMF Ikora patinated metal vase, ovoid shape, inlaid with a figure on horseback in silver, gilt and dark grey, 20.2cm. high. £425

A silver enamelled bud vase, by Tiffany & Co., N.Y., circa 1893, 5³/₈ in. high, 5oz.10dwt. £920

A Continental inverted pear-shaped vase on mask and paw feet, the body cast and chased with exotic birds, flowers and scrolling foliage, bearing import marks, 9¹/₄ in., 21oz. (Christie's S. Ken) £550

A pair of Viennese silver-mounted enamel vases, each painted overall with various allegorical scenes, the mounts enamelled and set with masks, late 19th century, 12in. high. (Bearne's) £3,500

Important Sterling silver trophy, 19th century, by Tiffany, cast handles in the form of angels holding children, either side with applied full, two-dimensional figures of women in diaphanous clothing, 24.8 troy oz. (Eldred's) £2,075

A vase by Tiffany & Company, New York, 1892, with two cast handles, each in the form of two swan's heads with elongated necks, 13¹/₄ in. high, 30 oz. (Christie's) £2,421

An enamelled vase by Gorham, Providence, 1897, with a flaring square rim and foot, the front and back cast with a pond and lilypads, 7³/₄ in. high, 16 oz. (Christie's) £1,440

An impressive W.M.F. two handled vase, the fascia depicting a maiden within entrelac and tendril borders, 50cm. high. (Spencer's) £520

19TH CENTURY

Italian .800 fine silver vase by Buccellatti, 10in. high, 24.2 troy oz.
(Eldred's)   £376

A pair of crocus-shaped embossed silver vases with leaf decoration, 6¼in. high.
£110

A late 19th century silver baluster vase with tall tapering hexagonal trumpet neck, signed Sadayoshi koku, 35cm. high.   £1,015

A Victorian Scottish two-handled vase, cover and rose-water dish, the dish on four shell feet and applied with four oval plaques with heads between, by Mackay Cunningham and Co., Edinburgh, 1880 and 1881, 30in. high, 213 ozs.
(Christie's)   £4,180

A pair of late 19th century Turkish vases, one for burning incense, the other for rose-water, 25cm. high - 50.5ozs.
(Phillips)   £1,900

A Japanese silver and polychrome enamel baluster vase, engraved with matted foliage, the body chased with a meandering stream, 10in. high, 20oz.
(Christie's)   £977

An Arts and Crafts electroplate vase, of tapering cylindrical form on short cylindrical foot with scalloped border, 24.5cm. high.
(Christie's)   £154

A pair of Eastern slender-necked vases decorated overall with birds, flowers, and scrolling foliage, 8¼in. high.
(Christie's)   £242

Dominick & Haff pierced sterling vase, with a cranberry glass liner, of trumpet form with a scalloped rim, 14in. high, approx. 16 troy oz.
(Skinner)   £377

20TH CENTURY

A silver overlay glass vase, maker's mark of Alvin Mfg. Co., Providence, circa 1905, 14in. high.
(Christie's) £1,781

A pair of Argentor silvered metal vases, after a design by Josef Hoffman, circa 1920, 17cm. high. £415

A Liberty & Co. 'Cymric' silver and enamel vase, the design attributed to A. Knox, 1902, 19.25cm. £5,000

An Edwardian silver-gilt gadrooned elongated campana-shaped vase, the body decorated with 18th century style figures, birds, flowers and scrolling foliage, D. & J. Wellby, London 1905, 7in., 12.75oz.
(Christie's S. Ken) £638

A matched pair of Neapolitan vases and covers, one repoussé with a bust portrait of Francis IV, the other repoussé with a victory scene depicting William of Orange, bears import marks for Birmingham 1902, 1714 grammes total.
(Spencer's) £2,500

A fine silver, enamel and stone-set "Viking" vase, maker's mark of Tiffany & Co., New York, circa 1901, designed by Paulding Farnham, the shoulder applied with stylised masks, 12in. high, 30 oz.
(Christie's) £13,000

An Arts and Crafts silver vase in the form of a castellated turret, the body with hammered finish, Birmingham 1902, 16cm. high.
(Christie's) £220

Pair of Japanese parcel gilt silver vases, circa 1900, with flat bases, tapering cylindrical sides, horizontal shoulders and everted mouth, height 11³/₄in., 53oz. 10dwts.
(Butterfield & Butterfield) £526

An unusual silver presentation vase, maker's mark of Mauser Mfg. Co., New York, circa 1903, 23¹/₂in. high, 191oz.
(Christie's) £11,871

20TH CENTURY

A tall silver vase, made by H. G. Murphy and R. M. Y. Gleadowe, 25.5cm. high, 29.5oz., maker's marks for London, 1935. £2,310

A pierced vase by Tiffany & Co., New York, 1902–1907, with fluted sides, scalloped rim, scrolling handles and a repoussé foliate base, 11½in. high, 51 oz. 10 dwt.
(Christie's)   £2,618

An electroplated vase, circa 1900, probably WMF, on an open four-legged base, 38.25cm.
£330

A silver vase, maker's mark of Gorham Mfg. Co., Providence, circa 1910, applied with acanthus leaves and acanthus and geometric strapwork, 12³/₄in. high, 52 oz.
(Christie's)   £2,156

A pair of Georg Jensen vases, stamped marks Dessin G J 925.S Georg Jensen 107A, 13.2cm. high, 332.5gr.
(Christie's)   £385

A Liberty & Co. 'Cymric' silver and enamel vase, the body decorated with a band of blue and orange enamelled stylised fruit branches, Birmingham hallmarks for 1905, 19.2cm. high.
(Christie's)   £990

A Liberty silver vase, the design attributed to A. Knox, stamped Cymric. L & Co within three lozenges and with Birmingham hallmarks for 1907, 17cm. high.   £300

A two-handled replica of the Warwick vase, the body chased and applied with masks, lions' pelts, foliage and trailing vines, by Barnard Brothers, 1908, height of vase 10½in., 118oz.
(Christie's)   £4,180

A vase by Towle, Newburyport, circa 1910, with a moulded circular rim and footrim, 9⁵/₈in. high, 30 oz.
(Christie's)   £654

20TH CENTURY

A cut glass and silver vase by Gorham, Providence; glass by Hawkes, circa 1912, 15in. high. (Christie's) £1,107

A silver twin-handled vase, 16.6cm. high, 12.5oz., stamped E.J.B. maker's marks, Birmingham, 1909. £310

A silver double vase on stand, by The Sweetser Co., New York, circa 1900-15, the stand of copper, 11½in. high, gross wt. of vase 20oz.10dwt. £1,195

A Liberty and Co. 'Cymric' three-handled waisted vase, the handles enamelled with entwined strap-work in shades of blue, green and purple, Birmingham 1901, 6¾in. high. (Christie's S. Ken) £1,540

A pair of Liberty & Co. 'Cymric' silver and enamelled vases designed by Archibald Knox, Birmingham marks for 1903, 12.5cm. high. (Phillips) £3,600

An Edwardian Irish spot-hammered flaring vase applied with foliate decorated scroll handles, Goldsmiths & Silversmiths Co. Ltd., Dublin 1903, 8¼in., 28.75 oz. (Christie's) £572

Black, Starr and Frost sterling vase, New York, early 20th century, with an overall chased flowering clematis vine, 14¾in. high, approximately 44 troy oz. (Skinner Inc.) £1,512

A fine Edwardian replica of the Warwick vase by Elkington & Co Limited, the body chased and applied with masks, lion's pelts, foliage and trailing vines, Birmingham 1904, approximately 6000 grammes. (Spencer's) £5,000

A large silver globular vase with trumpet-shaped neck, signed Takasaki Koichi koreo seizo and dated Meiji 33 (1900), 63cm. high, 210oz. £3,565

423

VESTA CASES

Also known as matchholders of fusee boxes, these consisted of a small container with a striking surface for holding and lighting matches. They were made from about 1830 onwards in two forms, a small portable variety and a larger type for standing on a desk or table. The basic form had a hinged lid at one end and a striking surface, sometimes concealed, of parallel ridges or, later, of glass paper, at the other. As the century progressed designs became more fanciful and elaborate and many novelty forms were produced.

An Edwardian circular vesta case, the front chased with a Victorian Rifle Volunteers shooting competition, Birmingham, 1906.
(Phillips)   £196

An enamelled oblong silver vesta case, probably German, importer's mark Simon & Alder, London 1903, 1¾in. high.   £1,000

A Continental gilt-lined vesta case, enamelled with a standing lady dressed in black stockings and a camisole holding a cat in the gathered folds, 2in.
(Christie's S. Ken)   £396

An unusual Victorian novelty vesta case-cum-cigar cutter shaped like an artist's palette, by Alexander Jones, 1884, with incised registration number and retailer's mark of *Asprey & Sons 166 Bond St*, 1.5oz.
(Phillips)   £420

A late Victorian 15ct. gold advertising vesta case of rounded oblong form, the cover decorated in polychrome enamel with a bottle and glass of 'Bass & Cº Pale Ale'.
(Phillips)   £400

A late Victorian plain vesta case, inset one side with a compass, makers Collins & Cook, Chester 1900.
(Woolley & Wallis)   £85

A late Victorian rectangular vesta case chased on the cover in relief with a horse-racing scene, Chester, 1895, apparently no maker's mark.
(Phillips)   £260

A Victorian engine turned vesta case, the cartouche with initials and date, maker S. Blankenzee & Son, Birmingham 1883.
(Woolley & Wallis)   £38

An Edwardian rectangular vesta case, the front enamelled with a two-horse carriage in a rural landscape, Birmingham 1901. (Christie's S. Ken) £165

A silver and coral guilloché enamel match box, workmaster's stamp of Michael Perchin and Fabergé in Russian script, Petersburg 1905, 3½ in. x 2¼ in. (Woolley & Wallis) £950

A Victorian novelty vesta case modelled as a milkman's hand can of oval cylindrical form, by William Leuchars, 1875, 5.6cm. high. (Phillips) £350

A Victorian combined vesta case and cachou box, engraved all over with leafage, 'Cachous', Birmingham, 1887. (Phillips) £130

A Victorian book vesta case, the cover enamelled 'en grisaille' with the cover of Punch magazine No. 2375, by Hubert Thornhill, 1887, 3.6cm. long. (Phillips) £440

An Edwardian novelty vesta case, depicting four people motoring along a country road in a vintage car, 5 x 4cm., maker's mark RB^s, Chester, 1906, 1oz. (Phillips) £280

An Edwardian rectangular vesta case, the front enamelled with an oval vignette of a dog, R.B.S Chester, 1906, 2in. (Christie's) £110

A novel late Victorian vesta case designed as an advertisement, of rounded oblong form, decorated in polychrome enamel with an oval cartouche, maker's mark *WJD*, Birmingham, 1894. (Phillips) £280

After Alistair for F.N., Pierrot vesta case, 1927, enamelled with a tipsy Pierrot seated at a banqueting table, 7.75 x 5cm. (Sotheby's) £1,840 $2,981

VINAIGRETTES

These are small, exquisite silver boxes which opened to reveal an inner, pierced and gilded lid, behind which there was a sponge soaked in aromatic vinegar. Vinaigrettes were the successors of pomanders, and served a similar purpose, used by ladies against faintness, and to ward of the many unpleasant odours which abounded in these less sanitary times. The earliest specimens date from the late 18th century and are round or oval, with flat chased or bright cut lids. More common, however, are rectangular types, or those made in some novelty design, imitating a miniature book, toy, watch or whatever.

Later Georgian vinaigrettes are characterised by highly ornamental filigree grids but those dating after the 1830s are simpler, with round drilled holes, in contrast to their elaborate rectangular lids with massive ornamentation. The fashion for such things was waning, however, by the mid 19th century perhaps as a result of improvements in sanitation at the time which made them increasingly superfluous. Late Victorian examples were also produced in silver mounted glass and ivory.

A French gold scalloped shaped vinaigrette chased at the hinge with foliage and shells, Paris, 1809-19, 1³/₄ in. long.
(Christie's)   £1,320

A good George IV silver-gilt vinaigrette, engine-turned base, heavily carved cover and thumbpiece, by Nathaniel Mills, Birmingham, 1826.
(Phillips)   £340

An unusual George III vinaigrette, shaped and engraved with asymmetrical patches of hatching and pricked dots to simulate a tortoise shell, 2.5 x 2.5cm., by Matthew Linwood, Birmingham, 1815.
(Phillips)   £240

A Victorian vinaigrette engraved with a view of Yorkminster, by Nathaniel Mills, Birmingham, 1843. (Phillips)   £350

A very rare early Victorian silver gilt cat vinaigrette, the oblong body engraved with peacocks and foliate scrolls, by James Beebe, 1837.
(Phillips)   £2,600

A Victorian oval vinaigrette, cover applied with the Scott Memorial within a surround of thistles and scrolls, by William & Edward Turnpenny, Birmingham, 1845.   £600

A George IV vinaigrette, engine turned with reeded sides, 1¹/₂in., maker Clarke & Smith, Birmingham 1825.
(Woolley & Wallis)   £90

A Regency purse vinaigrette, the gilt interior with pierced grille, 1in., maker Lea & Co., Birmingham 1818.
(Woolley & Wallis)   £160

An oblong silver gilt vinaigrette with pierced foliage panel on the cover, by J. Bettridge, Birmingham, 1827.   £175

Silver gilt cushion-shaped vinaigrette, by John Shaw, circa 1810, 3.2cm. wide. £165

A Victorian Scottish thistle-shaped vinaigrette, on matted stem with naturalistically chased flower, Edinburgh, 1881, maker's mark A F, 1⁷/₈in. long (Christie's) £770

A 19th century Chinese oblong silver gilt vinaigrette with chased body, unmarked. £380

An early Victorian vinaigrette, the gilt interior with a foliage engraved pierced grille, 1¹/₂in., maker Edward Smith, Birmingham 1843. (Woolley & Wallis) £95

A Scottish silver mounted mottled jasper vinaigrette with chased foliage rims, circa 1820, unmarked. £360

A William IV book vinaigrette engraved with foliate scrolls, cover inscribed *J. Bonny* in a shaped cartouche, by Taylor & Perry, Birmingham, 1836. (Phillips) £240

A George III oblong vinaigrette, engraved on the cover with a woodsman in 18th century costume, by Matthew Linwood, Birmingham, 1809. (Phillips) £200

A Victorian shaped oblong vinaigrette, engraved on the cover with the Crystal Palace on a rayed background, by Nathaniel Mills, Birmingham, 1850, 4.5cm. long. (Phillips) £700 $1,164

A Victorian vinaigrette, of rectangular form, formed as a book, the lid and base forming the 'covers', by Edward Smith, Birmingham 1846, 1¹/₂in. (Lawrence Fine Art) £330

A Regency rectangular vinaigrette, the gilt interior with a pierced engraved grille, maker possibly Wm. Shaw, London, 1813, 1.15in. long. £70

A William IV silver-gilt vinaigrette, rectangular, engine-turned, carved thumbpiece, by Nathaniel Mills, Birmingham, 1835. (Phillips) £200

A gold rectangular vinaigrette, the slightly sloped lid inset with a garnet and engraved with flowerheads circa 1840, 1.4in. (Christie's S. Ken) £418

VINAIGRETTES

Victorian shaped rectangular vinaigrette, by Yapp & Woodward, 1848, 3.5cm. wide. (Christie's) **£165**

A silver gilt rectangular vinaigrette, by William Boot, circa 1820, 4cm. wide. **£275**

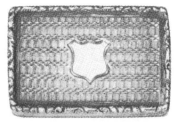

An early Victorian rectangular vinaigrette, by Francis Clarke, Birmingham 1843, 4.3cm. **£155**

A silver gilt vinaigrette of scallop shape, by Matthew Linwood, Birmingham, 1802. **£330**

A Victorian combination horn-shaped scent bottle and vinaigrette applied with lattice-work decoration, T.J., London 1873, 4¹/₅in. (Christie's S. Ken) **£264**

A silver gilt shell vinaigrette, the body formed from a small cowrie, circa 1800. **£475**

A George IV rectangular silver-gilt vinaigrette, the lid chased with flowers and foliage, the grill pierced and engraved with scroll work, Nathaniel Mills, Birmingham 1826, 1⁷/₁₀in. (Christie's S. Ken) **£440**

A George IV silver-gilt rectangular vinaigrette, the lid applied with a cast model of a Papillon dog, its back applied with a blister pearl, James Beebe, Birmingham 1824, 1¹/₂in. (Christie's S. Ken) **£2,200**

A George III silver-gilt vinaigrette, the cover cast with a shepherd piping beneath a tree with goats and cows, by Joseph Wilmore, Birmingham, 1813, 2in. long. (Christie's) **£880**

A Continental oval silver-gilt vinaigrette, the lid inset with a black pietra dura panel inlaid with two vari-coloured hardstone butterflies, circa 1800, 1⁴/₅in. (Christie's S. Ken) **£550**

A very attractive William IV silver gilt oblong vinaigrette, engine-turned and with floral borders, by Thomas Edwards, 1832. **£1,300**

A William IV oval silver-gilt vinaigrette, the lid applied with a carved cameo plaque depicting Venus and Cupid within a cast border, Nathaniel Mills, Birmingham 1836, 1⁷/₁₀in. (Christie's S. Ken) **£990**

A large oblong silver gilt vinaigrette, by Samuel Pemberton, Birmingham, 1814. £380

A 19th century Continental vinaigrette, the top inset with a fossilized quartz stone, 2⅝in. overall. £1,485

A William IV tartan engraved silver vinaigrette, by N. Mills, Birmingham, 1837, 1.5in. long. £110

A Victorian oblong vinaigrette, the gilt interior with a pierced foliage engraved grille, 2½in., maker Edward Smith, Birmingham 1859. (Woolley & Wallis) £200

An unusual, silver gilt vinaigrette chased as a crown, by Joseph Willmore, Birmingham, 1820, with suspension ring. £880

A Victorian gilt lined vinaigrette in the form of a book, the 'covers' engraved with foliage, Joseph Wilmore, Birmingham, 1841, 1½in. (Christie's S. Ken) £242

An attractive 19th century Swiss gold and enamel vinaigrette, the engine-turned surfaces enamelled in a translucent flesh pink, maker's mark *MB & C* in lozenge, circa 1840. (Phillips) £950

A George III oblong vinaigrette engraved with a portrait of Nelson in uniform within an oval surround inscribed with *England expects everyman will do his duty*, by Matthew Linwood, Birmingham, 1805, 3.5cm. long. (Phillips) £1,500

A George III rectangular silver-gilt vinaigrette, chased with a basket-weave effect, the lid inset with an oval micro-mosaic of a chariot, possibly Birmingham 1809, 1½in. (Christie's S. Ken) £198

A Continental gilt-lined casket-shaped vinaigrette, the base, sides and lid enamelled with blue foliage, possibly French, circa 1800, 1½in. (Christie's S. Ken) £572

A Swiss gold rectangular vinaigrette in the form of a book, the covers with rayed engine-turning, circa 1840, 1¼in. (Christie s S. Ken) £528

A George IV oval silver-gilt vinaigrette, the lid cast with two wading birds within a heavy shell, scrollwork and floral border, Birmingham 1829, 2in. (Christie's S. Ken) £825

CASTLE TOP

An oblong silver castletop vinaigrette chased with a view of Windsor Castle, by Nathaniel Mills, Birmingham, 1837. £495

An early Victorian silver castle top vinaigrette, of rounded rectangular form depicting St. Pauls Cathedral, Birmingham 1842, probably by John Tongue. (Spencer's) £360

A William IV vinaigrette, the cover chased in relief with a ruined building, by Taylor & Perry, Birmingham, 1835. £550

An oblong silver castletop vinaigrette chased with a view of Kenilworth Castle, by Nathaniel Mills, Birmingham, 1839. £380

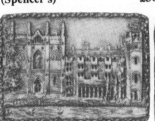

An oblong silver castletop vinaigrette chased with a view of Newstead Abbey, by Nathaniel Mills, Birmingham, 1838. £495

An oblong 'castle-top' vinaigrette chased with a view of Litchfield Cathedral, by N. Mills, 1843-4. £1,190

A Victorian shaped rectangular silver-gilt vinaigrette, the lid chased in high relief with a view of St. Pauls, Nathaniel Mills, Birmingham 1852, 1⁴/₅in. (Christie's S. Ken) £2,530

A Victorian vinaigrette, the lid embossed with a view of Abbotsford, the grille foliate and dot pierced, by Edward Smith, Birmingham 1839, 1¹/₂in. (Lawrence Fine Art) £330

A Victorian rectangular silver-gilt vinaigrette, the lid chased in high relief with a view of York Minster within a cast border, Nathaniel Mills, Birmingham 1841. (Christie's S. Ken) £1,430

York Minster, an early Victorian rectangular vinaigrette, the gilt interior with a pierced grille of a basket of flowers, 1³/₄in., John Tongue, Birmingham 1843. (Woolley & Wallis) £580

A Victorian rectangular gilt-lined vinaigrette, the lid chased in high relief with a view of Westminster Abbey, J.T., Birmingham, date letter indistinct, 1⁹/₁₀in. wide. (Christie's S. Ken) £528

A Victorian silver-gilt vinaigrette, the cover chased in low relief with a view of Yorkminster, by Joseph Willmore, Birmingham, 1844. (Phillips) £520

WAX JACKS

Also known as taperstands or, in America, as pull-ups, wax jacks could be made of silver, Sheffield Plate or brass and were used in the 18th and 19th century for holding wound sealing wax taper. They came in various forms – sometimes a reel holding the taper mounted vertically on a circular base or horizontally between two uprights. The taper end was held between scissor-like grips attached to the reel or projected through a small nozzle above.

WHISTLES

Silver whistles came mainly as children's novelty items, alongside coral rattles and silver bells in the 18th century, and no doubt parents, then as now, quailed inwardly as well-meaning relatives bestowed them upon their little darlings. Whistles were particularly popular in America, and were made there in the three main centres of Boston, Philadelphia and New York.

A late Victorian beaded and pierced cylindrical waxjack in the 18th century taste, James Dixon & Son, Sheffield 1897, 3¼in. high.
(Christie's) £308

A George II wax-jack, on three claw-and-ball feet and with cylindrical stem, maker's mark C.N., circa 1755, 5½in. high.
(Christie's) £1,430

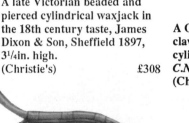

Rare George II bosun's whistle, London, 1740, 4¼in. long. £2,000

A Victorian cast whistle formed as the head of a dog, by Samson Mordan, London, 1886, 2½in. long. (Christie's) £462

Victorian silver whistle and penknife, London 1879. £200

Silver bosun's whistle, unmarked, 19th century, English or American, cylindrical tube ending in a ball form hollow chamber, with cut scrolling strut below, 6¼in. long, 1oz. 16dwt.
(Butterfield & Butterfield) £206

A goldwashed silver and coral rattle whistle, hallmarked Birmingham, 1862, 6in. long. £260

A George V rattle/whistle, the collar stamped 'darling' on a mother of pearl teething stick, Birmingham 1920.
(Spencer's) £40

A Royal Irish Rifles officer's silver (J. & Co. Birmingham, 1893) whistle with holder, chains and chain boss.
(Christie's S. Ken) £143

An Edwardian child's silver rattle, stamped in the form of Mr Punch, Birmingham 1908, maker's mark G & N, 14cm. high. (Henry Spencer) £120

WINE COOLERS

These two-handled gold, silver or silver-gilt vessels on a low foot were used to cool single bottles of wine. They may be of vase, urn or tub shape, usually with a detachable liner and sometimes with a stand, and came into fashion around 1780, though a few earlier examples do exist. They were particularly popular around the turn of the century, when the wine cistern fell from favour, but were in common use until the mid 19th century.

One of a pair of Queen Anne cylindrical wine coolers, by J. Bodington, circa 1710, 9½in. high, 216oz.   £254,100

An Austrian wine cooler, maker's mark G.H., Vienna, 1795, 120oz. excluding plated liner, 12½in. high.   £3,270

A Regency two-handled campana-shaped wine cooler on a rising circular foot, William Burwash, London 1813, fitted with a metal liner, 75.25oz. free. (Christie's S. Ken.)   £3,080

A pair of fine George III two-handled vase-shaped wine coolers, chased with bands of fluting and with lion's mask, shell and foliage bracket handles, by Paul Storr, 1810, 10in. high, 279oz. (Christie's)   £39,600

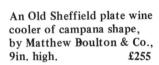

An Old Sheffield plate wine cooler of campana shape, by Matthew Boulton & Co., 9in. high.   £255

One of a pair of electro-plated Victorian wine coolers, by Elkington & Co., 1873, 22cm. high.   £1,430

A pair of Old Sheffield plate two-handled wine coolers, the partly-fluted vase-shaped bodies applied above with a band of vines, circa 1820, 10in. high. (Christie's)   £1,650

One of a pair of George III campana vase-shaped wine coolers, by Philip Rundell, 1819, 11¼in. high, 186oz.   £13,070

19TH CENTURY

One of a pair of campana-shaped wine coolers, by Wm. Elliot, London, 1829, 11½in. high, 276oz.12dwt. **£10,890**

A pair of 19th century Sheffield semi-lobed wine coolers. (Greenslade Hunt) **£720**

One of a pair of wine coolers with detachable rims and liners, by Paul Storr, London, 1817, 285oz.11dwt. **£43,560**

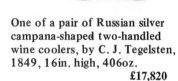

A Victorian silver gilt two-handled vase-shaped wine cooler, by A. Benson and H. H. Webb, 1893, 12½in. high, 106oz. **£2,905**

A pair of George III two-handled vase-shaped wine coolers, each on spreading circular foot, by Samuel Hennell and John Terrey, 1814, each with copper liner, 8½in. high, 241oz. (Christie's) **£11,500**

One of a pair of Russian silver campana-shaped two-handled wine coolers, by C. J. Tegelsten, 1849, 16in. high, 406oz. **£17,820**

One of a set of four George III silver gilt two-handled wine coolers, collars and liners, by Paul Storr, 1813, 11in. high, 689oz. **£242,000**

A pair of Old Sheffield plate inverted pear-shaped wine coolers applied with shell, flute and foliate handles, 8½in. high. (Christie's) **£1,210**

One of a pair of Sheffield plate two-handled campana-shaped wine coolers, by T. & J. Creswick & Co., circa 1820, 26.5cm. high. **£1,430**

WINE COOLERS

19TH CENTURY

A George IV silver-gilt two-handled campana-shaped wine cooler, collar and liner, by Paul Storr 1825, 11¹/₂in. high, 157oz. (Christie's) **£12,650**

A pair of William IV style two-handled Warwick vase wine coolers on square bases, 10¹/₄in., 231.50oz. (Christie's S. Ken.) **£4,620**

A Victorian two-handled campana-shaped wine cooler, collar and liner, by James Garrard, 1889, 10¹/₄in. high, 138oz. (Christie's) **£11,500**

Pair of Regency silver wine coolers by Robert Garrard, London, 1817, neoclassical urn shapes, with circular feet rising to a squat pinched waist, height 7³/₄in., 132oz. 6dwts. (Butterfield & Butterfield) **£12,778**

Pair of Sheffield plated wine coolers, first quarter 19th century, shaped as classical bell kraters, fluted lower body over a knopped squat stem, plain sides and gadrooned border, 9¹/₄in. high. (Butterfield & Butterfield) **£900**

A pair of Old Sheffield plate wine coolers, collars and liners, each form as a pail with reeded bracket handles and engraved with two crests beneath Earl's coronet, circa 1820, 7³/₄in. high. (Christie's) **£4,830**

A pair of two-handled spool-shaped wine coolers, chased with fluting and applied with vine tendrils between tendril scroll handles, by James Dixon & Sons, Sheffield, circa 1835, 10³/₄in. high. (Christie's) **£2,200**

A Victorian two-handled campana-shaped champagne cooler, the rockwork and scroll base on three shell and scroll feet, by John Hunt and Robert Roskell, 1865, 16¹/₂in. high, 214oz. (Christie's) **£6,900**

Pair of Sheffield plate wine coolers, early 19th century, crested, bracket handles with foliate attachments, gadroon edge, 11in. high. (Butterfield & Butterfield) **£1,135**

19TH CENTURY

An Old Sheffield plate part-fluted and gadrooned campana-shaped wine cooler, 10¼in. high. (Christie's) £385

An attractive pair of Old Sheffield plate wine coolers, 11½in. high, vase-form with two leaf mounted side handles, circa 1860. (Bonhams) £1,800

One of a pair of George IV two-handled vase-shaped wine coolers, by Matthew Boulton & Plate Co., circa 1825, 9½in. high. £4,600

A pair of George III two-handled partly-fluted wine coolers, the reeded angular handles springing from bearded male masks, by William Frisbee, 1807, 9¾in. high, 185oz. (Christie's) £19,800

A pair of fine George III silver-gilt two-handled campana-shaped wine coolers, stands, collars and liners, by Benjamin Smith, 1807, 11in. high, 348oz. (Christie's) £159,500

A pair of old Sheffield plate wine coolers, with rounded shoulders and everted stamped and filled stiff leaf border with acanthus leaf sheathed reeded handles, 19.5cm. high. (Spencer's) £530

A pair of George IV Sheffield plate wine coolers, having fruiting vine handles and borders, detachable liners, 10in., circa 1825. (Woolley & Wallis) £1,650

A Victorian two-handled campana-shaped wine cooler, on spreading circular foot and with dolphin and scroll handles, by Benjamin Smith, 1840, 11½in. high, 74 oz. (Christie's) £4,400

A pair of George III two-handled campana-shaped wine coolers and covers, each on a spreading circular base with rim foot, by Matthew Boulton Plate Co., Birmingham, 1818, 14½in. high, 339oz. (Christie's) £36,700

20TH CENTURY

Sterling silver two-handled champagne cooler by Shreve, Crump & Low, chased medial band, 10³/₄in. high, 36.8 troy oz. (Eldred's) **£496**

One of a pair of wine coolers, stamped Georg Jensen GI 925S 289, 9.8cm. high, 29oz. 9dwt. **£4,160**

Fine silver plated champagne bucket, 20th century, with applied vintage decoration, engraved inscription, 11¹/₂in. high. (Eldred's) **£432**

American Sterling Arts and Crafts wine cooler by Shreve & Co., San Francisco, California, circa 1909–1922, with pair bracket handles at sides, overall peened finish, 8¹/₂in. high, 45oz. 12dwts. (Butterfield & Butterfield) **£1,557**

A pair of tapering cylindrical wine coolers, each in the form of a bucket, by Garrard & Co. Ltd., 1973, 7¹/₄in. high, 118oz. (Christie's) **£5,280**

Art Nouveau Sterling wine cooler by Mauser Mfg. Co., New York, circa 1900–1910, with outwardly tapering sides rising to an irregular pierced lip applied with grape clusters and leaves, 10in. high, 72oz. 9 dwts. (Butterfield & Butterfield) **£1,150**

An American silver wine cooler, Gorham Mfg. Co., Providence, RI, 1906, derived from the Florentine pattern, 104oz., 12³/₈in. high. (Sotheby's) **£3,896**

Edwardian silver wine cooler, Edward Barnard & Sons, Ltd., London, 1901-02, 7³/₄in. high, approx. 29 troy oz. (Skinner) **£790**

An Indian silver wine cooler of urn shape, the body decorated with various wild animals, stamped on base *CKC & Sons, Silver, Bangalore*, 100oz., 14in. diameter. (Peter Francis) **£560**

WINE FUNNELS

These were cone-shaped silver funnels fitted with a removable strainer for decanting wine and sometimes came with a domed, saucer-like dish on which the funnel rested when inverted. The funnel rims were sometimes gadrooned or beaded. They became popular in the 1760s, and were made in the greatest numbers between then and the mid-19th century.

A George III reeded wine funnel with curved spigot and shaped clip, Peter and Ann Bateman, London 1792, 4¾in. (Christie's) £638

A George III silver wine funnel and stand by James Le Bass, Dublin 1822, 4oz. (Riddetts) £140

A good George III silver wine funnel, the rounded bowl with a part fluted and curved spout, London 1805, maker William Allen III, 6¼oz. (Phillips) £460

A George III silver wine funnel, London 1810, makers Peter and William Bateman, 4½oz. (Phillips) £310

A George III/IV silver wine funnel of conventional form, 4¾in., London 1820, makers Rebecca Emes and Edward Barnard, 4¼oz. (Phillips) £330

A good George IV floral and foliate-chased and part-fluted wine funnel with curved spigot, Rebecca Emes and Edward Barnard, London 1827, 6in., 7oz. (Christie's S. Ken) £1,155

A William IV melon-fluted wine funnel with shaped rim, curved spigot and shell clip, John & Henry Lias, London 1836, 5¾in. (Christie's) £605

A George III wine funnel, crested within a scroll cartouche and chased with scrolls and foliage, 5.5in. long, Thomas Wallis and Jonathan Hayne, London 1818, 182gms., 5.8oz. (Bearne's) £620

WINE FUNNELS

A George III campana shaped wine funnel, the upper part fluted, with tongue and dart border, by Chrispin Fuller, 1811, 5.5ozs. (Phillips) £500

A rare George III magnum wine funnel, by Paul Storr, with fluted body and frieze of shells, 1816, 30cm. high, 13.25ozs. (Phillips) £12,500

A George III silver wine funnel with gadrooned edge, 4¼in., marks rubbed, 1¾oz. (Phillips) £100

A good George III silver gilt wine funnel, the spout half fluted, by Michael Plummer, 1792, 8.75oz. (Phillips) £1,900

A George IV part-fluted and gadrooned wine funnel with curved spigot and scrolling foliate clip, maker's initials possibly *G.H.*, London 1826, 5½in., 5oz. (Christie's) £715

A George IV gadrooned wine funnel with curved spigot and shaped clip, William Bateman, London 1825, 4¾in. (Christie's S. Ken) £462

Early 19th century Chinese Export silver wine funnel, by Sunshing, Canton, 5¾in. long, 4oz. (Christie's) £2,063

A George III wine funnel, 4½in. high, plain circular with reeded rim and shaped rectangular hook, London, 1781, by Luke Hebden, 2½ozs. (Bonhams) £250

A George III beaded wine funnel with curved spigot and rounded clip, maker's initials possibly *I.L.*, London 1776, 4¾in. (Christie's S. Ken) £198

Silver wine labels for bottles began to be used in the early 18th century and by and large can be dated by their shape. Plain rectangular or crescent shapes were favoured in the 1730s, and escutcheon shapes in the following decade. Feather edging too dates from the 1740s, piercings and crestings from around 1770 and embossing from around 1790. Oval labels date mainly from the late 1770s, and pointed ovals from the 1780s. Plain rectangular labels continued popular throughout, however, and there is an increasing amount of saw-cut lettering. Plain neck rings, with the name of the wine engraved in two places, also date from the 1780s.

Those labels associated with glass decanters tend to be larger and more ornate from the 1770s. Before 1800, the labels were hand worked, but die-stamped thereafter in a process developed by Matthew Linwood in Birmingham. Labels from the Regency period often have soldered borders cast in relief with scenery, foliage and masks, with vine leaves and perforated lettering dating from 1824. After 1840 production and workmanship deteriorated and ceased in 1860 when the Licensing Act called for paper labels on bottles.

A Victorian Provincial escutcheon wine label, possibly by Thomas Wheatley of Newcastle, circa 1850 (Phillips) £65

A George II Provincial wine label, formed as two putti, by Isaac Cookson, Newcastle, circa 1750. (Phillips) £210

A set of four Victorian wine labels, each engraved with a crest, by Rawlings & Sumner, London, 1859 and 1860. (Christie's) £176

A George III wine label modelled as a putto, by Peter, Anne and William Bateman, 1799. (Phillips) £820

One of a matched set of four George III armorial wine labels, modelled as a sun with twenty-four rays, by John Rich, 1792. (Phillips) £850

One of three George III silver gilt wine labels for Port, Claret and Champagne, by Benjamin Smith, 1808, 3in. high, 7oz.5dwt. £2,735

One from a set of five Regency silver gilt wine labels by Paul Storr, circa 1811-14, 7oz.4dwt. **£2,620**

A Victorian wine label of fruiting vine and leafy scroll design, circa 1840. £120

One of a pair of George IV Irish oval wine labels, by James Scott, Dublin, circa 1825. (Phillips) £320

WINE TASTERS

As their name suggests these were used by vintners for tasting wine, and were made in Britain and Europe from the Middle Ages, though earliest extant examples date from the 17th century. Tasters come in the form of a small plain or embossed vessel with a slightly domed bottom.

A Russian silver gilt and champleve enamel wine taster, probably Moscow, circa 1900, maker's mark KA, 3⅞in. diam. (Christie's) £1,031

A Charles II two handled circular wine taster, punched with bunches of grapes, 1675, 3¾in. diam. (Christie's) £1,100

A Louis XVI silver wine taster, maker's mark TN, cockerel between, Reims, 1781-89, 4in. long, 1oz.15dwt. (Christie's) £1,069

A George III silver wine taster, maker's mark apparently that of Joseph Steward II, London, 1764, 4⅛in. diam., 2oz. (Christie's) £5,480

A French 18th century wine taster, engraved with the owner's name, with scrolling oval thumbpiece, 11.5cm. long, 79gr. (Henry Spencer) £1,500

An Austrian silver parcel gilt wine taster, Vienna, 1676, maker's mark FV, also struck with later control marks, 5½in. long, 3oz. (Christie's) £1,160

A German silver-gilt two-handled wine taster, the base chased with a flower, by Wolff or Georg Rotenbeck, Nuremberg, 17th century, 4⅝in. diameter, 60 grs. (Christie's) £1,100

An Italian parcel gilt circular wine taster, the centre chased with a recumbent sleeping dog within a border of stylised foliage, Turin, probably mid 17th century, 5¼in. diameter, 117grs. (Christie's) £12,100

A Louis XV silver wine taster, possibly by Chas. Despots, with the charge and discharge of A. Leschaudel, 4½in. long. (Christie's) £612

An 18th century English wine taster, part lobed decorated border, the reverse engraved with a coronet within a grape border. (Woolley & Wallis) £560

A Louis XVI silver wine taster, Provincial, circa 1780, with stylised snake handle, 4in. long, 1oz.5dwt. (Christie's) £515

INDEX

441